THE
CITY OBSERVED:
NEW YORK

THE
CITY OBSERVED:
NEW YORK

A GUIDE TO
THE ARCHITECTURE
OF MANHATTAN

PAUL
GOLDBERGER

PHOTOGRAPHY BY
DAVID W. DUNLAP

RANDOM HOUSE
NEW YORK

Text Copyright © 1979 by Paul Goldberger
Photographs Copyright © 1979 by David W. Dunlap

All rights reserved under International and Pan-American Copyright Conventions.
Published in the United States by Random House, Inc., New York, and
simultaneously in Canada by Random House of Canada Limited, Toronto.

Library of Congress Cataloging in Publication Data

Goldberger, Paul.
The city observed, New York.

Includes index.
1. Architecture—New York (City)—Guide-books.
I. Title. II. Series.
NA735.N5G64   917.47′1′044   78-21795
ISBN 0-394-50450-X

Manufactured in the United States of America

3 5 7 9 8 6 4 2

FIRST EDITION

Designed by Carole Lowenstein
Cartography by David Lindroth

To my parents

PREFACE

This is a personal guide: it is not meant to be comprehensive, and includes only those buildings I find significant, distinguished, amusing, or instructive. These criteria yield some 400-odd entries and perhaps twice that number of buildings. Some of the buildings are good and some of them are terrible, and I have not hesitated to be frank in expressing my views. When the idea for this guide was first conceived, it was intended to be a book that would be both amusing to read at home and functional to carry along on architectural walks around the city, and thus its tone has deliberately been kept conversational. I admit to a prejudice in favor of the walker—New York is a city meant to be seen on foot, a city in which having the right pair of shoes is the equivalent of having the right kind of car in Los Angeles.

The City Observed: New York is to be the first of a series of such personal guidebooks, and I should mention here that it is restricted to Manhattan not out of any disrespect to the other boroughs of New York City. Quite the contrary: the outlying boroughs are so rich in architecture that it is impossible to discuss them in the sort of detail this book requires, and it is planned that the series will eventually include the other boroughs.

The format here is to group short essay-like entries by geography. I have always hated organized walking tours—I always wanted to go off and look at something else that had caught my eye—so you will find no "Turn left at the white cast-iron building" instructions here. The entries tend to be longer than those in that encyclopedic and helpful general reference work the *AIA Guide to New York City,* but they are in fact listed in an order that makes for logical walks, so this book should be as helpful to those readers in search of more formal tours as I hope it will be for more casual wanderers.

Some notes on using this book: the entries are presented in geographical order from the southern tip of Manhattan to the northern end, and they are grouped into five major sections—each denoted by a roman numeral— Lower Manhattan, Midtown, Uptown, Upper Manhattan, and Roosevelt Island. Within each large section are several subsections, each covering a neighborhood and denoted by a capital letter. Individual entries—which may be single buildings, streets, parks, or collections of buildings—are indicated by arabic numerals. Thus, in I H 17, the Federal Archives Building in Greenwich Village, the roman numeral I indicates that the entry is in the Lower Manhattan section, the H indicates that it is in the Greenwich Village subsection, and the 17 indicates that it is the seventeenth entry in the Greenwich Village sequence.

This is a record of what has moved, excited or infuriated me in five years as architecture critic of *The New York Times*. The editors of the *Times* have been gracious in encouraging me to write to my heart's content about this extraordinary city, but I owe other debts as well: to Christopher Gray of the Office for Metropolitan History, whose research assistance has been invaluable; to David Dunlap, for his excellent photographs; to Vincent Scully, who, more than anyone else, taught me how to look at architecture; to Ada Louise Huxtable, who made it clear that serious architectural writing need not be incompatible with the demands of daily journalism; to Daniel Okrent, who first conceived the project, Jason Epstein, Gail Winston, Carole Lowenstein, and Sono Rosenberg, who saw it through to completion, and Georges Borchardt, who helped in innumerable ways; and to Alex Garvin, Eden Ross Lipson, Bridgit Potter, Steven Rattner, Jonathan Rogers, Charles Kaiser, Richard Meislin and Steven Robinson, who have joined me on walks around New York that were as important as any formal research ever could be.

A final debt is owed to several people whose writings on New York over the years have helped me form my own sense of the city: the late Meyer Berger, Francis X. Clines, McCandlish Phillips, Jonathan Raban, Richard F. Shepard, Kate Simon, Gay Talese and, finally, E. B. White, whose great essay, "Here Is New York," remains the finest single commentary on the city in our time.

PAUL GOLDBERGER

New York, December 1978

CONTENTS

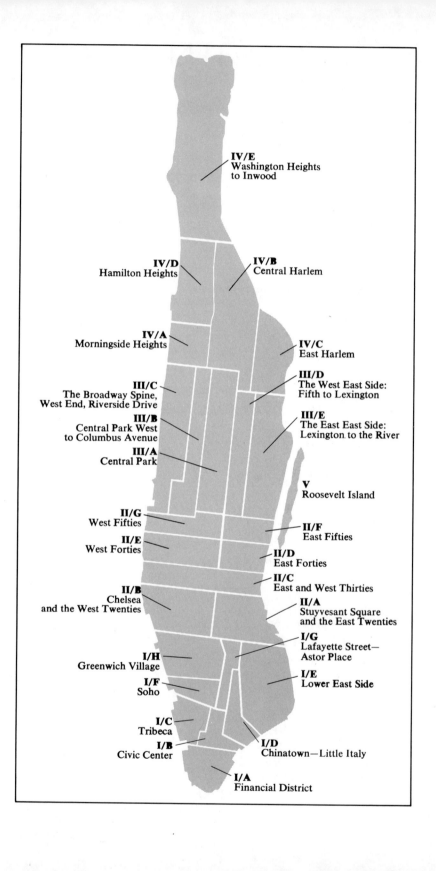

IV/E
Washington Heights
to Inwood

IV/D
Hamilton Heights

IV/B
Central Harlem

IV/A
Morningside Heights

IV/C
East Harlem

III/C
The Broadway Spine,
West End, Riverside Drive

III/D
The West East Side:
Fifth to Lexington

III/B
Central Park West
to Columbus Avenue

III/E
The East East Side:
Lexington to the River

III/A
Central Park

V
Roosevelt Island

II/G
West Fifties

II/F
East Fifties

II/E
West Forties

II/D
East Forties

II/C
East and West Thirties

II/B
Chelsea
and the West Twenties

II/A
Stuyvesant Square
and the East Twenties

I/G
Lafayette Street—
Astor Place

I/H
Greenwich Village

I/E
Lower East Side

I/F
Soho

I/C
Tribeca

I/B
Civic Center

I/D
Chinatown—Little Italy

I/A
Financial District

INTRODUCTION

New York is easy to criticize and it is easier still to romanticize, though fewer today seem to choose that option—it is no longer enough to be told merely that New York is the city of hansom cabs and headwaiters, or even that it is the city of ethnic diversity and cultural splendor. These characterizations are too easy, too glib, to describe a place where ethnic diversity can often mean ethnic turmoil, cultural splendor can often become cultural poverty, and even hansom cabs are as likely as not to be cramped and unpleasant.

New York is an arrogant city; it has always wanted to be all things to all people, and a surprising amount of the time it has succeeded. It has always been a city of commerce, and the values of commerce have tended to supersede other values. There has been no pretense here of excessive gentility, and the rush was always to the new, the large, the prosperous, the fashionable. It is not only in our time that New York's desire to make itself rich has led to an utter indifference to the better values of the physical environment—*Harper's Monthly* in June 1856 observed that "New York is notoriously the largest and least-loved of any of our great cities. Why should it be loved as a city? It is never the same city for a dozen years altogether. A man born in New York forty years ago finds nothing, absolutely nothing, of the New York he knew. If he chances to stumble upon a few old houses not yet leveled, he is fortunate. But the landmarks, the objects which marked the city to him, as a city, are gone."

We are accustomed to thinking of New York as unplanned chaos, and in many ways it is, but this is in fact one of the world's most planned cities. In 1811 the city commissioners adopted a plan for street patterns that laid the numbered grid of streets and avenues up the length of the island, from 14th street—a point which the ruthlessly northward thrust of development had not quite reached—all the way through Harlem. The grid was a somewhat cynical plan, for it was intended to maximize land use and, hence, real estate values; it generally ignored natural topography in favor of its own rigid, man-made order. The effect of the grid on the cityscape has been vast—far vaster than the designs of any one architect or of any generation of architects, and it has not really been so negative at all.

The straight streets provide a remarkable number of stunning vistas, not great axial views as along the boulevards of Paris, but neat, tight, ramrod-straight views that stretch from river to river. From almost every part of midtown Manhattan one can see at least one river at the end of the street canyon, and there is often a view of both rivers.

The grid has also made the New York "street wall"—the even line of buildings extending block after block—a crucial part of the city's visual identity. A period of flirtation with setback "plazas" breaking the street line, a result of the 1961 zoning ordinance's misguided desire to see the successful Seagram Building repeated, led to broken street walls all over town, but now planners and architects have come to a realization that every building has a responsibility, encouraged by the grid, to line up with its neighbors and be part of a greater whole.

But the grid has functioned most importantly in a more subtle, symbolic way. It is really a frame, an enclosure, a Cartesian anchor for the irrational impulses of this impulsive, active city. It is like an abstract drawing sketched not on a plan sheet but on graph paper; the grid of the graph holds the abstraction, defining its lines of force and keeping its movement in check. It is the subtle balance of the rational and the irrational; without the grid, New York's intensity and idiosyncrasy would be uncontainable.

New York is too often misunderstood as having a strong, clearly defined character. The city is itself strong, but its character is not; it is changeable and malleable. Like all great cities, New York takes on a different character for each of its occupants, and what it does that no small city can do is provide them with choice: the graph paper is there to be written on.

Such vast size—it is worth remembering that New York is more than twice the size of Chicago, the nation's second largest city—means that the city can embrace everything, and it often does. It is a place where culture is not merely consumed but manufactured, and to do that in quantity seems to take a certain anarchy. There has rarely been a clear political order here, nor, surely, so rigorous a social order as in Boston or Philadelphia, and there is by no means an architectural order.

In part, expediency has dictated the city's architectural form. New York has always had an eye for economy, and the quickly built houses of the early nineteenth century are in this sense no different from the crass towers of glass and steel of the mid-twentieth century; each was a speculator's way of making the most money from his land that the laws and the technology of his time would permit.

But it has never been expediency alone. New York's ambition was always raw, but never simple, and as the city grew its vision of itself became more complex. The nineteenth century was a time when all of Western architecture was looking toward the past, and the architectural styles of history were especially appealing to a city eager to prove its cultural maturity. Almost every prosperous American city of the late nineteenth century sported buildings in a variety of historic styles, but as the nineteenth century turned into the twentieth, the variety and intensity of this eclecticism in New York were unmatched. History was like a great smorgasbord to the architects and the clients who were building up New York; they wanted every dish, and they cared little whether the combinations were right.

What was important was to be masters of history—to confirm the power of their city and their culture by picking something Gothic here, something Georgian there, something classical as well. The styles thus lost their ideological meaning—the architects were free agents, so to speak, able to use a Gothic detail not for its ecclesiastical significance but purely for its formal appeal. It was an indulgent, almost hedonistic kind of an attitude, but its freedom from ideology could permit the best architects to let their essential quest be directed toward the making of compositions, the arranging of parts. It is this act of composition-making in fact, that might be said to be the essential element of New York's eclectic architecture.

The city's attitude is worth contrasting with that of Chicago, where the modern skyscraper was born. The great Chicago architects, men like Louis Sullivan and John Wellborn Root, believed that the new technology and program of the skyscraper demanded a new style, and they created buildings that eschewed historic precedent. New Yorkers, on the other hand, cared not at all for such ideology; they took the details they chose and adapted skyscrapers to them. The controlling force in New York was theater, not theory, and by the early 1930's the skyline of New York had become a dazzling, utterly fanciful array of pinnacles and turrets and crowns, all standing for little but visual pleasure.

New York through the 1930's was a magical vision, and it worked because the architects who made it were—for the most part—very, very good. New York has only a handful of truly great buildings of the sort that will find a place in histories of architecture three generations from now, but it has more very good buildings than any other city in the United States. The city's economic arrogance, cultural ambitions and overall theatricality combined to create a skillful, intense, and, for the most part, jealous eclecticism. The making of compositions, the making of streets, and the making of theater—it is these things that define the architecture of New York far more than does any single style.

"New York has changed in tempo and in temper in the years I have known it. . . . The city has never been so uncomfortable, so crowded, so tense," wrote E. B. White in 1949. It is easy to infer from this that things never change, that the city has always seemed on the brink of collapse, and that disaster is more in the eye of the beholder than in the reality of the city. But things *are* different in the New York of the late 1970's, and not only because of the mood of economic and social crisis. The physical city is different as well from that of a generation or two ago, and most of the difference is not to the good. Although the planners who created New York's first zoning ordinances in 1916 envisioned even greater densities, it is clear already that much of midtown Manhattan is too big, too heavily built up. While it is romantic to talk of Manhattan as being continually unfinished, there are such things as too many buildings and too big buildings—there are limits to growth in cities as much as in economies, and there is no question that the spirit that has sustained this city through all of its growth until now cannot be expected to continue indefinitely and still retain its strength.

But more important still to the city's spirit is the question of what, rather than how much, we are building. The joy that characterized New York's architecture for so long, the zest of the skyscrapers of the 1920's that made one forget how harsh was the city of which they were a part, seems lost. What joy is there in Third Avenue? What presence, even, is there in Third Avenue?

We are learning, but slowly, and probably too late. The housing of the last few years, places like Riverbend and East Midtown Plaza, is better than most of what came before; the Citicorp Center, while hardly Rockefeller Center, at least acknowledges with its generous public space the need of a city to have more than office blocks. Newer buildings planned, such as the IBM headquarters by Edward Larrabee Barnes and the AT&T headquarters by Philip Johnson and John Burgee, both of which will soon rise on Madison Avenue in the Fifties, show further improvement and a still more mature sense of what makes a city civilized. But a lot of what the city has always been is gone forever, and it is not merely an exercise in sentimentality to mourn it: we cry not because we think the architectural past was so good, but because we cannot believe that the architectural future will be better.

But it is unfair to conclude on such a note. A great deal of this city is left—far, far more than it looked as if there would be a decade ago, when there was both greater prosperity and a weaker Landmarks Preservation Commission. This remains one of the richest urban landscapes on earth, a city whose greatest characteristic may be its ability to inspire constant wonder and unending surprise. And there are some splendid signs of energetic renewal: for every new office tower today there are a dozen fine old commercial buildings being renovated into housing; for every bank that shoves its blank façade onto a lively retail street there are six restaurants and two bookstores opening a block away. New York remains what it has always been: a city of ebb and flow, a city of constant shifts of population and economics, a city of virtually no rest. It is harsh, dirty, and dangerous, it is whimsical and fanciful, it is beautiful and soaring—it is not one or another of these things but all of them, all at once, and to fail to accept this paradox is to deny the reality of city existence.

SOME NOTES ON
MOVEMENT

If it is best to read *Tender Is the Night* on the Riviera and Homer in
Greece, then probably the right place for Dante is the New York subway.
The underground transit system of New York City is a physical wreck—it
is dirty, smelly, and ugly. It *is* efficient, and there is a pleasing modesty to
the Metropolitan Transportation Authority's brief slogan "MTA gets you
there": MTA knows well it cannot promise anything more.

Most of the stations are extremely old—those, for example, on the
original sections of the IRT lines (the Lexington Avenue line below 42nd
Street and the Broadway line above 42nd Street) date from 1904. They are
cramped and ill-ventilated, with steel columns coming down every few feet
onto every platform. The stations feel like forests of columns, in fact, and
some years ago the MTA made it all worse by painting the columns a shade
of bright blue that manages to be both dirty and ugly. There is a lot of silver,
too, which surely someone thought would make all the stations look sleek,
but since the silver paint gets dirty even faster than the blue, it just makes
the stations look all the more like slums.

There are some promising signs so far as the stations are concerned—the
one major improvement in recent years, the passageway under 42nd Street
connecting the Sixth Avenue line with the Fifth Avenue station of the
Flushing IRT No. 7 line, is brightly colored, brightly lit, and filled with
large blowups of prints of neighborhood landmarks, such as the Crystal
Palace that once stood on the site of Bryant Park. And the MTA has been
painting a few of the stations, such as the 50th Street stop on the Seventh
Avenue IRT line, in tones of brown and orange, which come off a good bit
cheerier than the official-looking blue and silver. Moreover, plans for the
Second Avenue subway—now indefinitely postponed, but still with us in
the form of remnants of the construction process on Second Avenue in
Harlem—called for elaborate, architect-designed stations that would have
felt like real places, not like dank corridors.

Oddly, there never was any real elegance to the New York subway, even
though the first phases of the system were constructed at a time when the
city's physical environment was far more elegant than it is today. The IRT
was decorated with rather handsome mosaics and, on occasion, with terra-
cotta plaques bearing some reference to the name of the station—a
locomotive at Grand Central, for example—but except for one elaborate,
vaulted station, now abandoned, at City Hall, the subway stations were
small, tight platforms, with none of the generosity of space common to the
architecture of their time. Later stations, such as those built by the city for

Plaque in the Columbus Circle IRT station

the IND lines in the 1930's, are larger but more institutional-looking—mezzanines of steel columns and tiled walls, like vast men's rooms in which someone took out all the plumbing.

The biggest stations, like the one under Herald Square (II C 2) or Times Square or 14th Street, are labyrinths, with changes in level and turns and passageways and mezzanines and shops and snack bars. They have a certain sleazy kind of life to them—on 14th Street, in fact, the world of the subway station underground is almost indistinguishable from the world of the street aboveground—but they can be trying indeed as a daily experience, for they assault the senses ceaselessly. Music blares from the tiny subway record shop, the crowds make a noise that is at once a shuffle and a roar, and always the trains screech and scream along the rails.

If the New York subway is the inferior of other major systems in the world in terms of the physical environment of its stations, it is worse still in terms of its graphics: it is no exaggeration to say that there is no subway system in the world with a more inadequate and confusing system of signs and maps. Part of the problem comes from New Yorkers' fondness for colloquial usages—where else would the terms "Broadway Local," "Seventh Avenue train," "West Side IRT," and "No. 1 train" all mean precisely the same thing? But the MTA has done little to help, and, indeed, has exacerbated the situation with confusing signs in some places and no signs at all in others.

Now a program is in effect to install new, color-coded signs in sans-serif type. The new graphics standards are handsome, but since there is nowhere near enough money to replace everything in the system, they are added piecemeal, and the end result is a lot of sleek new signs next to a lot of old signs which the new signs are expected to supplement but all too often contradict.

The small, weak gestures toward improvement extend also toward the subway cars themselves. The newest models are quieter, and have seats of orange plastic and interior panels of fake-wood Formica. It is indicative of how really gruesome the subway environment is that one greets the presence of imitation wood with pleasure—only here can that be considered a happy alternative.

Older cars, nearly all of which are covered with graffiti, tend to be metallic and harsh, with seats set parallel to the sides so that riders are lined up like prisoners positioned always to face the guards. The graffiti on the outsides can be elaborate, colorful and rich; on the insides, it is inevitably messy and trivial and merely enhances the sense of squalor.

Aboveground, it hasn't been the same since the old double-decker buses disappeared. The ubiquitous MTA blue extended to the buses as well, but just last autumn the agency, in another surprising flurry of good sense, started painting a lot of its buses white, a color that may not last long in the New York air but looks a lot better in the short run. The glass-and-metal bus-stop shelters, which began appearing all over midtown Manhattan about three years ago, have had a remarkably positive effect on the cityscape— they are elegant, light objects (sometimes a bit too fragile to offer proper protection in bad weather, unfortunately) with a style and grace that is altogether uncharacteristic of the New York street. And the lighted advertising they contain seems not a commercial intrusion but a rather joyous presence, like the colorful posters on Paris street kiosks.

I/LOWER
MANHATTAN

A/FINANCIAL DISTRICT

Here, past and present come together, not in the gentle partnership of the ideal city, but in the dramatic clash of the city desperate to make itself new at the expense of the old. This is a part of town of immense visual power but—can one say this without making it sound like a commentary on the evils of capitalism?—precious little soul. Here, at the southern tip of Manhattan, New York began; as in virtually every major city in the world, the financial community found the original downtown to its liking and gradually turned the turf into its own.

The process was slow; even into the 1960's the waterfront was still lined with three- and four-story nineteenth-century commercial buildings, many of which, like those still standing as Schermerhorn Row in the South Street Seaport area, were fine Federal structures. They contained a mix of uses— spice merchants and shippers' offices, with storefronts making an active streetscape. The solid skyscrapers of the banks and brokerage houses clustered together in the inland blocks, with the intersection of Broad and Wall streets their symbolic as well as geographic center. It was a visually ordered world, in its heyday in the 1920's—a strong and solid center of hushed towers losing their dignity only in their exuberant crowns, surrounded by a lively, disheveled ring of littler and older buildings. The world of Louis Auchincloss and that of Horatio Alger kept each other in check.

All of this fell apart in the 1960's, when development, which had been virtually nonexistent in the financial district since the 1930's, exploded. It

I A · *Lower Manhattan skyline*

was the Chase Manhattan Bank's new headquarters in the center of the district that started the boom, but most of the expansion occurred in the only place where there was room—around the edges. Massive, boxy buildings, parodies of the worst of commercial architecture of the postwar period, obliterated the old structures of Water and Front streets on the East River, and the World Trade Center did the same with the Hudson riverfront. By the late 1960's, the sense of balance that had characterized Manhattan's tip was gone. Its once subtle profile is now crude, its life almost entirely that of bankers, lawyers, stockbrokers, and floors and floors and floors of computer clerks.

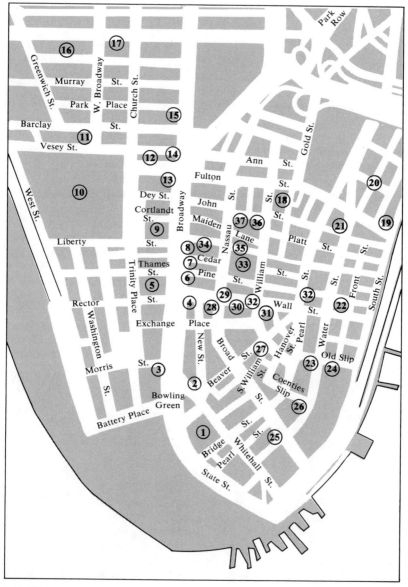

I / LOWER MANHATTAN **A / FINANCIAL DISTRICT**

I A 1 · U.S. CUSTOM HOUSE
between Bowling Green, State, Whitehall, and Bridge streets
Cass Gilbert, 1907

In a city rich in monumental Beaux-Arts architecture (New York is rich in a more paradoxical-style, nonmonumental Beaux-Arts architecture) Cass Gilbert's Custom House of 1907 would not be considered extraordinary. It would be appreciated, but not be the subject of awe.

Here, however, it *is* the subject of awe, and after looking around Lower Manhattan, it is difficult not to share that feeling. This is a distinguished granite palace, an ode to the city's role as a great seaport. A monumental flight of steps, four heroic sculptures by Daniel Chester French representing four continents, forty-four massive Corinthian columns, and a noble arched entrance mark the exterior. Within is a splendid oval rotunda with murals by Reginald Marsh.

There is not the originality and grace here of Gilbert's Woolworth Building, nor the absolutely overpowering monumentality of, say, Grand Central Terminal. One always senses in the Custom House just the tiniest hint of the federal government's heavy, unimaginative hand. And it is worth noting that this house, created to monitor the commerce of the oceans, is turned away from the sea: the building's back is to the harbor.

But none of this obviates the Custom House's vital and pleasing role as an anchor to the past in a part of town that has precious little sense of any past, particularly one so grand as what this building summons up. The Custom House has been empty since the U.S. Custom Service abandoned it for the World Trade Center in 1973; happily the federal government has now caught on to its own stupidity, and plans are afoot to rehabilitate the building for federal offices.

I A 2 · 26 BROADWAY
NE corner, Beaver Street
Carrère & Hastings; Shreve, Lamb & Blake, 1922

This is one of New York's great unappreciated buildings: an object lesson in what urban architecture should be about. The base of 26 Broadway slides uptown in a gentle curve, defining the shape of Bowling Green park and providing enough formal interest to be lively without being eccentric. The tower of 26 Broadway is set atop the curving base at what appears at first glance to be a curious angle; in fact it is related to the grid of the streets uptown. What the architects were doing is worth noting: it is clear that they made a conscious decision to treat the building as two separate elements, a base related carefully to its context and a tower related to *its* context, which was the overall skyline.

Carrère & Hastings' skill was such that the total composition never appears disjointed. Indeed, the building is a powerful presence in and of itself, an apt retort to those who argue that architecture based on relationship to context can never have a strength and a presence of its own.

The building was originally the headquarters of the Standard Oil Company. The Renaissance lobby, which contains the names of the founders of the company carved in the frieze, is a splendid space—immensely dignified, yet light and welcoming.

I A 1 · *U.S. Custom House*

I A 2 · *26 Broadway*

I A 3 · 25 BROADWAY
SW corner, Morris Street
Benjamin Wistar Morris, 1921

This powerful façade is the natural complement to the curves of 26 Broadway across the street. Built originally for the Cunard Line, 25 Broadway is of interest chiefly for the great hall inside, once Cunard's booking office. It is as good a space as the Custom House's rotunda, and it is somehow more pleasing (and typical of New York) to find that the space is not the centerpiece of a commercial palazzo but is the main floor of a skyscraper.

The hall is 65 feet high, with a magnificent dome, marble walls, and vaults, adorned with murals on sailing themes by Ezra Winter and maps by Barry Faulkner. It bespeaks the imperial innocence of its time—surely one owns the world when one can buy a steamship ticket in a room like this.

For quite a while Cunard has not been selling enough tickets to require a room 185 feet long (indeed, the line moved to midtown years ago) and the room lay empty for some time. In 1977 the U.S. Postal Service moved in, taking over the space in a deal that was hailed as a noble act of preservation. The intent was right, but the results, unfortunately, are disastrous: tacky, fake-wood Formica, standardized metal postboxes, and a huge metal space-frame truss from which floodlights are suspended. The space-frame makes it impossible for visitors to perceive clearly the overall space, and one cannot avoid the sense that the Postal Service's architects, Handren Associates, entirely misunderstood the masterpiece they were dealing with.

I A 4 · ONE WALL STREET
SE corner, Broadway
Voorhees, Gmelin & Walker, 1932
addition: Smith, Smith Haines Waehler & Lundberg, 1965

Wall Street in the thirties—this building, with a handful of others, summarizes it. The limestone skyscraper is at once a symbol of the financial community's solidity and of its aspirations—strong, conventional, solid, yet pushing onward and upward. Ralph Walker made a larger contribution to architectural history in his building for the New York Telephone Company at 140 West Street (I A 11), but the romance is just as strong in his careful massing at 1 Wall Street.

The banking space just inside the Wall Street entrance is Art Deco–inspired and altogether wonderful, the exuberance of that style crossed, if this can be imagined, with bankers' conservatism. It all comes off; why weren't more bankers like this? Just as much of a coup is the later addition by Voorhees, Gmelin's successor firm, which respectfully continued the building's limestone façade in an age when glass and steel would have been so much easier.

I A 5 · TRINITY CHURCH
Broadway, opposite intersection of Wall Street
Richard Upjohn, 1846

Trinity Church's tower was the Empire State Building of the mid-nineteenth century, the spire that symbolized the entire city. Its urbanistic role today is no less vital—by the luck of its siting at the head of Wall Street, Trinity, though dwarfed by skyscrapers, remains a commanding presence. The tower is everything to this building—an immense square that rises to four points and shoots out a spire to thrust higher still. Forthright and powerful, the tower stands in front of the building, and today it closes off the vista down Wall Street's canyon with just the right amount of emphasis. The base is solid, but the spire is narrow enough to permit the vista to continue around it. That the somber Gothic Revival should provide what amounts to an exclamation point in the urban context is one of Lower Manhattan's most pleasing ironies.

Upjohn's Trinity is the third church to have stood on this site on Broadway at the head of Wall Street; it replaced a church destroyed by fire in 1776 and another torn down because of structural failure. Trinity may well be New York's most famous church, and it was certainly a crucial structure in the development of the Gothic Revival in America.

Inside is a handsome—but not remarkable—nave, recently cleaned and restored. The plaster ceiling is hung from wood trusses, something never done in real Gothic churches, which, of course, have stone vaults in the ceiling. Trinity's buttresses are thus mere decorative echoes of the real thing. This may be disturbing to the rationalist; I find it comforting to be reminded that Upjohn knew the value of a stage set when he saw one.

I A 6 · 100 BROADWAY
SE corner, Pine Street
Bruce Price, 1896
renovated for Bank of Tokyo, Kajima International, 1975

This shows what can be done when a decent architectural firm approaches a decent old building and shows a decent respect. One hundred Broadway was built as the American Surety Building; it is a fine example of the Beaux-Arts-influenced commercial style common around the turn of the century. There is a base of majestic two-story Ionic columns, a row of full-scale classical figures above, a marble-fronted midsection, and an ornate multistoried cornice.

The Bank of Tokyo did all the right things. Its architects, Kajima International, cleaned and restored the façade, then removed the original ground-floor front behind the columns and created a new glass wall several feet back. The result is a welcome covered arcade behind the columns. Behind that is a splendid banking space, in which four massive Corinthian columns define a volume within which is suspended an utterly cool, brushed-aluminum sculpture by Isamu Noguchi. The room is one of the city's most subtle juxtapositions of new and old; but in fact, given how well the façade still works, with the Ionic colonnade in the foreground and the glass wall in the background, the same can be said of the entire building.

I A 7 · 120 BROADWAY (EQUITABLE BUILDING)
between Pine and Cedar streets
Ernest R. Graham, 1915

What an absolute monster this must have been when it was finished in 1915! Forty stories and 1.4 million square feet of office space, a whole city block, a huge mass effacing a piece of the sky. The Equitable Building is in every way the predecessor of such latter-day behemoths as Emery Roth & Sons' 55 Water Street; it is not a bad thing for us to be reminded that greed did not enter the real estate business in the last decade.

Still, greed was a fresher idea back in 1915 than it is today, and the city was shocked at the overwhelming mass of Equitable. The result was New York's, and the nation's, first zoning resolution in 1916, an attempt to restrict height and bulk in such a way as to assure that light would penetrate freely into downtown's narrow streets.

Equitable still appears massive, even to eyes accustomed to 40-story boxes. It is really more important for its historical role than as a piece of architecture, but the lobby, where Muzak booms through vaulted, coffered ceilings, is not without a certain power. Constant crowds move rapidly through the block-long space; it is an early vision of the romantic metropolis, something out of famous turn-of-the-century visionary drawings like "King's Dream of New York."

I A 8 · 140 BROADWAY
between Liberty and Cedar streets
Skidmore, Owings & Merrill (Gordon Bunshaft, partner in charge), 1967

Lever House may have been Skidmore, Owings & Merrill's most influential work in New York, but 140 Broadway is the best. Here, the glass curtain wall is dark and refined; more important, it is discreet. This is a soft building, in spite of the sharp and technological feeling of its materials, and there are almost no other glass buildings in town about which that can be said.

No. 140 is subtly shaped to reflect the trapezoidal configuration of the block on which it sits. It is thus a responsible building urbanistically, since it willingly molds itself to what is around it rather than defying its context, as virtually every other Skidmore building in New York has done. The taut, stretched glass skin has been copied in other buildings (notably Skidmore's own at 919 Third Avenue and 1166 Avenue of the Americas), but nowhere has it come off as well as here. Not the least of this building's virtues is the sculpture by Isamu Noguchi on the plaza on the Broadway side; the cube-like orange form, balanced on a corner, is a perfect counterpoint to the building's almost mellow presence.

I A 5 · *Trinity Church, at the foot of Wall Street*

I A 8 · *Plaza of 140 Broadway, sculpture by Isamu Noguchi*

I A 9 · ONE LIBERTY PLAZA
between Broadway, Cortlandt, Liberty, and Church streets
Skidmore, Owings & Merrill, 1972

The Singer Building may be gone, but what other building will be remembered by a 54-story tombstone? One Liberty Plaza, built on the site of Ernest Flagg's gentle, graceful, and utterly humane Singer Building, is aggressively anti-urban. Here all of modern architecture's hubris comes clear—an arrogant form, indifferent to its surroundings; immense bulk, but never anything approaching a generously scaled space inside; outdoor public areas that resemble prison yards.

The outdoor areas are particularly galling, since the building's bulk was permitted by the city's planners in part as a result of a trade-off, in which the developers agreed to create public open space in exchange for the right to add more rentable floor area. They kept their bargain literally—there is something that legally qualifies as public open space—but it is paved, barely landscaped, and uncomfortable for any sort of lingering. The complexities of the zoning amendments of the 1960's are considerable, and in some cases the notion of trade-offs yielded elements to the public good; here, however, one can only feel that the city was had.

I A 10 · THE WORLD TRADE CENTER
between Church, Vesey, West, and Liberty streets
Minoru Yamasaki & Associates; Emery Roth & Sons, 1970–77

It is big. It is bigger than anything you thought could be, and ultimately it proves that human beings can adapt to anything. There is both more and less to say about the World Trade Center than about any other complex of buildings in Manhattan. Its impact on the city, in terms of everything from the skyline to the ambience of downtown to the state of the office rental market, has been overwhelming. But the buildings themselves are boring, so utterly banal as to be unworthy of the headquarters of a bank in Omaha. Two big, tall boxes, with a few dainty, short boxes in a front yard too big and uncomfortable for any of them; absolutely no relationship to anything around the site—to either the river or the surrounding streets. Of course, relating at this vast scale is nearly impossible, which is another argument against the whole place. But then again, since when has the Empire State Building looked too big for its surroundings?

We could leave it at that, but there is more. The buildings are pretentious and arrogant; it is hard not to be insulted by Minoru Yamasaki's belief that a few cute allusions to Gothic tracery at the bottom and top could make a 110-story tower humane. While the load-bearing walls are a remarkable engineering accomplishment—they are, in effect, like a mesh cage supporting the weight of the entire building, making these towers a different breed entirely from conventional steel-frame construction—their structure has led to windows that are mean slivers, unconscionably denying office workers the panoramic views that should be their just compensation for putting up with the place.

The plaza is a windswept football field; it may well be, as one prominent

I A 10 · *World Trade Center*

I A 10 · *Plaza of the World Trade Center*

New York realtor proudly told a gathering of newspaper editors, "even bigger than the Piazza San Marco," but that remark, far from eradicating the Trade Center's stigma, merely helps to confirm it. The complex was built to be big, and it was set into motion by institutions—the Port Authority of New York and New Jersey foremost among them—that seem unable to see quality as anything but bigness.

The rest of the story? The towers have been up for several years now; the memory of the pleasant, disheveled neighborhood of electronics stores it replaced has faded; the republic has survived. A few good things have happened—the underground concourse has begun to put back some of the urban life the Trade Center took away; the gaudy 107th-floor restaurant by Warren Platner has served as a magnet to bring thousands of tourists downtown who might otherwise never have crossed 14th Street; the mountain climber George Willig and the tightrope walker Philippe Petit have brought some of the romance and drama to the towers that the architects left out.

By now the twin towers are icons, as familiar in souvenir shops as those little miniatures of the Empire State Building. We have all come to some sort of accommodation with the towers, God help us, and there have even been moments when I have seen them from afar and admitted to some small pleasure in the way the two huge forms, when approached from a distance, play off against each other like minimal sculpture. But the buildings remain an occasion to mourn: they never should have happened, they were never really needed, and if they say anything at all about our city, it is that we retreat into banality when the opportunity comes for greatness.

I A 11 · NEW YORK TELEPHONE CO. BUILDING (Barclay-Vesey Building)
140 West Street between Barclay and Vesey streets
Voorhees, Gmelin & Walker, 1926

The neighboring World Trade Center now makes this building look like a toy, but it was once a grand presence on the lower Manhattan skyline. The Barclay-Vesey Building, as the New York Telephone Company's old headquarters structure was long known, is one of the truly distinguished skyscrapers of the 1920's. Its massing is mountainlike—sumptuous masses piled on top of each other for an overall effect of immense repose. The chief influence here was Eliel Saarinen's celebrated design for the Chicago *Tribune* building of 1922, which was never built but which won second prize in the nationwide competition for the *Tribune*'s headquarters: a powerfully vertical structure with lilting masses setting back as they rose.

Barclay-Vesey was one of Ralph Walker's earliest efforts, and always recognized as his masterpiece. Lewis Mumford, who said that the building "expresses the achievements of contemporary American architecture better than any other skyscraper I have seen," nonetheless complained about the uneven configuration of the site, which led to a parallelogram-shaped base on which is set a rectangular tower; today, that form seems more an intelligent adaptation to a difficult site rather than a compromise of aesthetic purity. The building is lavishly decorated with some of the finest Art Deco detail in the city, with a lobby of special richness and gusto that, like the building itself, manages to achieve spirit at no expense of dignity. As further icing on the cake, the Vesey Street side has a covered arcade at sidewalk level—a civilized amenity, even if its relative emptiness makes it qualify for the title of New York's most de Chirico–like place.

I A 11 · *New York Telephone Company Building (Barclay-Vesey Building)*

I A 14 · *St. Paul's Chapel; ATT Headquarters to the left*

I A 12 · 20 VESEY STREET (old New York Evening Post Building)
between Broadway and Church Street
Robert D. Kohn, 1906

This is one of New York's few Art Nouveau buildings, and it is livelier and more graceful than Kohn's better-known Society for Ethical Culture uptown on West 64th street (III B 7). The old *Evening Post* headquarters is a fourteen-story office building, its façade a composition of three bowed bays per floor, culminating in an elaborate top with four sculpted figures and a fine, high copper mansard roof. Four statues ornament the façade near the top; two are by Gutzon Borglum, and they all stand on strong stone bracket bases.

This is not the lilting, fragile Art Nouveau of Hector Guimard in Paris; it is something firmer, less lithe, more formal. If you doubt that 20 Vesey Street has anything to say that is out of the ordinary for the New York streetscape, cast an eye next door to the eclectic skyscraper at No. 30 Vesey Street, where a roughly similar three-bay façade is covered with mounds of fussy classical detail. No. 30 is a grandmother's attic; No. 20 is an atelier, bursting forth with freshness. Kohn's work tends, at first glance, to appear flatter and more lacking in movement than it really is, perhaps because we are accustomed to thinking of Art Nouveau only in terms of Guimard's famous buildings and Metro entrances in Paris. This building does not prance as they do, but it flows, strongly and evenly.

I A 13 · AMERICAN TELEPHONE AND TELEGRAPH BUILDING
195 Broadway, between Dey and Fulton streets
William Welles Bosworth, 1957

A temple to the god of the telephone. There are eight Ionic colonnades, one atop the other, and on the roof is Evelyn Longman's famous sculpture "Spirit of Communication," which will eventually be moved to the lobby of the new AT&T headquarters uptown, removing a splendid skyline element from the financial district.

The lobby is everything here. It is a maze of fluted columns, curiously shaped to splay off at the top, without capitals. The room is a fascinating space, since it chooses to awe not in the conventional way—with grand scale—but in the far more complex and subtle way of creating genuine sculptural interest. One wanders around those columns as through a forest of polished marble. The room is hushed and dignified, as if to tell us that AT&T's power is so vast that it need not indulge in foolish, flamboyant gestures to gain our respect. It all feels a bit like a mausoleum (somehow, somewhere, there *must* be a catafalque bearing the remains of Alexander Graham Bell), but when all is said and done, the room is oddly comfortable.

I A 14 · ST. PAUL'S CHAPEL
between Broadway, Fulton, Church, and Vesey streets
Thomas McBean, 1766
tower: James Crommelin Lawrence, 1794

St. Paul's is eighteenth-century New York, as good an example as remains in this city in which late nineteenth-century structures are so often looked upon as remnants from the Middle Ages. St. Paul's really *is* a remnant, but a distinguished one. Its model was James Gibbs's masterpiece, the Church of St. Martin's-in-the-Fields in London, and it is no exaggeration to say that St. Paul's is New York's premier Georgian church, much as Trinity is the city's premier Gothic Revival church. The interior, in spite of the pink-and-blue paint job which gives it a bit of the air of a nursery, is gracious and welcoming, and good enough to be worth a look at as architectural space, not as a mere anachronism.

It is the outside that is best, however. Lawrence's tower, added almost thirty years after the church itself was completed, is of rough stone, a lovely counterpoint to the carefully wrought quoins of the main building. The surrounding cemetery is a gracious oasis in a pressured part of the city; there is drama in the view of the World Trade Center towers through the trees of the churchyard, the great metal hulks looming over eighteenth-century gravestones. The passage of time could not be made more visible.

I A 15 · WOOLWORTH BUILDING
233 Broadway, between Barclay Street and Park Place
Cass Gilbert, 1913

The lot of the architectural masterpiece in New York is not always a happy one, and it is tempting, therefore, to talk first of this building's remarkably untroubled history. The Woolworth Building was erected by Frank Woolworth in 1913 as the headquarters tower for his chain of variety stores; Woolworth wanted a building that would symbolize both his own commercial success and the glory of the city of New York, and paid $13 million in cash for it. The building has never had a mortgage, the Woolworth Company is still in it, and it has been kept in splendid physical condition.

And few buildings have so deserved to live happily ever after. Woolworth is the Mozart of skyscrapers, a lyrical tower that weds Gothic ornament to exquisite massing and scale. It is typically American, and typically New York, in its use of history—Gothic details were chosen for their picturesque quality, for the ease with which they could be applied to the basically vertical form of the skyscraper, and not for any deeper association they might have. The slogan "Cathedral of Commerce," then, made so popular when the building was new, was somewhat misleading; Gilbert was after beauty of composition, not religious associations.

The utter gracefulness of the form, light without any of the phony appliqué delicacy of Yamasaki's Trade Center, remains stunning today. The tower rises naturally from the large base, and it culminates in a crown that is superbly proportioned to the rest of the building. Here, fancifulness and inventiveness are in perfect balance with discipline and control; there is a sense of the imagination soaring, yet never becoming frivolous. It is all enough to make one believe, just for a moment, in that insipid phrase about architecture being frozen music.

The lobby is almost as good, and at first glance it is even more awesome. The ceiling, three stories up, is set with glass mosaic; the walls are of golden marble, and the details are superbly executed, whimsical versions of Gothic detail. There are caricatures in bas-relief of Frank Woolworth counting nickels and dimes, of Cass Gilbert holding a model of the building, of the renting agent closing a deal, and of others involved in the creation of the structure—all a reminder that architecture can encompass self-irony, and that great architecture in no way compromises itself by having a sense of humor.

I A 16 · 75 MURRAY STREET
between Greenwich Street and West Broadway
James Bogardus (?), 1857

The blocks to the west of City Hall contain some superb cast-iron buildings, in many cases the equal of those uptown in SoHo. Among the earliest and best is 75 Murray Street, a five-story Italianate palazzo built in 1857 to house the glassware business of Francis and John Hopkins. The composition is suave, the details precise, and the especially attractive Medusa heads used as keystones for the arched windows on the third and fifth floors have led Margot Gayle, New York's zealous cast-iron preservationist, to suggest that the building may have been the work of the celebrated James Bogardus.

Once these blocks were full of buildings like this, and a number of them remain, although few are in quite the good state that 75 Murray is in. In most cases ground floors have been altered to accommodate new retail uses, and in many cases details have been stripped away. Even 75 Murray is not entirely free of that disease—it is most likely that the simple fluted columns on the façade once had Corinthian capitals.

I A 15 · *Woolworth Building*　　　　I A 15 · *Lobby of the Woolworth Building*

I A 17 · 50 WARREN STREET
120 Chambers Street
pre-1865

How remarkable the cast-iron designers were as compositionalists! Here, in this commercial building with identical façades on Warren and Chambers streets, pilasters soar for two stories to join together adjacent floors of arched windows, creating a delicate and lively play of scales. The building reads both in the small scale of each individual floor and in the larger scale of the joined floors. It is a compositional technique we were to have more of in brick a few decades later, but in the early 1860's, the closest this building can be dated, it was inventive. The detail itself is good, although the foliated decoration in the arched spandrels is a bit on the routine side.

I A 18 · EXCELSIOR POWER COMPANY
33 Gold Street, between Fulton and John streets
William C. Grinnell, 1888

A hidden, little-noticed gem—a powerhouse, both literally and figuratively, of the Romanesque Revival. This is one of New York's finest examples of nineteenth-century brickwork, with superbly crafted brick ornament and wonderfully enveloping arches that call to mind Richardson. But the building also suggests the great mills of New England, and it ranks with them as an urban version of those great industrial relics—cruel places to the people forced to labor in them, exquisite palaces to those who come upon them in a later age. Excelsior is as good as anything its time produced in Lower Manhattan; it was owned for years by Consolidated Edison Corp., which let it languish in wretched condition, but it is now to be converted into housing.

I A 19 · SCHERMERHORN ROW
2–18 Fulton Street; 91–92 South Street; 195 Front Street
1811–12

Once the whole neighborhood looked like this good row of Federal and Greek Revival commercial buildings. Now they are relics. The uninitiated, learning that there is an intact row of 1812 buildings in Lower Manhattan, rush to see what they expect will be a neat and perfect world of genteel brick houses and cobblestone streets; such are the effects of Williamsburg on our culture. The reality, of course, is that Schermerhorn Row is a messy, lively jumble of buildings, some with signs, some with fire escapes, some with storefronts, some with skylights. The row is technically part of the South Street Seaport Museum, a splendid institution that is acting as catalyst for the preservation of the nineteenth-century structures that dot this small part of New York. The group is owned by the State of New York, which plans a restoration—may the state resist the temptation to make this a pure and perfect Williamsburg, and may it remain a lively and active neighborhood.

I A 20 · WATER STREET

Taken as a whole, this is as futuristic and terrifying an environment as exists in New York. Water Street was once full of small-scale nineteenth-century buildings, but development pressures of the 1960's burst it open. There are a few things worth looking at in themselves (see below), but most of Water Street should be viewed not as architecture but as an object lesson in real estate speculation gone wild. Almost nothing pays any attention to anything else; the buildings fight each other as much as they fight the street and the rest of the city. Laissez-faire planning yields little, it would seem, in the way of public amenity; this is a row of horrors, a testament to arrogance rather than civilized urbanity.

Like the World Trade Center, it is a missed chance; never will so much development happen again within a short period of time. In a sense it is worse than the Trade Center, for the twin towers at least offer a new, if troubling, sense of place to replace what was lost. Here, there is only a sense of emptiness, of confusion, of discord. Sadly, the last few years have made Water Street even worse than it was at the completion of the last boom: the depressed real estate market of the mid-seventies led to a certain amount of demolition of small and unprofitable buildings, adding gaping holes and parking lots to the visual joys already present.

I A 21 · 127 JOHN STREET
NW corner, Water Street
Emery Roth & Sons, 1972

This is Disneyland come to Wall Street, and it is desperately needed. No. 127 John Street is the project of one of New York's most remarkable developers, Melvyn Kaufman, a proud man who at once dislikes fancy architects and is prepared to offer an alternative. Kaufman agrees with all of the aesthetes that most speculative office building is sterile at best, oppressive at worst. What he has done, instead of commissioning buildings from architects with reputations for doing things beyond the ordinary, is to invite Emery Roth & Sons, purveyors of bargain-basement Mies to the masses, to design simple structures, which he proceeds to embellish with the work of consultants of his own choosing.

The results are not half bad, and at 127 John Street they are in fact very good. No. 127 has an open ground floor which replaces a conventional lobby; there are bright canvas canopies, metal seating, pleasing changes of level, and, outside, an enormous digital clock set like a huge billboard on the façade. Visitors move through corrugated metal tubes lined with neon to reach the elevators; the mechanical equipment on upper floors is brightly painted and made visible through special lighting. It is a long way from the sobriety of 23 Wall Street, and if J. P. Morgan would not have commissioned 127 John Street, no matter—the building is pleasing and humane, and these characteristics are in short supply in this neck of the urban woods.

A lobby plaque states that "this building was designed to create an atmosphere of pleasure, humor and excitement for people," and goes on to credit Corchia de Harak Inc., lobby designers; Pamela Waters, who did the roof and mechanical space; and Howard Brandston, the lighting consultant. Curiously, the architects are omitted. That might seem like poetic justice—given Emery Roth's poor record in providing public amenities in its buildings—but it is worth noting that both the skin of 127 John Street and the massing are superior to the Roth firm's usual effort.

I A 22 · 88 PINE STREET
between Water and Front streets
I. M. Pei & Partners, James I. Freed in charge, 1974

Like all of Pei's work, this is conservative by today's standards—it is a "modern" building, concerned more with purity of form than with references to context or social amenities. But it is surely the most refined tower built

I A 20 · *Water Street, looking south toward New York Plaza* (I A 25)

I A 22 · *88 Pine Street; South Street Seaport in the foreground* downtown since 140 Broadway, and one of the Pei firm's more significant works anywhere.

No. 88 Pine Street is a pristine white tower, set down precisely on a larger site. The metal cladding is all of white, and the windows are set into the bays with butt joints rather than mullions, so the façade consists of nothing but white solid and glass void, as if an early Chicago School skyscraper were translated into the language of high technology. There are no real advances here, but there are cosmetic ones—and the cosmetics are free of the affectation that burdens so many other recent skyscrapers. The result is a structure that is unpretentious, civilized, and dignified.

I A 23 · ENGINE COMPANY NO. 10
Water Street at Old Slip
Department of Public Works, 1962

Robert Venturi could not have done it better. Here a "dumb and ordinary" firehouse manages to say something, and to say it without a false note anywhere. This is just a plain building with life to it, thanks to a skillful combination of colors (white and gray marble, breaking at an unexpected point), attractive proportions, and the cutting of a driveway into the bottom rear section to liven up a side elevation. This is one of the best nonentities in New York, and an utter relief in the midst of Water Street.

I A 23 · *Engine Company No. 10*   I A 24 · *First Precinct Police Station*

I A 24 · FIRST PRECINCT POLICE STATION
Old Slip between South and Water streets
Hunt & Hunt, 1909

The Palazzo Strozzi—sort of. The city has better Italian Renaissance palazzi in the form of several banks, but this is an appealing piece of architectural imagery nonetheless. And it is made more significant than ever by virtue of its presence amid Water Street's desolation. What a city New York once wanted to be, to give a local police station such noble quarters!

I A 25 · NEW YORK PLAZA
Water Street, Coenties Slip to Whitehall Street
· 1 NEW YORK PLAZA
William Lescaze and Kahn & Jacobs, 1968
· 2 NEW YORK PLAZA
Kahn & Jacobs, 1970
· 4 NEW YORK PLAZA
Carson, Lundin & Thorsen, 1968

There really isn't any plaza at New York Plaza, and there is surely no New York. This is fake addressmanship combined with pretentious architecture, all adding up to very little except the destruction of a valued part of the city. Each building has its own plaza, in fact—which is probably just as well, since the buildings make no effort whatsoever to relate to one another. No. 1 looks like fifty stories of Otis elevator buttons (or blank TV screens), while No. 4 is a brick fortress. No. 2, now known as American Express Plaza, is sheathed with a dreary skin of vertical stripes which indent in an exaggerated expression of exhaust equipment on mechanical floors.

From Kahn & Jacobs one expects no better than this sort of ordinary commercial work. But William Lescaze was, in his day, a modern architect of more than passing interest, and it is unfortunate that he (so like Walter Gropius in the fiasco of the Pan Am Building) should have chosen to lend his name to such a set of design errors.

The lobby of 2 New York Plaza, to take a typical space, is an ugly mix of granite and white marble. Columns come down through the room, and the entire configuration of the space is awkward and senseless. Outside, the so-called plaza is a windswept wasteland. Granite benches directly face a huge waterfall, the back of which is a solid wall lining the street. Each building is seen as a world unto itself, responsible to nothing but itself. Of the three New York Plaza buildings, No. 4 is probably the best, since although its brick façade clashes utterly with its neighbors, the castle-like quality of this building seems to be making a fighting try at expressing the building's role, which is as a housing for Manufacturers Hanover Trust's computer equipment.

Incidentally, the rear of two of the buildings face Jeannette Park, an old neighborhood park renovated by M. Paul Friedberg & Associates. It has been done all in brick, and it is not one of that landscape architect's better efforts. Moreover, it is hard not to raise the question: Why do two huge skyscrapers turn their backs on this park in favor of nonexistent "plazas" from which they gain their false addresses? One can hardly imagine a stronger argument for comprehensive planning than this absurd situation.

I A 26 · FRAUNCES TAVERN BLOCK
the square block bounded by Pearl, Broad, and Water streets, and by Coenties Slip

This is the only full block of old low-rise commercial buildings—which is to say all four sides of a square—still standing in the financial district. Its name comes from the presence of a false, overly genteel, but altogether

I A 26 · *Fraunces Tavern block, with the reconstruction of Fraunces Tavern at the corner*

earnest reconstruction of Fraunces Tavern, the Georgian building in which Washington made his celebrated farewell to his officers. The other buildings are less elegant but more authentic—similar, in fact, to those of Schermerhorn Row. The block has been threatened with destruction a number of times, but it seems to survive—an architectural equivalent of the pigeons and the rats, similarly indestructible, which continue to thrive in Manhattan's difficult environment. Without a larger context the Fraunces Tavern block cannot have the meaning it deserves nor give the pleasure it is capable of, but there is some compensation in the drama of the juxtaposition of its nineteenth-century brick buildings against the massive towers of the New York Plaza grouping just to its south.

I A 27 · CORNER OF WILLIAM, SOUTH WILLIAM, AND BEAVER STREETS

It is worth standing on this corner for a moment, for here, even more than in the conventional vista down Wall Street, the power and aura of the old financial district comes through. The streets are narrow and tight, the buildings excessively built up. Everything is made of stone, solid, hard, absolutely unshakable. There is the venerable old headquarters of Lehman Brothers, gracefully meeting the corner at 1 William Street, the more fanciful corner entrance of the old Delmonico's Restaurant, where brick, terra cotta, and brownstone do a light and pleasing dance together, and the curious mix of sleekness and classical solidity that is 15 William Street. And there is 20 Exchange Place, Cross & Cross's fine, slender limestone tower of 1931, offering its rear entrance to the intersection, and vistas up to the tower of 40 Wall Street. One senses here, as in few other parts of the financial district now, how self-assured a world this was, how utterly closed to those who did not meet it on its own terms.

I A 28 · NEW YORK STOCK EXCHANGE
8 Broad Street, SW corner Wall Street
George B. Post, 1903
addition, Trowbridge & Livingston, 1923

The pasted-on pediment is the thing here—a classical temple to give authenticity to the doings of commerce. Once again, stage-set architecture is the mode in this Wall Street neighborhood which so prides itself on being rational and down-to-earth, and once again, it is done well enough so as to make us want to be forgiving. The building is worth entering, by the way, for a view of the trading floor: it would be one of the grandest interior spaces in Manhattan if empty, and when bustling with activity it is positively staggering.

I A 29 · FEDERAL HALL NATIONAL MEMORIAL
28 Wall Street, NE corner Nassau Street
Town & Davis, John Frazee and Samuel Thompson, 1842

A very fine Doric temple—a real one this time, not a pasted-on front—that served as the Custom House from 1842 to 1862, as the U.S. Subtreasury from 1862 to 1920, and since then as a federal monument to Washington's inauguration (he took the oath of office on this spot). There is an incongruous and excellent but cool rotunda inside; the building is very much worth a careful look, since there is the curiosity of a second portico at the north end on Pine Street.

I A 29 · *Federal Hall National Memorial*

I A 28 · *New York Stock Exchange*

I A 30 · MORGAN GUARANTY TRUST COMPANY
23 Wall Street, SE corner Broad Street
Trowbridge & Livingston, 1913

The intersection of Broad and Wall streets is the heart of the financial district, yet none of the buildings there—Bankers Trust's old headquarters at 14 Wall Street, the New York Stock Exchange, Federal Hall, and the Morgan Guaranty—is a particularly large building. Each, however, is imposing in a way that befits this corner, and perhaps Morgan, as befits its name, is the most imposing of all. The Morgan headquarters is really an exaggerated vestibule; most of the work of the bank is carried on in anonymous buildings next door, and the function of the corner building is to act as symbol. It carries off its mission well: the room is grand, but never altogether intimidating—the 16-foot high chandelier in the middle (added as recently as 1962) brings a certain odd domesticity to the space.

I A 31 · CITIBANK
55 Wall Street, between William and Hanover streets
Isaiah Rogers, 1842
McKim, Mead & White, 1907

Yes, you can add to an old building in a consistent style; no, you won't violate the integrity of your own period by so doing; and who will know who did what seventy years later anyway? Such are the lessons offered us by this fine piece of architectural surgery performed by McKim, Mead & White, who added a huge Corinthian colonnade in 1907 to the equally huge Ionic colonnade that had been built to Isaiah Rogers' designs between 1836 and 1842. The Rogers building was constructed as the Merchants' Exchange and later served as the Custom House, and McKim was called in for what today would be called an adaptive re-use job, refitting the building to house the First National City Bank, now Citibank.
   The feat was pulled off with deftness and skill. All of the integrity of the lower portion remains, yet McKim, Mead & White managed to make a statement of their own nevertheless. They did so by taking their cues from the Rogers building—not always literally (the change from Ionic to Corinthian columns was a conspicuous one), but in deciding to use a roughly similar kind of colonnade, to use a similar system of proportion, and to emphasize, as Rogers did, depth and shadow as well as surface detail.
   The main banking space is Wall Street's grandest and most welcoming; just as pleasing is the sense of making one's way through the colonnade toward the front door. The space between the columns and the entrance door is one of the city's great architectural interludes.

I A 32 · 40 WALL STREET
H. *Craig Severance and Yasuo Matsui, 1929*
· 70 PINE STREET
Clinton & Russell, 1932

These two are Wall Street's entries in the skyscraper sweepstakes that emerged out of the boom of the 1920's—flamboyant, rich towers that do for downtown what the Chrysler Building does for midtown. No. 40 Wall is the more restrained, its inventiveness limited largely to the elaborate, lantern-topped tower sixty-six stories above the street. No. 70 Pine, built as the headquarters of the Cities Service Company, is a wild celebration of Wall Street's riches—an Art Deco–inspired lobby that is as good as anything downtown, and a nobly massed profile culminating in a strong crown that one can only call Jazz Gothic.

No. 70 Pine Street was clearly built as an object of great pride—the Cities Service Company had its logo worked into much of the lobby detailing, and the entries contain a thoroughly appealing piece of architectural narcissism—limestone models of the tower set over the doorways. The building was once connected to a lower structure across the street at 60 Wall Street (indeed, it was once known as the 60 Wall Tower). When Cities Service decided it no longer wanted to service cities and abandoned New York for the Middle West, it ordered the smaller Wall Street wing demolished, leaving just the tower. Lighter brick on a spot fifteen floors up in the tower still marks the spot where a bridge once connected the two buildings.

I A 33 · *One Chase Manhattan Plaza, sculpture by Jean Dubuffet*

I A 33 · *One Chase Manhattan Plaza, with 40 Wall Street (I A 32) in the foreground*

I A 33 · ONE CHASE MANHATTAN PLAZA
between Nassau, William, Liberty, and Pine streets
Skidmore, Owings & Merrill (Gordon Bunshaft, partner in charge), 1960

This is the box all the others came in, so to speak: the first major new building, and the first notable example of the International Style, to be built in the financial district. It had the important result of anchoring a neighborhood already troubled by an exodus to midtown; it offered open space where none had existed before; and it brought a few of Gordon Bunshaft's careful details to downtown. But the positive side of the ledger stops there.

Chase's boxy form dealt the first blow to the financial district's classic skyline profile, a romantically jagged edge now turned into utter banality by all of this building's progeny. The plaza, a welcome place in principle, has been only partially successful, since Bunshaft was more interested in a platform to set off the tower than in creating usable space; as a result, the plaza takes no cognizance of changes in grade around the building, and it is as much as a full story above the street on some sides.

What Chase did succeed in doing was to bring a new prestige address to Wall Street; this bank headquarters is shared by many of New York's most venerable law firms, who gave up old Wall Street quarters to move here. Curiously, what seems to have attracted them was affectation not only of an architectural sort but also of a verbal sort: it is 1 Chase Manhattan Plaza that initiated the pretentious and confusing custom, now imitated all over the nation, of calling new office towers One This-or-That Plaza. Why aren't street addresses good enough any more?

Altogether to be praised, by the way, is the splendid Dubuffet sculpture, "Four Trees," which brings much joy to the plaza.

I A 34 · NEW YORK CHAMBER OF COMMERCE
65 Liberty Street, between Broadway and Nassau streets
James B. Baker, 1901

A Beaux-Arts fantasy, too precious to be significant, yet infinitely more likable than the grandiose Custom House a few blocks to the south (I A 1). Once there were three monumental sculpture groups on the façade in the blank spaces framed by the high Ionic columns; air pollution and pigeons, it is said, did them in. The off-center entrance is a curiosity, and suggests comparison with the New York Yacht Club by Warren & Wetmore (II E 8), a still more fanciful exercise on a similar scale. The Chamber of Commerce has an interior room of extraordinary opulence, off limits, unfortunately, to the public.

I A 35 · FEDERAL RESERVE BANK OF NEW YORK
33 Liberty Street, between William and Nassau streets
York & Sawyer, 1924

One's money *has* to be safe here. That, after all, is what Florentine palaces are all about. The Strozzis and the Medicis were around a bit before the Federal Reserve, and why not pick up a few of their tricks?

A decade ago such words would have been written in obvious sarcasm; today they are meant seriously. Image *is* important, often far more important than formal purity. York & Sawyer, New York's most prominent firm of bank architects, had an understanding of the value of image combined with the gift of composition, and as a result, their works are convincing on all levels. The Federal Reserve is a handsome building, freely adapting Italian Renaissance precedent to the demands of twentieth-century New York. There are not many things downtown as successful.

The adaptation gets freer the more you look at the building, of course. Not only is the size different, but so is the shape. The most appealing view of the Federal Reserve is from the east, where the building narrows considerably to conform to an awkwardly shaped site. From there the building looks like the bow of a ship of rusticated stone, sailing forthrightly down Maiden Lane, with a rooftop castle as the cabin on its deck. All of the solemnity of the façade is gone, and to make this view still more appealing, there in the distance is the Gothic top of Henry Ives Cobb's 1910 tower at the corner of Liberty and Nassau streets.

I A 36 · 100 WILLIAM STREET
SE corner John Street
Davis, Brody & Associates, 1974

Sheathed in slate, this boxy building harks back to the days when everything in the financial district was built of solid masonry. It is discreet and appealing, a welcome relief from the shrieking eccentricities of such confections as the New York Plaza grouping.

No. 100 William Street is most notable, however, for its pedestrian arcade. The building's design was among the first to take advantage of special zoning legislation encouraging covered public space instead of open plazas; Davis, Brody's skillful mix of chrome, glass, and slate has made for a lively place, an altogether pleasant interlude in the relatively dreary streetscape of the blocks just north of Wall Street.

I A 37 · JOHN STREET METHODIST CHURCH
44 John Street, between Nassau and William streets
1841

This is a pleasing façade of brownstone, unremarkable but excellent. It is most appealing for its strong austerity, a welcome moment of quiet in a visually chaotic part of town; there are few buildings that can evoke as pleasant a sense of surprise as this unexpected church in the midst of the bustling financial district. The Georgian interior is excellent.

I A 34 · *New York Chamber of Commerce*

I A 37 · *John Street Methodist Church*

B/CIVIC CENTER

The term "civic center" is a bit formal for the City Hall–Foley Square area, but it does sum up the neighborhood's prime function, the housing of government. Moreover, it suggests the aspirations, generally misguided, which bureaucrats have had for generations to give the area more coherence. Some of the early schemes were provocative, most of the recent ones dreadful, such as the Edward Durell Stone plan to demolish the Tweed Courthouse and several blocks north of Chambers Street to create an immense open plaza, within which would be set a single tower, a near twin to the same architect's General Motors Building uptown.

That has now, finally, died, but it was too slow a death, for the years when the plan was considered official city policy were time enough for the city to allow several fine buildings on the sites slated for demolition to

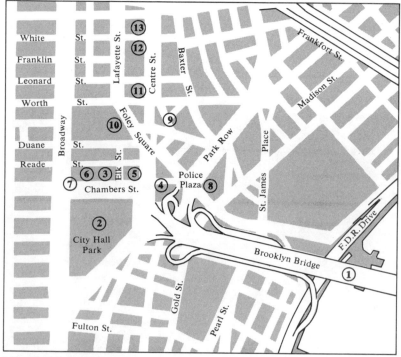

deteriorate to the point where, today, costs for restoration are unreasonably high. The civic center is now a mix of distinguished old buildings, distinguished new buildings, mediocre new buildings, mediocre old buildings, and empty lots. There is not much coherence to it all, although in its architectural pluralism it stands as a far better expression of New York than any of the replacement plans could ever be.

I B 1 · *West pier of the Brooklyn Bridge*

I B 1 · BROOKLYN BRIDGE
John A. and Washington A. Roebling, 1883

It would not be unreasonable to say that the two greatest works of architecture in New York are things that are not buildings at all—Central Park and the Brooklyn Bridge. Each is a magnificent object in its own right; each was the result of a brilliant synthesis of art and engineering after which the world was never quite the same.

To tell the story of the bridge in a brief essay is impossible, and to add substantially to what has been said already is barely less difficult. I can quote a few favorite remarks about the bridge, such as James Marston Fitch's observation that "the nineteenth century saw three great developments in structural theory: the enclosure of great areas in the Crystal Palace, the spanning of great voids in the Brooklyn Bridge, and the reaching of great heights in the Eiffel Tower." I also like Kenneth Clark's remark that "all modern New York, heroic New York, started with Brooklyn Bridge."

The bridge, thus, is an icon. It stands for movement, for thrust, for the triumph of man over nature, and, ultimately, for a city that prized these qualities above all other things. Today suspension bridges are a commonplace, and there have been bridges longer than the Brooklyn for fifty years, yet this bridge still holds an immense sway over our imaginations. It is not merely the result of the dramatic story of its construction, which took

I B 1 · *Pedestrian walk on the Brooklyn Bridge, looking west toward the Financial District skyline*

sixteen years and more than twenty lives, including that of its designer, John A. Roebling. It is only partially the result of the bridge's role as a cultural symbol, a piece of the landscape to be sold to the gullible, a part of the language to millions of people who will never actually see it.

All of these things play a part, but the reason most of us are so unutterably moved when we stand before the bridge is that, when all is said and done, it is an object of startling beauty. The road leaps with immense grace, the towers hold strong (how remarkable they must have looked, in 1883, when they were far and away the highest things on the skyline), and the cables join the parts of the structure together in a pattern of stunning delicacy.

The Gothic arches of the towers remind us that the bridge, for all the technological advance it represented, was very much a product of the nineteenth century. They were thought by modernist critics to hold the bridge back and compromise its meaning—Montgomery Schuyler complained in 1883 that the towers should have been simple piers, which would "assert themselves starkly and unmistakably as the bones of the structure." In the present arrangement, Schuyler felt, romantic form had been substituted for pure expression of function, and the result prevented the bridge from being a great work of architecture.

That is ideological hedging, and the fact of the matter is that the Gothic towers *do* express function—the function of the bridge as a symbolic gateway between two cities. The great arches do that well; to post-modern eyes, there is nothing wrong with a building functioning on both a romantically expressionist level and a technological one, and indeed, the bridge's ability to do both at once can be said to be still further enhancement of its appeal. The bridge is a tie not merely between two shores, but between two ways of seeing the world—the certainty of solid form as expressed in the Gothic towers, the risk of technology as expressed in the soaring roadway. Both are real, both were parts of their time as they are of ours, and in revealing its struggle to be both old and new at once, the bridge becomes a humane object.

A walk across the Brooklyn Bridge is not like any other experience in

New York, or in any other city. You are at once immersed in the life of the
city and above it: the view of the skyline is stunning; of the river, exciting;
and of the bridge itself, pleasingly intimate. You want not only to touch the
great stone towers but also to feel the panorama of the city at a distance,
and you can do both, all at once. The city gleams through the shimmering
cables, and it is only the incessant sound of the traffic that brings you back
to earth.

I B 2 · CITY HALL
City Hall Park, between Broadway and Park Row
Joseph F. Mangin, John McComb, Jr., 1811

It makes no sense at all that the largest city in the nation is still run from
the same small building that housed its headquarters in 1811, and that fact
is absolutely wonderful. City Hall is a splendid little palace, a bastard born
of French Renaissance and Georgian parentage; it is both delicate and self-
assured—a rare combination indeed. The building was always a bit too
refined for this harsh, aggressively growing city, which makes the nature
of its use today merely the continuation of a historical irony.

The building sits well in City Hall Park, its steps offering views of the
Brooklyn Bridge to the east and the Woolworth Building to the west. When
City Hall was new, it was at the uptown end of New York, and the city
fathers were so certain that the city's growth would ebb that they decided
to save money by facing the rear in brownstone instead of marble, on the
theory that no one would be likely to view the building from the north.
Once, then, the city practiced economy before hubris.

The building's quality is not limited to its superb façades. The central
hall, with its twin spiral, self-supporting marble stairs under a dome, is one
of the city's finest public interiors. And the Board of Estimate chambers
on the second floor, reached by a Corinthian-columned gallery, is a splendid
public chamber, grand in more of an eighteenth-century way than a
nineteenth, and a superbly anachronistic setting for the testimony of angry
citizens come to complain about the failings of twentieth-century bureaucracy.

I B 3 · TWEED COURTHOUSE
52 Chambers Street, between Broadway and Centre Street
John Kellum, 1872

Boss Tweed was modest enough not to give his name to the building his
administration erected just behind City Hall, but history has done it for
him. A building may have been put up to house criminal courts, but when
a city administration manages to use it as the funnel for such scandal that
its final cost is more than twenty times the projected budget, it is only fair
that the structure stand as a memorial to such greed.

The problem is, the Tweed Courthouse has been remembered for too
long just as a receptacle for Tweed's payoffs and paddings, and the
distinction of its Anglo-Italianate exterior and the potential of its fine central

well are often overlooked. The city has mistreated the building for years, beginning with an unmatching (though excellent) Romanesque wing by C. L. W. Eidlitz added just after the main building was finished, and continuing through the destruction of the great entrance stair in the 1940's. Now the building is a near ruin; one must enter it through an unpleasant basement, and it is no wonder that it is less than beloved. This is unfortunate, since the city really did get quality for all of Tweed's kickbacks (if you pay a carpenter $360,747 for a month's work and a plasterer $2,870,464 for nine months' work, they have to do *something*), and the building is in fact one of the most distinguished structures in the civic-center area. Indeed, there are few better Anglo-Italianate public buildings anywhere.

I B 2 · *City Hall in the foreground, with the Municipal Building* (I B 4) *in the background*

I B 4 · MUNICIPAL BUILDING
1 Centre Street, at Chambers Street
McKim, Mead & White (William M. Kendall in charge), 1914

This is no Woolworth Building, but it is nonetheless one of the finest eclectic skyscrapers in Manhattan. The challenge McKim, Mead & White faced was a subtle one—to create a large building on a difficult site straddling Chambers Street that would not overwhelm City Hall. It was pulled off so deftly that the result, more than sixty years later, remains an object lesson in sensitive urbanism.

The building is shaped like a somewhat flattened "U," which, from the south, creates the sense that it is embracing the far smaller City Hall. From the west, however, it sits solidly and symmetrically over Chambers Street, which proceeds below it with newfound dignity. (The street is now closed to through traffic under the building, but the sense of procession under the great vaulted space still remains.)

The Municipal Building was as serious an attempt as any other to interpret the skyscraper form in terms of historical style, and while it lacks the unusual grace of Woolworth, it is nonetheless a building of inventiveness. The top is a wedding-cake sequence of colonnaded towers surmounted by Adolph Weinman's statue "Civic Fame"—the innocently grandiose vision of the City Beautiful movement come to New York in skyscraper form. Daniel Burnham would have liked it.

I B 5 · SURROGATE'S COURT
31 Chambers Street, NW corner Centre Street
John R. Thomas, Horgan & Slattery, 1911

A lavishly detailed pile of Beaux-Arts detail that is bigger than the Chamber of Commerce, smaller than the Custom House, and as good as either one of these. The façade is an especially appealing composition: a heavy base containing a triple-arched central entrance two stories high, over which is a three-story Corinthian colonnade flanked by side sections unprotected by columns. Cornices run over this, then another floor, another cornice, and, finally, a richly ornamented mansard at the top. It is all superbly balanced and controlled, rich yet never excessive.

The Surrogate's Court has a central hall that is far and away one of the city's finest Beaux-Arts rooms. It is the grand foyer of the Paris Opéra in miniature, though hardly a literal reproduction. But there is a splendid staircase and a finely colonnaded upper story, and the delightful sense of reduced scale—it feels as if it should be bigger, but it isn't, and thus has an exquisite and unexpected intimacy.

I B 6 · EMIGRANT BANK BUILDING
49–51 Chambers Street, between Broadway and Elk Street
Raymond F. Almirall, 1913

An intended backdrop to City Hall, this commercial building, now owned and largely occupied by the City of New York, was designed with considerable respect and cordiality toward its small and distinguished neighbor. There is a double tower topped by eagles and globes, and the building is on axis with the center of both City Hall and the Tweed Courthouse. Most impressive, however, is the banking space on the first floor—a majestic hall that is among the best banking rooms left in New York.

Unlike such better-known banking spaces as the Bowery on East 42nd Street and the Central Savings Bank at 73rd Street and Broadway, the Emigrant's room is gentle and gracious rather than grandiose and awe-inspiring. It is a formal room, but made soft and almost sensual thanks to the flowing elliptical shapes repeated throughout. They hint at the feeling of Art Nouveau. There are four large oval skylights of stained glass that represent facets of the economy; figures in the glass are labeled "Mining," "Agriculture," "Banking," "Transportation," and the like, and the bronze and marble counters are especially fine. The city now uses the room as a place in which the Parking Violations Bureau collects fines; it is a banal use, but at least the room is intact. The upper floors are used for city offices and rented out to private tenants. These offices are entered through once-elegant elevator lobbies, now shabby and full of the feeling of old-time politics—it is clear that the cigar-chomping criminal lawyer rents space here, not the Wall Street deal-maker.

I B 7 · 280 BROADWAY (Sun Building)
NE corner Chambers Street
J. B. Snook and Joseph Trench, 1846 onwards

Like the Emigrant Bank, this, too, has passed into city hands. And, like the Emigrant Bank, the city has abused it, toyed with demolishing it, and now lets it languish on minimal maintenance. The building deserves better: built in 1846 as the headquarters for the A. T. Stewart Department Store, 280 Broadway was a marble palace of commerce, among the very first Italianate commercial buildings anywhere in the nation and a dazzling presence on the then small-scaled Broadway. It was taken over by the New York *Sun* in 1917 (which added the clock with its legend "The Sun It Shines for All"). The city has owned it since 1966. No. 280's influence was considerable in spreading the Italianate style through the city and, ultimately, around the nation, so this can truly be said to be one of the few buildings in the civic center not only with intrinsic quality, but with genuine significance in the history of architecture.

I B 8 · BEYOND THE ARCH OF THE MUNICIPAL BUILDING: "GRUZEN COUNTRY"

There is one architectural firm in New York City that has been notably successful in obtaining commissions in the civic-center area, so much so that the blocks behind and just north and south of the Municipal Building seem at first glance to consist entirely of structures of its design. The firm is Gruzen & Partners, and unlike most of the other politically well-connected architects who operate in New York, the standard of design has been relatively decent.

The firm's impact here has been enormous. Most notable is the Police Headquarters, completed in 1973, its entrance right on axis with the great

I B 8 · *Police Headquarters*   **I B 8** · *Chatham Terrace*

central arch of the Municipal Building. A plaza by M. Paul Friedberg & Associates connects the Municipal Building to the new Police Headquarters; the building is a dignified structure of red brick and concrete. A grid of windows, attractively detailed, encloses the upper floors which house office space; below this waffle-like façade the scale changes, enlarging to reflect the civic functions of lower floors. The style is a kind of mild Brutalism—the Boston City Hall tamed. It is not as daring or important a building as Boston's, but, curiously, it succeeds best where Boston's monument fails, as a provider of decent pedestrian open space.

The police headquarters could have pulled the entire area together. As it is, it makes an effort, but the eastern segment of the civic center remains jumbled. Gruzen's additions to the U.S. Courthouse on Foley Square, completed in 1974, alleviate the problem somewhat. They are simple structures of striated concrete, discreet and helpful in providing a sense of overall continuity in the area, and good reminders of how additions can be presences in themselves and yet not detract from the main event.

Gruzen has also wrought the decent but undistinguished Southbridge Towers housing complex just below the Brooklyn Bridge and the low concrete structure, which is Bache & Co.'s headquarters, at 100 Gold Street, also just below the bridge. Far more interesting are the firm's two housing projects northeast of the Municipal Building: Chatham Green, a great undulating wall of red brick built in 1961, and Chatham Terrace, a group of powerfully articulated towers of raw concrete completed in 1965. Chatham Green is dated now: too earnest, too eager to be "designed" to be convincing, though it is a well-meaning attempt at innovation. But Chatham Terrace has aged well, and even though it could be called heavy-handed Corbusier (which it clearly is), it is well-scaled, comfortable, and visually attractive—qualities which help any building survive the passage of time.

Gruzen's other effort in the blocks east of the Municipal Building is the Murray Bergtraum High School, built in tandem with the vast tower by Rose, Beaton & Rose that houses equipment for the New York Telephone Company. Neither segment of this unfortunate marriage is very attractive: the Gruzen school is a dark brick fortress, while the Rose, Beaton & Rose tower is a massive and utterly banal intrusion into the skyline, performing what can only be called an act of urban cruelty, as it cuts off much of the view of the Brooklyn Bridge.

I B 9 · *New York County Courthouse*

I B 9 · U.S. COURTHOUSE
Foley Square, SE side, south of Pearl Street
Cass Gilbert, Cass Gilbert, Jr., 1936
· NEW YORK COUNTY COURTHOUSE
Foley Square, E side, north of Pearl Street
Guy Lowell, 1912

Foley Square's two Corinthian-columned courthouses taken together give definition to this amorphous open space. The Cass Gilbert building wants to be a skyscraper, and in his old age Gilbert seems to have lost the ability to let it soar, as he could do with his Woolworth Building twenty-three years before. The result is an awkward compromise, a pyramid-topped tower set on a classical temple base. It is one of those buildings that are always all right, never inspired, and it is sad to see Gilbert's romanticism made into something so forced, so hardened, at this point in his career— Mozart become Tchaikovsky.

Not that there is so much heart to Guy Lowell's New York County Courthouse next door. But there is a liveliness to the hexagonal plan, and at least this time the Corinthian colonnade seems right—this building is a real temple in its massing and scale, not a tower trying to look like one.

I B 10 · FEDERAL BUILDING AND CUSTOMS COURTHOUSE
Foley Square, W side, between Duane and Worth streets
Alfred Easton Poor, Kahn & Jacobs, Eggers & Higgins, 1967, 1976

Whatever the U.S. Courthouse and the N.Y. County Courthouse do to bring coherence to Foley Square, this building undoes completely. It consists of a glass box (the court) set in front of a decorative checkerboard-skinned tower (the offices), and surely the architects are full of all sorts of clever theories about how well the low, separate, and more formal courthouse and the bigger, blander office area behind it are appropriate expressions of their different roles. Claptrap. Both are designed with the subtlety of an airport concourse—each, in its own way, strikes a deep blow at the compositional order of Foley Square as a whole, which is hardly given coherence by a pair of clashing boxes.

Discord seems to have been consciously sought here—it is achieved so often. Not only does the courthouse wing clash with the office tower and both of them clash with the old courts across the square, but the rear section of the tower (added a few years later) clashes entirely with the front section. There are two skins used, both of them ugly, and they fight each other as much as they fight everything around them.

The final, and cruelest, irony of all of this is that this project happened at the same time that Chicago was getting Mies van der Rohe's Federal Center. Maybe the federal government *does* have it in for New York after all.

I B 11 · CRIMINAL COURTS BUILDING AND PRISON ("THE TOMBS")
100 Centre Street, between Worth and Leonard streets
Harvey Wiley Corbett, Charles B. Meyers, 1939

From a distance, this is a handsome composition—a granite base, limestone top, casement windows, and a few Art Deco curlicues. It could be an uptown apartment house. It could be, that is, until you get to the entrance.

The front door of the Tombs is one of the most brilliantly contrived, if evil, stage sets in the City of New York. It is set back in a court, the opening of which contains two thirty-foot-high square granite columns, supporting nothing. One can go straight in between them and thence, on axis, to the door, or one can enter beside the columns and around a slight bend on which is inscribed on one side, "Where Law Ends There Tyranny Begins," and on the other, "Only the Just Man Enjoys Peace of Mind." Once past the columns and in the court, a kind of roofless vestibule, the

I B 10 · *United States Customs Courthouse, with the Federal Building in the background*

I B 11 · *Criminal Courts Building and Prison*

vast height of the building suddenly becomes clear; the immense doors set into a three-story-high entrance loom ahead with the words "Criminal Courts Building" carved in huge letters above.

No one, I would suspect, could pass through that entrance without feeling himself guilty. It is architecture out of Kafka; one can admire the skill with which it has been put together at the same time one mourns for those who pass through it without the luxury of contemplating its meaning disinterestedly.

I B 12 · MUNICIPAL AND CIVIL COURT BUILDING
III Centre Street, SW corner White Street
William Lescaze and Matthew Del Gaudio, 1960
· FAMILY COURT BUILDING
60 Lafayette Street, between Leonard and White streets
Haines Lundberg Waehler, 1976

There are many generations of courthouse design around Foley Square, and these two are the latest. The Lescaze building is what happens when the modernists make it clear that they know better than all that old fancy stuff and try to strip it down; the Haines Lundberg Waehler building is what happens when somebody tries to put it all back. Neither is very successful.

The Lescaze building is just a bland box, period. The Haines Lundberg Waehler building is more interesting but, ultimately, not much better—it is so contorted, so needlessly agonized, as to be more a piece of narcissism than of architecture. The Family Court is a huge box of polished gray granite, its shiny dark surface reflecting neighboring structures. There is a high entrance colonnade, several 45-degree cuts into the façade that reflect interior rooms set at 45 degrees off from the main axis of the building, and a few projecting windows up high. It is all abstract, and all pretentious— although one cannot deny the good intentions of the architects, who realized

I B 12 · *Family Court Building*

I B 13 · *Engine Company No. 31*

that a strong masonry box is an appropriate expression of civic architecture and tried to restore some dignity—robbed by so many recent efforts—to the notion of the courthouse.

I B 13 · ENGINE COMPANY NO. 31
87 Lafayette Street, NE corner White Street
Napoleon Le Brun, 1895

This is a French Renaissance château and it served just fine as a firehouse, thank you. It is tempting to look at this now empty building as an eccentric confection, but it is in some ways far more appealing than the old Vanderbilt mansion of similar style, on Fifth Avenue, was. There is less pretension here, yet great scale in detailing—absolutely lovely scale—and fine massing. This is a gem by any standard: the best of the many eclectic firehouses around town done by the Le Brun firm in the 1890's. That was a time when first-class architecture for civic purposes was considered as much of a necessity as fire protection itself.

Plans call for the eventual re-use of this building as some sort of community service center; it has been unused by fire engines for several years.

C/TRIBECA

This is what SoHo once was: the industrial neighborhood of glorious industrial architecture that still remains just about that. No other city in the world has as much fine cast-iron architecture as New York does, and while SoHo is more famous for it, some of the very best examples—along with much fine masonry construction—can be found in the blocks below Canal Street and west of Church Street.

The neighborhood is right now in the process of either slipping or improving, depending upon who you are and what you want from it; there is no question that the SoHo-ization has been proceeding in earnest for some time now. The new name is indicative of that: TRIangleBELowCAnal Street, cute enough to make the name SoHo sound like Wall Street by comparison.

Now the area is full of living lofts, many of them occupied by the artists driven out of SoHo by the price of their own success at making that a viable neighborhood. Soon, if the process keeps up, they will be forced away from Tribeca, too, for the buildings are as desirable here, the atmosphere quieter and more attractive, and the prices firmly on the rise.

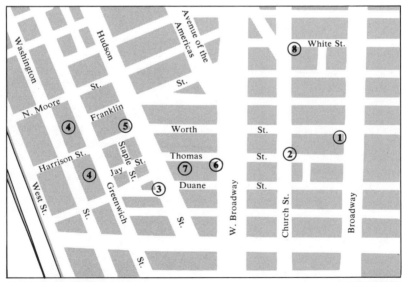

I / LOWER MANHATTAN   C / TRIBECA

Hanging plants now appear in the windows of buildings where machinery and warehoused goods used to sit—the ultimate test of the presence of the middle class. (Indeed, hanging plants are considered such a giveaway that residents say the City Planning Commission checks on the number of lofts being used as residences by sending people up and down the streets of Tribeca, counting plants in the windows.)

The ebb and flow of the city is ceaseless; this is the shore upon which the wave is now breaking.

I C 1 · AT&T LONG LINES BUILDING
Broadway at Worth Street
John Carl Warnecke & Associates, 1974

Built and owned by the New York Telephone Company for lease to its parent AT&T, this is the only one of the several windowless equipment buildings around town that make sense architecturally. The other such structures either try to look like conventional buildings (even down to fake windows) and fail miserably at it, or are just ugly bunkers. Here, however, Warnecke has made the building itself an enormous piece of equipment— the sides rise as walls of granite, neatly articulated, and the building culminates in huge vents at the top. It is admittedly sculptural, but it is restrained and carefully proportioned, and the warm color of the stone used helps a great deal. One might say, in fact, that the form attempts to express the building's role as a piece of equipment, and the stone sheathing expresses its role as a part of the cityscape—a successful and visually pleasing way of pulling off a double-barreled challenge.

I C 2 · STATE INSURANCE FUND
199 Church Street
Lorimer Rich Associates, 1955

This is Funky Bauhaus: a nice, relaxed air where it is least expected. There is nothing remarkable about this building except for the fact that it is visually pleasing, which few fifteen-story white-brick structures with horizontal strip windows in New York are. The metal sunscreenlike devices above the windows do not appear to be terribly effective, but they look good, and at least they represent an effort to acknowledge the existence of the sun—something that makes this building still more of a standout by comparison with others of its style. The canopy, brick exterior and mosaics, along with the strip windows, mark this firmly as a 1950's project, but it is far superior to its contemporaries from that generally fallow period.

I C 3 · DUANE PARK

This is the sort of place cities around the country struggle to create; New York has had it all along, and it is ignored. Duane Park is one of those

I C 1 · *AT&T Long Lines Building, with the State Insurance Fund Building* (I C 2) *in the foreground*

I C 5 · *Mercantile Exchange*

accidents in a city which cannot be planned, and perhaps it is just as well that not too many people know about it, because this is one place that could never survive the madding crowd.

All it is, is a little triangle left over by the oddly shaped intersection of Duane and Hudson streets. Now, the city is filled with such intersections, and many of them try to be parks. This one succeeds where most of the others fail because, first, it is surrounded—tightly—by superb buildings, all of which work together to create a coherent whole, and second, because it is furnished attractively, but utterly unpretentiously, with a few simple benches and landscaped with a few trees. There are no tricks, no gimmicks— just the sense of what makes an oasis.

Not that the park would be easy to miss, given the quality of the buildings that surround it. While none is remarkable in itself, all are good, and they represent a range of nineteenth- (and in one case, twentieth-) century architecture. There are Italianate, Romanesque, Greek Revival, and Art Deco–inspired buildings; almost everything is in masonry, helping to pull the group together, and everything is in more or less similar scale, but there were never any deliberate attempts to carry along any stylistic motifs from building to building.

Probably the best single building on the square is the red-brick structure at No. 169 Duane Street (c. 1880, Stephen D. Hatch), a grand and self-assured mix of rounded arches, Romanesque and Italianate details, topped off with a mansard roof. The brickwork is especially fine.

Next door is 171 Duane Street, a delicate five-story cast-iron front built onto the structure of a three-story Federal house in 1859. Fluted piers rise for the upper four stories, giving the entire structure an elegant and subtle verticality that prefigures the skyscraper detailing of Sullivan; the base is the loading dock of M. J. King, the wholesale egg firm that has been in the building for nearly fifty years.

Other buildings of note: 173 Duane, a brick structure more frankly Romanesque than 169; 63 Duane, an excellent Romanesque structure with rich, deep-red sandstone contrasting warmly with tan brick, and an appealing castellated top; and 60 Hudson Street, Voorhees, Gmelin & Walker's building of 1930 for the Western Union Company, which powerfully closes off the vista from Duane Park to the north. Like Ralph Walker's other major buildings downtown (I A 4 and I A 11) Western Union is Art Deco in inspiration, and deeply concerned with problems of massing. Here, the use of different colors of brick—a favorite 1930's decorative gesture—gives the building a variety of shadings from brown to pink.

As significant as the buildings themselves around Duane Park are the views: the tower of the Woolworth Building is visible to the southeast, the tip of the Municipal Building's tower can be seen to the east, and the new towers of Independence Plaza housing project are visible to the west. The immediate surroundings are thus largely of the nineteenth century, but the views encompass more of the ciy, saving Duane Park from becoming a place of illusion. There is, however, just the right amount of illusion—from most benches in the park the angle of the surrounding buildings makes it impossible to see the World Trade Center. Otherwise, Duane Park is real— the buildings around it are full of companies wholesaling butter, eggs, and cheese; the streets are active with commerce, yet are never frenetic; the place is a world that works. It puts such artificial nineteenth-century contraptions as Seattle's Pioneer Square to shame.

I C 4 · INDEPENDENCE PLAZA NORTH
Washington Street between Duane and North Moore streets
Oppenheimer, Brady & Vogelstein; John Pruyn, 1975

It was not so many years ago that the warmth and serenity of Duane Park extended west to the Hudson River. There was Washington Market, the city's wholesale food district, New York's equivalent of Covent Garden and Les Halles. Never let it be said that we were behind London and Paris in anything; at roughly the same time as Paris and London New York made the same irrational decision that the presence of such facilities was a detriment to a dense urban area rather than an asset to it. Off went Washington Market to Hunts Point in the Bronx, and in came the bulldozers. The result is a housing project called Independence Plaza, and it is not a terribly happy place to be.

It bursts suddenly upon you as you come to Greenwich Street, the north–south street that forms the border between the extant old neighborhood to the east and the urban renewal site to the west. The two worlds confront each other across Greenwich Street, the new one in the form of three huge brick towers splayed out at the top à la Waterside (II A 17). But these are not nearly as good as Waterside as formal objects—there is too much concrete, too much of an institutional, public-housing aura to them. The buildings never lose this feeling as one walks through the project, up and down stairs and across terraces and plazas that have dramatic city and river views but are, at bottom, cold places. The instinct behind all of this— to bring housing to Lower Manhattan—was a good one, but the utter failure to recognize the workings of a neighborhood was sadly typical of its time. This is surely not worse than most housing contemporary to it, and it is better than a great deal of it—it is Independence Plaza's fate to stare across

Washington Street at one of New York's most appealing places, making its own good points all the harder to perceive.

There is a group of "restored" eighteenth-century town houses in the middle of the project site, brought there from elsewhere in the urban renewal area as a gesture toward neighborhood preservation. It was an earnest, well-meaning idea that has turned out disastrously—the houses huddle beneath the towers, looking like children cowering in the presence of stern adults. There are façades at Disneyland that look more real, and all that these houses make you want to do is run back again across Greenwich Street where old buildings are still real and not kept alive by artificial respirator.

I C 5 · MERCANTILE EXCHANGE
6 Harrison Street, NW corner Hudson Street
Thomas R. Jackson, 1886

This is a posh glory, not great architecture but utterly likable, much like an overdressed woman whose wardrobe manages to show just enough style to save her from vulgarity. There are arches and gables and columns and cornices and a clock tower culminating in a wonderful fanciful roof. The materials are red brick and granite; in the late afternoon sun on the right sort of day the light brings color worthy of Monet. There is no true inspiration here, but there is something humane and loving in this kind of opulent, singing pile of masonry—just those qualities missing in the place for which the New York Mercantile Exchange abandoned this building in 1977, the World Trade Center.

I C 6 · 147 WEST BROADWAY
SE corner Thomas Street
John O'Neil, 1869

A very special little piece of cast iron, as good a reminder as anything in New York of what a splendidly illusionistic material that metal could be. This looks for all the world like a five-story building of blocks of stone, finely articulated with quoins at the corners. The façade is really of cast iron, however—it gives itself away to the careful observer who notes how precise and perfect all of the rusticated quoins are, as well as to those who can see bits of rust.

All cast-iron architecture depended in part upon the illusion of stone, of course. But normally the architect's interest was in using cast iron to simulate columns and arches and porticoes, whereas here O'Neil actually simulated a conventional stone wall. New York as stage set is a notion that, plainly, began long before Stanford White.

I C 7 · 8 THOMAS STREET
J. Morgan Slade, 1875

A cast-iron storefront for the bottom, a Ruskinian Gothic commercial building for the top. The cast-iron columns are unusually slender and

I C 6 · *Detail of 147 West Broadway*

I C 7 · *8 Thomas Street*

I C 8 · *10 White Street*

delicate, but the main interest is in the façade, robust and lyrical at the same time. I hesitate to use the word "charming," and it is one that is rarely applicable to any first-class building, much less a Ruskinian Gothic one, but it seems appropriate here, where town-house scale joins with Gothic earnestness to create a civilized façade. It is an altogether atypical building, and even in the cast-iron-rich terrain of the blocks below Canal Street, it is a treasure.

I C 8 · WHITE STREET
West Broadway to Avenue of the Americas

Not the most perfect of the Tribeca loft blocks but a typical one, with the mix of styles and periods of the area, which contains, as well, a sense of the onward ebb and flow of the entire city: the cutting through of the Avenue of the Americas led to many oddly shaped lots and blank sides of buildings within view of this block.

Among the more notable buildings is 10 White Street (Henry Fernbach, 1969) which has finely crafted mock-rusticated stonework in segmental arches over the windows. As in all of the better cast-iron buildings, the detail is strong, the feeling robust, and yet there is a somewhat malleable air to it all, too: we feel as if the thing had been made out of a huge mound of clay by a giant who possessed the perfect molds. Across the street is 17 White Street, another loft building, this one with a cast-iron base and a mansard roof with oculi poking through.

D/CHINATOWN—
LITTLE ITALY

Tight, compressed areas—they have uneven, shifting borders, yet you always know when you are there. Chinatown begins just east of the civic center, starting out on a plot of land that was once called, after an intersection, Five Points, and was the worst slum in the city in the mid-nineteenth century. The rear walls of the county and federal courthouses are Chinatown's own west wall; it is remarkable how suddenly the heavy ambience of official granite disappears on the other side.

Both Chinatown and Little Italy are neighborhoods of street life—Little Italy so much so that at semiannual festival time merely finding a place to walk on a street, let alone drive, can be an effort. The architecture of interest is minimal. Chinatown's best housing, Chatham Terrace and Chatham Towers, is really part of the civic-center area (I B 8). Much of the housing is of the tenement variety, and there are relatively few public buildings of note.

It is all really the streets here. There is a particular Chinatown style of restaurant; it is in no way Chinese and resembles a miniature version of an American cafeteria—fluorescent lights, Formica fixtures, vinyl floor. There is not only no elegance, there is no quaint old-world charm, either. What there is, is vibrancy and life, and that is more important than any kind of design.

It was once the case that Chinatown existed south of Canal Street and Little Italy to the north. Canal still has a symbolic role as a divider, but it is functioning less and less like an inviolable border. Chinatown has been expanding for years, and many of the buildings to the north of Canal Street are now in Chinese hands. As a result, there are curious and pleasing cultural clashes—storefronts with Chinese lettering on them cheek by jowl with old Italian social clubs.

I D 1 · ALFRED E. SMITH HOUSES
between South, Madison, and Catherine streets, St. James and Robert F. Wagner, Sr., places
Eggers & Higgins, 1952

The Ville Radieuse comes to New York—not for the first time, and not at the greatest scale or in the most creative way, but in as clear a fashion as anywhere else. This is public housing, at the very lowest edge of the Lower East Side where it tucks around to be part of Chinatown.

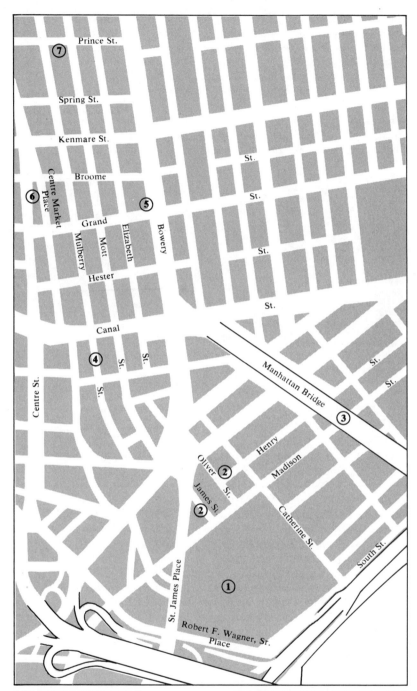

I / LOWER MANHATTAN   **D / CHINATOWN—LITTLE ITALY**

It is worth seeing, mainly because it is not so terribly bad—yes, Jane Jacobs, there *is* light and air made available to people who never had it before—but also because of the juxtaposition its site offers with other, more conventional parts of the cityscape. When red-brick cruciform towers rise in Harlem, we have little to compare them with save for other such projects down the block or tenements across the street. But here the towers have the Brooklyn Bridge to one side, the buildings of the civic center to the west, and the skyline of the financial district to the south. They play off not against a grid but against a complex urban landscape, and as a result, their own absolute order becomes all the more insistent by contrast.

Other projects, such as Stuyvesant Town (II A 18), offer a better opportunity to ponder the wisdom of the tower in the park. It was a naïve dream of the modernists, anti-urban at its core, and full of ignorance about what streets and neighborhoods should be.

I D 4 · *Mulberry Street, during the festival of San Gennaro*

I D 2 · *Mariners' Temple*

I D 2 · MARINERS' TEMPLE
12 Oliver Street, NW corner Henry Street
Minard Lafever, 1842
· ST. JAMES' CHURCH
32 James Street between St. James Place and Madison Street
attrib. to Minard Lafever, 1837

The area's two venerable Greek Revival churches. Both are worth noting, but the fact of the matter is that they perform their greatest service not to the cause of architecture but to the cause of a neighborhood in need of landmarks. Each of the churches has an entry flanked by two columns—Ionic in the Mariners' Temple, Doric in St. James'—with the rest of the façade brought out to the front line of the columns. The entries thus feel like alcoves cut into the mass of the building, something altogether different from the conventional temple portico. It gives the churches a bit of the aura of barns, a pleasant contrast to the austere pomposity of so many Greek Revival churches.

I D 3 · MANHATTAN BRIDGE AND APPROACHES
east end, Canal Street
O. F. Nichols, engineer, with Carrère & Hastings, architects, 1909

More advanced technologically than the Brooklyn, but aesthetically a step sideways. The open steelwork of the towers prefigures that of the George

I D 3 · *Approach to the Manhattan Bridge*

Washington Bridge so many years later, and it has a certain grandeur to its form. But there is a lot of fussy decorative work around the edges of this bridge, and the approaches by Carrère & Hastings are pure Beaux-Arts, making for an odd stylistic leap from a grand stone portal to a modern steel bridge.

Still, the architects do celebrate the notion of entrance in a city all too indifferent to its gateways, and for that they deserve to be remembered. The scale of the approaches is really too small for the bridge, although it was probably less of a problem when Daniel Chester French's monumental sculptures "Manhattan" and "Brooklyn" were part of the composition. The bridge was completely redesigned three times in its nine-year construction period to meet the whims of each succeeding mayor's chief engineer— Nichols followed Gustav Lindenthal, who did get his design for the Queensboro Bridge (II F 6) built—so, in the end, we are probably lucky that this bridge has even as much order as it does.

I D 4 · MULBERRY STREET, Canal Street North: the Morsa Restaurants; the Haas Mural

This street is to Little Italy what Mott Street is to Chinatown—the spinal cord of the neighborhood. Until recently, virtually every Italian restaurant and café was designed as a free-for-all of colored ceramic tile, fake-wood furniture and plastic—as with the Chinatown cafeteria style, there wasn't even anything that could credibly be called "old-world charm" to make up for the lack of more serious architectural interest.

Enter Donato Savoie and Antonio Morello, two young architects who live in the area and who saw their mission as that of persuading the neighborhood that modern design was not only acceptable, it was actually Italian. They showed slides of Milan restaurants and cafés, and finally won over one restaurateur who invited them in 1975 to design Il Cortile at No. 125. It has an elegant front of dark-stained oak and a lot of exposed brick and glass—nothing special by uptown standards but a shock in Little Italy.

Emboldened, the partners got sleeker, creating a gem of a lamp shop on Hester Street just west of Mulberry, and a slew of other restaurants. The Caffe Biondo at 141 Mulberry is perhaps the best summary of the Morsa style. It has a glass front, with lacquered black cast-iron columns; the sleek new forms play off well against the preserved older ones. Inside, there is a white and black checkerboard floor of marble; counters of brass, marble, and black Formica, and exposed brick walls with old pieces of architectural ornament hung as decorations.

The effect manages to be cool and handsome without ever becoming mechanical—modernism is romanticized, made gentle through the careful juxtaposition of new and old elements and through a constant awareness of the importance of scale and texture. The café's front is a sheer surface of glass, but since it is fit within the existing cast-iron columns, it remains respectful of the street.

Morsa was a bit more daring at the Ristorante La Griglia, a clean white sliver of a room at 117 Mulberry Street, with a glass front projecting out onto the sidewalk. There is another continuation of the same theme at the Caffe Primavera at Mulberry and Spring streets.

Also on Mulberry is a fine trompe l'oeil mural by Richard Haas, the illusionist of city walls. On the block between Hester and Grand streets he has painted the side of an old warehouse to resemble a grouping of storefronts; more amusing still, architectural details are carried from the old building onto the mural. It is witty, sweet, and never overbearing—something one could not say for the shrill abstract murals that have popped up on brick walls around town in recent years.

I D 5 · BOWERY SAVINGS BANK
130 Bowery, NW corner Grand Street
McKim, Mead & White, 1894

Big and grand and imposing, the way a bank is supposed to be. It would be stirring on Wall Street; on the Bowery amidst winos and junkies it is a staggering presence. The Bowery entrance is a vast, barrel-vaulted space, set at a slight angle because of the need to align with the banking room, which is lined up with Grand Street. There is another entrance on Grand Street: this is classicism in the shape of an L.

I D 6 · OLD POLICE HEADQUARTERS
240 Centre Street, between Grand and Broome streets
Hoppin & Koen, 1909

The most remarkable thing about this is not the building itself—which is very good—but the way it bursts out of the tortuous, narrow streets of Little Italy. It is the Invalides set in the middle of the Marais, an ornate French Renaissance pile dropped where it is least expected. You can do this only once in a city, or at most once in a neighborhood, since grand civic palaces like this, when they are within view of one another, need some axial planning and distance to keep order. But here, not only is the lack of a great vista not disturbing, but it is somehow liberating, as if we were given both the spontaneity of an Italian hill town and the grandeur of a Renaissance palace—contradictory things made possible all at once.

As a composition, the building is rich yet restrained, and it holds the street well on an awkward wedge-shaped site—it is clear that the architect knew what he was doing when it came to urbanistic relationships. The

I D 6 · *Old Police Headquarters*

interior is lavish but somehow far more institutional than the outside; when the police department was still there (up to 1973), the sense of lineups and interrogations was never quite absent. The building stands for police work as drama, whereas the new police headquarters (I B 8) is a symbol (more accurate, surely) of police work as bureaucracy. There are plans to convert this building into a community center for the Little Italy neighborhood.

I D 7 · OLD ST. PATRICK'S CATHEDRAL
between Mott, Prince, and Mulberry streets
Joseph Mangin, 1815
restoration: Henry Engelbert, 1868

This is just a remnant, awkwardly rebuilt after a disastrous fire. It looks more like a Gothic Revival barn than a major cathedral, but it is possible to get a hint of the Gothic Revival curiosity contrived by Mangin, co-architect of City Hall. The original cathedral was among the very first Gothic Revival churches in the United States (second only to the 1807 Chapel of St. Mary's Seminary in Baltimore) and had a façade that innocently combined Gothic Revival elements with classical ones. There was an entablature and balustrade atop the columns that still frame the front door; on top of that was a bizarre composition consisting of a central pointed window surrounded by a broken pediment and topped by a spire. Now all of that is gone, and the rebuilt church has neither the curious stylistic clash of the original nor the skillful detailing of a good copy. It is even duller, in its way, than the grander St. Patrick's uptown, to which the Archdiocese of New York removed in 1879. Of more interest, incidentally, is St. Michael's Chapel up the block at 266 Mulberry Street. Completed in 1850 to the designs of James Renwick, it is a slice of ecclesiastical architecture cut to tenement-lot size.

E/LOWER EAST SIDE

It is a sad and lonely place today, a neighborhood of drab shops and tenements, the tight streets broken by an ocean of red-brick towers of public housing toward the eastern edge. The Lower East Side does not look as harsh and cruel as it once did, back when it was awash with immigrants from Eastern Europe. Time and urban renewal have mitigated some of its roughness, but they have also taken away much of its romance, and what is left today is merely shabby, less interesting physically than the first-time visitor who formed his impressions from Harry Golden or Irving Howe might expect. Some of the tenements are still there, and some of the people who could have been their original occupants and many of the institutions they created—the synagogues and the stores and the community centers—remain.

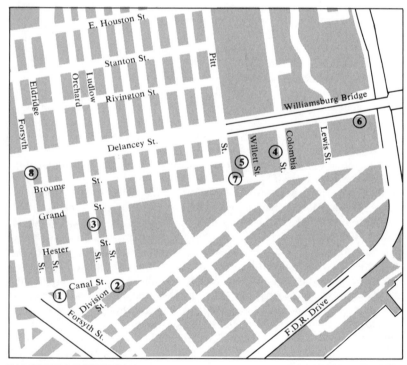

I / LOWER MANHATTAN   E / LOWER EAST SIDE

Some of the synagogues are still active; others are empty and desolate; still others have become churches to serve the area's growing Puerto Rican population. (Above Delancey Street the neighborhood is now largely Puerto Rican.) Many of the familiar parts of the Jewish neighborhood—I think in particular of an extraordinary delicatessen, Schmulke Bernstein's on Essex Street—remain lively and good places, but are run by former occupants of the neighborhood who have made enough money to move to the suburbs and patronized by a clientele that is much the same. It is too real to be false, yet it is not a natural state of affairs, either—Schmulke Bernstein's and other places on the Lower East Side are where people gather to have their emotions jogged by madeleines they call blintzes.

But it is hard not to be moved by a visit to this place. As much as anywhere else in the United States, it is a neighborhood of beginnings and dreams. It is where the "wretched refuse" of Emma Lazarus's poem—the Jewish immigrants of Eastern Europe—came to start their new lives in the years from the 1870's through the 1920's. They made of this slum a place that, at its height, was a fountainhead of culture and community. But it was always an intermediate step in the process of assimilation—a place to get out of as much as a place to come to, and that shows in every street, in every brick, and on every face.

I E 1 · ELDRIDGE STREET SYNAGOGUE (Congregation Khal Adas Jeshurun—Anshe Lubz)
14 Eldridge Street, between Canal and Forsyth streets
Herter Brothers, 1887

This is one of New York City's finest houses of worship, and it is falling apart. Once this was the pride of the Lower East Side, a grandiose façade mixing Romanesque, Gothic, and Moorish elements in a glorious testament to this congregation's faith in the New World. There is a rose window in the center, and there were once ornamental finials atop a parapet, making the overall composition of the façade more graceful than it now appears. Most remarkable is the sanctuary, an immense and opulent room with elaborate brass chandeliers with Victorian glass shades hanging in the midst of a huge, barrel-vaulted space. Ornate walnut carving covers the front of the balcony and the ark where Torah scrolls are stored, and there are small domes over the balcony areas along the sides of the large room.

Khal Adas Jeshurun was the first major synagogue constructed on the Lower East Side by Jews from Eastern Europe—earlier ones had been built by Western Europeans—and it is clear that the building, down to the choice of the fashionable firm of Herter Brothers (better known as interior decorators to the likes of the Vanderbilts), was an attempt to establish a strong presence. It would have been a good building in any part of town; rising on a side street of tenements, it has a greater drama still, much like that of the old Police Headquarters on Centre Street.

The sanctuary has been abandoned since the thirties, and the front doors sealed. All that is used is a plain basement room, where services are held under the light of a bare bulb when a group can be assembled. Funds are being sought for a restoration, but the outlook is grim; now the building stands brooding and silent, its remarkable grandeur ebbing away, a touching reminder of a time when the Lower East Side was a neighborhood of hope.

I E 2 · *Division Street, looking west toward the World Trade Center*

I E 1 · *Eldridge Street Synagogue*

I E 2 · DIVISION STREET

Division, Ludlow, and Canal streets come together in a triangle just a couple of blocks east of the Eldridge Street Synagogue, and it is worth pausing for a moment to look at the view west down Division Street. It is one of those vistas that in an instant sum up so much of New York: tenements are in the foreground on both sides of Division Street, while in the far distance are the towers of the World Trade Center. Chatham Towers and the towers of the U.S. Courthouse and Municipal Building are in front of the Trade Center, and closer still, the approach to the Manhattan Bridge cuts a bold swath across Division.

It is a bit too glib, if one can call a view that—a bit too facile a juxtaposition. But the composition saves it from being trite—the tenements form a powerful frame, the Trade Center is just the right distance back, and the bridge approach cuts across to give the view some horizontal force.

I E 3 · ORCHARD STREET

Orchard is the market, the bazaar, the event of commerce that is clearly also an event of urban design. Neither the shopkeepers nor the patrons are exclusively Jewish, as in days of old, but the tradition of the Sunday market still remains. For block after block, retail establishments line both sides of Orchard Street, the storefronts themselves appearing to jostle for space just as the patrons do, who, on fair Sundays, turn the street into New York's real pedestrian mall.

Each store has an outdoor display as well as an indoor one, and the overall effect down the long street is dazzling: tables of merchandise piled high with dresses and coats and shoes and sneakers, spilling out from the stores and looking at the same time like endless rows of pushcarts caught in a traffic jam. None of it was ever designed, unlike all of the pretentious (if well-meaning) downtown malls which try so hard to revitalize other American cities. This one just happened.

I E 4 · AMALGAMATED HOUSES
between Grand, Broome, Willet, and Lewis streets
Springsteen and Goldhammer, 1930

This is truly excellent courtyard housing, better than Knickerbocker Village down a few blocks at the edge of Chinatown. Brick and stucco join to create lively, vaguely Art Deco façades, and there is a large central garden with a fountain, a great deal of light, and a pleasant arched entrance at the end. The scale is modest and humane, and the overall effect altogether civilized and dignified. It must have been a startling breakthrough in the neighborhood of rookeries that the Lower East Side was in 1930; even now it has a certain freshness.

I E 5 · BIALYSTOKER SYNAGOGUE
7 Willett Street, between Grand and Broome streets
1826

This modest but self-assured Federal-style church was originally the home of a Methodist Episcopal congregation, and was purchased by the Bialystoker Synagogue (the name refers to the fact that the congregation is made up of immigrants from the Bialystok province in Poland) in 1905. It is more a country church than an urban synagogue, but the fieldstone façade is warm and attractive. The interior is more lavish than the outside would lead one to expect, and has an almost sprightly quality. Bialystoker is one of the few synagogues on the Lower East Side that have remained well attended and relatively prosperous; one feels here some of the sense of current life that is missing in so many other parts of the neighborhood.

I E 6 · WILLIAMSBURG BRIDGE
east end, Delancey Street
Leffert Lefferts Buck, 1903

The second bridge to cross the East River, and a visual curiosity—there is almost no feeling of suspension to this suspension bridge. The towers are of steel (among the earliest examples of such) in a shape that splays out to

I E 5 · *Bialystoker Synagogue*

I E 8 · *Forsyth Street Synagogue (now Seventh Day Adventist Church)*

the sides, and the end spans are not suspended, hence the absence of supporting cables hanging to the roadway in these sections. Structural problems led to the addition of extra trusses in the years after the Williamsburg's completion, making its form still more ungainly. As it is now, it has neither the lyrical romance of the Brooklyn or the George Washington nor the tough machine quality of the Queensboro—a so-so compromise instead—although, like all of the East River bridges, it rises out of the confused cityscape with a considerable presence.

I E 7 · HENRY STREET SETTLEMENT—ARTS FOR LIVING CENTER
466 Grand Street, between Pitt and Willett streets
Prentice and Chan, Olhausen, 1975

A part of the Lower East Side with so little left that a cluster of old tenements nearby looks almost quaint. This building, a major addition to the venerable settlement house established by Lillian Wald, tries to bring definition to the area via a strong brick mass, its plan scooped out in the center with a great quarter arc. The arc keeps the brick form from being too intimidating on the street and also yields an attractive courtyard space with terraced seating; inside, it provides light and creates a sense of rapport with the street.

The interior is a bit on the concrete-block institutional side, but it is not too bad, and the building works well with the Greek Revival townhouses that form the original section of the settlement house. If it looks forbidding, look again at the warmth of the curving façade—and also compare the building to the brick fortress of the new 7th Precinct Police Station down Pitt Street just west of here, which makes the Arts for Living Center look like a gingham-curtained farmhouse.

I E 8 · FORSYTH STREET SYNAGOGUE (now Seventh Day Adventist Church)
Forsyth and Delancey streets, SE corner
J. C. Cady & Co., 1890

Good urbanism, way ahead of its time: not only was this old synagogue designed neatly in scale with its neighbors, but it has a row of stores set into its base on the Delancey Street side, not a bad way for a religious institution to render unto Caesar that which is Caesar's. Indeed, it prefigures such latter-day mixes of commercial and nonprofit real estate as Kahn's Yale Center for British Art in New Haven, where a row of stores on the ground floor sits beneath a museum.

The façade on Forsyth Street makes it clear that this is not just a commercial building, though—a high flight of steps leads to a grand entrance and there is a relatively elaborate cornice. The stores on the other side fall away, and you know you are entering a temple.

F/SoHo

Robert Moses viewed the blocks below Houston Street as a wasteland of useless industrial buildings, and proposed to level much of the neighborhood and replace it with the Lower Manhattan Expressway. The ludicrous expressway scheme was finally abandoned in 1965, and the old loft buildings in the area people were starting to call SoHo began to be occupied by artists in need of large, cheap space. The rest is history: where artists went, galleries, boutiques, and restaurants followed, and the most frequent complaint heard in recent years is that it has all become so fashionable that few of the people who made the neighborhood possible can any longer afford it.

But it is this neighborhood's fate to be misunderstood. If SoHo is not the slum that Moses thought it was, neither is it the Madison Avenue that so many New Yorkers today fear it has become. SoHo is something unique in New York. It was built as an industrial quarter, and it will never have the light, glittering elegance of certain parts of the Upper East Side. It is heavy, solid, dense, and the fancy shops and galleries and living spaces are only an overlay. SoHo is now fashionable, but it is not elegant in the conventional sense, and it probably never will be. It will also—probably—never be terribly clean, either.

Yet this is far and away one of the most beautiful neighborhoods in New York. It possesses not only the conceptual beauty of the phoenix, but the actual beauty of the strong, finely detailed, self-assured place. Nowhere in the United States is there as rich a concentration of cast-iron buildings as here, where you can walk for blocks and see a nineteenth-century cityscape essentially intact.

Cast iron was a curious material—a technological advance in the mid-nineteenth century that permitted cheap and mechanical reproduction of columns, moldings, lintels, arches, cornices, doorways, and entire façades, it represented a move toward standardization and prefabrication. But at the same time it made possible a richness of detail that acted as a brake against the rush of standardization. Ultimately, by permitting details to be stamped out mechanically and combined at the architect's whim, the use of cast iron furthered the values of composition; to us today the cast-iron fronted buildings of SoHo are less interesting as technological objects and proto-steel skeletons (which they are) and more compelling as pure compositions.

There are only a handful of very great buildings here, but there are more very good ones than it is practical to list. There is a temptation to say that it is all a little bit like Belgravia, a set of exquisite variations on a single

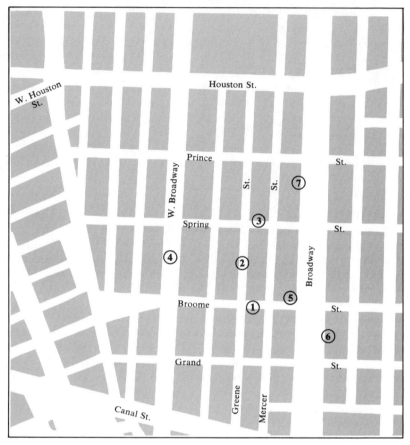

theme, but that would sell SoHo short, for the variations are more complete and the theme much more meaningful. There is nothing neat or prim about this neighborhood—it is robust before it is anything else, and one senses that it decks itself out in Italianate and neo-Grec and Second Empire decoration out of brashness, not timidity. Visitors are often surprised to realize how much of the neighborhood, for all its fame as an art center, is still industrial—and New Yorkers are grateful, for the surprise juxtapositions between the dingy warehouse of a cardboard-box shipper and sleek white quarters of an art bookstore are important to the area's special quality. Tip the balance either way, and something is lost.

There is drama to these brooding façades, and a tension between the richness of their detail and the strength of their overall masses. The buildings want to be strong and they want to be pretty; their genius is in their ability to make you wonder why you had ever imagined there was a contradiction between these things. It is more important to wander the streets than it is to go in search of a group of individual buildings; it does not take too many minutes on Greene Street or Broome Street to perceive the power of the ensemble overall, and to feel how brilliantly the tension is resolved.

I F 1 · BROOME STREET

This is SoHo before the boutiques—blocks of virile cast-iron buildings which have been converted into living lofts inside, but which, owing to a location just a bit south of the neighborhood's tourist center, have remained fairly free of galleries and restaurants at street level. So it looks more or less as it always has, save for the ubiquitous hanging plants in the upper windows.

The blocks are better than typical, because they are so much of a piece, but what they share with typical SoHo blocks is the sense of ensemble—not the planned ensemble of a single architect or builder's edict, but the casual ensemble that comes to be when a group of architects work in a place over a period of time and all show a respect for each other's work and for the basic verities of urban manners.

There are no remarkable buildings here, but there are many excellent ones. Of special note are three by Griffith Thomas, one of the city's better architects in cast iron: No. 453–455 (1873), with central groupings of four windows on each floor flanked by strongly articulated end windows; No. 469–475 (1871), with a wonderful rounded corner that deftly celebrates the potential of cast iron; and No. 476–478, a fine, controlled composition.

No. 484, by Alfred Zucker (1890), is a powerful brick pile of fine Romanesque-inspired detailing. It doesn't belong in the land of cast iron but it fits in perfectly all the same—a good lesson that there are many roads to urban coexistence.

I F 2 · GREENE STREET

Like Broome, this is an extraordinary street, only slightly altered at ground level. There are still many buildings with industrial uses; though artists and chic émigrés from Park Avenue may live upstairs, the streetscape is still more or less as it was. Greene has buildings that would stop you dead in

I F 1 · *469–475 Broome Street*

I F 2 · *114 Prince Street, mural by Richard Haas*

your tracks anywhere else—here, on a narrow street, cheek by jowl and with dirt and debris all around, they are almost overlooked.

· 72 GREENE STREET
J. F. Duckworth, 1872

This is cast iron at its grandest—and at its most pompous. But it is in the nature of this material that pomposity is never intolerable. Five stories, piled sumptuously one atop the other, with a central pedimented porch at the ground floor, porticoes on each middle floor, and a pedimented top. It is enormous, bulbous almost, yet with the graciousness and even a touch of the lightness of most cast-iron façades. This building is like the old uncle who wears a three-piece suit and a watch chain, but who smiles and winks when you misbehave—he *wants* to be liked, and in the end, he is.

· 28–30 GREENE STREET
J. F. Duckworth, 1872

The triumph of Second Empire cast iron. It is touchy to imply that architecture can suggest gender, but this seems to play female to Duckworth's male at No. 72 down the street. It is smaller and more delicate, but is a similarly conceived composition, also emphasizing slightly projected central bays. In each case, the compositional hand is sure, and here, in fact, the details are finer—although there is a certain bravado to No. 72 that is missing here. But no apologies are necessary; this is a wonderful addition to the streetscape.

At the corner of Greene and Prince streets, on the side wall of No. 114 Prince Street, is Richard Haas's other great gift to New York, still better than his Mulberry Street mural—New York's ultimate piece of trompe l'oeil art. What better thing to do with the dreary brick side wall of a cast-iron building than to carry the cast-iron front around the side in paint? The cat in the window is too cute and a giveaway, but this is still witty and attractive and lovable and full of understanding of what makes a city block work.

I F 2 · *28–30 Greene Street*

I F 3 · *101 Spring Street*

I F 3 · 101 SPRING STREET
Nicholas Whyte, 1870

What lightness, what strength! Cast iron permitted great expanses of glass, for it was a kind of skeletal frame construction, and here one sees the potential—a glassed urban palazzo. Its true comrade is a building like Skidmore, Owings & Merrill's Olivetti Building on Park Avenue of 1960 (II F 9). The details are simple and geometric, not imitations of classical capitals but an attempt to do something that would look, at least to the nineteenth-century eye, like an appropriate expression of iron construction. The pediments atop the second- and fourth-floor windows are the only fussy detail, the sort of thing that would work in another architect's façade but, here, seems only a useless compromise, a concession, perhaps, to some guilt about the purity of the overall design.

I F 4 · WEST BROADWAY

Not too much architecture here—at least not of the kind one finds on Broome and Greene streets and on Broadway. Most of West Broadway is uneven; it was the western edge of the industrial district, and it did not develop with quite the same kind of quantity of first-class cast iron. But this is the Main Street of SoHo, and it has become one of those extraordinary New York streets that, at the right time, are a cultural experience impossible to duplicate anywhere else. West Broadway on a fair Saturday afternoon is not Madison Avenue, though it is full of art galleries and fashionable strollers; it is not Washington Square, though it is full of students and people one might, a few years ago, have called hippies; it is not 57th Street and it is not Times Square and it is not Union Square. It is a little bit of all of these places, the one place where people who would normally not be caught dead promenading can promenade, and where people who promenade all the time can just shuffle along instead.

There is just one building of special note here, No. 468, and it is one of SoHo's most unusual landmarks, for it is of masonry. It is a red-brick composition of arches, on the west side of West Broadway just a few doors south of Houston Street; like so many late-nineteenth-century brick buildings, the structure is massive and heavy, but this one has sleek, smooth surfaces. It is more like the refined, weightless glass buildings of the 1970's, for the brick creates a thin, taut wall, and the arches have the feel of holes punched, not of caverns dug into a deep, solid surface. Just as interesting is the rear façade around the corner on Sullivan Street—here the base is a series of tall, tall arches, so much out of proportion to the rest of the structure that they make it look as if the building were standing on legs.

I F 5 · HAUGHWOUT BUILDING
488 Broadway, NE corner Broome Street
J. P. Gaynor, 1859

This is the Platonic cast-iron building. It is one of those rare pieces of architecture in which everything fits together perfectly and yet with room left for passion. There is real emotion here, and there is utter discipline and control; the balance between them is extraordinary.

The design is heavily Italianate and relatively simple: five stories of windows, each within an arch set on Corinthian colonnettes and flanked by large Corinthian columns set on paneled bases. There is an entablature and balustrade atop each story, and a rich cornice at the top of the entire building.

That is the recipe. They are all standard elements from classical architecture, none of them invented here. What makes the result so fine, aside from the high level of the detailing, is an altogether remarkable sense of balance between, first, the façade as a horizontal element and as a vertical one, and second, between the overall building as a volume and as a planar surface. You read Haughwout's front now as horizontal, now as vertical; you read the whole building now as a deep mass, now as a stretched skin. It is never more one than the other, and not out of architect's indecision— it is clear that, here, all of the terribly difficult, subtle things that we mean when we use the word "harmony" were completely understood.

I F 6 · ROOSEVELT BUILDING
478–82 Broadway, between Grand & Broome streets
Richard Morris Hunt, 1874

This tries too hard and never makes it. It is not terribly fair for any cast-iron building to be a stone's throw from Haughwout, and this one is hardly a failure, but it has none of the utter grace of its neighbor to the north. The composition of the façade into three-window bays visually foreshadows the Chicago School of skyscraper design, and it is clear that Hunt was working toward some kind of expression of iron as a material, and not trying just

I F 5 · *Haughwout Building*   **I F 5 ·** *Detail of the Haughwout Building*

to imitate stone, so in these senses the building can be said to be advanced. What is missing is some sense of magic in all of this conscientiousness—it is never there, and you are left with the feeling that it is just as well that Richard Morris Hunt gave up trying to innovate and sought refuge in imitating French châteaux for the Vanderbilts. There was skill in this cast-iron effort, but Hunt's heart was clearly still in the Loire.

I F 7 · "LITTLE" SINGER BUILDING
561–563 Broadway, between Spring and Prince streets
Ernest Flagg, 1904

This is really the only Singer Building, not the little one, since Flagg's big Singer Building on lower Broadway was torn down. But even though this was the smaller and less famous of the two, it was surely the better one architecturally. Big Singer was a gracious but less than perfect mansarded French building stretched into a tower that related to the overall structure as a giraffe's neck does to its body. Little Singer is something much more credible—a noble street façade of terra cotta, glass, and steel, lavishly decorated with wrought-iron balconies.

The composition is genuinely graceful; it climaxes in an arch expressed in iron on the next-to-the-top floor, with a cornice and one other floor above. There is clearly much Parisian inspiration here, though in the arch one feels hints of Richardson, here made light and dreamlike. The façade is one of the most significant forerunners of the curtain wall to be found anywhere, and ultimately it is unclassifiable—an original gem.

G/LAFAYETTE STREET—ASTOR PLACE AREA

New York's most fashionable neighborhood, for an hour or two, in the fickle nineteenth century. Actually, it was desirable for long enough in the 1830's for Edith Wharton to get it all down in *Old New York*; by the 1840's, however, society had moved to Washington Square, and then the long climb up Fifth Avenue began. There is almost nothing left of Lafayette Street's days in society—Colonnade Row and the Old Merchant's House are the best of the remnants—but what makes the place so wonderful are the leftovers from the neighborhood's next incarnation, as an industrial district. Now that, too, is changing, and the loft buildings are being reclaimed for housing and artists' studios; moreover, the presence of the Public Theater in the old Astor Library has sparked a certain amount of other Off-Off Broadway activity here. It is a place of past glories that will never return and of a constant sense of revival—ghosts and phoenixes are the neighborhood's symbols.

I G 1 · PUCK BUILDING
295–309 Lafayette Street, SE corner Houston Street
Albert Wagner, 1885, 1892

Nineteenth-century brickwork at its best—strong arches, elaborate cornices, and everything made of a rich, red brick except for a few terra-cotta brooches pinned on as an afterthought. The composition is basically Romanesque and built around arches—two-story arches at the base, with arched windows half as wide for the next two floors, then a third as wide for the next three floors. It is a bit too fussy for Sullivan, too active for Richardson, but still very much a descendant of his great Marshall Field Wholesale Store in Chicago. The building was once the home of the humor magazine *Puck,* hence the characters that look gleefully out to Houston Street from the north corners of the building—a bit of Disneyland in a Romanesque Revival context, making this building even more appealing than it is to start with.

It is worth stepping back a block to the corner of Crosby and Houston streets and looking north to Sullivan's Bayard Building at Crosby and Bleecker streets. Sullivan is immensely more graceful, and far more serious about expressing his structure and telling us what he is about. But is he better? The Puck Building, conservative as it is by comparison, is every bit as dignified a presence on the cityscape—a noble thing, really.

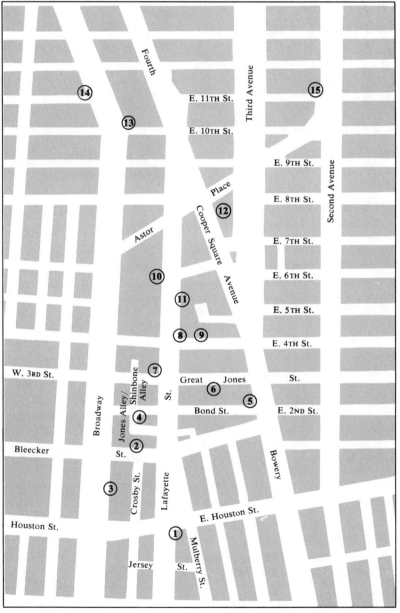

I / LOWER MANHATTAN   G / LAFAYETTE ST.—ASTOR PL. AREA

I G 1 · *Entrance of the Puck Building*

I G 2 · *Bayard Building*

I G 2 · BAYARD BUILDING
65 Bleecker Street, between Broadway and Lafayette streets
Louis Sullivan, 1898

The only New York work of the man Frank Lloyd Wright called Master. It is a delicate poem, yet a strong one, an ode to Chicago's love for structural expression—the structural columns are shown fat and solid, the columns that merely divide windows are lithe. It all culminates in one of the richest and most lyrical cornices New York has ever seen, in which a sextet of angels (added over Sullivan's objections, it is said) fly from the structural columns to the cornice.

The cornice is sweet; the rest of the building is more profound. It is unfortunate that the whole thing had as little impact as it did—Sullivan appears not to have been asked back to design anything else in New York, and no one else took his lead. By the turn of the century the decorated skyscrapers of Richard Morris Hunt and Cass Gilbert and Ernest Flagg were the city's trademarks; had a few architects paid some attention to what was going on on Bleecker Street, New York's architectural history might have been different.

The building is best perceived looking north along Crosby Street—it appears to be slid into its tight space neatly, like a large piece of furniture.

I G 3 · 628 BROADWAY
between Houston and Bleecker streets
Herman J. Schwarzmann, 1882

This is fussy, nice cast iron. No imitation of classical stonework this time, and no serious attempts to express the nature of ironwork, either. What 628

Broadway is, is a playful game, a set of floral and natural motifs which all come off looking more geometric than they should, but are appealing nonetheless. The blocks of Broadway just above Houston Street are almost as good as those below; these are a highlight, but worth looking for are 648 Broadway (Cleverdon & Putzel, 1891); the old Brooks Brothers at 674 Broadway (George E. Horner & William Paulding, 1873); and 678 Broadway (David & John Jardine, 1874), just as fussy and just as simplistically likable as No. 628.

I G 4 · 1 BOND STREET
SE corner Jones Alley
Stephen D. Hatch, 1871

This is grandiose cast iron in the manner of the Duckworth buildings on Greene Street in SoHo (I F 2). All very Second Empire, and all very grand, culminating in a mansard roof of immense size. The broken pediment at the entrance portico is a pleasing and unusual detail. But this is most interesting as cast iron just out of context—without other similar buildings on either side, it looks startling in a way that the SoHo buildings do not. In general, surprise breaks with context are not the best prescription for urban design, but let this stand as the exception that proves the rule.

I G 5 · BOUWERIE LANE THEATRE
330 Bowery, NW corner Bond Street
Henry Engelbert, 1874

Long and slender: Cast iron as stage set. This is good Second Empire, fine in its details, but like most cast-iron buildings it is most interesting of all as a study in composition. Engelbert varied the details subtly so as to play down the extreme narrowness of the Bowery façade; in brief, his method consisted of wrapping the longer Bond Street façade around the Bowery side, although in fact he was really playing a more complicated game, which involved using quoins, usually an expression of a corner, as modulating elements on the long side. The rhythms are subtle and effective throughout, and worth a careful look.

I G 6 · ENGINE COMPANY NO. 33
44 Great Jones Street, between Lafayette Street and the Bowery
Ernest Flagg and W. B. Chambers, 1898

The glory of the address would be almost enough, but the building lives up to it. This is whammo Beaux-Arts, a little firehouse that brings flamboyance and dazzle to civic architecture. The trick here is not overdecoration but grand scale—an immense arch swoops up one, two, three stories to an elegantly carved keystone above an ornate cartouche. But the arch itself is deep and smooth and strongly spatial in feeling, not decorative.

Alas, the arch with its wonderful French windows set into it does not serve the building's main function: it begins only on the second floor, above a rusticated stone base, and so it does not act as a portal for the fire engines themselves. They enter and leave through more conventional doors in the base. But no matter. This is rich and happy civic architecture at its best, full of the flamboyance you want to believe that firefighting consists of, and all the order and dignity you want to believe that the city consists of.

I G 5 · *Bouwerie Lane Theatre*   I G 6 · *Engine Company No. 33*

I G 7 · 376 LAFAYETTE STREET
NW corner, Great Jones Street
Henry J. Hardenbergh, 1888

This is of interest more because of its architect than because of its inherent architectural quality, although there is plenty of that here. Hardenbergh, like the cast-iron architects, was a compositionalist before he was anything else—what mattered to him was not purity of style or adherence to historical precedent but intuitive feelings of order, scale, and proportion. He showed that best in his first major work, the Dakota Apartments (III B 9), and almost as well in the Plaza Hotel (II G 12) and the Art Students League (II G 18). Here, in this warehouse designed just a few years after the Dakota, nothing went wrong, all the skill is clearly visible, yet it somehow didn't come together to mean terribly much.

No. 376 Lafayette Street is richly ornamented, far more so than the Puck Building and the DeVinne Press Building, its two logical comrades in the neighborhood. Much of the ornament is first-rate, too, but it seems curiously underscaled and much more of an afterthought than it should be. I am the last to argue for structural expression, but the problem here is that the building seems to argue for that all by itself, and the architect just wasn't willing to listen.

I G 8 · 399 LAFAYETTE STREET (DeVINNE PRESS BUILDING)
NE corner, East 4th Street
Babb, Cook & Willard, 1885

A couple of years before Hardenbergh's 376 Lafayette, and very much better. Nothing fancy here, just superb and utterly powerful brickwork, making you feel in an instant the weight of the massive bearing walls. It is plain and utilitarian, and so convincing that you are ready to start believing in modernist doctrines about purism. What makes this work where a Miesian glass box doesn't, however, is the richness and depth of the brick itself. It is a material that can do things that steel and glass cannot, and purism here is solid and opaque and mysterious, not cold and austere. This is truly New York's equivalent of the great nineteenth-century brick mill structures of New England. And it is far and away the finest work of the architects who a few years later were to produce the fussy and dull Carnegie Mansion (III D 44).

I G 7 · *376 Lafayette Street*   I G 8 · *DeVinne Press Building*

I G 9 · OLD MERCHANT'S HOUSE
29 East 4th Street, between Lafayette Street and the Bowery
attributed to Minard Lafever, 1832

This is a remnant—and a perfect one—of the Greek Revival origins of this neighborhood. Once it was the city's most fashionable quarter, and houses like this lined all of the streets. The Old Merchant's House is now a museum, and it is a perfectly furnished period piece. One is tempted to think of house museums as curiosities in rural New England presided over by genteel old ladies who are more concerned with galoshes tracking mud than with the history of architecture; this place, perhaps because of where it is, rises above all that.

I G 10 · COLONNADE ROW (LA GRANGE TERRACE)
428–434 Lafayette Street, between East 4th Street and Astor Place
attributed to Alexander Jackson Davis, 1833

Once there were nine houses in this group; five were demolished to make way for the John Wanamaker Co. warehouse. Now there are four, and they are landmarks, so there will never be none. But the four remaining houses are in wretched condition, and only dimly recall the grandeur that the row had when it was the most fashionable group of houses in the city.

But it still does wonders for the streetscape. The notion of sliding a row of Corinthian columns across a row of townhouses does two things: it brings monumental scale to the houses and it brings texture and depth to the façades. The scale is the most pleasing thing, for it lets the single row house (not small to begin with, but hardly the size of the Fifth Avenue mansions that would come a few decades later) gain a degree of urban importance it could not otherwise have. There is grandeur and monumentality, and there is still the pleasure of townhouse proportions—a wonderful chance to have your cake and eat it, too. It is sad that the second wave of classically inspired townhouse building in New York at the beginning of the twentieth century was to serve a clientele too obsessed with individual expression to permit this civilized urban idea to have a more modern echo.

I G 10 · *Colonnade Row* (*La Grange Terrace*)

I G 11 · PUBLIC THEATER (originally Astor Library)
425 Lafayette Street, between East 4th Street and Astor Place
south wing: Alexander Saeltzer, 1853
center section: Griffith Thomas, 1859
north wing: Thomas Stent, 1881
conversion to theater: Giorgio Cavaglieri, 1966

Several Victorians' version, over time, of an early Italian Renaissance palace. It is a good building, well-detailed and decently proportioned, but it is most important as an early example of what has come to be called

I G 9 · *Old Merchant's House*   I G 12 · *Cooper Union Foundation Building*

"recycling"—the conversion of old buildings to new uses, often unintended by their original architects. Giorgio Cavaglieri took the old Astor Library (which had served as the headquarters for the Hebrew Immigrant Aid Society for an interim period) and carved theaters and office and rehearsal space out of its large rooms, creating, as he did in the Jefferson Market Courthouse in Greenwich Village, something that has been deservedly viewed as an icon of the preservation movement.

That said, there is not, unfortunately, all that much style to the renovation. Cavaglieri is a just hero of preservationists for his early championing of re-use of old buildings, but in the years since the Public Theater conversion somewhat more sophistication has come into the business. There is neither an unusual sympathy for the older building nor a particularly strong new personality evident in the renovation—it seems a compromise, and one with an oddly institutional air to it. Several of the theater spaces, however, are first-rate—there was great respect for the work of the original architects there, and it shows.

I G 12 · COOPER UNION FOUNDATION BUILDING
East 7th Street, between Cooper Square and Third Avenue
Frederick A. Peterson, 1859
reconstruction: John Hejduk, 1974

This was drastically rebuilt not long ago, and the results are superb, a total reversal of the frequent pattern in which an original building is of interest for its architecture and a later renovation for its technology. Here, the old Cooper Union was of more technological interest—it was among the first buildings anywhere built with the aid of wrought-iron beams. The brown-stone façades, however, are fairly routine Italianate designs. The renovation by John Hejduk, which involved a virtual gutting of the original structure, is splendid. It is white and pure as the driven snow, and it has relatively little to do with the original building save for basic similarity in plan. But if the whole thing resembles, as Russell Sturgis wrote long ago of McKim, Mead & White's Century Club, "a box with a pretty inside put into a larger box with a pretty outside," that makes it no less valid, and no less interesting. Indeed, the success with which Hejduk has managed to make his Corbusian vocabulary feel like a box with a pretty inside, and the extent to which he has managed to make that vocabulary meld comfortably with the box with the pretty outside, offer pause for thought: it reminds us that the Corbusian vocabulary need not be an entity unto itself, but in the right hands can be joined gracefully to that very larger stylistic whole which—ironically—it tried so firmly to reject.

I G 13 · GRACE CHURCH
800 Broadway, NE corner East 10th Street
James Renwick, Jr., 1846
· GRACE CHURCH RECTORY
804 Broadway
James Renwick, Jr., 1846

It is all in the tower, which is set perfectly to take advantage of the bend in Broadway at 10th Street. This is perhaps New York's best Gothic Revival church, more graceful than Upjohn's Trinity, more inventive than Renwick's later, dryer St. Patrick's on Fifth Avenue. Renwick was only twenty-five when he designed Grace, and he was at once in love with Pugin and unbound by Gothic Revival dogma; the result was a building utterly faithful to Gothic details and to the Gothic spirit, and yet fresh and free in its own special way. The rectory next door is distinguished, yet discreet—the perfect counterpoint to the exuberance of that vast, shimmering tower.

Around the back on Fourth Avenue is a group of fine Gothic Revival houses designed years later by Renwick's firm, Renwick, Aspinwall & Russell. They do not equal the quality of the original grouping, but they are

I G 13 · *Grace Church*   I G 14 · *Cast Iron Building*

fine nonetheless, and were the deserved subjects of a major preservation controversy in 1974, when the Grace Church School proposed to replace them with a new gymnasium. Preservationists rallied round, and the gym was set into the shell of the older buildings, preserving them for the streetscape.

I G 14 · CAST IRON BUILDING
807 Broadway, NW corner 11th Street
John Kellum, 1868
renovation: Stephen B. Jacobs, 1973

This is a good, but not exceptional, Italianate cast-iron façade, notable mostly for the extreme length and splendidly soft rhythm of its 11th Street façade. It is worth a look, however, for its present use, which is that of a more or less conventional apartment house—among the very first of the city's immense old commercial buildings to be so converted. The units inside are decent, and mark a significant early break from the low-ceilinged sheetrock box of most postwar apartments in Manhattan. Here the space soars, and there are sleeping lofts, split-level arrangements, and Corinthian columns coming down right in the middle of living rooms. None of it is extravagant, but this was an important step. It is a shame that the developers felt it necessary to add a floor on top for extra income; the banal penthouse compromises the building considerably.

I G 15 · ST. MARK'S-IN-THE-BOWERY
NW corner, East 10th Street and Second Avenue
1799 steeple: Ithiel Towne, 1828
portico: 1854

This is a country church and a building with urban social aspirations at the same time. It wants to be rural, or at least it did when its original late-Georgian structure was built in 1799. Later the church got uppity and wanted to join the Greek Revival and did so with its fine steeple, added by Ithiel Towne atop the main pediment, while later still an Italianate portico in cast iron was added to the assemblage, reflecting the latest architectural fashion. What is remarkable is how well all of these elements manage to work together, and how little sense of shifting gears there is to St. Mark's. The pure and strong simplicity of the original building is compromised, to be sure, but the hybrid is a wonderful example of New York doing what it has always done with history—take it wherever and whenever it is wanted, for whatever purpose.

Not the least of the pleasures this building offers, it should be mentioned, is the element of surprise—it is in the middle of what came a few years ago to be called the East Village, a mix of honky-tonk and slum, and this vision of both Christian order and social climbing is delightfully out of place.

A tragic fire did severe damage here in 1978. Restoration is promised, but is doubtless far off for this no-longer wealthy church.

H/GREENWICH VILLAGE

Every New York neighborhood is as much a state of mind as a physical place, and it is the extraordinary ability of Greenwich Village to be any state of mind at all. The Village can be contorted into whatever you want it to be; it can be twisted and bent and turned inside out and it will never break. It is tranquil to those who come to it as a refuge from downtown and midtown skyscrapers, and it is frenetic to those who seek in it an escape from the boredom of suburbia. By reputation it is the hotbed of radicalism, but its residents are as conservative as any in Alabama when they feel their rights are being threatened. It is old and messy and disheveled and chic and sleek and new; it is flamboyant, and it is strangely private.

This is a neighborhood that looks unlike the rest of New York and yet attracts the most chauvinistic New Yorkers, a further paradox. Once there was a time when it was possible to live a certain kind of life only in the Village, a life filled with bars and small restaurants serving ethnic food and shopkeepers who remembered your name and kept you stocked with fresh pasta. This attracted a kind of population that wanted such unconventional things and was itself less than superstraight; now the sort of people who once seemed to live only in the Village live everywhere, and there is little available to the Village resident that does not have at least a rough equivalent elsewhere in Manhattan.

But this place remains special, even unique. Part of it is the physical reality of the Village—crooked streets asserting themselves against the grid, small Federal and Greek Revival townhouses, lively shops and cafés. It is never so picturesque as Beacon Hill nor so chic as Georgetown, although there are some aspects of the Village that resemble these places. But it is less definable, less graspable than its equivalents in other cities, in part because in a characteristically New York way it changes its mood every couple of blocks, in part because, for all its fabled intimacy, it is really sprawling and rambling and disorganized. Never do the best blocks of the Village look like the perfect stage sets of the East Seventies, yet never could the neighborhood be mistaken for Times Square either, although it has become honky-tonk enough to make this not so unlikely a confusion.

Perhaps the essence of Greenwich Village is that all of its elements are utterly interdependent. The genteel Federal houses would mean less without the loud 8th Street shops, which save them from being Williamsburg at the same time the houses are saving 8th Street from being Times Square. Similarly, the mad rush of Washington Square and the quiet blocks of Bedford and Commerce and Grove streets work together, as do the people—

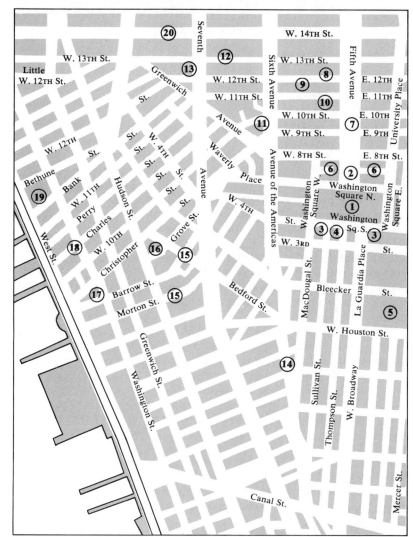

I / LOWER MANHATTAN   H / GREENWICH VILLAGE

the gays of Christopher Street and the Jane Jacobs homeowners of West
11th Street all would be stereotypes if they existed on their own; together,
they save one another from cliché.

The Village's history is well known—it began as a true village, a refuge
north of the city of New York. It grew dramatically during the yellow-fever
epidemic of 1822, when the well-to-do fled the existing city, and while
fashion did not come to the Village until the 1830's and 1840's, it was firmly
established as part of the city by then, not as an outlying district. Many of
the houses that are so highly prized today were put up quickly by
speculators, the Levittowns of the early nineteenth century.

What is important to remember is that New York grew around the Village,
not through it, as the neighborhood itself was filling up with Federal and
then Greek Revival row houses. There was physical isolation from the rest

of the city until the subways came and Seventh Avenue South slashed its way mercilessly through the Village's crowded streets after World War I. But its isolation, its sense of being an island in the midst of the teeming city, was and is still crucial to the Village's identity.

I H 1 · WASHINGTON SQUARE PARK
arch: McKim, Mead & White, 1892
redesigned by committee, 1964–69

It's wrong, it always was wrong, and the fact that it is famous and venerable and a necessary bit of open space in the dense Village doesn't make it right. The problem is that Washington Square Park is too big to be a square, too small to be a park, and it ends up as an awkward compromise. There is neither the intimacy of Gramercy Park (or of a good London square) nor the expanse of Central Park or Riverside Park. Washington Square Park tries to behave like a square, but the buildings can't seem to enclose it properly, and the space seems to flow out like water from a tank that has too many holes in it.

The park started out as a potter's field, and became a parade ground in 1826; it became a real park in 1828, and not long afterward the city's most fashionable houses were built around its perimeter. Perhaps in the small-scaled city of the mid-nineteenth century the park felt like real open space; today it doesn't. The square was used as a bus turnaround for years, and in 1964 community activists in the Village succeeded in persuading the Transit Authority to do its turning elsewhere and managed to restore the park to pedestrians. But, unfortunately, redesigning the park to accommodate its higher uses opened up a Pandora's box of local community involvement. Ultimately, the park was redone by a committee consisting of Martin Beck, Harold Edelman, Robert Michaels, Joseph Roberto, Norman Rosenfeld, Robert Nichols, Edgar Tafel, Robert Jacobs, and Robert Weinberg, and nothing in New York stands as better proof of the old adage about committees—Washington Square Park is a camel. There is too much paving, too many of those clichéd street lamps with round tops, too much overall sterility. Nowhere is there the sense of refuge from the city that a park should be expected to provide.

The best thing is still the Arch, as much a symbol of Greenwich Village as there is. It is ironic that the city's iconoclastic neighborhood should be symbolized by one of its very few pieces of monumental, formal sculpture, but so it is, and in the desolation of the park, one is grateful. The Arch was the work of Stanford White of the McKim firm, and it has his characteristic deft, light detail, self-assured yet not overbearing. It is worth viewing from a few blocks up Fifth Avenue: it pulls you to the square like a magnet.

I H 2 · WASHINGTON SQUARE NORTH
1831
· 2 FIFTH AVENUE, at Washington Square
Emery Roth & Sons, 1952

"The Doctor built himself a handsome, modern, wide-fronted house, with a big balcony before the drawing-room windows, and a flight of white-marble steps ascending to a portal which was also faced with white marble. This structure, and many of its neighbors, which it exactly resembled, were supposed, forty years ago, to embody the last results of architectural

I H 1 · *Washington Square Park Arch, looking north up Fifth Avenue, with 2 Fifth Avenue* (I H 2) *at the left*

I H 3 · *Bobst Library, New York University campus*

science, and they remain to this day very solid and honorable dwellings,'' wrote Henry James in 1881 of the houses that still stand, though altered and incomplete as a grouping, on the north side of Washington Square.

There have been compromises—about which more in a moment—but this still remains the noblest row of Greek Revival houses in New York. They are formal and dignified and yet welcoming; to twentieth-century eyes accustomed to the stares of Park Avenue doormen it is hard to see how intimidating these buildings must have been in the 1840's, when they were occupied by the most fashionable families in the city. The houses join to make a unified, yet lively and rhythmic, streetscape, and the row of marble steps and the trees and the generous sidewalk seem to make being in front of these houses even more relaxing than actually being within Washington Square Park across the street.

Much of the east end of "The Row"—the houses at Nos. 7 to 13—were gutted in 1939 and converted into an apartment house. The façades remain intact, however—the job was as sensitive as any such conversion done since. More dramatic was the change that came to the west side of Fifth Avenue, where houses were demolished to make way for Emery Roth & Sons' massive apartment tower, 2 Fifth Avenue, of 1952. Originally, plans called for the tower to be set directly on the square, but villagers protested violently; the builder, Samuel Rudin, compromised by suggesting the five-story mock-Federal wing of red brick along the square, tied into the larger gray-brick tower behind it. It may be heresy to say so, but the fraud comes off—it is good urbanism, respectful of the square and of its neighbors, and the low wing does a substantial job at reducing the mass of the tower as viewed from the park. There are lessons in all of this that were forgotten for years and are only being rediscovered today, in buildings such as Ulrich Franzen's 800 Fifth Avenue tower (III D 3).

I H 3 · ELMER HOLMES BOBST LIBRARY
70 Washington Square South, between West Broadway and Washington Square East
Philip Johnson and Richard Foster, 1973
· HAGOP KEVORKIAN CENTER FOR NEAR-EASTERN STUDIES
50 Washington Square South, SW corner Sullivan Street
Philip Johnson and Richard Foster, 1973

Philip Johnson's two efforts for New York University on Washington Square (there are others, less interesting, down the block at 40 West 4th Street and 707 Broadway). The little one on Washington Square, the Kevorkian Center, is discreet and sensitive to what is around it; the big one, the Bobst Library, is not. Villagers hate it, although not always for the right reason. The red sandstone is rich and warm, an altogether appropriate material and a nice echo to the red brick of the houses on Washington Square North. The problem with Bobst is partially the result of its bulk, which is simply too large for its neighbors on the south side of the square to handle (although it is not too large for the square itself).

Worse still is the interior. Johnson designed it in 1964, back in his decorative phase, and the 150-foot high central court is fussy and pretentious. New York needs grand spacè, and N.Y.U. certainly needed a monumental centerpiece, but how much better this would have been if the architect had been content to leave it alone and not fuss it up! Glitter is everywhere, with only the trompe l'oeil floor pattern of white, gray, and black marble (copied from Palladio's San Giorgio Maggiore in Venice) an element with enough strength for a room of this enormous scale—and even it clashes with the other details. Bobst is the sad story of a missed chance—made sadder still by N.Y.U.'s placement of a tennis court on the roof, denying the building what integrity it does have.

I H 4 · JUDSON MEMORIAL CHURCH, JUDSON HALL and TOWER
McKim, Mead & White, 1892
· LOEB STUDENT CENTER
Harrison & Abramovitz, 1959
· HOLY TRINITY CHAPEL, NEW YORK UNIVERSITY
Eggers & Higgins, 1964
· VANDERBILT LAW SCHOOL, NEW YORK UNIVERSITY
Eggers & Higgins, 1951
all on Washington Square South between MacDougal Street and LaGuardia Place

How to do and how not to do on Washington Square South. The first is the best: McKim, Mead & White's gracious, generous historicism both respects the square and enlivens it with an essay in Italian Renaissance design that is far lighter, if less serious, than the firm's Villard Houses (II F 18), on Madison Avenue of a few years before. The campanile is just right, a

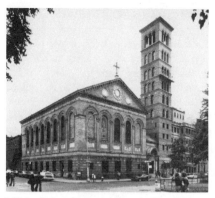

I H 4 · *Judson Memorial Church, New York University campus*

I H 5 · *100–110 Bleecker Street; 505 LaGuardia Place*

punctuation mark, a second voice to shout out after a theme established by the Arch within the square.

In 1951 Eggers & Higgins did a decent, if dull, job with the law school of New York University, an unabashedly late example of no-nonsense historicism. It is altogether capable, respectful of its context, but it lacks the verve of Judson down the block. Whatever sense of context that firm had in 1951, however, it lost by 1964—its Holy Trinity Chapel for N.Y.U. is an outspoken piece of sculptural exhibitionism, and a pitifully weak building to close the vista through the Arch. No better, alas, is the Loeb Student Center next door—why couldn't these architects look to the north side of the square and see how it's done?

I H 5 · 100–110 BLEECKER STREET; 505 LaGUARDIA PLACE
Bleecker to West Houston streets, Mercer Street to LaGuardia Place
I. M. Pei & Partners, with James I. Freed in charge, 1966

Three concrete towers, arranged pinwheel fashion with an enlargement of a Picasso sculpture in concrete as the centerpiece. No one is much for towers in the park these days, and with good reason, but while these have all the weaknesses we expect of that sort of planning, they are dignified and sophisticated as architecture. In a city with hardly more than a handful of decent postwar apartment houses, these stand out. Pei's ability to bring rhythm and texture to a façade that is just a grid of concrete is absolutely superb.

The towers are a generation apart from the immense Washington Square Village to the north, just across Bleecker Street (S. J. Kessler, Paul Lester Weiner, 1958), where roads going under white-brick slabs bring a certain drama, but not enough to make up for the impersonal hugeness of the place. The spots of colored brick don't do enough, either—and in the end it is the Pei project, though it is far more abstract, that is the more humane.

I H 6 · WASHINGTON MEWS / MacDOUGAL ALLEY

These are the stables behind the great Greek Revival houses of Washington Square North. Everyone, from your Aunt Agatha who has been to New York only once to your friend who looks longingly from her West Village high-rise studio, wants to live there. And everyone describes these places as "charming."

They *are* charming, even if often overpraised. They are intimate and nice and friendly and ever so slightly unreal, which is perhaps why they appeal to non–New Yorkers and dyed-in-the-wool New Yorkers alike. MacDougal Alley is more interesting, for a reason that probably makes it less appealing to fans of these places—the immense mass of 2 Fifth Avenue's rear façade backs up against the alley, closing it off and tightening the space. One would think 2 Fifth Avenue would be an intrusion, but it is an unexpected help: a mews doesn't work if it feels too open.

I H 7 · LOWER FIFTH AVENUE: Washington Square to 14th Street

This somehow ends up as one of the most delightful stretches of street anywhere in New York, let alone in the Village. It is really too large in scale for the Village—most of the avenue below 14th Street contains apartment houses and office buildings. But these are both good buildings in themselves and arranged in such a way as never to be oppressive. Churches break the masses of the apartment towers, storefronts come in at the upper end just when (if you are walking uptown) their absence would begin to be noted and cause a sense of uptown sterility.

The highlights of these blocks: 1 Fifth Avenue (Helmle, Corbett & Harrison, 1926), a finely massed apartment tower that curiously mixes neo-Georgian with Art Deco motifs; 40 Fifth Avenue (Van Wart & Wein, 1929), a Park Avenue building that must have come loose in a storm and dropped anchor down here; and two Gothic Revival churches, Richard Upjohn's Church of the Ascension of 1841 at 10th Street, and Joseph C. Wells's First Presbyterian Church of 1845 at 11th Street. The Upjohn church, redecorated by McKim, Mead & White in 1889, is known for its LaFarge murals, but the Wells church, a strong echo of the tower of Magdalen College, Oxford, is the finer. McKim, Mead & White did the south Parish House in 1893, but of more interest is Edgar Tafel's discreet and sensitive Church House on the 12th Street side: it is perhaps Tafel's most successful work, striking just the right balance between repeating themes established in the original building and offering new ones of his own.

I H 8 · BUTTERFIELD HOUSE
37 West 12 Street
Mayer, Whittlesey & Glass; William Conklin and James Rossant in charge, 1962

One of the city's very few decent new apartment houses. The bay windows in the low 12th Street wing are a perfect and respectful counterpoint to the

I H 6 · *MacDougal Alley*

I H 8 · *Butterfield House*

old houses which line that fine block off Fifth Avenue. The scale is just right, and the building appropriately gets bigger on 13th Street to match the larger, more industrial scale of that block. There is a pleasant courtyard in between as yet another reminder that this is not your basic white-brick box.

I H 9 · NEW SCHOOL FOR SOCIAL RESEARCH
66 West 12th Street
Joseph Urban, 1930
additions: Mayer, Whittlesey & Glass, 1958

Urban's Bauhaus for New York. Like so many works of that period, it not only does not shock anymore, it appears rather quaint today, almost as capable of inspiring affection as his altogether different, and now demolished, Ziegfeld Theater on Sixth Avenue. The striated brickwork is good, and Urban's attempts to render the scale acceptable to the building's townhouse neighbors generally succeeded. The oval auditorium inside is of note.

I H 10 · 18 WEST 11th STREET
Hardy Holzman Pfeiffer Associates, 1979

This was almost architect Hugh Hardy's Waterloo. He designed this house for himself to occupy the site made vacant by the explosion caused by radicals' bomb-making in 1970; by the time the Landmarks Commission finished debating the question of whether this design could be considered acceptable within a row of Federal houses, Hardy could no longer afford to build. By extraordinary luck a new set of clients came along years later with a request to build the same house. The Landmarks Commission chose to open the whole matter up again, and the community, which never wanted the building to begin with, was up in arms. Again the go-ahead came, and now it is difficult to see quite what the fuss was all about. This is not a needless expression of modernism, but merely the absence of false, Williamsburg-like kowtowing. It is perhaps a bit stronger a form than the block needs, but its dynamic shape is respectful of what surrounds it, and that is what matters.

I H 11 · JEFFERSON MARKET COURTHOUSE
Sixth Avenue at 10th Street
Frederick Clarke Withers and Calvert Vaux, 1876
remodeling into library: Giorgio Cavaglieri, 1967

This is the epitome of what a local landmark should be. It has a prominent site, providing a hectic neighborhood with a visual anchor. It is an anchor in time. And as a neighborhood library (it was converted in 1967) it plays an active role in the Village life of today.

Jefferson Market is one of the city's best examples of Ruskinian Gothic. Its gables, towers, arcades, and arches are richly red, strong, and yet fanciful at the same time. There is more whimsy here than one usually expects from this style: the building laughs and jokes with you as you walk up Sixth Avenue. The only problem is that when Giorgio Cavaglieri converted it into a library (in one of the pioneering acts of the current

I H 9 · *New School for Social Research*   I H 11 · *Jefferson Market Courthouse (now Jefferson Market Library)*

I H 13 · *National Maritime Union (now Edward and Theresa O' Toole Building, St. Vincent's Hospital)*

I H 12 · *Village Community Church*

generation of preservationists) he took the building too seriously. He has put Serious Modernism into it, and the large, single-pane windows turn the old courthouse's smile into a blank stare. Not that the building isn't so strong that it wins in the end, of course.

I H 12 · VILLAGE COMMUNITY CHURCH
143 West 13th Street
Samuel Thomson, 1846

A Doric temple given Village informality. What makes it feel so comfortable from the street is worth pondering, for the church shouldn't be so likable. It has a hexastyle colonnade and all the austerity one would expect of the Greek Revival in the 1840's. But the proportions are gracious and the overall scale modest enough to permit the building to blend comfortably with the townhouses on either side of it. On an avenue this would be lost, but on a side street it becomes a pleasant, benign surprise. It is a true side-street building—the Doric colonnade exists only in the front, and even the entablature does not return around the sides: a Greek temple made over graciously for a tight New York site.

I H 13 · EDWARD AND THERESA O'TOOLE BUILDING, ST. VINCENT'S HOSPITAL
36 Seventh Avenue
Albert C. Ledner, 1964

This was built originally by the National Maritime Union, and it is unfortunate that a labor union willing to do something out of the ordinary should have been taken in by such pretentious claptrap. Maybe this white building with round holes and round versions of sawtooth cornices is trying to make us think of ships; maybe it is trying to make us think of space travel; maybe it is trying to make us think of how nice the Village used to look before it got modern architecture. At the latter it succeeds; it is the sort of arrogant building that leads one to take on an unnatural degree of sympathy for its opposite number, a banal but good-mannered building like N.Y.U.'s Vanderbilt Law School on Washington Square (I H 4). This was taken over by the ever-expanding St. Vincent's Hospital a couple of years ago, and that has made it somehow less disturbing. Is it that all those round holes in the white façade seem more right for hospital functions than they did for a union hall? Or is it that we have come to expect so little architecturally from any hospital that we are programmed to be more forgiving in that category?

I H 14 · REDESIGN OF SIXTH AVENUE, West 4th Street to Canal Street
Frank A. Rogers, urban designer
Department of Highways, City of New York, Manuel Carballo and Anthony Ameruso, commissioners, 1976

Our perceptions of our urban surroundings are shaped by a myriad of small details: sometimes a shop window or a signpost can affect us more than a skyscraper can. Frank Rogers understood this, and somehow he persuaded the financially strapped City of New York to agree with him. The result was Rogers' redesign of the blocks of Sixth Avenue south of 3rd Street, and it is one of the best things the municipal bureaucracy has produced in years.

What was done was, first, a redirection of the street itself, eliminating some unnecessary spurs and side alleys and turning them into miniparks. Then, new street furniture—benches, lampposts and so forth—was added along the length of the project area. And the street was repaved, in part with conventional asphalt paving and in part with an unusual concrete paving block, which denotes bus stops and crosswalks in alternating light and dark striping. The paving block is splendid visually, good from a safety standpoint, and easy to maintain, since it requires no painting.

There are other details of equal quality—benches of wooden slats in a comfortable contour shape, their legs anchored directly into the paving so that they appear to be standing on elegantly thin spindles, for example. The benches are set to permit group conversations as well as street watching, and that is the sort of seemingly tiny detail that, ultimately, makes this project so remarkable. New York, whatever its virtues, has never paid much attention to the niceties of a public environment; as a city, we are the ultimate example of Galbraith's observation about private affluence and public squalor. Here, an attempt was made to deal on the small scale of daily life and to find therein some way to have an impact on the larger environment. Lower Sixth Avenue is not epoch-making, but it works, and thus the city becomes a tiny bit more civilized.

I H 15 · MORTON STREET / BEDFORD STREET

Here are the classic places in the West Village, the blocks where people who have always said they dreamed of living in Greenwich Village want to be, the places that are just enough off the tourist route to be quiet and serene. Morton and Bedford are not absolutely typical of this area west of lower Seventh Avenue—Commerce Street and Grove Street and Charles and Bank streets farther uptown probably qualify better on that score. These streets are worth looking at because they are *not* typical, but are just a bit eccentric in ways that make them, if abnormal, all the more characteristic of New York.

I H 14 · *New street furniture from the redesign of lower Sixth Avenue (Avenue of the Americas)*

I H 15 · *59 Morton Street*

Morton Street, first, has a bend, and that makes it loved in this Cartesian city. It also has tenements, which makes it less loved in the townhouse-oriented Village. And it has some fine Federal houses, too, and everything runs together and jostles side by side and somehow seems right. Only the doorway at No. 59 Morton is of serious individual architectural interest— it is quite possibly the best Federal doorway in the Village, a poem of Ionic columns and an elegant fan window and a six-panel door that come together with a grace seen almost nowhere else. But Morton Street is itself a kind of poem, not always quite in meter and never rhyming, but worth coming back to, if only because, when all is said and done, it feels comfortable in a way few other places do.

Bedford Street northwest of Seventh Avenue is longer, yet more intimate. It is narrower than Morton Street, more the sort of experience one would expect from a village with a small "v" than from an urban neighborhood. Once again, things that don't quite fit have come together—in this case frame houses, brick houses, tenements, and total oddities like the former Edna St. Vincent Millay house at No. 75½, a 9½-foot-wide sliver, and "Twin Peaks," at No. 102, the wonderfully ludicrous mock half-timbered fantasy row-house castle remodeled in 1925 by Clifford Reed Daily from an 1835 Federal house.

It all holds together; the buildings are set in rows on a narrow, treeless street, almost like pieces of furniture arranged for sale in a store. It is, too, a little bit like the back alleys of Venice—one has the same sense here that it is all a kind of interior, that you are walking down a corridor in some vast building. The reason may be the surprising absence of trees in this immediate area; Bedford Street's ambience is the sort that one would expect to find trees in.

The juxtaposition of No. 17 Grove Street, at the corner of Bedford, a frame house built in 1822 and still essentially intact, with the five-story tenement beside it on Grove Street—not to mention with the toylike frame workshop at 100 Bedford behind the house—is as dramatic as any you will see in the Village. What is most remarkable, though, is how unexceptional the combination seems. We are accustomed to such meetings across time and style in this part of town, and even such drastic adjacencies as this one seem not to clash.

I H 16 · GROVE COURT
enter between 10 and 12 Grove Street, east of Hudson Street
1854

This is one of the half-dozen most civilized places in New York, period. Six generous Federal houses set behind a welcoming forecourt hidden from the clamor of the street, it feels more like an urban version of Brattle Street in Cambridge than like a part of New York. It is utterly restful and gracious, and the houses are big enough and dominate the court enough so that they manage to discourage the word "charming." They are serene, not charming, and their site plan, which places them back at the end of a V-shaped court so as to create maximum privacy with minimum use of land, is a masterpiece of urban design.

I H 17 · FEDERAL ARCHIVES BUILDING
641 Washington Street, between Christopher and Barrow streets
1899

This competes with the DeVinne Press Building (I G 8) for the title of New York's best piece of nineteenth-century industrial brickwork, and it probably

I H 17 · *Federal Archives Building*

I H 16 · *Grove Court*

I H 19 · *Inner court at Westbeth*

wins. It is massive, more so than DeVinne, and its debt to Richardson's great Marshall Field Wholesale Store still clearer. There is a fine base of rounded arches, then a single horizontal story, topped by five-story arched bays of two windows each, with two two-story bays and then a delicate top. The rhythm is strong and sure, and yet the mass is never oppressive. The building is clean and strong, its brick forming arches and walls as solid, as silent, as graceful as those of Kahn seventy years later. It is the best, almost, that this style could yield—rich without ever being fussy, powerful without ever being overbearing. It breaks the scale of the West Village, and it is so good that this matters not a wink.

The origin of the design is an area of some uncertainty. The plans were drawn by various supervising architects for the United States government and, in true bureaucratic fashion, altered from one administration to the next. The lower two stories are known to be the work of Willoughby J. Edbrooke; Marjorie Pearson, who has done the most extensive research on the building, asserts that no records exist to determine who the architect of the handsome upper floors is.

I H 18 · WEST VILLAGE HOUSES
Various sites along Washington Street, Morton to Bank streets
Perkins & Will, 1974

This is a sad story. This project was going to save the Village, and it was going to show everyone that Jane Jacobs was right and that people—or at least Villagers—didn't want fancy modern apartments but wanted unfancy old-fashioned ones. The Village group that developed this complex, intended originally to be sold as co-ops, believed it could create a modern equivalent of Jacobs' ideal. Alas, political squabbling and rising costs led to drastic compromise, and the result is a set of dreary, dreary boxes, with—dare one say it?—less life to them than there is in any of the high rises these were to be the antidote to.

The West Village Houses are five-story walkups. They are in scale, all right, but so what? The starkness of the forms is terrifying, and the blank brick walls on Washington Street facing the rest of the community are a special problem. Here, politics and economics put an end to good intentions.

I H 19 · WESTBETH
463 West Street, at Bank Street
Cyrus L. W. Eidlitz, 1900
renovation: Richard Meier, 1965

A distinguished relic by now, the venerable leader in recycling. This was once the Bell Telephone Laboratories, and under the guidance of the Kaplan Foundation it became housing for artists after Bell moved to New Jersey. Richard Meier opened up the huge building in just the right way, with round balcony fire escapes bringing life to the inner court. The outdoor plazas are a bit more sterile than they might be, but this remains a major pioneering effort—the spiritual father of all the commercial loft conversions that have created a whole new housing type for Lower Manhattan in the last decade.

I H 20 · 14th STREET

Like all of the major crosstown streets—23rd, 34th, 42nd, 57th—this has a distinct personality, and one that changes as the street moves across Manhattan. Fourteenth Street's western end is occupied by the city's wholesale meat district, and the old brick buildings clustered tightly together have something of the air of the old, departed Washington Market that once filled several blocks of Tribeca (I C). The meat district sprawls onto a few of the tight, crooked little streets just south of 14th Street here (among them is the wonderfully named Little West 12th Street), and here, in the buildings if not in the populace, there is something of the feeling of the rest of Greenwich Village. But as 14th Street moves eastward it comes close to losing its neighborhood identity altogether: the Village's northern border seems to have given up even trying to pretend to any of the atmosphere of this part of town, and has fallen into uptown ways instead. But they are not the fancy uptown ways of the gentry avenues; the rest of 14th Street is more like a shopping street in the Upper West Side or Washington Heights, messy and sleazy and yet full of energy. There seem to be more bargain stores per square foot on this street than in any other part of town, and there are surely more old ladies with shopping bags who wander aimlessly, muttering to themselves.

There is not much architecture of note, save for the sudden break in the street's hectic rhythm caused by the executive offices of the Salvation Army in Centennial Memorial Temple at No. 120, between Sixth and Seventh avenues (Voorhees, Gmelin & Walker, 1930). Here, the architects who brought so much fine commercial Art Deco architecture to Lower Manhattan (I A 4, I A 11, I C 3) tried their hand at making a monument. The cavernous entrance and overblown scale is what the Art Deco style wanted all along, and here, unrestrained by the functional demands of commercial building, it all comes rather grandly into its own. Too grandly, perhaps, since there is little of the rigor and the discipline here that is to be found in the other Voorhees, Gmelin & Walker buildings, but if this is all just a stage set, it is an amusing and strong one. The Centennial Temple faces the 42nd Division Armory of the New York National Guard across the street at No. 125 (Charles S. Kawecki, New York State General Services Administration, 1971), an altogether overbearing, hostile pile of concrete; the two buildings stare each other down like opposing ranks of soldiers, each waiting for the other to fire the first shot across 14th Street.

II/MIDTOWN

Plaza at the end of the Promenade at
Rockefeller Center (II G 1), sculpture of
Prometheus by Paul Manship, with the RCA
Building in the background

A/UNION SQUARE, STUYVESANT SQUARE, AND THE EAST TWENTIES

II A 1 · UNION SQUARE: Intersection of Park Avenue South and Broadway: 14th to 17th streets

Union Square was named as the joining of the Bowery Road and the Bloomingdale Road (Broadway), the city's main routes early in the nineteenth century. It was an elegant square in the pre–Civil War days, and 14th Street, which forms its southern boundary, was long a theatrical center— once the Academy of Music, the city's most fashionable pre-Metropolitan opera house, was the area's grandest magnet. Later on, into the twentieth century, the square became a center for radical activities, where speech-makers spoke on soapboxes and where protest marches begin.

Union Square's past, be it in either its formal or its Hyde Park Corner incarnation, is more interesting than its present. Now the square is just a dreary park, one of the least relaxing green spaces in Manhattan. The square was redesigned around World War I to accommodate a huge BMT subway station underneath, and the result is ungainly. Nothing, in fact, seems correctly proportioned, from the oddly deep benches to the overall shape of the "square" itself. Like Washington Square, this is too big to be a square, too small to be a good park, although the uneven shape does make this a bit more parklike than Washington Square.

The location of Union Square is unfortunate. Heavy truck and bus traffic on all sides means that the city intrudes aurally as well as visually. Much of the area at the park's edge has been paved for parking, and the surrounding precinct is tawdry with no particular charm. The best buildings are on the west side (see below), although there are a few of note on the east side.

Most pleasing is the nice four-story mansard roof of the Guardian Life Insurance Company at 201 Park Avenue South (D'Oench & Yost, 1911); it sits comfortably on the square with none of the pretentious fussiness one often finds in elaborate mansards. The addition is by Skidmore, Owings & Merrill, dating from 1961, and while its Miesian style is surprising beside the main building, it comes off—largely, one suspects, because it is low and deferential to the main building in scale, if not in style.

The old Century Building, headquarters of the long-gone *Century Illus-*

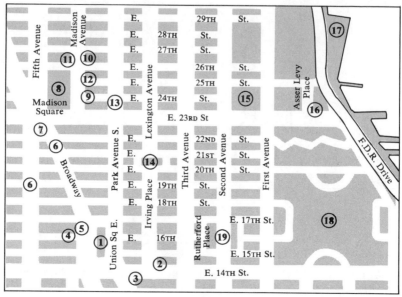

trated Magazine, is across the street on the south corner of 17th Street facing Union Square. It was built in 1881 to the designs of William Schickel, and while the Queen Anne pile might have worked somewhere else, it seems oddly uncomfortable here. Union Square can accommodate flamboyant show-offs and it can accommodate derelicts, but not genteel matrons.

Far more satisfying is the fine and dignified Union Square Savings Bank at No. 20 Union Square (Henry Bacon, 1907). The Corinthian-columned exterior is all that is left, alas; the bank has been given a motel-modern inside. Still there, though, is the lettering to the left of the front door indicating the place's former name: The Institution for the Savings of Merchant's Clerks.

For all that has gone wrong here, there are still reminders within the square itself of what a grand civic environment this once was. There are bronze fountains and some of the city's finest statuary. The best of the statues are Henry Kirke Brown and John Quincy Adams Ward's equestrian statue of Washington, with a Richard Upjohn base, and Karl Adolf Donndorf's mother and children atop a bronze fountain base. There is also an immense flagstaff base, 9½ feet high and 36 feet in diameter, with bas-reliefs by Anthony de Francisci symbolizing the forces of good and evil in the Revolutionary War; even if a derelict is relieving himself beside it, it has a rather majestic presence.

II A 2 · CONSOLIDATED EDISON COMPANY BUILDING
4 Irving Place, NE corner 14th Street
Henry J. Hardenbergh, 1915–29
tower: Warren & Wetmore, 1926

Henry Hardenbergh was at the end of his career when he designed the main building of Con Edison's headquarters, and it is hard not to feel that he must have been very tired by then. There is none of the life of Hardenbergh's Dakota, Plaza, or Art Students League in this heavy, ponderous mass. The Warren & Wetmore tower is actually better, although all of the columns and statuary melded into its upper portions give it rather an air of the Vittorio Emanuele monument in Rome. It seems to represent an awkward moment just between Beaux-Arts monumentality and modernist sleekness, and by no stretch of the imagination does the tower demonstrate the better side of either style. Indeed, it is more like a fight between the two, with the elaborate top fighting the austerity of the shaft, and the shaft itself fighting the heavy details up and down its corners. One is thankful, though, for the grand clock atop the tower; it gives the building at least one benign role in the cityscape.

II A 3 · 145 FOURTH AVENUE
SE corner 14th Street
Horace Ginsbern & Associates, 1965

Worth looking at for the zigzag along Fourth Avenue, which provides visual interest as well as diagonally set windows to give south light and views to west-facing apartments. More important still, it is an attempt to accommodate the building's overall form to the bend of Fourth Avenue: good urbanism, not unlike the similar gesture at 240 Central Park South (II G 13). A rare piece of thoughtful postwar apartment design.

II A 4 · 31 UNION SQUARE WEST (Bank of the Metropolis)
NW corner, 16th Street
Bruce Price, 1902

This narrow old bank is one of the city's more appealing smaller towers, a lovely eclectic creation. There is a wonderful, gently bowed Ionic portico at the bottom, a slender, almost sleek shaft, and an enormous, elaborate cornice. It feels like a building Louis Sullivan would have designed had he been a Beaux-Arts architect; some of the ornament even seems a watered-down version of Sullivan's, although the overall aesthetic is clearly a more classical and academic one. Price never quite found a style and never did a truly great building, but he was a deft, intuitive maker of compositions, and this is one of his best works.

II A 5 · 33 UNION SQUARE WEST
between 16th and 17th streets
Alfred Zucker, 1893

This is one of those buildings that are entertaining more than seriously good; on the other hand, there is nothing really wrong with it, either. It is wildly eclectic, almost hysterical in its stylistic swings and absurd excesses, yet it retains a certain slender poise in spite of itself. If the Siegel-Cooper

II A 4 & 5 · *Bank of the Metropolis (now 31 Union Square West) and 33 Union Square West*

II A 6 · *156 Fifth Avenue*

department store (II B 11) is an overweight glutton, this building is like one of those people who eat and drink and debauch and manage never to let any of it show.

If 33 Union Square West is anything, it is a mix of Moorish and Venetian Gothic. But there are pieces of ornament, like the framing around the large second-story window, that prefigure Art Nouveau. There is every kind of lintel, molding, spandrel, colonnade, and balcony; it gets very Venetian Gothic for a part of the way up, and then, in an arcade near the top, suddenly classical. The top itself bursts into a wild fury of every style that came before; what was it, you wonder, that was once at the bottom where a bad corrugated metal storefront now holds forth.

II A 6 · FIFTH AVENUE AND BROADWAY—Union Square to Madison Square

These are wonderful, surprising streets—one can look uptown on Fifth Avenue from 15th Street and not see a new building through Madison Square. It is the sort of assemblage of fine nineteenth-century buildings that suggests SoHo, although here the buildings are, of course, later, are mostly of masonry, and cannot in truth command quite the significance for the history of architecture as SoHo's masterpieces can. As with the Sixth Avenue stores (II B 11), these are best seen as a group, but the quality is higher here. There is less pretension, more of a sense of solidity and a sense of knowing direction, yet there is more imagination, too. These are good buildings individually and they strengthen one another to form an even better whole.

Romanesque with a certain classical variation is the basic theme, and it is a free and pleasing eclecticism, done for compositional and urbanistic ends above all. There are a lot of arches here, a lot of Corinthian columns and pilasters—they all manage to fit together, to make a place that is a remarkable relic of New York streets as they once were. But why phrase it that way? This is, happily, a New York street as it *is*.

R. H. Robertson's MacIntyre Building at 874 Broadway (northeast corner of 18th Street) of 1892 is one of the area's best: a narrow, elaborate Romanesque tower, it begins with almost Sullivanesque ornament at the base, then becomes more conservative and devotedly Romanesque as it rises—a remarkable case of an architect who seems to have gotten religion somewhere in the middle of his job.

The old W & J Sloane store at the southeast corner of Broadway and 19th Street (W. Wheeler Smith, 1882) is a six-story mix of Chicago School and classical details—large windows, wide brick columns, narrow mullions—one of the strongest and most controlled compositions here. Almost as good is the Arnold Constable store on the southwest corner of Broadway and 19th Street (Griffith Thomas, 1869, extended 1873, 1877), a dignified mix of Second Empire and Italianate details with a brutalized ground floor but one of the city's very finest mansard roofs, two stories high. On the same intersection is the Victorian trifle of the Gorham silver company's old store (Edward H. Kendall, 1883), a delicate if slightly strained counterpoint to the more robust buildings it faces.

Just above the old Gorham building is a sliver of a building, roughly five stories high, that is entirely covered in a punched-out decorative metal sheathing. It looks like Edward Durell Stone from a distance; it was a 1977 renovation, and as the only intrusion on this block, it is worth pondering. The form is vulgar and unpleasant; yet, since it has an even texture, it is in fact less jarring than glass would have been.

Corners seem to be all in this section of Broadway, and the most pleasing are at the intersection of Broadway and 20th Street. Lord & Taylor's former store at the southwest corner (James H. Giles, 1869) meets the corner with a mansarded tower set at a 45-degree angle to the intersection; it manages to be respectful of the street grid nonetheless, and the cast-iron façade recedes gracefully on both sides from its powerful centerpiece. Once again, a ground floor that has been brutalized.

The McKim, Mead & White building at the southeast corner, 900 Broadway, which dates from 1887, meets the corner more calmly—it just swings around in a gentle curve. There is superb brickwork here, mounting up from a base of arches, and the upper sections (some of which are floors added later) have a bit of the air of a Chicago School skyscraper to them, although the building overall is far too picturesque to really deny its New York eclectic origins.

Yet another corner treatment is visible just to the west at No. 141–147 Fifth Avenue (R. Maynicke, 1897). This is an overdone, rather pretentious, but nonetheless pleasing mass, and it works because the fine rounded corner provides a focus for the entire overactive composition of pilasters and oculi and corbels and laurels and cartouches and balustrades and pediments. The ornament heightens in intensity at the corner, and the corner itself mounts to a high tower. The façade suggests more a decorator's two-dimensional sense of composition than a real architectural mind at work, but the building is such a devoted and cooperative part of the street that one welcomes it.

The other structures of note in this stretch are the Romanesque Revival Methodist Book Concern at No. 150 (20th Street) (Edward H. Kendall,

1889), the two-story arched entrance at No. 156, a coffered-ceilinged reminder that lobbies do *not* have to be low and lined in acoustical tile to work (Rowe & Baker, 1895), and the original headquarters of the Scribner publishing firm at No. 153–157, an 1894 structure by Ernest Flagg, who designed the later and better-known current Scribner building on Fifth Avenue (II D 4). And just up the block at the corner of West 23rd Street is No. 186 Fifth Avenue, one of the few buildings by Henry Hardenbergh left in New York. This is early Hardenbergh, completed in 1884 for the Western Union Company; its façade is a taut composition of brick and stone, with two-story arches creating an arcade at the base, an unusual chimney mass at the western end, and a dormered top. It is more severe than its Hardenberghian contemporary, the Dakota, and less fanciful than the Plaza, but it aptly demonstrates Hardenbergh's not inconsiderable ability to bring order out of diverse parts.

II A 7 · *Flatiron Building*

II A 9 · *Metropolitan Life Insurance Company Headquarters*

II A 7 · FLATIRON BUILDING
175 Fifth Avenue, at Broadway and 23rd Street
D. H. Burnham & Co., 1902

This was once the city's most famous skyscraper, and its triangular shape quickly gave it a name other than that which had been intended for it—the Fuller Building. The triangular plan is an apt response to the awkward site left at the intersection of Broadway and Fifth Avenue; it may seem like the most natural solution in the world, but later architects, so intent on pure forms ignorant of context, could never match it—as in the insipid Gulf & Western Building (II G 14) which totally ignores the shape of Columbus Circle.

The Flatiron's shape creates interesting effects from certain angles. When viewed from certain positions, for example, it appears more as a thick wall, not as a volume—an effect similar to that achieved by the parallelogram of the John Hancock Tower in Boston, seventy years its junior. But the Flatiron is good enough so that it deserves to be remembered for reasons other than its shape. The façade is a richly detailed tapestry of rusticated limestone, with gently undulating bays in the midsection that break the sense of sheer wall, yet still keep in balance with the overall shape of the tower. The French Renaissance detail is ornate, and reflects the historicist—and somewhat pompous—leanings of Daniel Burnham, who started as one of Chicago's great modernists and then, after the death of his brilliant partner John Wellborn Root, grew stodgy and conservative. But this is one of Burnham's best, livelier by far than most of his output could ever have hoped to be.

II A 8 · MADISON SQUARE (Intersection of Broadway and Fifth Avenue: 23rd to 26th streets)

This is what Union Square might have been, if things had worked out. Madison Square, which dates from 1847, is a comfortable, unpretentious park, defined mainly by what surrounds it—the Metropolitan Life Tower, the Flatiron Building, the New York Life Insurance Co. headquarters. The east side of the square is marred only by the Merchandise Mart at No. 41 Madison Avenue (Emery Roth & Sons, 1973), an anonymous tower of dark glass that pays no attention whatsoever to its rich context. The Mart replaced the old Jerome Mansion, as of this writing the only city landmark yet destroyed under a loophole in the landmarks law permitting demolition if no commercially viable use can be found for a landmark structure. The Mart does more damage to the buildings around it than to the square itself, however; Madison Square has a kernel of serenity that is hard indeed to crack. Worth noting are the benches set in tiny alcoves within the park rails—a clever, sensible, and self-assured design gesture.

II A 9 · METROPOLITAN LIFE INSURANCE COMPANY HEADQUARTERS
1 Madison Avenue, between 23rd and 25th streets
east side, 1893; tower, 1909, Napoleon Le Brun & Sons
north building, (11–25 Madison Avenue), Harvey Wiley Corbett and D. Everett Waid, 1932
remodeling, Lloyd Morgan, 1962

The 700-foot-high tower, New York's great campanile, was once the world's tallest building. The early 1960's remodeling, which saw the base structures entirely rebuilt, also brought a simplification of the tower, with a great deal of its ornament stripped off. But enough of the building's integrity remains, and it is worth comparing with the awkward Con Edison tower (II A 2). Here, the architects were doing something "wrong"—imitating a historic model directly—whereas at Con Edison they were being original, which was thought to be better. But the building that breaks the rules works in this instance, and the one that follows them doesn't. The reasons have to do with basics—with notions of proportion, scale, and so forth. The Metropolitan tower looks graceful even after the needless renovation it received; Con Edison would look heavy even if every bit of its ornament were stripped off.

The North Building is handsome indeed—a limestone mass, mounting up and up in a manner that recalls the drawings of Hugh Ferris. The four great arcaded entrances join with the many setbacks in creating a visually interesting and relatively unoppressive mass, given this building's enormous size. And it is a good neighbor to the venerable tower beside it, too, despite their difference in style. Indeed, only one thing can be held against this building: it replaced the Madison Avenue Presbyterian Church, a McKim, Mead & White temple that was Stanford White's last—and among his very finest—buildings. It was on the site for only thirteen years after its completion in 1906.

II A 10 · NEW YORK LIFE INSURANCE COMPANY BUILDING
51 Madison Avenue, 26th to 27th streets
Cass Gilbert, 1928

This solid limestone mass joins with the Metropolitan Life Insurance Co.'s North Building (II A 9) to create the splendid east wall of Madison Square. Gilbert's work declined in quality in his later years, and this building is just at the edge—there is some of the sense of life and movement of his Woolworth Building, but it is not hard to feel the beginning of the hardening of the arteries that was to be apparent in the later, final works, such as the Supreme Court in Washington. The New York Life building is best at ground level, where the Italian Renaissance base gives into a noble and grandiose lobby, as good as any early twentieth-century bank in New York as a reminder of the power and glory of a financial institution. The gilt pyramid at the top is appealing because of its bright gold tone, but it is in fact rather awkward—it seems one size too small, and does not grow gracefully out of the tower as does the top of, say, Gilbert's Woolworth Building. Whatever its faults, the New York Life building shines beside its tacky annex across the street at 28 East 28th Street (Carson & Lundin, 1962). This is a banal box, with a limestone sheathing that comes off as a cheap attempt to show sympathy with the older building; the addition's tawdry metal heart shows through, both literally and figuratively.

One cannot leave this subject without observing, as at the Metropolitan Life Insurance Co.'s North Building, the site's distinguished past. Here stood not only the original terminal of the New York and Harlem Railroad, the Union Depot, but the original Madison Square Garden, the lavish palace completed in 1890 to the designs of Stanford White of McKim, Mead & White. It was on the Garden's roof that White was shot in 1906 by Harry K. Thaw, husband of Evelyn Nesbitt, White's former mistress.

II A 11 · 50 MADISON AVENUE
NW corner East 26th Street
Renwick, Aspinwall & Owen, 1896

This Italian Renaissance palace sits properly and discreetly at the northeast corner of Madison Square, and it holds its own superbly among its much larger neighbors. It is a building that is urbane in the best sense—it is high, strong, and respectful of the street, the square, and everything else around it. It is detailed with liveliness—the elaborate cornice is especially good— but with restraint. And not the least of this fine building's attractive features is the dignified lettering set into the façades above the first floor indicating "Madison Avenue" and "26th Street"—a European model other New York buildings would have done well to emulate.

II A 12 · APPELLATE DIVISION, NEW YORK STATE SUPREME COURT
Madison Avenue, NE corner 25th Street
James Brown Lord, 1900
addition: Rogers and Butler, 1954

What is so marvelous here is not just the much-talked-about sculpture (though that is very good indeed) but the small scale. This building feels tiny, absolutely delicate, in a way that almost no other Beaux-Arts structure in the city manages to do. Narrow stairs lead to narrow doors; even the statuary, which includes Frederick Ruckstahl's "Wisdom" and "Force" flanking the portal, Karl Bitter's "Peace" on the balustrade facing Madison Square, and Daniel Chester French's "Justice" on the East 25th Street side, is not so very much bigger than life size.

Lord was onto something here. We are taught by the example of most Beaux-Arts work that grand scale is all, and that immense size is crucial to a sense of civic importance. Here, there is small and comfortable size, yet we feel no diminution of civic dignity. It works in part because of the sculpture, in part because the elements of the building are all in scale with one another and there is an impressive sense of control; the end result is still a bit unreal, as if Grand Central Terminal had shrunk itself to dollhouse size and invited us in to play. The combination Lord achieved here of modest size and civic grandeur is as good an image for the court system as one could ask for. And to make this situation pleasanter still, the addition by Rogers & Butler is respectfully deferential, yet dignified.

II A 13 · PARK AVENUE SOUTH

Once it was Fourth Avenue, then it wanted class. Not surprising: the buildings here, full of historical cribbings, are all rather eagerly striving for some sort of social acceptance themselves. But they are good, lively examples of New York commercial eclecticism, and they make a reasonably coherent whole. Indeed, Park Avenue South is really an early twentieth-century equivalent of the nineteenth-century large-scale commercial rows of Fifth Avenue and Broadway above Union Square (see II A 6).

There is a good tradition of elaborate cornices here, and, indeed, in many of the buildings the detail gets better toward the top, in spite of the fact that these tend to be boxy, loft structures, with no pretense toward the elaborate tops given to their skyscraper contemporaries. This is get-down-to-business architecture—but these architects clearly had a very good time getting down to business.

No. 381 Park Avenue South (Charles A. Valentine, 1910) is topped by an unusually pleasing polychromed array of cartouches, arches, egg and darts and colored panels. No precedent here, no serious intent, just a lot of things taken whimsically out of a lot of books, one suspects, but the architect got away with it. At No. 419 (Walter Haefeli, 1927) there is a lovely Art Deco top, resting above a rather industrial-like mass, as if the building really wanted to be a factory, but could not resist joining in with the street's strong tradition of cornice ornament.

Two other buildings of note here were designed by architects whose reputations were made with more serious buildings elsewhere, and in each case they seem to have tossed off a bit of classicizing ornament rather casually, as if to suggest that they were above the whole idea of working in this not entirely fashionable quarter. No. 432 Park Avenue South (Warren & Wetmore with Robert T. Lyons, 1914) has its corner marked by huge, upright round shields surrounded by intricate ornament. No. 440 (Cross & Cross, 1913) is topped by a startlingly grandiose Corinthian colonnade, a temple set atop a tower and matched to its bulk.

II A 14 · *Players Club on Gramercy Park South*

II A 12 · *Appellate Division, New York State Supreme Court*

II A 14 · GRAMERCY PARK
foot of Lexington Avenue, 20th to 21st streets

Here is the proof—and there are few enough of them in New York—that
real estate developers are not all bad. Gramercy Park was laid out in 1831
by Samuel Ruggles, who drained an old marsh (the name is a corruption of
a Dutch phrase meaning "crooked swamp"), laid out sixty-six building lots
around the central open space, and then sold them on the premise that they
would have access to a perpetually private park in the center. Miraculously,
the system still works today: the park is immaculately kept by its private
owners, and the value of the real estate at its periphery has remained high.

It is common to hear people speak of Gramercy Park as the part of
Manhattan that most resembles London, and there is some truth to that.
The park is really more of a square, and the entire quarter has that sense
of tree-lined restraint characteristic of London streets and squares. But
Gramercy Park's identity derives as much from New York as from London;
its brownstones and loose eclecticism could only be American.

Change has come slowly here; except for the construction of large
apartment houses on the north side of the park in the 1920's, there has been
relatively little altered around the park during this century. It is a quiet
place, free of through traffic thanks to the fact that Gramercy Park blocks
Lexington Avenue, and this, almost as much as the architecture, creates
the extraordinary sense of tranquillity here.

The row of houses on the west side of the park is excellent. Nos. 3 and
4 Gramercy Park date from the 1840's and are attributed to Alexander
Jackson Davis, one of the city's leading architects of the pre–Civil War
period; the elaborate cast-iron porches are special indeed. There are two
brownstones of note on the south side; the National Arts Club at No. 15
Gramercy Park (remodeled in 1884 by Calvert Vaux for Samuel J. Tilden,
the 1876 presidential candidate), and the Players Club at No. 16, remodeled
in 1888 by Stanford White for Edwin Booth. Across Irving Place at No. 19
is a vast house that has been given a Second Empire top; it is silent and
dignified, its perfectly polished brass lamps and door knockers a symbol of
what the park area can be at its best.

Down the block is a fine, austere Italianate structure, the Brotherhood
Synagogue at No. 28. It was built in 1859 to the designs of King & Kellum
as the Friends' Meeting House and renovated in 1975 by architect James
Stewart Polshek. The parade of eclecticism continues: No. 34 on the east
side of the park (George DaConha, 1883) is a fine red-brick apartment
house, one of the city's earliest and, with its octagonal turret corner, one
of its most appealing. The lobby, with a richly polychromed mosaic floor,
is one of the city's best. There is an ancient cable-controlled Otis elevator
here, and the general attitude of the residents is such that they tend to look
down on the Dakota (III B 9) as something of a parvenu.

No. 36 Gramercy Park, next door, was built in 1908 to the designs of
James Riely Gordon. The armored knights standing guard at the entrance
have given the building the reputation of being rather more unorthodox
than it truly is; No. 34 is really the better work. But the white terra-cotta
Gothic ornament of No. 36 is good, and worth noting. The last structure
of any distinction to go up in the park itself was No. 1 Lexington Avenue,
the apartment house of 1910 by Herbert Lucas. It is solid in the very best
uptown manner, but already a bit of the gentleness of the earlier Gramercy

Park buildings is ebbing away. The later additions—the other apartment houses on the north side and the Gramercy Park Hotel—are decent, but they could be anywhere in Manhattan.

The park's periphery can be strolled in just a few minutes, and it can be done by arriving at any of the six entrances to the square—the four corners or Lexington Avenue from the north or Irving Place from the south. It is best to enter from a corner, though; there one sees only a sliver of the park as one approaches, and the immense gracefulness of the place comes as just a bit more of a surprise.

II A 15 · EAST MIDTOWN PLAZA
East 23rd to East 25th streets, First to Second avenues
Davis, Brody & Associates, 1974

This is really the best urban housing Davis, Brody & Associates has done since Riverbend (IV B 15). It is assertive, yet welcoming; these brick towers feel like *houses,* not like institutions, for all their size. The success comes from two aspects of the design: the shapes of the buildings themselves, which have chamfered corners and low brick walls instead of balcony rails, and from the arrangement of the buildings on the site, which creates generous open space and yet works carefully with the existing street and building pattern.

This is all harder to do than one would think; if you doubt it, look at the housing tower on Second Avenue above 25th Street, just north of East Midtown Plaza. There, a banal tower is plunked down with no recognition whatsoever of what is around it. At East Midtown Plaza, the relatively low wing along 23rd Street, the anchoring corner towers and the good central space all show a real willingness to recognize context. The exposed concrete reads as ornament here, not as structure, a further plus in that a utilitarian aspect of the building has been contorted into a happily nonutilitarian role. The design was imitated just up the street by Frost Associates in the Phipps Plaza housing complex on Second Avenue between East 26th and East 29th streets, completed in 1976. The knockoff isn't quite as good, but it, too, comes a long way from the scaleless boxes of most publicly assisted housing.

II A 16 · PUBLIC BATHS, CITY OF NEW YORK
East 23rd Street at Asser Levy Place
Arnold W. Brunner and William Martin Aiken, 1906

Roman baths were the model for railroad stations and art museums, so why not for American baths? Thus reasoned the good Mr. Brunner and Mr. Aiken, and they came up with this lovely, pretentious little pile. It speaks of a day when New York was full of tenements with no baths of their own and public bathing facilities had to be provided. Of course they were going to be in the grandest Roman style, civic pride being what it was in those days; the irony of a city willing to give its residents such an opulent facility and yet not think of improving their housing so that they might have baths

II A 16 · *Public Baths, City of New York*

II A 15 · *East Midtown Plaza*

of their own was not, one supposes, perceived by many in 1906. Now it is a public swimming pool, and a handsome one indeed. It remains hard for late twentieth-century eyes, trained to see such classical structures as buildings intended for the most formal of events, not to be amused by the lettering on the frieze: FREE PUBLIC BATHS.

II A 17 · WATERSIDE
F.D.R. Drive, East 25th to East 30th streets
Davis, Brody & Associates, 1974

This is one of the city's most acclaimed housing developments, and the praise it has received is partly justified, partly not. It was a daring idea, put forth by developer Richard Ravitch and architects Lewis Davis and Samuel Brody: housing on a platform site in the East River. And the towers themselves are good—Davis, Brody's square brick is handsome, and the change in plan as the towers rise, from cut-in corner to chamfered corner to full corner, is a good way to vary the form visually at minimum expense, as well as an appealing reversal of the usual setback idea, since these buildings are set *out,* not back.

But the immense concrete plaza is psychologically cold on even the warmest summer's day, and while recent exhibitions of large-scale sculpture have been helpful, there is a desperate need for landscaping. Further problems are the institutional public spaces within (though they lead to decent apartments) and the isolation from the rest of the city. One feels all too much on an island, cut off from the very city life these buildings presumably exist to enrich. The tiny bridge over the Franklin Delano Roosevelt Drive is especially irritating, since it feels like a drawbridge over a moat—how much better the whole place would have been if the bridge had been wide and lined with shops.

But the waterfront promenade, down a flight of steps from the plaza, is a delight, and makes up for many of the sins of the rest of the public space. One can walk the length of the complex at the water's edge, away from the view of the towers and the plaza, and at the north end of the walk the view of river and skyline is extraordinary—an end-on view of the United Nations joins with the towers of a Con Edison plant to form an unusually good composition.

II A 18 · STUYVESANT TOWN
First Avenue to F.D.R. Drive, East 14th to East 20th streets
Irwin Clavan and Gilmore Clarke, 1947

This is Le Corbusier's Ville Radieuse minus the highways—and thank goodness for that, for the separation of automobiles and pedestrians is one of this complex's strongest points. Towers in open space, away from streets, are not very fashionable to praise these days—Jane Jacobs and her followers, correct most of the time, denounce Stuyvesant Town as monstrous and anti-city. When it was new, Lewis Mumford got his licks in by saying that the place had the architecture of a police state.

The fact is that this place really works—the curving walks, play areas, lawns and benches promote interaction, and the towers, while all too similar in design, are given variety by placement, grouping, and landscaping. They are solid masses of red brick, hardly imaginative but not hostile, either, and the apartments within are decent and well planned. Doubtless it is easier to praise the place now that the trees are thirty years old and grown, but it is hard to believe that this pleasant, light, and airy park was quite so brutal as critics have suggested it was when new.

If the Corbusian dream of towers in the park is working here, let it be remembered, of course, that this is the exception that proves the rule. The isolated tower is generally a destructive urban model, and its success here was due, surely, as much to the good intentions of Stuyvesant Town's middle-income tenancy and the good maintenance of its landlord, the Metropolitan Life Insurance Company, as to any ideas the architects may have had. Maybe these factors counted for more, in fact, than the architecture—perhaps Stuyvesant Town's most important lesson is that architecture is not always crucial.

II A 18 · *One of the towers of Stuyvesant Town*

II A 17 · *Waterside*

II A 19 · STUYVESANT SQUARE
East and west of Second Avenue, 15th to 17th streets

This is a survivor, and it comes off well—far better, in fact, than the more familiar Union Square to its southwest. Stuyvesant Square was once, like all of this area's open spaces, an elegant residential quarter, and it is still a surprisingly pleasant refuge from the city's tumult. The neighborhood, especially to the east, has slipped, but the immediate surroundings of the park have more or less held their own. The square was a gift of Peter Stuyvesant to the city (a shrewd one, since it increased the value of the property he intended to develop around it), and it was always split in two by Second Avenue. The presence of a busy street bisecting the square makes the relative tranquillity of the square all the more impressive.

The Friends' Meeting House and Seminary on Rutherford Place, the square's eastern boundary, is a spare, strong gem, completed in 1860 to the designs of Charles T. Bunting. It is a bit more New England in feeling than the Friends' Meeting House on Gramercy Park, but it exists in an oddly comfortable truce with the overpowering St. George's Church and Parish House next door (see below).

Seventeenth Street is especially appealing to the northwest of the square, with a Richard Morris Hunt house of 1883 at No. 245. East of Second Avenue Beth Israel Hospital's expansion has damaged the area considerably—there is a ghastly metal bridge over 17th Street that slices right into one brownstone, and a school of nursing at No. 317 East 17th Street (Schuman & Lichtenstein, 1963) that is utterly brazen in its disregard for its handsome, but delicate, context. It is a building that seems designed as a declaration of war on its neighbors. What is the point of such architecture?

St. George's, on the other hand, manages to be powerful without ever being hostile. This was J. P. Morgan's church, as if anyone had to be told: it is heavily Romanesque brownstone, old New York and the Church of England joined in contented wedlock. The design, by Leopold Eidlitz and Otto Blesch, dates from 1856; it was rebuilt, after a fire in 1866, according to the original plans. Two other buildings complete the St. George's group, the Parish House of 1888 by Cyrus L. W. Eidlitz, a dignified, taut urban palace of Gothic Revival, and the Chapel of 1911 by Matthew Lansing Emery and Henry George Emery, a Byzantine overachiever.

B/CHELSEA AND THE WEST TWENTIES

Not, alas, as good as its London namesake. New York's Chelsea is a mix of industrial buildings, tenements, churches, and some very fine row houses. The lots were laid out around 1830 by Clement Clarke Moore, who inherited the family holdings that comprised most of the area. For all his efforts to spur the development of Chelsea—he also donated the land on which the General Theological Seminary now stands—it was Moore's fate to be remembered more as the author of the poem "A Visit from Saint Nicholas" than as a figure crucial to Manhattan's growth.

Chelsea has had a history of ups and downs, but has always managed to avoid the extremes of either considerable wealth or complete poverty: it was never either Fifth Avenue or Hell's Kitchen. The neighborhood has had a recent, limited resurgence as row houses have been redeveloped in the blocks of the low Twenties east and west of Ninth Avenue, and while it lacks the easy charm of the West Village, it has none of the sometimes intimidating heaviness of the townhouse blocks of the Upper West Side.

Chelsea's problem is one of definition: there doesn't seem to be enough there there, to paraphrase Gertrude Stein. The neighborhood has no real center, save for the very private seminary block. It has no real edges, either. The grid, such a strength in so much of Manhattan, seems an enemy here, for it prevents a sense of surprise and assaults the small scale of Chelsea's better row-house blocks. Wound around crooked Village streets, Chelsea's houses would have more appeal; stretched out on the grid, they

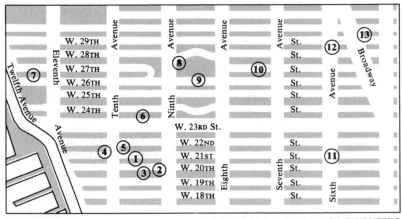

seem weakened. A grid neighborhood, especially one with such long blocks as this one, needs a major focus to give it coherence, as Central Park, Broadway, and Riverside Park all do for the Upper West Side. And it needs larger scale as well. Without these things, nothing holds together quite as it should—a shame, because there are the seeds of a very likable neighborhood here.

II B 1 · GENERAL THEOLOGICAL SEMINARY (Chelsea Square)
Ninth to Tenth avenues, 20th to 21st streets

This is one of New York's true treasures—private, but viewable through fences à la Gramercy Park, and enterable as well. It is a square block, surrounded for much of its perimeter by buildings; inside is a pleasant campus. The space is not that large, but it is divided by a chapel and by a few smaller structures so that it feels much bigger and more complex than it is—like a real campus, in which you never know what is around the next bend. Not the least miraculous thing about this place is how it achieves its sense of utter refuge from the city without fully cutting itself off—much of the south side of the block is open to 20th Street, offering a view in to passers-by and, more important from the standpoint of Chelsea Square's design, offering a view of the fine row of houses across 20th Street, which function as a means of closing off the square on that side.

The buildings themselves are not distinguished, but they are good, and they are made better—*pace,* Frank Lloyd Wright—by their coverings of ivy. What is more important than any single building here, however, is the overall ensemble—as well as the fact that this place sustains the pastoral illusion better than anything else in Manhattan except Central Park.

The only recent building, closing off the square on Ninth Avenue (O'Connor & Kilham, 1960) is dreadful—a real reminder of how difficult the business of relating skillfully is. It is done in light brick, clashing with the dark tones of the older buildings elsewhere in the complex. There is a gray-stone base, and the exterior is full of cutesy little pointed windows, which are obviously supposed to be Gothic. This is not serious historical allusion; it is crudeness.

But the rest of Chelsea Square is good enough so that this does a minimum of damage. Most of the buildings are by Charles C. Haight and were completed between 1883 and 1900; typical is Hoffman Hall (1899) at the west end of the campus, with a grand entrance and stairway to take you through a deep Victorian Gothic mass. It is somber and heavy, yet never oppressive. It is never particularly historicist in its detailing, either—Haight's work always had a more institutional air to it than a seriously Gothic one.

Also of note are the West Building of 1836 (it once had a matching East Building), one of the city's earliest surviving pieces of Gothic Revival architecture. It is a fieldstone box with Gothicized window details, but a massing that feels still caught in Greek Revival. Seabury Hall (1931) just to the west of the overscaled chapel, is a remarkably nice piece of industrial Gothic—that is, a bold and plain building, free of fussiness, yet willing to work with its neighbors in a way that the front building doesn't do.

II B 2 · 402 WEST 20th Street
C. P. H. Gilbert, 1897

This is a wonderful lesson in urbanism—a relatively routine late nineteenth-century house that has a concave curve in its façade to make a gentle transition from the building line of one of its neighbors, a tenement on Ninth Avenue, to the setback line of the Greek Revival row to the west. There is a handsome curved cornice and curved bays as well, so the whole building really *is* the curve. Necessity has been a good mother of architecture here. The name on the façade, DONAC, commemorates Don Alonzo Cushman, the builder who developed many of Chelsea's townhouse rows, including the one next-door to No. 402.

II B 3 · 404–418 WEST 20th STREET
1830, 1840

No. 404 West 20th Street is the earliest Greek Revival house in the area. Ten years later Don Alonzo Cushman built what is occasionally known as Cushman Row next door, and that remains the finest Greek Revival row in Chelsea, and surely the best in the city after Washington Square North. The feeling of these houses is more delicate than at Washington Square; everything is a bit smaller and a bit less formal. The attic windows, encircled by wreaths, and the splendid ironwork are the best details here—the iron banisters, newels, and fences form a gentle and sweet rhythm down the street. Here, it becomes clear that destruction or loss of one house destroys all—the lesson of the *tout ensemble* is irrefutable.

II B 4 · GUARDIAN ANGEL CHURCH
193 Tenth Avenue, NW corner 21st Street
John Van Pelt, 1930

This is a curiosity, a small but exceedingly elaborate Romanesque-Byzantine hybrid. The combination of red brick and limestone is an odd one for a church in this style, as if the materials intended for a Georgian church had

II B 3 · *404–418 West 20th Street*

II B 1 · *Campus of the General Theological Seminary*

ended up being used for this one. If the style is anything, it could be called Picturesque Romanesque, and if the building looks like anything else, it is what one would imagine a Romanesque chapel in Bronxville or Greenwich to look like. To find it on Tenth Avenue in Chelsea heightens the oddity, and also the pleasure. For whatever its suburban yearnings may be, this is an appealing building from that too-little-appreciated period of late American eclecticism between the wars.

II B 5 · 188–192 TENTH AVENUE
between 21st and 22nd streets
Andrew Spence, 1891

This is an ordinary, row-house-size retail and tenement block. What makes it special are the absolutely enormous pilasters set into the façades and painted gray against the red-painted brick of the rest of the buildings. They are wildly monumental, totally on the scale of a civic building, not of a three-story tenement block. They may be gas flues or they may be simply a flamboyant gesture; the point is that they utterly transform this building into something grand. It is Pop Art, really, so out of scale are these ordinary elements made extraordinary. But there is a dignity they bring which makes them still better than Pop Art. Not the least of the reasons for their appeal is that the pilasters seem based upon an understanding of the nature of New York avenues—they are clearly intended for a *wide* street; the gesture would never have worked on a narrow street around the corner.

II B 6 · LONDON TERRACE
Ninth to Tenth avenues, 23rd to 24th streets
Farrar & Watmaugh, 1930

Fourteen buildings with 1,670 apartments, making a great wall across Chelsea. One thing like this is acceptable in each part of town; two can destroy a neighborhood, as happened in the East Sixties after other buildings set out to imitate Manhattan House, itself a postwar version of London Terrace.

Happily, there is only one London Terrace in Chelsea, and thus the effect of the monster is not so disturbing as it might be—although it is obviously far worse on the dark north side of the complex than it is on the sunny south side. And any monster with Romanesque details and decent apartments is not, by definition, quite so much of a monster. Imagine London Terrace's bulk in raw concrete or unrelieved red brick, and then the complex as it now stands seems far more palatable.

II B 7 · STARRETT-LEHIGH BUILDING
Eleventh to Twelfth avenues, 26th to 27th streets
Russel G. and Walter M. Cory, with Yasuo Matsui, 1931

This is New York's great monument to industrial modernism, a square-block factory with ribbons of glass zipping across it and around rounded corners. It is best, however, from a distance—what admirers of this building

II B 7 · Detail of the Starrett-Lehigh Building

II B 8 · Church of the Holy Apostles

often forget is that the base is rather conventional, with solid columns breaking up the strip windows for the first three floors so that it looks like any old factory. Also, a section in mid-block is cut up in a similar fashion, so nowhere does the horizontal sweep of glass extend for a full block.

But if this is more an ad hoc object than a pure statement of modernism, it remains a powerful and wonderful thing, far and away *the* industrial monument of the far West Side. It is curious, though, that Starrett-Lehigh's major imitator, Philip Johnson and John Burgee's Post Oak Central building in Houston, is an office tower, not a factory. The Starrett-Lehigh Building's aesthetics, wonderful as they are, had little to do with the idea of a factory building, and thus did not become a model for other structures of its type.

II B 8 · CHURCH OF THE HOLY APOSTLES
300 Ninth Avenue, SE corner 28th Street
Minard Lafever, 1848
transepts: Richard Upjohn & Sons, 1858

This church is what historicism really should be about. There is nothing directly imitative about it, and it is not a collection of disparate details from disparate periods put together for their own sake. Rather, it is an attempt to forge a genuine new statement out of pieces of different old ones, and, astonishingly, it works. The Italianate style is what predominates; the interior has allusions to the Italian Renaissance but without classical details, and there are hints of Romanesque on the façade. The tower is a marvelous composition in itself, jaunty and smooth at the same time, like something made of rubber.

The Church of the Holy Apostles is a survivor: its neighborhood is one of industry, trucking, and housing projects. It wants to be part of one of the splendid Greek Revival rows of houses just a few blocks downtown in the heart of Chelsea, but like a good missionary, it does its work here, instead, where it is most needed.

II B 9 · PENN STATION SOUTH
Eighth to Ninth avenues, 23rd to 29th streets
Herman Jessor, 1962

This massive project of cooperative housing for garment workers is the best of its breed, which is to say the enormous housing complexes of the post–Stuyvesant Town era. That praise doesn't mean too much, since most of what has come in Penn Station South's generation has been terrible. But the Corbusian scheme is helped enormously here by the casual placement of the towers off a grid, and by the reworking of the street plan to give some streets a curve as they pass through the multiblock site. Also, the towers themselves are decent. The balconies are given vertical slats for fences, a tiny detail that makes a vast difference in the façades' overall appearance. More important still are the setbacks near the top, creating at least some sense of profile, as well as broad terraces and variation in plan for upper apartments.

II B 10 · FASHION INSTITUTE OF TECHNOLOGY COMPLEX
Seventh to Eighth avenues, north and south of West 27th Street
DeYoung & Moscowitz, 1958–59
DeYoung & Moscowitz, Lockwood & Green, 1969–74

It is astonishing that one architectural firm supervised virtually all of the development of this campus where aspirants to fashion careers are trained, for it looks at first glance not only as though every building were designed by a different architect, but as though every architect were forbidden to look at any of the other buildings before he set out to design his own. There is a sense of confusion here perhaps unmatched in any other single complex in Manhattan.

Moreover, the buildings themselves are dreary at best, silly at worst. They are a mix of Neo-Nursing Home, Downtown Parking Garage, Middle-American Convention Center, and Fancy-Pants Brutalism. Not a single building looks as if it belongs in New York—the origami-fronted metal building with the arched canopy might be the best hotel in Dubuque, there is a Detroit parking garage and a Bronx nursing home. The big new section is a cross between a megastructure (it spans 27th Street and joins other sections of the campus to one another) and Lincoln Center. It even has a big, empty open ground-floor colonnade to boot, just the thing for rushing between classes in February.

What is most intriguing about this place, though, is the utter non–New

Yorkness of it. It is not just that these buildings are bad, but that they are bad in a way so uncharacteristic of New York. They are innocent, almost—they think they are neat and almost arty. Oh, well. It was a try, clearly.

II B 11 · SIXTH AVENUE, 18th to 23rd streets

This was once the city's most fashionable shopping district, a portion of what was known in the late nineteenth century as the Ladies' Mile. It was all gone by World War I, by which time fashion had decreed more northerly locations, but, remarkably, these buildings have survived. Most of them function as warehouses, offices, and light-manufacturing structures, and they have far more of an aura of ghostliness about them than do the buildings in SoHo, in many ways their counterparts architecturally.

Sixth Avenue in its heyday was a row of merchandising palazzi, a Grand Canal of retailing. The buildings are almost without exception pretentious, lacking the restraint and the skillful composition of most SoHo structures—these buildings were where the Gilded Age bought its gilt, and their architects had to let you know it.

The buildings are a bit better in the Fifth Avenue and Broadway portions of this area (II A 6), but the grand pomposity of the Sixth Avenue buildings does give a certain pleasure. They make awfully good ruins, if nothing else.

The grandest of them all was, and is, Siegel-Cooper (DeLemos & Cordes, 1896) on the east side of the avenue between 18th and 19th streets. This is a true overachiever—a triple-arched entry, three stories high, with a balustrade above that; on top of that, a central window with its own balcony, then more columns and arches and what have you. It is all a rather vulgar assemblage, since it never manages to convince you that it is other than a great big barn. It is heavy, bloated, and totally without subtlety. But who can deny that it must have been a lot more fun to shop here than in a Formica-covered Korvettes?

The old Altman's across the street (David and John Jardine, 1876; William H. Hume, 1877) is more restrained and far more gracious. It would mean little in the context of SoHo's cast-iron buildings, but on Sixth Avenue it shines as a model of dignity and control.

The best this stretch has to offer is the Hugh O'Neill Store, at No.

II B 10 · *Fashion Institute of Technology, corner of Eighth Avenue and 27th Street*

II B 13 · *Gilsey House*

II B 11 · *Hugh O'Neill Store (now 655–671 Avenue of the Americas)*

655–671 Sixth Avenue (Mortimer C. Merritt, 1875), an exceedingly amiable block-front of cast iron anchored by round towers at either end and topped with an immense pediment. The towers once culminated in bulbous, almost Byzantine domes, but except for their disappearance, the façade is intact. This one *does* rank with SoHo in quality; it is surely Sixth Avenue's only distinguished piece of retail architecture.

II B 12 · FLOWER DISTRICT
Sixth Avenue around 28th Street

Remarkable for what it does to a walk, or even a ride, up Sixth Avenue. There is no "flower market" per se, no open space or square or central building; all it is, is a lot of wholesale and retail establishments bunched together, with flowers and greenery overflowing out to the streets. It isn't the buildings, which are as dreary as they were for the previous few blocks, and it isn't the people and it isn't really the amount of activity, although that does increase slightly here. But you still feel, in a manner that is wonderfully surprising no matter how many times you pass this way, that something unexpected has happened above 27th Street. The flower district just slides gently into the grid of Manhattan's streets, making no real changes, and yet somehow changing everything.

II B 13 · GILSEY HOUSE
1200 Broadway at 29th Street
Stephen D. Hatch, 1869

This former hotel is one of the grandest pieces of cast-iron work in the city, easily ranking with the grandiose Duckworth buildings of Greene Street (I F 2). The Gilsey House is all Second Empire, floor after floor mounting with a delicious kind of sumptuousness. As in the best of the cast-iron buildings, there is richness and yet total control; there is never a sense of vulgar excess. The best thing of all here is the corner tower, a three-story mansard including a fine pair of arched windows topped by a broken pediment containing a bull's-eye window that is itself topped by a pediment; on top of that pediment is a clock.

The tower, and the entire corner of the façade, is set at a 45-degree angle in plan, emphasizing its role as a corner element. Indeed, the entire building pivots around the corner—it recognizes that its role in the cityscape is to turn a corner, and everything is given over to that.

C/EAST AND WEST THIRTIES

II C 1 · HERALD SQUARE: Intersection of Broadway and 6th Avenue: 32nd to 35th streets (including Greeley Square)

This is two triangles, not a square: Herald Square forms the north end of the intersection of Broadway and Sixth Avenue, Greeley Square is the south portion. It is not particularly distinctive architecturally—the best building to have stood here was McKim, Mead & White's Venetian palazzo headquarters for the New York *Herald* (gone since 1921, though its clock remains as ornamental sculpture). There is one good bank, the Corinthian-columned Greenwich Savings Bank at the corner of 36th Street (York & Sawyer, 1924), but that is about it. The department stores define the place, and they could be in Cleveland or Detroit or any old city's downtown but for the vast crowds. But maybe that is what defines Herald Square—other parts of New York are crowded, but this one has that particular energy that distinguishes shopping crowds from commuters' crowds or theatergoers' crowds: it is the push and shove of Filene's basement, spread out over several blocks.

Herald Square is another of those parts of Manhattan that are often said not to be what they used to be, but the criticism seems exaggerated here. Herald Square has been most famous as a shopping district, which it still is, and it was known for its proximity to Pennsylvania Station, which is still, in a mannner of speaking, nearby. The area *is* a bit rundown, but then again, Herald Square was never really posh, and so it has hardly undergone a dramatic transformation.

What has changed, though, is the sense of this as a place of night life. There are far fewer hotels, thanks to the decline of train travel—the vast McAlpin is closed, and the Pennsylvania has become the mediocre Statler Hilton, no longer the sort of place to inspire a song, as it did when Glenn Miller wrote "Pennsylvania 6-5000," based on the hotel's telephone number.

But the stores go on, and this remains a stronghold of middle-class shopping—Gimbels, Korvettes, and the currently rising Macy's, a venerable New York institution that fell to discount-store mediocrity a few years back, but lately has been filled once again with first-class merchandise and the sort of customers willing to pay for it. That may signal a general upgrading in the quality of the Herald Square area, which now teeters between middle-class propriety and sleaziness.

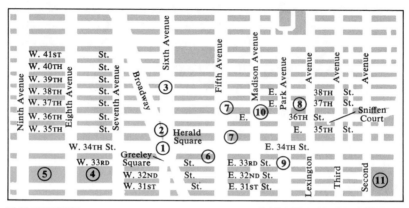

II C 2 · 34th STREET SUBWAY STATION, HERALD SQUARE

The 34th Street subway station is like every other New York subway station, only more so. It is so vast and so old and so complex that one suspects that there are segments of it as yet unexplored by modern man; there are surely segments of it as yet *uncleaned* by modern man (although, to be fair, it is not nearly so dirty as the labyrinth under Times Square). But what makes this place truly special is one great architectural experience, and that is the connection between the tracks serving the BMT trains and the rest of the station on the IND lines. These are several levels apart from one another, and the BMT trains are reached by a long escalator or by a series of ramps that double back and forth, cutting the distance into several runs. In either case one passes through an immense space, unlike most of the station dimly lit. The ramps are enclosed in cagelike iron fences, and there are shadows and odd, broken vistas. It is best of all to ascend into the space by escalator; you rise slowly through this chopped-up space past ramps and fences and dim lights, and the effect is absolutely Piranesian.

II C 3 · GARMENT CENTER
Sixth Avenue to Broadway, 34th to 42nd streets

This neighborhood is crucial to the city's identity, yet nowhere else in New York is a sense of identity so little expressed as here. The garment center is big buildings on the avenues, factory loft buildings on the side streets; none of them says anything about the nature of the people they contain, the industry they shelter, or even the city they are so significant a part of. One somehow expects them to be more flamboyant, more like a row of Miami Beach hotels; what they are instead are masonry boxes, one after the other, making streets that are tight and dark and have none of the sense of the hushed power of Wall Street. Maybe that is the problem—we expect the kind of designing and manufacturing and deal-making that goes on here to be showy and dramatic, but the architecture of matter-of-fact business buildings does not allow for it. The venerable garment-center scene of a young worker pushing a rack of clothes through the streets—now fast disappearing—doesn't fit as naturally into a heavy, canyon-like New York street as does the picture of the runner for a brokerage house scampering down Wall Street; there is a culture clash here between the architecture and the events that go on within it.

There are a few—very few—things worth looking at specifically here. The Nelson Tower at 34th Street and Seventh Avenue has a decent profile, not unusual but characteristic of the well-massed but more subdued towers of the early 1930's (H. Craig Severance, 1931). Much of the garment center was designed by Ely Jacques Kahn, but little is up to the standard of his 2 Park Avenue building (II C 9) except, perhaps, the startlingly jazzy "530" above the entrance to his 530 Seventh Avenue (1924). Too often overlooked is the red-and-green horizontally striped tower at 1407 Broadway (Kahn & Jacobs, 1950), an excellent example of the work of that postwar period when architects were using more and more glass in horizontal ribbons, yet still held back from embracing the glass curtain wall. The 1407 tower has the added appeal of a set of zigzagged storefronts along Broadway, a sensitive recognition of the oddly shaped site. It stands in sharp contrast to the attitude of the Chanin organization, architects and developers of 1411 Broadway next door (1969), where a dull white box sits squarely on its site, ignoring completely the fact that the plot is not itself square but trapezoidal. What is left over is a dull, awkward "plaza" and the wall of buildings along Broadway is broken—a sad event, especially considering that the site has a distinguished heritage, for it previously contained the Metropolitan Opera House.

II C 4 · MADISON SQUARE GARDEN CENTER
West 31st Street to West 33rd Street, Seventh to Eighth avenues
Charles Luckman Associates, 1968

For this, there is no excuse. Even if one surmounts the prejudice with which an evaluation of any building that replaced the extraordinary McKim, Mead & White Pennsylvania Station must begin, it is still terrible—a graceless, sloppy, cheap entertainment and office complex that would be an insult to an empty site in the middle of nowhere, let alone the site that contained Penn Station.

Madison Square Garden is housed in a precast concrete-clad drum that is reasonably functional but utterly banal. The 2 Penn Plaza office tower is its mate in dullness, with a vast, windswept open arcade at ground level that is just the thing for pedestrians in a New York winter. Its skin, a tan precast concrete, is at least less offensive than the glaringly metallic One Penn Plaza next door (Kahn & Jacobs, 1972), a tower which aims low, yet somehow rises all too high. None of the buildings, it should be mentioned, work very well together, and they all ignore the street and the larger urban context completely.

As for the station—well, it is now entirely underground, a subway station with terrazzo floors and slightly cleaner shops than in the real subway. It permits train riders to enjoy all of the vulgarity and oppressiveness of airports right in the middle of town. One can only recall the old station and think of Vincent Scully's properly bitter obituary: "Through it one entered the city like a god. . . . One scuttles in now like a rat."

II C 4 · *Madison Square Garden Center*   II C 6 · *Empire State Building*

II C 5 · GENERAL POST OFFICE
Eighth Avenue, West 31st to West 33rd streets
McKim, Mead & White (William M. Kendall, partner in charge), 1913

This is good but not that good—given the choice, any New Yorker would have kept Pennsylvania Station and let its echo across the street go. But if we got the short end of the stick in what remained, this is a decent urban building, with a real sense of dignity, as good a staircase as one can find in any public building in Manhattan—it really functions like a plaza—and, of course, that endless inscription about rain and snow and gloom of night.

II C 6 · THE EMPIRE STATE BUILDING
350 Fifth Avenue, SW corner 34th Street
Shreve, Lamb & Harmon, 1931

This is famous for being tall, but it is good enough to be famous for being good. The profile of the Empire State Building, with graceful setbacks set in perfect balance to sheer rise, has been a symbol of New York, and indeed of romantic skylines everywhere, for something close to fifty years. The massing is more skillful than it looks at first glance—the five-story base holds the street line well, and assures that the huge hulk of the tower is a safe visual and psychological distance from passersby; the main shaft has its mass correctly broken by indentations running its full height; and the top is a perfect balance between liveliness and dignity. The limestone, granite, aluminum, and nickel of the façade create a sleek, grayish tone that is appropriate both for New York and for the idea of height, and there is just the right hint of Art Deco ornament. This success came not from a pure

II C 5 · *General Post Office*

aesthetic concept, nor as the accidental product of a commercial outlook, but was the result of a lucky balance of objectives—the developers, John J. Raskob and Pierre S. duPont, wanted something big, and went to William F. Lamb, a commercial architect with a reputation for efficient, straightforward designs. Lamb's preference was for clean lines and simple structures; had it been a few years later, with the International Style in dominance and a different set of zoning laws, he might well have produced a plain box, but no one but the avant-garde was doing that in 1929. So Lamb created an Empire State of ornament and texture and immensely solid dignity, and one must therefore add to the list of elements contributing to the Empire State's success the lucky accident of timing.

II C 7 · B. ALTMAN & CO.
Fifth Avenue, 34th to 35th streets
Trowbridge & Livingston, 1906, 1914
· GORHAM BUILDING
390 Fifth Avenue, SW corner 35th Street
McKim, Mead & White (Stanford White, partner in charge), 1906
· former TIFFANY & CO.
409 Fifth Avenue, SE corner 37th Street
McKim, Mead & White (Stanford White, partner in charge), 1906

These were three of the first commercial palaces on Fifth Avenue above 34th Street, which until Altman's made the move was still a solidly residential quarter. The Altman's store was designed in deliberately restrained style by the architects who were to do the headquarters of J. P. Morgan & Co. seven years later (I A 30); perhaps Benjamin Altman felt he would offend the Astors less if the architecture could resemble the dignified Renaissance piles of Fifth Avenue's mansions. Altman's remains handsome and intact on the outside (the interior once had an atrium, now filled in); the two Stanford White buildings up the block, finished just afterward, have been less lucky. Gorham's is a fine Italian Renaissance pile of columns and arches; Tiffany's, modeled after the Palazzo Grimani in

Venice, is a more passionate mounting of pairs of columns upon pairs of columns, rising sumptuously and lushly to an elaborate cornice. Horrendously unsympathetic alterations have taken away much of the pleasure these buildings once conferred, but some remains.

II C 8 · MURRAY HILL

A neighborhood, yet not a neighborhood; as in Chelsea, space seems to flow out from it, and nothing is pulled in. There is no focus, no center, just a few streets that for a certain part of their long length are clearly part of Murray Hill and not of someplace else. Park Avenue, for example, is neither so grand here as it is uptown nor so commercial as it is above Grand Central Terminal; it is something in between, and yet somehow—perhaps because it is quieter here than on any other part of its length—it is different.

There is an elegance to Park Avenue here, more understated than elsewhere, yet real. McKim, Mead and White's fine J. Hampton Robb residence at No. 23 Park Avenue (1898), later the Advertising Club and now cooperative apartments, is a discreet Italian Renaissance palazzo with more style and dignity than many McKim houses uptown; the Union League Club (Morris & O'Connor, 1931) is pompous neo-Georgian, but as good as any of the uptown clubs by Delano & Aldrich except the exquisite Knickerbocker (III D 3). And even the apartment houses here choose not to shout, as so many of their uptown brethren do.

The side streets are good, especially between Park and Third from 35th through 38th streets—surprisingly fine brownstones and a few anomalous gems, like good carriage houses and the handsome old house of 1857 at 152 East 38th Street, transformed into something in the Federal style in the 1930's, and set back from the street by a welcoming forecourt. And there is lovable Sniffen Court, a mews of tiny carriage houses at 150–158 East 36th Street, a place that is delicate and intimate and restful as the city at large so rarely manages to be.

II C 9 · 2 PARK AVENUE
between 32nd and 33rd streets
Ely Jacques Kahn, 1927
· 3 PARK AVENUE
SE corner 34th Street
Shreve, Lamb & Harmon, 1976

Two generations of lower Park Avenue office buildings, as different from each other as either of them is from what is built uptown. The Kahn building is one of the city's finest Art Deco pieces, with a richly polychromed terracotta top—as good a way as any to bring life to a matter-of-fact brick box of a building. There is a good lobby, too, and it has been restored with love and care by the current owner, who has added period pieces not initially intended for the space, such as the chandeliers. The clock at the rear is especially good, and original.

No. 3 Park is another matter. It is one of several buildings in town done as a project of the Educational Construction Fund, which sponsored mixed-use towers combining schools with commercial facilities (I B 8), and the

II C 7 · *Tiffany & Co. (now 409 Fifth Avenue)*

II C 9 · *Detail of 2 Park Avenue*

Norman Thomas High School is at 3 Park's base. The tower is of reddish brick, and it is set at a diagonal to the street grid. There is a sort of mansard roof, lighted a garish orange at night. There is nothing else in town that looks like it, and it is all rather puzzling—was Shreve, Lamb & Harmon trying to recapture some of the sense of daring it had not had as a firm since the Empire State Building? Is it a statement against the monotony of the standard uptown International Style tower, so many of which that firm has itself designed? Is it a statement against the rigid order of the street grid itself?

It is hard to be sure, and it is harder still to make any sort of absolute judgment about this building. It is both too somber and too garish, and the arrogant break it makes at ground level away from the corner of 34th and Park is inexcusable. But there are some good ideas here—if only the diagonal tower had been set on a square base, for example, and if only the top, a welcome attempt to create *some* sort of pinnacle in a flat-topped age, had been better thought out.

II C 10 · MORGAN LIBRARY
33 East 36th Street, NE corner Madison Avenue
*McKim, Mead & White (Charles F. McKim, partner in charge), 1907
addition: Benjamin W. Morris, 1928*

· LUTHERAN CHURCH IN AMERICA (former J. P. Morgan, Jr., residence)
231 Madison Avenue, SE corner 37th Street
1852

Built of marble blocks laid in true Greek fashion with no mortar, McKim's Roman villa for J. Pierpont Morgan's collection of manuscripts and art objects is at once sinfully opulent and utterly dry. It is, in its way, as rich

II C 10 · *Morgan Library*

II C 9 · *3 Park Avenue*

an experience as anything to be found in New York—grandly scaled rooms, extraordinarily detailed and containing a collection that is unequaled. McKim's work was grander and solider than his partner White's; his detail was more elaborate and his overall conceptions more sweeping. What is missing is White's lyricism. This is in many ways a place that approaches greatness, but its beauty is that of prose.

The old brownstone next door is one of the city's earliest and best Italianate mansions, freestanding as few brownstones are. It was the subject of a significant landmarks case. The Lutheran Church in America, owners of the house since 1944, brought suit to have its landmark designation withdrawn; the suit was won, but the church gave up its plans to erect a high-rise tower, and the house remains, joining with the Morgan Library to create one of Madison Avenue's only open, low-scaled block-fronts.

II C 11 · KIPS BAY PLAZA
East 30th to East 33rd streets, First to Second avenues
I. M. Pei & Partners, S. J. Kessler, 1960, 1965

These concrete slabs with their handsomely detailed gridded façades seemed significant in the early 1960's. They remain an architectural improvement over the standard New York apartment tower, but the urbanistic values they represent—the freestanding tower in open space, the ignorance of the life of the street and city around it—are so disturbing today that their value is diminished. Now they look old-fashioned, polemics left over from a revolution that happily never fully succeeded.

The project looks as if Kessler's Washington Square Village and Pei's Bleecker Street towers (I H 5) had been crossbred, for it has the twin-slab site plan of the Kessler project and the sharply outlined concrete façades of the Pei project. It is curious that Kips Bay Plaza was built in between those other two housing complexes—but gratifying that Pei was wise enough to pick up on the most successful aspect of this project, the concrete-grid façades, for use on Bleecker Street while discarding the long slabs.

D/EAST FORTIES

II D 1 · GRAND CENTRAL TERMINAL
42nd Street opposite Park Avenue
Reed & Stem, Warren & Wetmore, 1913
viaducts completed, 1919

> *As a bullet seeks its target, shining rails in every part of our great nation are aimed at Grand Central Station, heart of the country's greatest city. Drawn by the magnetic force of the fantastic metropolis, day and night great trains rush toward the Hudson River . . . dive with a roar into the two and a half mile tunnel beneath the swank and glitter of Park Avenue, and then—Grand Central Station!—Crossroads of a million private lives, gigantic stage on which are played a thousand dramas daily.*

There are few trains now, and they tend to be things like the 5:10 to Westport instead of the *Twentieth Century* to Chicago, but Grand Central remains as potent a symbol of the power of its city today as it was thirty years ago, when the passage above came booming over the CBS radio network to introduce *Grand Central Station,* a radio drama program. Grand Central Terminal (as it is properly called: it is the end of a line, not a station) is the nation's most famous railway depot, and it is one of those

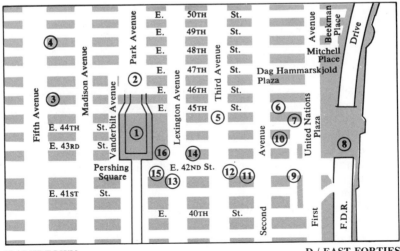

II D 1 · *Grand Central Terminal, with the Pan Am Building (II D 2) in the background*

II D 1 · *Detail of Grand Central Terminal*

structures, like the Empire State Building and the Brooklyn Bridge, that identify New York in the minds of people around the world who have never been to the city and probably never will go to New York in the future. Grand Central's legendary power transcends actual experience.

It would be naïve to attribute all of this building's significance as a symbol to its architecture. But it would be absurd to minimize the role the architecture has played in fixing Grand Central's image in the minds of New Yorkers and non–New Yorkers alike. The building is not quite so awesome as Pennsylvania Station was, but it is massive in scale, handsome in proportion and dignified and restrained in detail. It is more innovative than Penn Station ever was—there was not only no direct model for Grand Central, as the Baths of Caracalla was for Penn Station; the overall plan of Grand Central and its surrounding blocks was a truly inventive work of urban design. If Penn Station represented wonderful, blessed excess of civic grandeur and a full understanding of the role of a station as a vestibule to a great city, Grand Central represents all of this plus a new set of ideas about how the rest of a city should interact with a great, symbolic building at its center.

The station and its surroundings are the work of several men, and they took their form for a number of reasons. The problems ensuing from the open cut of the New York Central's railway tracks along Park Avenue and the subsequent decision in 1889 to electrify the lines into the existing Grand Central led to a proposal by the railroad's chief engineer, William Wilgus, for an entirely new terminal, with the air rights over the tracks around the terminal to be used for real estate development. The firm of Reed & Stem won a limited competition for the design, which included ingenious separation of automobile, pedestrian, subway, and train traffic, as well as the connection of various levels of the complex with gently sloping ramps. Later Warren & Wetmore, the distinguished New York Beaux-Arts firm, was brought in to add a touch of class to the project, and the terminal's

II D 1 · *Main concourse of Grand Central Terminal*

sumptuous façade is largely Whitney Warren's. It is relatively stark, a simple pavilion blown up to a scale that, for this sort of building, is gigantic. The façade is marked by three great arched windows, columns grouped in pairs, and an elaborate central sculpture group by Jules Coutan.

If the conceptual high point of Grand Central is its innovative planning, the architectural triumph is the main concourse. It is 275 feet long, 120 feet wide, and 125 feet high, almost—but not quite—too big to be perceived comfortably as a single space. Oddly for a Beaux-Arts building, it is best entered from a corner, where its proportions can be better felt than when seen on axis; coming in along either of the two low arcades connecting the concourse with Lexington Avenue to the east creates the best sense of surprise at the grandeur of the space, although there is a particular, and different, joy to entering from the west, at the Vanderbilt Avenue doors a level above the floor, which permit one to descend grandly into the space.

The concourse has had its share of trouble in recent years—it seems to have housed more advertising than Times Square, and even so strong a room as this cannot fail to suffer somewhat in such circumstances. It is not so much that the huge signs are vulgar as that they are distracting, just as the presence of a piece of serious art at that scale would be distracting. The signs flood the room with light and loud colors and movement; the space was meant to be quiet, soft, even a bit mysterious and shadowy—a discreet background for human movement, not a room with movement of its own.

A recent cleaning at the hands of the Metropolitan Transportation Authority, which operates the station under lease, has helped; the quasi-public agency has proven a more thoughtful custodian than the Penn Central Company, which, in the now famous case, sued to have the building's landmark status withdrawn. The Supreme Court upheld the city's right to declare the building a landmark in 1978, quashing the now bankrupt railroad's plan to place a huge tower, designed by Marcel Breuer, over the concourse. The future of the building now seems safe, Kodak signs and all.

II D 2 · PARK AVENUE IN THE FORTIES (north of Grand Central)

The New York Central Railroad conceived of Grand Central as the focal point of "Terminal City," a vast real estate development on Vanderbilt Avenue, East 42nd Street, Lexington Avenue, and Park Avenue. The name never caught on, but over the years the buildings were built, and most of them are, or were, excellent—soberly classical brick and limestone structures like the Biltmore Hotel (Warren & Wetmore, 1914) and the Yale Club (James Gamble Rogers, 1915).

The major focus was Park Avenue, though, a street which until Grand Central Terminal was built was blighted by the presence of open railway tracks. Once the tracks were covered it was clear that, with development pressure from both south and west, Park was ripe to become expensive real estate.

In its heyday, from 1929 until after World War II, this was one of the great pieces of urban design in the world. A roughly even cornice line— more or less at thirteen stories—tied one fine masonry mass to another, and they marched down, block by block, to 46th Street. There, astride the avenue, the New York Central set its own headquarters (now the Helmsley Building) designed by Warren & Wetmore and completed in 1929, a perfect punctuation mark in the midst of Park Avenue's sobriety. The New York Central Building rose higher than the others, as befitted not only the railroad's headquarters but the building in the center of the avenue; it culminated in a great pyramidal roof topped by an elaborate cupola. At the tower's base were set two great arches, vehicular tunnels which completed the impressive system of access and bypass roadways to bring traffic around the terminal. The building provided the perfect focus for the southward view from upper Park Avenue; it pulled the eye down that long line of apartment houses, gave it a moment of joy as it reached the exuberant top, then sent it on its way again, moving down the avenue.

II D 2 · *Park Avenue, looking south toward the Helmsley Building and the Pan Am Building, with the Racquet and Tennis Club* (II F 16) *in the foreground*

It is all gone now. The building, of course, is still there—and it has recently been renovated and rather grandly floodlit—but the meaning of Park Avenue as it was created through the 1920's has evaporated. First came the Pan Am Building, the precast concrete monster that was set in between the New York Central Building and Grand Central Terminal; at fifty-nine stories it soars way above the pyramidal top and steals from the sky the role of backdrop. And it is wide, so wide that the eye can no longer travel around the older tower and have a sense of Park Avenue's continuity to the south. In short, it blocks everything.

The architects for this behemoth, completed in 1963, were Emery Roth & Sons, Pietro Belluschi, and Walter Gropius. It is said that Gropius turned the building's great mass so that it would block Park Avenue, which makes his participation in this act of destruction of the cityscape even more disturbing; it is ironic that the apostle of Bauhaus social responsibility should have ended his career by collaborating on a building that is the epitome of irresponsible planning and design. If Pan Am, an arrogant, oversize intruder, represents the contribution one of modern architecture's great theorists could make to the city, it is hard not to call that entire theory into question.

Above 46th Street, 250 Park Avenue (Cross & Cross, 1925) remains to indicate the scale and design of the buildings that made the great march together down the avenue. Most of the rest is enough bargain-basement Mies to keep the master whirling in his grave for years, and the differences from one to the next are slight. It is true that Skidmore, Owings & Merrill's Union Carbide Building (now Manufacturers Hanover Trust, 1960) at No. 270 is possessed of more carefully wrought details than, say, Shreve, Lamb & Harmon's 245 Park Avenue (1967), but they are both so ruthless in their disregard of the ideas that made Park Avenue such a remarkable lesson in urban design that this distinction becomes merely academic.

There is still, of course, a certain dignity to Park in the Forties; the avenue's generous width, center island, and generally moneyed aura make it more acceptable than it deserves to be. Ultimately, the best building on Park in the Forties is the Waldorf-Astoria Hotel, (Schultze & Weaver, 1931), which manages to work both as a powerful sculptural mass in itself, thanks to its pair of nicely molded Art Deco towers, and as a good citizen of the old, even-corniced Park Avenue, thanks to its base on the avenue scaled to the height of its former neighbors. The public spaces inside are overdecorated and have lost their original Art Deco tone, but most are still good—the Waldorf is too often underrated, and really deserves to be considered among midtown's better skyscrapers.

II D 3 · FRED F. FRENCH BUILDING
551 Fifth Avenue, NE corner 45th Street
Sloan & Robertson, 1927

This is typical of the massing of the Fifth Avenue towers of the 1920's— base built out to the street, setbacks beginning around the thirteenth floor, then an oblong tower rising for the rest of the height, which in this case is to thirty-eight floors. The Chase Manhattan Bank down the block at No. 535 (originally the Bank of the United States Building), completed to the

II D 2 · *New York Central (now the Helmsley) Building, with the Pan Am Building in the background*

II D 3 · *Fred. F. French Building*

designs of H. Craig Severance in 1926, is similar, though *that* building's shape led to a lawsuit when *The New Yorker* wrote that its tower "has the grace of an overgrown grain elevator." Severance, not amused, filed suit, and the magazine printed a retraction. Score one against architectural criticism.

Fred F. French is better than the usual building of this genre, however. As the headquarters of a major real estate firm, it was designed to be unusually opulent, and contains not only a lavishly decorated lobby, still largely intact, but a set of multicolored faïence ornaments decorating the

II D 4 · *Charles Scribner's Sons*

upper floors. The design at the top resembles a sun rising or setting, and it is among the more genuinely original pieces of façade decoration in Manhattan.

II D 4 · CHARLES SCRIBNER'S SONS
597 Fifth Avenue, between 48th and 49th streets
Ernest Flagg, 1913

The storefront is everything here. It is ornate and barnlike at the same time, a tough thing to pull off. Interior renovations have been respectful, but the place still feels far too new inside. But Flagg's splendid black-and-gold iron-and-glass front still makes the purchase of a book seem like a great ceremonial event.

II D 5 · THIRD AVENUE

When the El came down, Third Avenue boomed, and while that may have helped the economy, it did nothing for the quality of urban design. Third Avenue in the Forties is midtown's worst major avenue—the one with the poorest individual buildings and the weakest sense of any ensemble. Here, nothing is much good on its own, and the buildings fail to make any effort to work together; Sixth Avenue is a picture of order by comparison. If it proves anything, it is that the Miesian mode, the standard glass box, isn't so neutral as is often pretended. It can be an aggressive, unpleasant presence, as it so often is here.

There are three things of note, however, amidst the overall desolation. No. 711 Third Avenue at 45th Street is a William Lescaze building (1956) with strong horizontals and a touch of color that suggest that somewhere there was some sort of architectural intelligence at work, even though the results are less than inspiring. No. 747 Third Avenue at 47th Street (Emery Roth & Sons, 1972) has a lively ground floor and lobby by Pamela Waters with an undulating sidewalk and plenty of chairs for passersby. The developer was Melvyn Kaufman, whose lively imagination brought 127 John Street (I A 21) to Lower Manhattan.

Finally, the Buchanan at 160 East 48th Street, at the SW corner of Third (Lafayette A. Goldstone, 1929) is a fine example of the sort of apartment house the Grand Central neighborhood used to possess. Its presence on Third Avenue was a bit daring, since it generally resembles the lost buildings of Park Avenue in the Forties—a strong brick mass with vaguely classical details, and a generous central courtyard.

II D 6 · TURTLE BAY

The blocks of Turtle Bay—never precisely defined but, by agreement, the mid to upper Forties, Third Avenue to the East River—still look more or less as much of the East Side of Manhattan once did. There is a mix of brownstones, small shops, and medium-sized apartment buildings, with relatively few of the massive white-brick intrusions that make the East Sixties, Seventies, and Eighties a different kind of city. There is a fair amount of commercial usage, which lessens as Turtle Bay turns into the Beekman and Sutton Place neighborhood of the East Fifties (II F 1,4).

There are two special enclaves that remain intact: Turtle Bay Gardens, between 48th and 49th streets and Second and Third avenues, and Amster Yard, 211 to 215 East 49th Street. Turtle Bay Gardens is a group of row houses from the 1860's that are not extraordinary in themselves. But behind them (unfortunately, invisible to the public) is a common garden running through the middle of the block, a splendid example of enlightened urbanism that resulted from the decision of Mrs. Walton Martin to buy all the houses in 1919 and join their rear yards together. The houses were also altered so that all living rooms face the garden instead of the street.

Amster Yard is another private midblock garden, but thanks to the placement of several commercial enterprises in space accessible only through the garden, it is public. It is tranquil and pretty and completely apart from midtown Manhattan; it drives one to utter trite phrases about how distant one feels in this garden from the city, and it is true.

Just beside Turtle Bay Gardens is William Lescaze's townhouse of 1934 at 211 East 48th Street. This was the residence and office of one of the city's pioneering International Style architects, and it is one of the city's earliest examples of International Style work. The stark white house with horizontal strip windows and glass block breaks sharply, even arrogantly, from the design themes set by its brownstone neighbors, and reminds us of the hubris of the early modernists. But it is a handsomely wrought composition in itself, and its top-floor living room and lower-floor offices bespeak intelligent planning, so the house represents the International Style's strengths as well as its weaknesses.

Down the block, at the corner of Second Avenue, is what the International Style brought us in a later time. One Dag Hammarskjold Plaza (Emery Roth & Sons, 1972) is a 49-story blockbuster, a building with no relationship whatsoever to the Turtle Bay neighborhood, to the spirit of Second Avenue or even, in fact, to Dag Hammarskjold Plaza, the strip of 47th Street that is within its view but in no way adjacent. It is a triumph for addressmanship, not for architecture.

One of the city's best housing conversions is Turtle Bay Towers at 310 East 46th Street, in an old industrial loft building that had been put out of commission by a gas explosion. It was purchased by the Elgahanyan brothers, who have actively ridden the boom in turning commercial properties into housing, and renovated admirably by Bernard Rothzeid & Partners in 1977. The best detail: the greenhouse enclosures on the upper-floor setbacks.

Two other multiple dwellings are worth a note. No. 860 and 870 United Nations Plaza (Harrison & Abramovitz, 1966) are a grandiose pair of Miesian boxes, sited to take particular advantage of United Nations and city views (though also to block the view of the U.N. from Beekman Place). They look handsome, and they are decent, but to say they are acceptable is more a comment on the wretched nature of most new luxury housing in Manhattan than a positive observation in itself.

Far more significant is the glittering, golden orange Beekman Tower Hotel at the corner of Mitchell Place (49th Street) and First Avenue, built as the Panhellenic Hotel in 1928 to the designs of John Mead Howells. It is a lovely little skyscraper, very much a tower for all of its modest 28-story height, utterly expressive of the desire to celebrate verticality. Howells, who with Raymond Hood won the famous Chicago *Tribune* architectural competition in 1924, was obviously influenced, as were so many architects, by the second-prize winning entry by Eliel Saarinen, and this is his sleek and soaring homage to it.

II D 7 · ONE UNITED NATIONS PLAZA
NW corner, 44th Street and First Avenue
Kevin Roche John Dinkeloo and Associates, 1976

This is arguably the best glass-curtain-wall structure New York has seen in a decade. It is a frustrating building, for Roche in his design ignores every proper rule of high-rise construction—the skin of blue-green reflective glass is arranged in a gridiron of panes that obscures any sense of floor divisions or any sense of anything at all from the outside. We cannot count the floors, we cannot tell what is a window and what is a spandrel, and we cannot relate any of the changes in the building's shape to changes in interior function.

But the skin is so beautiful that one is tempted to let all of these things pass, to let this exquisite tower be the exception that proves the rule. The building is a combination hotel and office complex serving the United Nations, and its design is an intelligent counterpoint to the U.N.'s Secretariat Building—the color relates well, the materials relate well, and the odd

II D 7 · *One United Nations Plaza, at the right, with the headquarters of the United Nations: the Secretariat, at the left, and the General Assembly, in the center (II D 8)*

shape, which involves a nipped-in corner at the southeast and some 45-degree setbacks on the north, provides an appropriate rhythm to play against the Secretariat's even slab.

The glass is like a great glass blanket, covering everything with the same even grid. Even the street-level canopy is of the same material in the same grid; a piece of the skin is set at 45 degrees, as if it had been peeled off and turned into an awning. It looks from some angles too much like a skirt, but it is a sensible response to a problem and, indeed, from an aesthetic standpoint, is probably the best way to mark the entrance to a reflective glass box, a significant improvement over the tacked-on bubbles used at the John Hancock Tower in Boston, for example.

The public spaces of the hotel, entered from 44th Street, are among the best new public rooms in New York. The lobby is sleek and absolutely dignified, a mix of green and white marble set in a checkerboard pattern and chrome and felt. It is a lush, sensuous kind of modernism, and Roche does it well. More spectacular but no less disciplined are the restaurant and bar, red rooms with dazzlingly intricate ceilings of trelliswork and mirrors.

II D 8 · UNITED NATIONS HEADQUARTERS
First Avenue, 42nd to 48th streets
International committee of architects under chairmanship of Wallace K.
Harrison, 1952

The United Nations complex was the city's most daring piece of modern architecture in the early 1950's; it brought the glass curtain wall to Manhattan, and was thought by most observers to be projecting an image of bold progress for the international organization. Today, however, it looks nothing if not old-fashioned, even a bit quaint. The glass box is a symbol now not of progress but of conservatism, and one is tempted to agree with Lewis Mumford, one of the few naysayers when the buildings were completed, who felt that the 39-story glass-walled Secretariat Building symbolized not political authority but "that the managerial revolution has taken place and that bureaucracy rules the world." At least Mumford was more prescient than architectural historian Henry-Russell Hitchcock, another critic, who noted the air-conditioning problems caused by the orientation of the Secretariat in a north–south direction, with long walls east and west, and suggested that "the most significant influence of the Secretariat will be to end the use of glass walls in skyscrapers—certainly in those with western exposures, unless exterior elements are provided to keep the sun off the glass."

Le Corbusier created the initial concept of three buildings: a dominant slab to house the bureaucracy, a monumental assembly hall, and a low conference wing. He lost out in political battles with the international committee, however, and renounced any association with the execution of the design, which was largely by Wallace K. Harrison. The details, which are not particularly distinguished, tend to be Harrison's, and the planning of the interiors is, unfortunately, especially confused. Le Corbusier can be blamed for the symbolic problem pointed out by Mumford, however: the symbol of the complex is the Secretariat, not the General Assembly Building; even from close up the green glass slab dominates. That Le

Corbusier meant this as an ironic reminder of the very fact of which Mumford complained—that the bureaucracy now triumphs—is possible, of course, but somehow the possibility of such wit here makes the result no more pleasing.

The great lobby of the General Assembly Building is the closest the complex comes to a successful monumental space, and it is a flawed one indeed, fussy and overbearing at the same time. The General Assembly hall, with two Léger murals that are among the poorest works any great twentieth-century artist has ever made public, has the same tendency to be overly theatrical. All of the spaces in this building are characteristic of the tendency toward a certain degree of romantic expressionism that was to become characteristic of the later 1950's, as in the works of Eero Saarinen; there is both more discipline and more sheer visual pleasure in the three chambers of the Conference Building next door.

The 17-acre site, donated by John D. Rockefeller, Jr., is really too small, and the addition of a library by Harrison & Abramovitz in 1963 hasn't made the complex seem any more open. Nonetheless, the Secretariat *is* the only skyscraper in Manhattan that stands free, with acres of space around it, and that does enhance it considerably.

II D 9 · TUDOR CITY
East 40th Street to East 43rd Street, between First and Second avenues
Fred F. French Co., 1928

"Tudor City is for people who spend carefully. Large scale production reduces overhead and cost. Tudor City offers people with modest incomes a home life in beautiful surroundings. . . ." began some promotional literature in the early 1930's, shortly after Tudor City's completion. This is a pioneering effort in private urban renewal by a real estate developer who thought that large-scale middle-class housing was feasible in midtown Manhattan, and bought up large tracts of slum housing to prove it. He replaced blocks of tenements with twelve high-rise towers, all arranged along a private street, Tudor City Place. The architecture is 1920's American Tudor—which is to say brick with a hint of Tudor appliqué—but it is appealing, and there is a pleasant park in the midst of the development that pulls the whole place together into a true village. The entire thing is raised above the level of the surrounding streets, and 42nd Street passes beneath.

When Tudor City was built, the rest of the neighborhood was still quite blighted—slaughterhouses occupied the site of the United Nations, for example. As a result, the project was designed to face inward, and almost windowless walls look east toward the U.N. and the East River. The period of design of the project can be excused for this isolation; that problem aside, this remains a model effort, and one which clearly transformed an entire part of town.

The park is now threatened—developer Harry Helmsley, the current owner, has nowhere near the Fred F. French Co.'s understanding of urban design, and he seems to see the central open space merely as a vacant lot. If it is built upon, as Helmsley now plans, the essential quality of the entire development will be destroyed, and Tudor City will become just another piece of real estate.

II D 10 · FORD FOUNDATION
320 East 43rd Street
Kevin Roche John Dinkeloo and Associates, 1967

The city's modern Medici palace, an appropriate housing for an organization whose philanthropic largesse rivals that of a host of beneficent dukes. The offices are arranged in an L-shape around a 130-foot-high interior garden atrium, one of the city's most spectacular interior spaces. The garden, which is visible through the glass walls from the street, serves both as a private park and as a waste-air chamber. Since most offices are visible to one another across it, the garden space also functions as a symbolic unifier of the building.

The building is constructed of a medium-brown brick, glass, and rust-colored Cor-ten steel, which Roche has managed to use in a particularly handsome and restrained way here. This building has been perhaps a bit overpraised by critics who, despairing at the virtual absence of anything decent in Manhattan in the years following its completion, pointed to it again and again, but that should not get in the way of the fact that this is very distinguished architecture indeed—one Ford Foundation philanthropy that, by its very presence on the streetscape, benefits the entire city.

II D 10 · *Ford Foundation*

II D 10 · *Atrium of the Ford Foundation*

II D 11 · DAILY NEWS BUILDING
220 East 42nd Street
Howells & Hood, 1930
addition: Harrison & Abramovitz, 1958

A major step toward the postwar slab, and—for all we may dislike its progeny—a remarkable building for its time. The Daily News Building soared, its white brick verticals expressing height in a way that, for 1930, seemed remarkably daring. It is not a pure slab, of course; there are setbacks, and they are carefully positioned to enhance the sense of pure height but still break up the form. Viewed from close up, there are sculpted red and black brick spandrels that carry considerable weight, and so the building does not appear as unrelievedly vertical as photographs would suggest. The detail over the front entrance is especially elaborate and impressive.

Harrison & Abramovitz's addition was a thoughtful but inadequate companion. The original building has a powerful force, a real sense of *Zeitgeist* to it—it knows it is the coming thing, and one feels Hood and Howell's sense of commitment to the new as they abandoned the Gothic style they used for their headquarters for the *Daily News*'s parent company, the Chicago *Tribune*. The 1958 addition is but a weak echo.

II D 12 · AUTOMAT
street floor, 200 East 42nd Street, SE corner Third Avenue
Horn & Hardart Co., 1958

The last of a great breed. The Automats, which began in Philadelphia, became as much a part of New York as Sabretts hot-dog stands. Only this one, which is too new to be part of the first generation but which does a decent job of replicating the general ambience, remains. Still there is the change booth with its very, very solid stone counter, still there are the many little contraptions, each with a piece of so-so pie or lukewarm casserole. It is the place where a child is brought to lunch in the shadow of a great stone skyscraper, to be awed at the technology of the little boxes that take his nickels and dimes. That is the substitute for the awe he would feel at the skyscraper and the city itself, were he able to express it; the Automat takes its place, in a way that McDonald's and Burger King will never equal.

II D 13 · CHANIN BUILDING
122 East 42nd Street
Sloan & Robertson, 1929

The headquarters of the Chanin real estate empire, another New York development firm that, like Fred F. French (II D 3), was better known to an earlier generation. This is one of the city's Art Deco triumphs, a proud building with a base of terra-cotta ornament in plant forms and a lobby of remarkably intricate detail (now altered with a dropped ceiling). There are mock buttresses above the fourth floor, and a carefully accented sense of height, indicating the attention Sloan & Robertson, like so many architects of the period, had paid to Eliel Saarinen's distinguished second-place entry in the Chicago *Tribune* competition. Chanin once had an elaborate auditorium on an upper floor, which has disappeared to make way for more commercial space, as a bus depot did on the ground floor.

II D 13 · *Bas-relief on the Chanin Building*

II D 14 · *Chrysler Building*

II D 14 · *Spire of the Chrysler Building*

II D 14 · CHRYSLER BUILDING
405 Lexington Avenue, NE corner 42nd Street
William Van Alen, 1930

Is it silly or is it real? It is hard, even after years of looking carefully at this and so many other buildings, to answer that question. Chrysler *is* absurd, in a sense; the notion of a skyscraper topped by six levels of stainless-steel arches wrapping triangular windows, all culminating in a spire, and all on top of a tower ornamented by brick designs taken from automobile hubcaps and gargoyles modeled after radiator ornaments—of course that is silly.

Why, then, has it lasted? Chrysler is not rational, it is not profound, it is not subtle, it is not, even, in the final analysis, very beautiful. But there is something that makes it wonderful, something that makes that odd silvery tower glimmer in the sun and thus bring a smile to our lips. The current rage for Art Deco has led to Chrysler's being overpraised, but even with the hyperbole put aside, this is a very good building indeed. Perhaps the reason is that it *does* express the romantic longings of a particular period, that it is, in its way, a more appropriate statement of what New York wanted to be about as the twenties turned into the thirties than any perfect box the International Style could dream of. The quality of Chrysler comes from its ability to be romantic and irrational and yet not quite so foolish as to be laughable; it stops just short, and therefore retains a shred of credibility amidst the fantasy—rather like New York itself.

The building changed hands not long ago—after several years as a property of the Goldman-DiLorenzo real estate empire, which treated it rather like a tenement in the South Bronx, the building is now in the hands of the Massachusetts Mutual Life Insurance Company, which seems to like it a bit more. A major rehabilitation is under way at this writing, and whether it cleans up the building or changes it is still unclear. The lobby, a fantastic triangle of African marble, and the richly paneled elevators are among New York's masterpiece Art Deco interiors, and they must be preserved at any cost.

II D 15 · BOWERY SAVINGS BANK
110 East 42nd Street
York & Sawyer, 1923

A triumph from New York's finest bank architects of the 1920's. This is, among other things, a clear rebuke to those who would suggest that a monumental bank can exist only as a freestanding building; here is one set into a larger structure, and it is among the city's very best. The arched entrance is noble and the richly ornamented Romanesque banking room more so; the exhortations on thrift and the protection of funds carved into the frieze inside seem clearly to have been ignored by the bank in planning this structure, and one can only be thankful for it. After more than half a century the room is intact, and still seems, as it must have from the day it opened its doors across from and echoing Grand Central, like the safest place in the world to place your dollars.

II D 15 · *Banking room of the Bowery Savings Bank*

II D 16 · HYATT REGENCY NEW YORK (under construction)
NW corner, 42nd Street and Lexington Avenue
Gruzen & Partners, with Der Scutt

A glass box, over the old brick sheathing of Warren & Wetmore's Commodore Hotel, a part of the original Grand Central grouping. The Commodore was not particularly distinguished, and everyone concerned about the depressed state of construction in New York in the mid-1970's welcomed this project, but did it have to be of bronze mirrored glass? The essence of the Grand Central area is defined in stone, in solid masonry masses, and a jazzy reflective glass box fights all of that. It might have worked elsewhere, but here it appears as a desperate, unnecessary striving for the new, and it is unfortunate.

E/WEST FORTIES

II E 1 · THE NEW YORK PUBLIC LIBRARY
Fifth Avenue, 40th to 42nd streets
Carrère & Hastings, 1911

This is, along with Grand Central Terminal (II D 1) the city's Beaux-Arts high point. The library manages to be both awe-inspiring and gracious, dignified and cheerful, in the way that only the best Beaux-Arts buildings of the early twentieth century could be. The façade consists of three deep-set archways flanked by paired Corinthian columns in the center and single columns at the ends, all under a substantial parapet and pediment. The building is set on a wide, expansive terrace—the triple-arched entrance is reached by a wide set of steps, guarded by E. C. Potter's famous sculpted lions—that has come over the years to function as one of the city's very finest outdoor plazas.

The rear façade is totally different. Vertical strip windows run up and down for seven floors, expressing the stacks within. It is a startling piece of proto-functionalism, and quite handsome in its own right; what is impressive today, however, is not so much that Carrère & Hastings would decide to do this as that they would see no contradiction between using one style for one part of the job and another style for the other. Their brand of

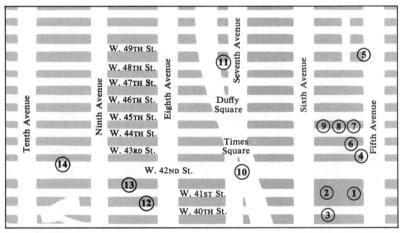

II / MIDTOWN   E / WEST FORTIES

II E 1 · *New York Public Library*

II E 1 · *Main reading room of the New York Public Library*

Beaux-Arts architecture, then, was not rigidly ideological; it was more concerned with stage-set ideas, with the notion of using Beaux-Arts tradition to establish a strong symbolic presence for the library on Fifth Avenue. Where the symbol was not needed, the Beaux-Arts was not needed, either— although the building is composed with such skill on all its façades that there is no jarring sense whatsoever from front to rear. The same Vermont marble and a certain amount of similar detailing provide continuity; the unusual stack side is a *different* façade more than it is in any way a "back."

The main reading room on the third floor is one of New York's nobler public rooms—grand like everything here, yet somehow relaxed. It is long and narrow and divided into two parts by the book delivery desk, which reduces the sense of sweeping space somewhat but makes the proportions of each side a bit better. One enters in the center of the long side, right on axis with the delivery desk; there is thus a moment before the entire space is perceived, and the enormity of the room comes as a pleasant surprise.

Thomas R. Hastings, the surviving member of the firm of Carrère & Hastings (Carrère died before the library was finished, one of the earliest victims on record of a fatal automobile accident) was never happy with the Fifth Avenue façade. He found the entrance too harsh, and considered having the stonework altered so that the Corinthian columns would not be set so deeply into a stark stone frame as they are now. It is said that Hastings left money in his will to have the library renovated according to a revised scheme; that was never done, and one suspects that it is just as well. Both Carrère and Hastings are memorialized in busts off the grand staircases rising from the main lobby, one of the very few cases of New York honoring its architects in a fitting manner.

II E 2 · BRYANT PARK AND SIXTH AVENUE, 40TH TO 42ND STREETS

The Crystal Palace was here from 1853 to 1858, hard by the Croton Reservoir, which occupied the east end of the huge square from Fifth to Sixth avenues where the public library now stands. The park on which the

Crystal Palace stood was named for William Cullen Bryant in 1884, and it became the public library's backyard in 1911. Its rather formal present design by Lusby Simpson was executed by the Parks Department in 1934.

The park is now, alas, best known for the attraction it holds for drug pushers and derelicts who wander toward it from Times Square and other areas to the west, and while office workers come out in sufficient numbers for lunch to effect a certain détente on pleasant days, most of the time it is the drug pushers who prevail. It is too bad; this is a formal square of a sort that is unique in midtown, and social problems have made its usage extremely low.

There is a mix of buildings around it that ranges from excellent to terrible, but it is the tightness of their arrangement that gives Bryant Park its definition, and makes its axial layout of fountain, statuary, and pathways appropriate. The best building is the American-Standard headquarters (II E 3); the worst is surely the Grace Building, 1114 Avenue of the Americas (Skidmore, Owings & Merrill, 1974), one of Skidmore partner Gordon Bunshaft's two swooping-front towers—the other is the Solow Building (II G 10)—that exists in utter disregard of its context.

The Grace Building's front—I call it swooping, others call it ski-jump—is an arrogant, exhibitionistic form that breaks the line of building-fronts that is important to any New York street, but is especially so as a definer of the edge of Bryant Park. Mr. Bunshaft, it would seem, cares nothing about Bryant Park or about anything except the shape of his own building, which from the northwest, at the corner of 43rd Street and Sixth Avenue, looks like nothing so much as an immense piece of furniture that has been squeezed awkwardly into the wrong place. At that corner, as a zoning bonus permitting extra height, is one of the coldest and most unwelcoming plazas any architect has created anywhere.

Things are not much better on the other side of Sixth Avenue. The New York Telephone Co.'s headquarters at No. 1095 (Kahn & Jacobs, 1974) is a pretentious white-marble box whose vertical lines make a shrill and unpleasant echo to the vertical windows of the west façade of the public

II E 4 · *Manufacturers Hanover Trust Company*

II E 3 · *American Radiator Building (now American-Standard Building)*

library. Here, too, extra height has been permitted via a trade-off that brings the public a dark, awkward, and thoroughly unappealing plaza; who really wins in such cases—the public or the real estate developer? East of the Grace Building along 42nd Street the pickings do get better. Next door to Grace at 33 West 42nd Street is the Graduate Center of the City University of New York, the old Aeolian Hall (Warren & Wetmore, 1912), remodeled in 1970 to the designs of Carl J. Petrilli & Associates. The ground floor has become a block-through mall, with stone floor and striated concrete walls; it is handsome and, for all its use of harsh materials, more welcoming than any of the public plazas in the neighborhood. Next door are two fine office towers that do a good job working with each other and, by creating a strong street wall, with Bryant Park: the Salmon Tower at 11 West 42nd Street (York & Sawyer, 1927 and 500 Fifth Avenue (Shreve, Lamb & Harmon, 1931), which uses in a 699-foot-high version a massing not so different from that which these architects were to use immediately thereafter in a 1,250-foot version called the Empire State Building.

II E 3 · AMERICAN-STANDARD BUILDING (originally American Radiator Building)
40 West 40th Street
Hood & Fouilhoux, 1924

This is Raymond Hood's first major building in New York, and it is something of a cross between his winning design for the Chicago *Tribune* headquarters and Eliel Saarinen's much praised second-place winner. The American Radiator Building is Gothic, like Hood's Chicago Tribune, but it is sleeker and more gracefully massed, suggesting the Saarinen scheme. The brick here is black, since Hood wanted the structure to appear as a sculpted mass, unbroken by the black holes that windows often appear to be; the top is of gold terra cotta. The profile is suggestive of a building much larger than this 21-story tower really is; it was Hood's gift that he could create so successful an illusion in massing, and also that he knew that the place for it was opposite Bryant Park, where the little tower could be seen from a distance. The showroom wing to the west is sympathetic, but not original to the tower.

II E 4 · MANUFACTURERS HANOVER TRUST CO.
510 Fifth Avenue, SW corner 43rd Street
Skidmore, Owings & Merrill, 1954

It looks pretty routine today, but this was a daring building for its time. Banks were supposed to be in Roman temples or Romanesque halls or Renaissance palaces; Skidmore hearkened to the call of Mies van der Rohe for a modernist vocabulary that would be universal, and persuaded the client, then called Manufacturer's Trust Company, to give it a whirl. The building was built to create an image, as surely as any York & Sawyer Renaissance palace was a bank built to create an image, and to be fair, this bank is successful at it, too. It is best, indeed, as a stage set; as a great

Miesian statement it comes off as second-rate and ordinary. The huge safe, oriented toward the glass wall to tantalize passersby and reinforce the image of openness, remains an eye-catching aspect of this influential building.

II E 6 · *Century Association*

II E 5 · *Goelet Building (now the Swiss Center)*

II E 5 · GOELET BUILDING
608 Fifth Avenue, SW corner 49th Street
E. H. Faile & Co., 1932
alteration of lower floors: Lester Tichy & Associates, 1966

This is now the Swiss Center, and the new base is routine modern merchandising. But the upper floors are a marvel—New York's real early modern gem, completed just one year after McGraw-Hill (II E 13). The massing suggests something a bit more old-fashioned, and the two central piers on the Fifth Avenue front create a classicizing effect that proves, upon examination, to be an illusion—this is a building very conscious of the International Style, with strong geometric lines and a façade that bespeaks what for 1932 would have been an almost purist sensibility.

II E 6 · CENTURY ASSOCIATION
7 West 43rd Street
McKim, Mead & White, 1891

Stanford White & Charles McKim were both members of this club, which has long encouraged intellectual pursuits, and while this was probably more White's building, records suggest a joint responsibility within the firm for the design. The Century is the first of McKim, Mead & White's many club designs to have been done as a grandly scaled Renaissance palace, in this case a Veronese sixteenth-century design adopted into a New York midblock site. It is a handsome and well-proportioned façade, here by virtue of the site turned into a plane rather than a mass. The spaces within are ample and relaxed, quite unlike the more formal public rooms in McKim's University Club (II G 8) or White's Metropolitan Club (III D 1). Those strike one as clubs for the newly rich who came to them from Richard Morris Hunt–designed châteaux; the Century, while still in the newly fashionable Renaissance style, seems more designed to keep the old New Yorker who comes to it from his brownstone at ease.

II E 7 · HARVARD CLUB
27 West 44th Street
McKim, Mead & White, 1894, 1905, 1915

If the Century and the University clubs were intended to bring some of the air of the Italian Renaissance to New York's growing upper class, the Harvard Club, designed largely by Charles McKim, had a simpler goal. Its Georgian design recalls the buildings of Harvard Yard, so this is architecture *à la recherche du temps perdu.* But in McKim's hands, this objective yields not a sentimental stage set but a strong and forceful original piece of architecture. There are a couple of major interior spaces, most notably Harvard Hall, that have a scale that is far in excess of anything the controlled and modest 44th Street façade might suggest, but which is visible from the rear on 45th Street.

II E 8 · NEW YORK YACHT CLUB
37 West 44th Street
Warren & Wetmore, 1899

This is one of midtown Manhattan's most likably eccentric buildings, and it is a wonderful surprise that it came out of the office of Warren &

II E 8 · *New York Yacht Club*

Wetmore, talented but not usually so inventive architects. What is best known about the Yacht Club are its three bay windows, carved to represent the sterns of eighteenth-century sailing ships; the voluptuously shaped windows are surrounded by sculpture of ocean waves and dolphins, but they are framed by columns which serve to temper the fantasy and, if one can possibly use this word, anchor the building firmly in the tradition of urban Beaux-Arts architecture. So this is at once a grand Beaux-Arts club and an oddly literal stage set. Architects tend to be fearful of such literalism as these ships' windows, though one happy development of the last decade is that they are getting less so; one can only be pleased that no such prejudice existed in the office of Warren & Wetmore in 1899.

II E 9 · ALGONQUIN HOTEL
59 West 44th Street
Goldwyn Starrett, 1902

An eclectic mix—cast-iron bay windows in vertical rows, red brick, a certain amount of quick-and-fussy classical detailing—but it is not the architecture that makes the Algonquin special. Here, not only has a building been preserved; so has a kind of place, the sort of hotel in which people really *do* sit in the elegant paneled lobby in wing chairs and chatter over whiskeys and Perriers. This was celebrated as the home of the great Round Table of the 1920's, but the visitor who goes in search of the contemporary equivalents to Dorothy Parker, Robert Benchley, and George S. Kaufman will not find them here: the crowd now is businessmen, tourists, theatergoers, publishers, and while the place is always filled to the gills, it does have a slightly stuffy, tired air that surely could not have been there in the grand old days. There is prosperity, but a hardening of the arteries. But then again, this place is myth and reality, in equal parts, and maybe the oak paneling always *was* more tangible than the *bons mots*.

II E 10 · TIMES SQUARE: Intersection of Broadway and Seventh Avenue, 42nd to 47th streets (including Duffy Square)

In New York a real square is called a park, and what is called a square is really a triangle. So it is here, in the most famous of all of Broadway's many intersections with the orthogonal street grid. The crossing of Seventh Avenue has been the center of the city's theater district since late in the nineteenth century, when legitimate theaters and music halls followed the Metropolitan Opera, which opened on Broadway at 40th Street in 1883. The intersection was then called Longacre Square; it was renamed to honor *The New York Times* in 1904, when the newspaper moved up from downtown to occupy the Times Tower, a triangular sliver of a building designed by Eidlitz & MacKenzie to fill the center of the intersection and, it was hoped, bring the newspaper the same sort of fame that McKim, Mead & White's Venetian palazzo had brought to the New York *Herald* at Herald Square.

Now *The New York Times* may well regret the association of its name with the quarter, so deteriorated has Times Square become and so connected is its name with vice and crime and urban decay in the minds of the public. This is no longer happy honky-tonk, as it was for so many years, when Times Square was filled with great hotels and restaurants and night clubs, and the sky blazed at night with the most elaborate and dazzling neon signs in the nation. The best signs are now in Las Vegas, the best hotels are now across town, and even Times Tower itself suffered an offensive remodeling into a banal marble box at the hands of Smith, Smith, Haines, Lundberg & Waehler in 1966. (The *Times* has long since moved to other quarters just off the square at 229 West 43rd Street, and the tower is now called simply One Times Square.)

Forty-second Street between Sixth and Eighth avenues, which slides by the south end of Times Square, is architecturally more intact than the buildings on the square itself. Most of the great theaters of the 1890's were built along here, and they survive, their façade details largely hidden behind new marquees advertising the sex-and-violence cinema that they now purvey. The lights are dazzling at night, but it is a sleazy and hostile street today. Also still there, but with its ground floor altered, is the ornately classical 142 West 42nd Street (Marvin & Davis, with Bruce Price, 1902), originally the Knickerbocker Hotel and still possessed of a rich mansard roof. The old Knickerbocker bears a resemblance to two of Times Square's best hotels, both now gone: the Astor of 1904, by Clinton & Russell, and the Claridge of 1911, by D. H. Burnham & Co.

The best building facing Times Square itself is the old Paramount Building (Rapp & Rapp, 1927) with fourteen setbacks mounting symmetrically toward a glowing bulb at the pinnacle. The Paramount Theater is gone from the main floor, but there is still a splendid sense of theatrics balanced with New York skyscraper traditions here. A block to the north is something called One Astor Plaza (Kahn & Jacobs, 1969), where there is no Astor, since this is the site of the old hotel, and there isn't much of a plaza, either. One Astor Plaza is a 50-story office tower that marked the beginning of the intrusion of office space into Times Square, a development which, unfortunately, has managed to remove much of the neighborhood's color without in any way detracting from its sleaziness. One Astor Plaza is significant, however, as a building in the history of New York zoning law—it is the first building to have taken advantage of the city's special zoning district intended to stimulate construction of new theaters. The tower contains one legitimate theater and one movie theater, for which the developer was permitted more than the usually acceptable amount of rentable office space in exchange. The theaters have proven large and uneconomical to manage, and the extra office space stayed empty in the depressed office market of the early 1970's, so the benefits of the district are questionable. The tower is topped by a set of concrete fins that are a well-meaning attempt to break away from the flat top; they come off looking cheaply futuristic, not inventive.

The Lyceum Theater (Herts & Tallant, 1903) across the square at 149 West 45th Street is the oldest theater in the Broadway area still used for legitimate productions, and one of the few of architectural merit. The strong Baroque columns and undulating marquee bring a certain lyricism to the façade, which is far more ornate than any of its successor theaters.

If the Lyceum is a remnant of the old Times Square, the TKTS booth at the north end of the square (technically in Duffy Square) is a sign of the new, and one of the more positive developments both architecturally and culturally that the neighborhood has seen in some time. Completed in 1973 to the designs of Mayers & Schiff, the booth, which sells half-price tickets to Broadway shows, is a metal-pipe and canvas structure, cheerfully industrial in a way that relates to nothing in Times Square's past, yet somehow seems at home and appropriate for its use.

II E 10 · *Paramount Building on Times Square*

II E 13 · *McGraw-Hill Building (now Group Health Insurance Building)*

II E 11 · 49th STREET STATION, BMT SUBWAY
Seventh Avenue, 47th to 49th streets
Johnson/Burgee, 1973

Federal funds permitted the total reconstruction of this subway station, the only one in the city's system to be so honored. It is hardly Philip Johnson's major work—the orange-brick walls and terrazzo floors give it something of the air of an airport—and it is a sign of how dreadful all of the other subway stations are that this appears quite pleasant by comparison. That may be a bit unfair; there *was* a serious effort here, and certain aspects of this design, such as the attempt at noise reduction within, are impressive. But it is hard to sense any real aesthetic ideas here, save for the one gesture of continuing the orange-brick motif up to the sidewalk in the form of low walls around the entrance stairs; that seems in theory like a wonderful example of thematic continuity throughout a design, but in practice it seems to have little point at all.

II E 12 · PORT AUTHORITY BUS TERMINAL
Eighth Avenue, 40th to 42nd streets
Port Authority of New York and New Jersey design staff, 1950, 1963, 1978

The latest expansion will turn the Port Authority Bus Terminal into a constructivist monster, with a two-block-long façade of diagonal steel bracing. It looks like a fortress intruding itself into the squalid Eighth Avenue neighborhood, as if it wished to protect the innocent commuters who scurry past the derelicts and give them the beginnings of the sanctuary they seek at home across the river in New Jersey.

At present, though, there is no sanctuary at all in the Port Authority Bus Terminal. It is a cold place, full of the glare of fluorescent lights and the stares of drifters, who, as in any city, make the bus terminal their home. The attempts at grandeur when the original building was completed in 1950, such as the central well open to the upper story, come off looking not elegant and generous but merely insipid. Nowhere, perhaps, is there as strong a reminder of how important color and materials can be—everything here is in varying tones of beige, and every material, from the walls to the floors, is harsh; it makes an airport seem inviting.

II E 13 · McGRAW-HILL BUILDING (now Group Health Insurance)
330 West 42nd Street
Hood, Godley & Fouilhoux, 1931

McGraw-Hill is one of New York's great modern buildings, the only structure in the city to have rated inclusion in Henry-Russell Hitchcock and Philip Johnson's classic survey, *The International Style,* of 1932. "The Mc-Graw Hill Building comes nearest to achieving esthetically the expression of the enclosed steel cage," Hitchcock and Johnson wrote approvingly.

Today, however, it is not just the International Style credentials—which were always just a touch suspect, for this is an individualized design indeed—but the other aspects of McGraw-Hill that seem most appealing. The bright greenish-blue terra-cotta sheathing, the lively setback form (Vincent Scully called it "proto-jukebox modern") and the Art Deco detailing of the entrance and lobby are all significant, as much so as the strongly expressive horizontal strips of windows so often pointed out in modernist architectural histories.

McGraw-Hill, the huge publishing company, located on 42nd Street west of Eighth Avenue partly in the hope of seeing land values rise there and partly out of the need to be in a neighborhood zoned for industrial uses, and it commissioned Hood to design a practical, industrial sort of structure. Nothing turned out quite as expected: the building came out an unorthodox masterpiece, the neighborhood never caught on, and the green tower's thirty-five stories commanded the skyline of the far West Forties virtually alone for most of the building's life.

McGraw-Hill lost patience after forty-two years, and moved to a new and dreary Harrison & Abramovitz building in Rockefeller Center in 1973; the "green building" lay empty for some time, then was taken over by Group Health Insurance. Ironically, McGraw-Hill's departure came at a time when the boom of interest in Art Deco was making the building a more and more significant object of study on the part of art historians, and it is probably fair to say that there is no other building in New York with so impeccable a modernist pedigree that is also so much fun to look at.

II E 14 · MANHATTAN PLAZA
West 42nd Street, Ninth to Tenth avenues
David Todd & Associates, 1977

Two red-brick towers, each forty-five stories tall and anchoring an end of a superblock. This was intended by its developer, the HRH Construction Company, to be the spur to improvement in the Clinton neighborhood—as the far West Forties have come to be called—that Tudor City was to the East Forties. Unfortunately, the buildings neared completion in 1975 as construction costs were skyrocketing and the housing market sagging; fair market rents would never have worked, since those who could afford the prices would not have wanted to be pioneers so close to Times Square, and those willing to live there could not afford the costs. An innovative plan rescued the project, converting it into "Section 8" federally subsidized housing, but for New Yorkers involved in the performing arts, not for welfare families, thus helping to stabilize the neighborhood with an infusion of people involved in this part of town's one real strength, the theater.

Architecturally, the towers are decent, with somewhat more flair than the average new apartment skyscraper on the East Side. But that is it—there is no real innovation here, and no real style, and good as the success of the development is for this troubled area, a neighborhood full of such buildings would be no neighborhood at all.

F/EAST FIFTIES

II F 1 · BEEKMAN PLACE

Beekman Place is utterly exquisite in a particularly New York way, distant as its tranquil two blocks may seem from the spirit of the rest of the city. For this tiny street, lined with good but not exceptional townhouses and with apartment buildings that work themselves in with reasonable deference to the small scale, is a mix of elements that do not really belong together at all. It is not the charm of a John Nash terrace in London, where identical houses form a perfectly matched unity, but the eclectic combination that is so representative of New York: an Italianate house here, a Georgian one there. Most pleasing are the double pediment over Nos. 25 and 27 and the ornaments on the façade of No. 33, but everywhere here, even Paul Rudolph's new attic on his house at No. 23 (1978) plays a role in the total composition. (The Rudolph house, incidentally, has been strongly criticized by its neighbors, who seem to have forgotten that their street is a mix of different styles put together over time. Still, it is a forceful intrusion, and acceptable though the vertical extension is in principle, it is hard not to wish that Mr. Rudolph had not been willing to show a bit more restraint in his overall massing, which cantilevers over the front of the existing townhouse.)

Contributing as much as the architecture does to making Beekman Place

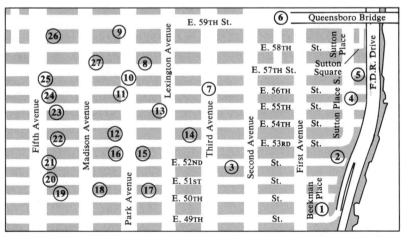

seem like a stage set for a quaint comedy about upper-class life in Manhattan is the extreme quiet—there is no through traffic, and it is remarkable to observe what a change that can affect in the general ambience of a neighborhood. The intrusion of the glass towers of 860 and 870 United Nations Plaza, which in some ways is a liability, since it removes Beekman Place's view south to the United Nations, curiously enhances the street's sense of privacy and isolation, making it seem all the more like a secret enclave.

II F 1 · *860 and 870 United Nations Plaza*

II F 2 · *River House*

II F 2 · RIVER HOUSE
435 East 52nd Street
Bottomly, Wagner & White, 1931

River House is the quintessential New York apartment house of a style and a period where the romantic ideal of the New York apartment comes home. It is a 26-story tower of limestone and gray brick, set just beside the East River—so close, in fact, that until the Franklin Delano Roosevelt Drive was completed in the 1940's, residents had a private yacht mooring. The building has a splendid profile, topping off with a rounded tower, and it may have the best entrance in New York—through gates to a private courtyard and automobile turnaround, then to a discreet, elegant lobby that opens onto a formal garden and a view of the East River. Nothing here advances the state of the art, and the apartments themselves, while elegant and spacious, are not in any way unusual. The point here is that the image of a certain kind of life, the 1930's New York of dashing, moneyed Wasps who played at "21" by night and at the stock exchange by day, was captured as concisely as if in a snapshot.

II F 3 · TOWNHOUSE, 242 East 52nd Street
Philip Johnson, 1950

Originally a guest house for Mr. and Mrs. John D. Rockefeller III, then owned by the Museum of Modern Art, and later the city home of Johnson himself, this is one of Manhattan's few distinguished postwar townhouses. It comes from Johnson's Miesian period, but it is more a proto-loft space inside than a perfectly detailed Miesian room. There is a kitchen just inside the front door, a huge living room with a glass wall facing onto a reflecting pool, and a bedroom in a separate wing reachable across the pool. Everything is deliberately turned inward, focusing on the pool, yet the façade is a lively enough composition to show some kindness to the street. This ranks with William Lescaze's house (II D 6) and George Nelson's house for Sherman Fairchild (III D 7) as a major attempt to bring the aesthetics of the International Style to the problem of the design of the New York townhouse; of the three, Johnson's house represents the most impressive rethinking, and it is far and away the most visually pleasing. It is the only one of the trio that today does not look old-fashioned.

II F 4 · SUTTON PLACE

This is a sort of grown-up Beekman Place—longer, wider, more built up and less charming. But it suffers only by comparison with its downtown neighbor; Sutton Place is, in fact, one of the most relaxed and pleasant streets on Manhattan Island. The lower end, Sutton Place South, has now been built up entirely with high-rise apartments which more or less resemble their mediocre counterparts elsewhere in town, but as at Beekman Place, the virtual absence of traffic transforms the street into something relaxing and pleasant. A small park at the south end at 53rd Street brings to the street some of the sense of the river that the great buildings have taken away from most of it.

The vista of the street itself is dramatic from the south end—the street rises gently, its sides defined by the strong lines of the apartment buildings on the right and left, and its end marked sharply by the soaring ironwork

II F 3 · *242 East 52nd Street*

II F 4 · *1 Sutton Place*

of the Queensboro Bridge (II F 6), as it leaps across Sutton Place on its way to the East River.

Sutton becomes more elegant as it moves north. No. 1 Sutton Place South, a 17-story apartment house completed in 1927 to the designs of Manhattan's great luxury apartment-house architect Rosario Candela, with the firm of Cross & Cross, is almost River House's equal in conveying an image of the life of the rich in New York in the 1930's—the building's elegant triple-arched porte-cochere opens to a lobby that, in turn, opens to a private garden on the East River.

There is a small balcony of a park projecting over the East River at the east end of 57th Street, just north of 1 Sutton Place South; north of that is Sutton Square, a remarkable block of townhouses with a common garden. The houses run the gamut from a lavishly decorated attempt at French provincial style that looks like a bit of Beverly Hills squeezed into a New York row-house plot to a pair of houses at the south end of the block that are excellent in their Georgian detailing. (No. 3 is now the residence of the secretary general of the United Nations.)

The 58th Street side of this group uses Sutton Square as an address, and just beyond it is one of the city's least-known and most appealing streets, really an enclave of an enclave—Riverview Terrace, a group of five ivy-covered brownstones fronting directly on the river. A private street, Riverview Terrace runs north from Sutton Square just on the river; since the houses occupy only one side of the street, all facing the river, this row clearly takes advantage of its river site to an extent even Beekman and Sutton fail to do.

The tranquillity of the neighborhood is shattered brutally by the Sovereign, just off Sutton Place at 425 East 58th Street (Emery Roth & Sons, 1973), a 48-story apartment house that bears a relationship to Sutton Place's delicate scale that is more or less similar to the relationship the *Queen Mary* would have if she were docked beside a little fishing village. Ironically, the Roth firm created in the Sovereign one of the few new luxury buildings in the city with a good floor plan—the apartments run through the building to have both north and south views, and there are separate elevator banks serving just two apartments per floor. But these private virtues do little to ameliorate the building's public sins.

II F 5 · 322 EAST 57th STREET
Harry M. Clawson and Caughey & Evans, 1930

The studio buildings of West 67th Street (III B 8) are more famous, but this ranks among the best of that small group of apartment houses distinguished by double-height living rooms in virtually every unit. Most such buildings were constructed as artists' studios and functioned at least nominally as such for the first decades of their existence; 322 East 57th had no such pretensions—everything about this building says it was constructed for the rich, not for any bohemian artist types. There is a limestone front, and the façade is styled in a cool Italian Renaissance, far from the tempestuous Gothic of the West Side studios.

Best of all are the apartment layouts themselves here. Many of the nineteen apartments are entered at the top, permitting visitors to pause at the upper balcony, survey the crowd, then make a proper entrance into the 18-foot-high living room down a curving staircase.

II F 6 · QUEENSBORO BRIDGE
east of Second Avenue and 59th Street
Gustav Lindenthal, engineer; Palmer & Hornbostel, architects, 1909

A heavy mass of cantilevered steel in a city of graceful suspension bridges. It should, therefore, be a ponderous intrusion, but it is not; the intricate web of steelwork adds a sense of movement, depth, and complexity to a part of town that, whatever its other virtues, possesses little in the way of dramatically expressive form. The bridge is best seen from the north or south, rather than from its entrance at 59th Street and Second Avenue, but even from there the great erector set that is this bridge's structure is clear. It is no surprise that Henry Hornbostel, the architect, is said to have exclaimed, "My God, it's a blacksmith's shop!" upon seeing the completed bridge for the first time, but one hopes that when the shock of all that industrial steel wore off he came to think more kindly of his work, for it deserves it.

II F 7 · THIRD AVENUE IN THE FIFTIES

Much of this stretch of Third Avenue has the same sense of confusion as Third Avenue in the Forties—it is no longer the casual, random street of bars and tenements and antique shops that it once was, but it is not quite comfortable being a street of new towers, either. This is best shown at 56th Street, where Skidmore, Owings & Merrill's 919 Third Avenue (1970) rises next to the tiny nineteenth-century remnant, P. J. Clarke's bar. P. J. Clarke's, which was excluded from the block assembled for 919 Third, has one of the city's most ornate cut-glass and mahogany bars inside; the outside now sits on the plaza of 919 Third like a piece of sculpture, and it is hard to say which seems more ill at ease, the new building or the old one. Clearly, for all the fuss about Clarke's preservation, Skidmore, Owings & Merrill was not prepared to do anything to take the old building into account in its design; 919 Third is a box of black glass, with a smooth façade modeled after the firm's success at 140 Broadway (I A 8). But that building is slender and delicate and this one is enormous and gross, with travertine spread around its base as if it were an insect repellent keeping the old honky-tonk Third Avenue at bay.

Above 57th Street, the avenue changes into something equally different from its past identity, but this time the role seems more fitting. Several theaters, Bloomingdale's, and fast-food outlets crowd the sidewalk for space. These blocks have become to today's city what Times Square was to the city of a generation ago, and while the scene has become too sleazy to be called good clean fun—there are sex and drugs to be bought here, as sure as in Times Square—there is a sense of energy that Times Square has lost, perhaps forever.

It is worth noting that the corner of 59th and Third has become the focus for the powerful attraction this neighborhood exerts on moviegoers, shoppers, and voyeurs alike, and that this corner is merely a normal corner in the Manhattan street grid, not a main axis or otherwise significant intersection at all. All of the energy concentrated in this part of Third Avenue came without any specific expression for it in the street plan; the area functions like a square, with all of the magnetic pull of a square and all of the symbolic value of a square, but it is just four plain corners, without any open space whatsoever. Rather like Murray Hill on a larger scale (II C 8) there is no center, no traditional sign that you are in a special place; you just feel it as you glide up the avenue into it, and when you pass you know that it is gone.

II F 8 · GALLERIA
117 East 57th Street
David Kenneth Specter, Philip Birnbaum, 1975

One of the city's two major new mixed-use buildings, it makes an interesting contrast with the Olympic Tower (II F 20). This one does what seems to be the right things—it is built out to the street on 57th Street, it expresses the change in use from office to apartments on its façade, and it has a complex, setback top. It still, alas, comes off as fairly ordinary. The Philip Birnbaum apartments are quite routine, save for those on the south side that have greenhouse-balconies; the public spaces at ground level by Specter are far superior, but still do not quite come off. One problem is that there is nothing inside to pull passersby through; plans for a café never materialized, and the doors on 57th Street instead of an open front suggest to the pedestrian that the central atrium is private space, not public (in spite of the symbolism of the gaping, mouthlike hole in the façade). But the atrium does have some handsome details, particularly in the granite and quarry tile paving.

The building became well known for one reason beyond its status as a trial for new zoning provisions. Millionaire Stewart Mott commissioned the multistoried penthouse, which was designed as an office, residence, and vegetable garden. He decided the price was too high and never purchased it; it was Mott's needs that gave the building its sculpted profile.

II F 9 · OLIVETTI BUILDING
500 Park Avenue, SW corner 59th Street
Skidmore, Owings & Merrill, 1960

What good work Skidmore, Owings & Merrill is capable of when the building is small! It seems no accident that this firm's best New York work—140 Broadway, Lever House, and this—is all relatively small in size. There is nothing overbearing about this, nothing aggressive—the Olivetti Building is an elegant box of glass and aluminum, floating on piers but respectful of the street and of the scale of its neighbors. Like the Seagram Building, it is a jewel of metal and glass that works best when it can be played off against older, masonry buildings beside it which set off its

II F 6 · *Queensboro Bridge*

II F 9 · *Pepsi-Cola Building (now Olivetti Building)*

detailing and materials. Seagram (II F 15) has lost its generational dialogue thanks to the construction of mediocre office towers to its north and south; Olivetti's original neighbors remain, and the buildings work together superbly.

This is one of the few instances of modern commercial architecture in New York succeeding at what it set out to do—create an elegant, refined, and civilized environment that would enrich the city at large. Curiously—and sadly—the client for whom the building was built, Pepsi-Cola, understood none of this, and fled New York for rural upper Westchester County not much more than a decade after this building was finished. The Olivetti Corporation was a willing purchaser, but in 1978 it, too, decided to leave, and this fine building's future is uncertain.

II F 10 · 445 PARK AVENUE
SE corner 57th Street
Kahn & Jacobs, 1947
· 450 PARK AVENUE
SW corner 57th Street
Emery Roth & Sons, 1972

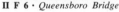

Two generations, and the contrast is illuminating. No. 445 Park Avenue was the first large postwar office building, and it is one of the best examples of a style that flourished for a brief period between the war and the advent of the glass curtain wall in the mid-1950's. The exterior wall is of limestone (it is more often in brick in such buildings), which is set in horizontal bands, alternating with horizontal bands of windows. The massing, which takes the building out to the property line for the first twelve stories, then sets back neatly a few times to reach the total height of twenty-two stories, is determined largely by zoning. But it is worth noting how compatible this massing makes the building with older Park Avenue structures—as well as how different the masonry façade treatment makes 445 Park from slightly newer, similarly massed glass-wall structures, such as 320 and 350 Park (both Emery Roth & Sons, 1961 and 1962).

The real contrast, of course, is across the street, with 450 Park Avenue, a tower constructed under newer zoning laws which call for a sheer rise, without setbacks, and a plaza on the site as a bonus in exchange for greater height. The Roth firm was trying one neat trick here—the floor divisions on the smooth façade of black steel and glass are articulated in a pattern of every three floors, then a single floor, then three more floors, presumably to reduce the scale of the building when viewed from afar. It doesn't work—partly because the building is never viewed from afar—and it comes off as rather arty and pretentious instead. The "plaza" behind the building is the worst thing of all, however—it is small, dark, and cramped, more like an airshaft than a public place. That it is called a civic amenity is absurd; that the builder was given additional floor space for this travesty is an insult.

II F 11 · MERCEDES-BENZ SHOWROOM
430 Park Avenue, SW corner 56th Street
Frank Lloyd Wright, 1955

Why Wright did this is a mystery; he didn't seem to need the work at that late stage of his career, and the design, which attempts to squeeze a ramp into a conventional ground-floor storefront, comes off as contrived and silly. The idea of having sleek European cars (the room was designed originally for Jaguars) appear to the purchaser to be gliding toward him off a curving ramp *is* an appealing one, but it doesn't stand a chance of working in such a low, cramped space.

II F 12 · LEVER HOUSE
390 Park Avenue, 53rd to 54th streets
Skidmore, Owings, & Merrill (Gordon Bunshaft, partner in charge), 1952

This ranks with McGraw-Hill, the Daily News, and Seagram in terms of influence—it is a building that really did help make an era. When Lever House was in the planning stage, Park Avenue in the Fifties consisted almost entirely of masonry apartment houses, buildings built out to the street line and carrying a more or less even cornice line down the avenue.

Bunshaft changed everything. He scooped out a block of Park Avenue and inserted two slabs of stainless steel and glass, one set horizontally on columns over an open first floor, the other poised vertically above. The result was not only a change in use of Park Avenue, from a residential street to a commercial one, but a dramatic new model for the office building. Suddenly the tight city was opened up, both at ground level and above. Light poured in, open space flowed around. To a city accustomed to blocks and blocks of limestone and granite, it must have been a dazzling vision of a new world.

It was a stunning act of corporate philanthropy, too. The Lever Brothers Company chose not to build as large a structure as was legally permissible, leaving much of the "zoning envelope," or total volume the building could occupy, empty.

Now Lever is old enough so that it contains many employees who were not even born when the building was finished; it is a historical structure in every sense of the word, and ready for an evaluation that is free of the romantic heroism the 1950's assigned to it. By today's standards, the building remains a handsome and impressive object, but there are problems. The break with the street wall of Park Avenue, so liberating in the 1950's, now seems needless and not a little narcissistic. The open ground floor, which seemed to be the very embodiment of enlightened urbanism when it was new, now seems dull and sterile, its public space little used.

And the premise of "structural honesty" on which the building was said to be based is, of course, an exaggeration: the double-slab form is a pure composition, and the use of spandrel glass—the glass that covers the structure between the floors, making the entire outside look like a window— is not structural honesty at all, but merely a modernist brand of ornament.

II F 12 · *Lever House*   **II F 14 ·** *Citicorp Center*

II F 13 · CENTRAL SYNAGOGUE
SW corner, Lexington Avenue and 55th streets
Henry Fernbach, 1872

A neo-Moorish synagogue with the exterior restraint of a proper Georgian church, this building just won't let go. It is a shame—Fernbach was a good architect, and did some of SoHo's best cast-iron buildings—but here he seemed almost desperately eager to prove that a synagogue could be a stuffy, respectable member of society. The result is a building of considerable quality and elegance but of little visible passion. The style calls for passion, but it all seems to be pent up somewhere, unreleased, and as a consequence Central Synagogue does not really hold its own very well among the

II F 14 · *St. Peter's Church, at the left, under the base of Citicorp Center*

skyscrapers that are now its neighbors. It is so much more stylish than anything nearby except Citicorp Center that it could have dominated the whole block, but it just doesn't. If more emotion had been put into this building when it was built, there might be more to take out of it now.

The twin octagonal towers, topped by onion-shaped domes, share the restraint of the entire building but manage a certain fanciful air nonetheless— they possess the lightness that the entire structure should have had. So, by the way, does the sanctuary inside, a brilliant array of stenciled polychrome that calls to mind the very best vibrant Victorian interiors.

II F 14 · CITICORP CENTER
Lexington to Third avenues, 53rd to 54th streets
Hugh Stubbins & Associates, 1977
· ST. PETER'S CHURCH
Lexington Avenue at 54th Street
Hugh Stubbins & Associates, 1977

The most talked-about building in mid-Manhattan in the 1970's, and not only because nothing else was getting built. Citicorp would have been significant even in a more productive decade: it is a mixed-use project combining offices, stores, and restaurants, as well as a church; it is the fourth tallest building in Manhattan, and it has a dramatic form that has made it highly conspicuous on the skyline. All of this adds up to a project that, whatever its faults, has provided a desperately needed shot of adrenaline to the city's architectural bloodstream.

The 900-foot tower is set on four great columns, each 22 feet square and

115 feet high. The columns are in the middle of each side rather than in the corners, freeing a considerable amount of space, which has been given over to a six-story retail wing with a central atrium, to a new structure for St. Peter's Church, and to a sunken entrance plaza. The entire structure save for the church is sheathed in whitish-silver aluminum, and the top 130 feet are sliced off at a dramatic 45-degree angle. It is the slanting top that is the building's most conspicuous formal gesture, and it has become Citicorp Center's visual trademark.

This is not brilliantly innovative architecture, but it is good architecture indeed, and intelligent synthesis of certain ideas which have been in the air for a long time but which have barely made themselves felt in Manhattan until now. The ideas, in brief, are that skyscrapers can have funny-shaped tops instead of flat ones, that they can have elegantly sleek skins instead of Miesian glass-and-steel ones, and that they can share some of their space with other uses, such as restaurants and churches, without any diminution of their value, economic or otherwise.

The skin is one of New York's handsomest, a far better evocation of "high-tech" imagery than Skidmore, Owings & Merrill's 919 Third Avenue. If the elaborate façade of the Woolworth Building suggests a draftsman's anguished hours of meticulous drawing, Citicorp's outside looks as if it could have been designed by a computer. Its light tone makes it glow slightly, which is much better than the glare that comes from towers of reflective mirror-glass. The aluminum skin covers even the bottom of the tower, visible under the projecting corners between the four legs—spots that are impressive for their powerful, yet unthreatening, futuristic imagery.

Nothing about Citicorp, in the end, *is* threatening. The shopping atrium is cool and pleasant, so lacking in real innovation that it seems at first glance like a mall in some Midwestern city designed to look like a sophisticated New York skyscraper. The church beside the tower (which is there as the result of a complex land transaction in which Citicorp bought the old St. Peter's on the site and promised to erect a new church) is also less imaginative than it might appear to be. It is a granite mass—a granite tent, almost—that sits like a sculptural object beneath one of the tower's corners; inside is a dramatic, angular space that is handsome and dignified but not in any way complex or profound. (St. Peter's also contains the lovely and modest Erol Beker Chapel, a sculptural work by Louise Nevelson.) One might further observe that there is a bit of disturbing symbolism to the church's position at the base of the tower—the granite church seems from some angles to cower beneath the huge skyscraper, a rather awkward reminder that the bank is big and rich and the church less so. It is hard not to recall here Hugh Ferris's visionary design of the 1920's that also joined a church to a skyscraper, but put the church on top as the skyscraper's crown—rather more comfortable a way to render unto God that which is God's and unto Caesar that which is Caesar's.

I may be being unfair, and perhaps it is best not to judge either Citicorp or its neighboring church by such tough standards. Surely it contributes immensely to the well-being of midtown Manhattan by virtue of the summary it offers of socially responsible large-scale design ideas of the 1970's, even if it does not advance these ideas dramatically. If one recalls the banal and awkward Miesian box erected in 1961 by Citicorp, which then called itself First National City Bank, next door to the new building at 399 Park Avenue, the significance of Citicorp Center becomes clear. It is worlds ahead of the old building in terms of both aesthetics and social relevance, and if the advances of Citicorp Center are what conservative clients now seek, then it means the rules of the game have changed for the better.

II F 15 · SEAGRAM BUILDING
375 Park Avenue, 52nd to 53rd streets
Mies van der Rohe, Philip Johnson, 1958

"Reason," Mies van der Rohe used to quote St. Thomas Aquinas as saying, "is the first principle of all human work." Seagram is a temple to reason, a tower built to elucidate the Miesian principles of order, logic, and clarity in all things. It is not quite what it would seem, however—Mies was far more interested in having his buildings appear to be structurally simple than actually be structurally simple. But if the myth that has surrounded this building (and the rest of Mies's work) is not entirely accurate, that does not diminish Seagram's standing as one of the great buildings of the twentieth century. The bronze curtain wall is serene, the proportions are sublime, and the detailing—well, if not perfect here, then where? So meticulous was the care that lavatory fixtures and lettering on the lobby mailboxes were designed specially for use here.

Seagram is set back from Park Avenue on a deep plaza, with green Italian marble rails as benches along its sides and two great fountains in its foreground. It is all done to show off the tower, yet, curiously, the narcissistic plaza has ended up being one of New York's most relaxed and welcoming public spaces. Mies conceived of it as a single spot of relief from the tight limestone canyons of Park Avenue; unfortunately, the brilliant success of Seagram led the city in its 1961 revision of the zoning code to encourage other tall towers on plazas. The result has been a slew of imitations, cheap Miesian buildings on uncomfortable, street-wrecking plazas.

The building is as good as it is largely as a result of the efforts of Phyllis Lambert, an architect and daughter of Samuel Bronfman, the late head of Joseph E. Seagram & Sons. She learned that her father had asked a routine commercial firm to design the building, and was so disturbed that she flew back from Paris to persuade him to hire an architect of international reputation instead. Father indulged daughter, putting her in charge of a search committee; she later wrote that she considered Frank Lloyd Wright but felt his work represented the frontier mentality of an America then gone, and that Le Corbusier's sculptural forms would not be a "good influence" in New York. Mies was the architect of the day, she felt: "Mies forces you in. You have to go deeper. You might think this austere strength, this ugly beauty, is terribly severe. It is, and yet all the more beauty in it."

All true—and yet. There may be few buildings in New York as beautiful as Seagram, and there are surely no postwar skyscrapers as truly exquisite, but it is not entirely the kind of beauty Mies intended it to be. Seagram is not only a bit of a trick structurally—Louis Kahn was fond of calling it "a beautiful lady with hidden corsets," for the "pure" Miesian skin hides lots of other kinds of supports—but it is, with its I beams running down the façade and its marble-paneled false windows on the sides, not a little mannered and ornamented. This is not the natural outgrowth of technology, as Mies pretended it was, and it is not the *Zeitgeist*. It was believed to be such, which led to wretched imitations and, even sadder, to a growing sense on the part of society at large that contemporary architecture was a faceless, styleless art.

In the end, Seagram, like all of Mies's work but like so little else the International Style produced, is true not to the rules of an abstract system but only to itself, like all great works of art.

The Four Seasons restaurant off the main lobby, designed by Mies's co-architect on the building, Philip Johnson, was New York's first consciously modern postwar restaurant, and it remains the best. Johnson's two great rooms, joined by a travertine corridor hung with Picasso's 1929 stage backdrop for *Le Tricorne*, are the finest echo our time has produced to Henry's Hardenbergh's great Oak Room in the Plaza Hotel or McKim's dining room on the University Club. These rooms make a significant departure from the austerity of the International Style, and in a sense begin the move toward sensuous restaurant design continued by Charles Gwathmey and Robert Siegel in Shezan (II G 11) and Warren Platner in Windows on the World at the World Trade Center (I A 10). The wood-paneled bar with its Lippold sculpture is at once warm and dignified; the main dining room with its central pool and vast space is luxurious, and every detail, from graphics to tableware, is superb.

II F 15 · *Seagram Building*

II F 17 · *St. Bartholomew's Church, with the General Electric Building in the background (right)*

II F 16 · RACQUET AND TENNIS CLUB
370 Park Avenue, 52nd to 53rd streets
McKim, Mead & White, 1918
· FISHER BROTHERS BUILDING
behind 370 Park Avenue
Skidmore, Owings & Merrill, scheduled for construction

Very mediocre McKim, Mead & White—this time the Italian palazzo has come out looking rather like a warehouse, and one yearns for the delicate touch of Stanford White, whose death twelve years before this commission put an end to what sprightliness this great firm's work may have had. But for all its ordinariness as a building, what importance the Racquet Club plays in the cityscape as a foil to the Seagram Building! The façade is the true west wall of Seagram's great plaza, anchoring it and holding it secure. And the success of the juxtaposition serves as a subtle reminder of how truly classicizing Mies van der Rohe's instincts were.

Scheduled to rise behind is an immense wedge, courtesy of the architects of Skidmore, Owings & Merrill and the zoning planners of the New York City Planning Commission. It is far too large for a mid-block site, and whether the public galleria space will mean enough to offset the loss in urban quality that this huge mass on the skyline will bring remains to be seen.

II F 17 · ST. BARTHOLOMEW'S CHURCH
Park Avenue, 50th to 51st streets
Bertram Goodhue, 1919
entrance portico from old St. Bartholomew's: McKim, Mead & White, 1902
· GENERAL ELECTRIC BUILDING
570 Lexington Avenue, SW corner 51st Street
Cross & Cross, 1931

Who says you can't put a 51-story skyscraper next to a Byzantine church? This is one of the most impressive juxtapositions of scale and style anywhere in New York. St. Bartholomew's is a richly detailed pile of limestone and salmon-colored brick, topped off by a low polychromed dome; the tower is Art Deco, topped by an elaborately detailed crown of laced stonework that seems to be an abstract representation of the radio waves associated with the building's original tenant, RCA. Cross & Cross used the same materials that Goodhue had used in the church, and the tower is massed so that its wide base is largely hidden behind the church from Park Avenue, and only the slender, graceful tower rises above St. Bartholomew's. Nowhere is there a sense of either scale or style clashing.

St. Bartholomew's itself set the pattern for sensitive juxtaposition, though. Goodhue, who was especially gifted at both detailing and sculpted masses, designed St. Bartholomew's to accept the Romanesque entrance porch that the congregation wished to save from its old McKim, Mead & White church, and the shift in style from McKim, Mead & White's Romanesque to Goodhue's Byzantine is handled with considerable finesse.

II F 18 · VILLARD HOUSES
Madison Avenue, 50th to 51st streets
McKim, Mead & White, 1884
· PALACE HOTEL
behind the Villard Houses
Emery Roth & Sons, under construction

Four houses arranged in a U around a central courtyard, and the project that started both the McKim firm and the rest of late nineteenth-century New York on a wave of neo-Italian Renaissance building. These are powerful, graceful brownstones, modeled roughly after the Palazzo della Cancelleria in Rome, but inventively molded into a presence that, at least now if not in the 1880's, seems particularly characteristic of New York. The houses are rich in history: they were built for Henry Villard, a journalist and owner of the New York *Post*; one section was once the home of Whitelaw Reid, publisher of the New York *Tribune;* one section became the offices of Random House, then the entire complex eventually ended up in the hands of the Roman Catholic Archdiocese of New York. It was the Archdiocese that negotiated with developer Harry Helmsley to build a hotel behind the property, using the houses as a formal entrance; preservationists battled the scheme, but gave in when Helmsley agreed to preserve the incomparable interiors as part of the hotel. The hotel tower now rising will be a neutral glass box—respectful of its great neighbor only by default.

II F 19 · ST. PATRICK'S CATHEDRAL
Fifth Avenue, 50th to 51st streets
James Renwick, Jr., 1879; towers, 1888
· ARCHBISHOP'S RESIDENCE
452 Madison Avenue, NW corner 50th Street
James Renwick, Jr., 1880
· RECTORY
460 Madison Avenue, SW corner 51st Street
James Renwick, Jr., 1880
· LADY CHAPEL
St. Patrick's, behind altar
Charles T. Mathews, 1906

St. Patrick's has neither the dark, theatrical passion of Upjohn's Trinity Church (I A 5) nor the graceful inventiveness of Renwick's own Grace Church (I G 13). It is a large, formal mix of English and French Gothic elements, and the end result is rather stuffy and dry. Part of the problem is that the building seems to want to be on an open site—it makes no attempt to relate to the Manhattan street grid, as at Goodhue's St. Thomas Church up the street (II G 4), and there is no element of it that works as a lively element in the cityscape, as the towers of both Trinity and Grace churches do. And the absence of flying buttresses makes for a certain blandness. But if the Lady Chapel added to the rear has a more pleasing delicacy, this is undoubtedly a major monument of the Gothic Revival. It is just the Gothic Revival grown too self-assured, too successful, too proud to prove itself.

II F 20 · OLYMPIC TOWER
645 Fifth Avenue, NE corner 51st Street
Skidmore, Owings & Merrill, 1976
public space: Chermayeff, Geismar & Associates; Zion & Breen; Levien,
Deliso's & White; Abel, Bainsson, 1977

This is the one that isn't the Galleria (II F 8), and it was far more successful economically, but, one suspects, for reasons of skillful marketing, not good architecture. All of the uses—ground-floor retail, public arcade, offices, condominium apartments—are covered in a bland skin of dark-brown glass. It is just one big slab, with no definition on the outside as to what is going on inside and no variation in the shape at top, middle, or bottom. The apartments are laid out like ordinary Third Avenue high rises, with the added amenities of floor-to-ceiling glass windows, marble bathrooms, and slightly better-detailed kitchens, but none of these do enough to remove this building from the high place it occupies on the If You Can Afford to Live Here You Can Afford to Live Somewhere Better list.

The public space, for which rentable space was granted, is better detailed than its opposite number at the Galleria, but empty of life—a big lobby with a chair or two. It is so uninviting from the outside that a sign had to be put up reminding the public that access to this through-block, waterfall-possessing arcade was permitted.

II F 22 · *Paley Park*

II F 19 & 20 · *Spires of St. Patrick's Cathedral, with Olympic Tower in the background, and, at the left, 650 and 666 Fifth Avenue (II G 3)*

II F 21 · CARTIER, INC.
651 Fifth Avenue, SE corner 52nd Street
Robert W. Gibson, 1905
remodeled as shop: William Welles Bosworth, 1917
4 East 52nd Street wing: C. P. H. Gilbert, 1905

The unused development rights over Cartier were transferred to the Olympic Tower (II F 20), helping it achieve its considerable height. Well, one cannot blame a decent Italian Renaissance mansion like this for the political manipulations surrounding its value as real estate; this is one of Fifth Avenue's better houses, and one of the only survivors of the age when

Fifth Avenue below Central Park was a residential district. The best detail is the set of pilasters and pediment set onto the middle of the 52nd Street façade, like a ghost of a portico, or like a piece of jewelry adorning a body. The shop was skillfully remodeled into Cartier's American headquarters after only twelve years as a townhouse.

II F 22 · PALEY PARK
3 East 53rd Street
Zion & Breen; Albert Preston Moore, 1967

Utterly dignified and restful, this is a model for understated, civilized urban plazas. The gray brick strikes a sophisticated tone that is appropriate for the East Fifties; the furniture is good, and the waterfall both screens out street noise and brings a sense of nature to a place that neither could nor should be lushly landscaped.

II F 23 · ST. REGIS HOTEL
2 East 55th Street
Trowbridge & Livingston, 1904
addition: Sloan & Robertson (?), 1925

That bulbous bronze sentry box out front is really the best thing about this hotel; along with the wonderful, anachronistic ST. REGIS CAB CALL sign above the marquee, it does more than the architecture to set the St. Regis's image. But the architecture is very good indeed—this building with its elaborate mansard roof and rich marble lobby comes closer, perhaps, than any other building in New York to resembling a Parisian apartment house of its period, stretched to a New York height.

II F 24 · CORNING GLASS BUILDING
717 Fifth Avenue, SE corner 56th Street
Harrison, Abramovitz & Abbe, 1959

This 28-story tower of green glass is probably Harrison & Abramovitz's best work in New York, small as it is compared with the firm's other projects, such as the western additions to Rockefeller Center (II G 1). Corning Glass is discreet and understated, as slick as Skidmore, Owings & Merrill's smooth glass-walled façades and a great deal less aggressive. The white entrance to the Steuben Glass showroom on Fifth Avenue is a reminder of how difficult the problem of punching an entrance into a sheer glass tower is; adding a doghouse as a vestibule, as was done here, isn't the solution. But the little reflecting pool is pleasant, and the overall feeling is one of a graciousness possessed by few other recent Fifth Avenue buildings.

II F 25 · BONWIT TELLER
721 Fifth Avenue, NE corner 56th Street
Warren & Wetmore, 1928–29
remodeled by Ely Jacques Kahn, 1930
· TIFFANY & CO.
727 Fifth Avenue, SE corner 57th Street
Cross & Cross, 1940

Bonwit's, built originally as the A. T. Stewart store and remodeled by Ely Jacques Kahn for Bonwit Teller, is Art Deco at its most grandiose and formal—figures in bas-relief and abstracted urns atop the façade piers. If the impulse was classicizing, it appeared almost flamboyant beside Cross & Cross's new home for Tiffany & Co. next door, where formality and order have become all. The ease with which Art Deco could slide into late classical is worth noting, however—as is the impressive compatibility of the two buildings, which join to form a handsome stone block-front that is the very image of chic Fifth Avenue. Oddly, the more stylized Bonwit Teller has the more modest and ordinary interior shopping space (remodeled into a mirror-filled floor in 1977 by Kenneth Walker), while Tiffany has a rather joyfully pompous main selling floor.

II F 26 · GENERAL MOTORS BUILDING
767 Fifth Avenue, 58th to 59th streets
Edward Durell Stone, Emery Roth & Sons, 1968

A decade has done little to ameliorate the damage this marble-clad pile of pretense has inflicted on the streetscape. General Motors is a 50-story slab, with marble-covered piers rising unbroken for the building's full height. The strong verticality gives it a bit of the air of an early modernist building, such as the Daily News (II D 11), whereas the marble and bay windows and huge round chandelier in the ground-floor auto showroom strike an entirely more pretentious and self-indulgent note. The whole thing ends up looking like what we might have gotten if Raymond Hood had designed a Miami Beach hotel.

But General Motors is less amusing than that, for its problem goes far deeper than incongruous architectural styles. The site is Grand Army Plaza, once one of the city's most civilized outdoor spaces, bordered and defined by the Plaza Hotel (II G 12), Bergdorf Goodman, 745 Fifth Avenue, and the Savoy-Plaza Hotel. The plaza was a true outdoor room, its walls the masonry walls of the buildings around it, its furniture the Pulitzer Fountain. General Motors occupies the site that once held the Savoy-Plaza, and instead of being placed out to the building line of Fifth Avenue, as the Savoy was, it has been set far, far back, with an unattractive hole of a sunken plaza in front. In one gesture the wall of Grand Army Plaza was taken away and the sense of a room was destroyed forever.

What, you wonder, is the point of adding another plaza to what had been New York's best plaza to start with? Making it bigger only destroyed it, and General Motors' own plaza, sunk below grade as it is, can hardly be considered a major amenity. Here, perhaps more than anywhere else in midtown Manhattan, the urgency of seeing buildings as parts of larger contexts and not as isolated objects unto themselves makes itself felt.

II F 27 · FULLER BUILDING
41 East 57th Street
Walker & Gillette, 1929

Good black-and-white Art Deco, with a fine, slender tower done in a sort of geometric, faintly Aztec motif. The top is neatly handled as a boxy, squared-off crown, and the entrance, with a clock and sculpted figures by Elie Nadelman, is grand in a rather romantic, voluptuous way that breaks slightly from the style of the rest of the building. Worth a look are the mosaic tile floors in the lobby, which in one panel attempts to picture in tile the Fuller Company's former home, the Flatiron Building.

II F 27 · *Detail of the Fuller Building*

II G 1 · ROCKEFELLER CENTER
Fifth to Sixth avenues, 48th to 50th streets
Reinhard & Hofmeister; Corbett, Harrison & MacMurray; Hood & Fouilhoux, 1931–40

> *Jim said he would not mind standing all day in Radio City, where the French and British shops and the travel offices were, and the evergreens at Christmas and the tulips in the spring and where the fountains in summer sprayed ceaselessly around Mr. Manship's golden boy and where exhibition fancy skaters salved their egos in the winter. If he grew tired of the skaters, Jim said he would not mind standing and staring up and up, watching the mass of building cut into the sky. It made him know what people wanted and what they thought.*
>
> —John P. Marquand, *So Little Time*

At Rockefeller Center, almost everything that a city—or at least New York—should be comes together: skyscrapers, plazas, movement, detail, views, stores, cafés. It is all of a piece, yet it is able to appear possessed of infinite variety at the same time. It is as much a part of the office worker's New York as of the tourist's, as much a part of the shopper's New York as of the skater's. It was conceived as a place in which monumental architecture would spur both business and culture to new heights, and it has come remarkably close to fulfilling that somewhat naïve goal. It is surely the parent of every large-scale urban complex every American downtown has built ever since—from Atlanta's Peachtree Center to Hartford's Constitution Center to San Francisco's Embarcadero Center—and it is no insult

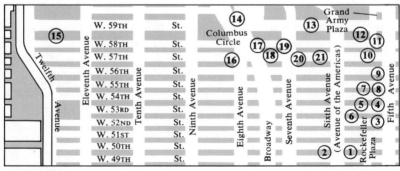

II G 1 · *Rockefeller Center*

to any of these to say that Rockefeller Center still remains far and away the finest such development ever built.

Designed and built throughout the 1930's by a consortium of architects which included Raymond Hood as its central design figure, the center grouped skyscrapers in a coherent plan, daringly innovating in terms of urban design by mixing retail, theater, and office use and including underground concourses and roof gardens, yet firmly basing itself in traditional Beaux-Arts principles with its axial arrangement of buildings, reliance on masonry and sculptural ornament. The Beaux-Arts quality of the original center grouping was long downplayed by critics eager to hail the complex as exclusively avant-garde. Today, with modernism not the appealing promised land it once was, these conservative aspects of the center are as pleasing as the advanced ones. The center's wealth of Art Deco detail is an example: nothing is more attuned to romantic fantasies of New York than the RCA Building's black-granite lobby, the Rainbow Room's ornamental framing of a seventieth-floor view, or the utter extravaganza of the Radio City Music Hall lobby, Art Deco's true shrine.

It is best to begin an exploration by giving in to the Beaux-Arts leanings of the complex and approaching it on its main formal axis—down the promenade which leads from Fifth Avenue to the sunken plaza between the Maison Française and the British Empire Building. The sense is of a clear order, the low, symmetrical masses of the French and British buildings defining a comfortable pedestrian street between them and enforcing a clear sense of direction toward the central plaza and the entire complex's major focus, the RCA Building at 30 Rockefeller Plaza.

Both the plaza and the RCA Building are strong magnets, pulling you down the gentle slope of the promenade toward them. The plaza is the only sunken plaza in New York that makes sense, and that is because it is really a piece of theater—we look down at the movement of the ice skaters within it, we do not go into it ourselves. (In the summer, when it turns into a café, it is far less successful, although still a great deal more pleasant than most sunken plazas.) The Paul Manship sculpture of Prometheus is a further aid to the plaza—it pulls the eye forward, and keeps it from looking only down into the center of the plaza floor.

From the promenade the Prometheus statue looks like a great brooch pinned to the bottom of the cascading mass of the RCA Building, and thus it serves visually to join the tower to the plaza in front of it. The tower itself is one of the best slabs ever built—it is a narrow slice of masonry, but its north and south sides avoid the look of too much sheer surface by virtue of their carefully wrought symmetrical setbacks. It shares with all the buildings skin of vertical strips of Indiana limestone with dark metal spandrels. Like the center itself, the form of 30 Rockefeller Plaza is a fundamentally modernist element, varied and made traditional to just the extent needed to provide visual, even romantic, interest.

From the walkway around the plaza, brilliant on a sunny day as flags flap in the breeze, the pinwheel arrangement of the main grouping of towers becomes visible. The RCA Building is the focus, the International Building at 630 Fifth Avenue is a balancing parallel mass, while One Rockefeller Plaza is set perpendicularly, bringing motion to the whole composition.

Four interiors are worth a look. The lobby of RCA is a setting for a 1930's movie about corporate power, pulsing with the energy of capitalism both real and romantic. (The murals, incidentally, by José Maria Sert, replaced an earlier set by Diego Rivera that was removed at the order of John D. Rockefeller, Jr., when the artist refused to alter a panel glorifying Lenin.)

The lobby of 10 Rockefeller Plaza, once Eastern Air Lines' headquarters, has a mural tracing the history of transportation and a rather pleasing stair, something of a miniature version of the grand staircase in the Radio City Music Hall foyer. The best stair in one of the office towers, however, is not a stair at all but the escalator in the lobby of 630 Fifth Avenue—it marches up powerfully, right on axis with Lee Lawrie's Atlas sculpture in front and

II G 1 · *RCA Building at Rockefeller Center*

II G 1 · *Promenade at Rockefeller Center, looking toward the RCA Building*

the view of St. Patrick's Cathedral through the window. Here, in one of the few such instances in modern architecture, the escalator has become a true triumphal staircase.

The most famous and, appropriately, the most beloved interior anywhere in Rockefeller Center is that of Radio City Music Hall. Designed by the center's architects with Donald Deskey, the music hall was a theater meant to bring into the lives of every moviegoer all the grandeur the 1930's could summon up. The Art Deco style as it is used here is innocent, but never corny. The grand foyer's sweeping staircase and precisely patterned Art Deco rug, the sleek black smoking lounge below, and the rest rooms that were once filled with fine murals (a Stuart Davis graced the men's room, and is now in the Museum of Modern Art) all remain as testaments to the Music Hall's design quality. Image was everything here—a world of sleekness and luxury, the life of long black Packards, top hats, champagne, and Lalique crystal. If it never really existed, no matter; it was the job of the Music Hall to sustain the illusion that it did, and that everyone could have a part of it.

But it is this very sense of there being something in this place for everyone that, ultimately, defines and ennobles Rockefeller Center. The meaning of this place comes from its ability to be so many things at once—a symbolic center of midtown Manhattan, yet a private enclave all its own; a formal array of majestic towers, yet a contemporary center of street life. None of the buildings is truly great by itself, but taken together the elements of the complex do become great: they are the finest reminder that exists of the principle that in the making of an urban place, the whole is more than the sum of the parts.

II G 2 · ROCKEFELLER CENTER EXTENSION
Sixth Avenue, west side, 47th to 51st streets
· TIME & LIFE BUILDING
1271 Sixth Avenue
Harrison & Abramovitz, 1959
· EXXON BUILDING
1251 Sixth Avenue
Harrison & Abramovitz & Harris, 1973
· McGRAW-HILL BUILDING
1221 Sixth Avenue
Harrison & Abramovitz & Harris, 1973
· CELANESE BUILDING
1211 Sixth Avenue
Harrison & Abramovitz & Harris, 1974

Westward flows Rockefeller Center, but not to the promised land. Harrison & Abramovitz, successor firm to Corbett, Harrison & MacMurray, was the only survivor of the original Rockefeller Center team, and so it got the job in the mid-1960's to expand the complex, and there may never have been a case in which a lesson that an architect was literally staring in the face—the original Rockefeller Center grouping—was so misunderstood. Here, largely due to the refusal of both architect and client to understand what

II G 2 · *Rockefeller Center extensions, from the left: Celanese Building, McGraw-Hill Building, Exxon Building*

II G 1 · *Associated Press Building at Rockefeller Center, sculpture by Isamu Noguchi*

made the original Rockefeller Center buildings so distinguished (although, to be fair, current zoning laws didn't help), we have four ponderous towers, three of which are almost identical. They are all set back from the street on wide plazas, with none of the life and joy of the original buildings. They are better than the incoherent mess of Third Avenue in that they do have a certain unified and, indeed, powerful presence, but that is all.

II G 3 · 650 FIFTH AVENUE
SW corner 52nd Street
John Carl Warnecke & Associates, 1978
· 666 FIFTH AVENUE
52nd to 53rd streets
Carson, Lundin & Shaw, 1957

From a purely aesthetic standpoint, these are just two clichés, each of its own era. No. 650 is for the 1970's—horizontal bands of windows alternating with reddish granite—while No. 666 is an embossed aluminum patterned skin that is a fine example of the decorative silliness common in the 1950's. The newer building is more dignified, certainly, and the solution it represents is surely better than the previous decade's cliché, the bargain-basement Mies of the 1960's. Whether this makes 650 Fifth Avenue—built for the Shah of Iran's Pahlevi Foundation—a good building is another matter.

Urbanistically, however, both buildings are decent. No. 650, thanks to provisions of the new Fifth Avenue Special Zoning District, is built out to the street, with a setback at a good mid-rise level. No. 666 anticipated these provisions: it is a very correctly massed building with a strong base holding the street line and a tower rising from the center. The ground floor is lined with stores and has a pedestrian arcade cutting through—an enlightened piece of urbanism indeed for the generally regressive 1950's.

II G 4 · ST. THOMAS CHURCH
Fifth Avenue, NW corner 53rd Street
Cram, Goodhue & Ferguson, 1914

This is surely the best Gothic church in midtown Manhattan, and a truly urban church like few others. St. Patrick's (II F 19) seems to want to be off in a tiny village somewhere, its towers rising over cottages set in crooked lanes; St. Thomas was made to be on a Manhattan street and nowhere else. It had no precise model—there are both French and English elements, brilliantly melded into a composition that sits with solidity and assurance on Fifth Avenue. St. Thomas is not symmetrical: the heavy tower on the left side of the façade exists to anchor the church on its corner site and act as a pivot around that corner. The building's urbanistic role, in other words, is to turn that corner, and it does it with such strength that St. Thomas easily holds its own amidst its skyscraper neighbors, though it was designed for a smaller Fifth Avenue of mansions.

Inside, the dazzling white reredos behind the altar is the work of Goodhue with Lee Lawrie, the sculptor; it is the central focus of a truly lush Gothic interior. The reredos is credited firmly to Goodhue, one of the greatest eclectic architects of American history, while the design of the building itself is a subject of some dispute, with certain scholars seeing it as the work of Goodhue's partner, Ralph Adams Cram, and others sure that it was Goodhue's own. Cram's work tended to be somewhat dry, and St. Thomas is so brilliant and original a composition that it is hard not to feel that it came from Goodhue's hand. And the tendency of the façade not merely to break from Gothic precedent, but also to mass intricate details together and play them off against larger, smooth surfaces—suggesting Goodhue's later Spanish Baroque work in California—seems to further underscore the notion that this is Bertram Goodhue's, not Ralph Adams Cram's, building.

II G 5 · THE MUSEUM OF MODERN ART
11 West 53rd Street
Philip L. Goodwin and Edward Durell Stone, 1939
additions: Philip Johnson, 1951, 1964

The original Museum of Modern Art building, designed by Philip L. Goodwin and, back before he turned to making pastry instead of buildings, Edward Durell Stone, is one of New York's great International Style structures. It enunciated a gospel that the museum, its staff, and its architects believed in fully; there was no question in any of their minds that this was what God had ordained the mid-twentieth century to be about, and this building was, as much as anything, a missionary center.

When it stood alone among the brownstones of West 53rd Street, it could make its statement with powerful drama. It was a bold box of opaque glass, marble, and strip windows of clear glass, topped off by a penthouse roofed by a portholed canopy that was itself like a cornice for the entire building. Side walls of tile, visible as the flat building projected out from the more articulated brownstone façades, enhanced the contrast with the existing buildings. It was not much of a formula—such breaks with context have generally been quite destructive—but this one got away with it.

It began to change when Philip Johnson added a Miesian wing to the west in 1951, and it lost still more of its character when the large Johnson wing to the east and the new canopy were added in 1964. The Johnson additions are handsome in themselves, but they have the unfortunate tendency to squeeze the original building like bookends.

Johnson's sins can be forgiven for his sculpture garden, however: as good an open space as exists in New York City. It is a sublime and graceful mix of fountains, platforms, pools, and plantings, all in perfect balance with one another and with the works of art displayed therein. The gray stone is rich, yet restrained, and the mood is one of utter tranquillity yet of urban presence at the same time. Plans for the museum's latest addition, to be built to the designs of Cesar Pelli, will alter the garden a fair amount, and will result in the replacement of Johnson's west wing and several neighboring buildings with a slick, glass gallery extension and a glass apartment tower.

II G 5 · *Museum of Modern Art*

II G 4 · *St. Thomas Church*

II G 6 · CBS BUILDING
51 West 52nd Street
Eero Saarinen & Associates, 1965
Interiors: Carson, Lundin & Shaw, with Knoll planning unit

CBS is decent architecture and terrible urbanism, the precise opposite of 666 Fifth Avenue (II G 3). Saarinen's only skyscraper has been overly praised, which, given the mediocrity of its neighbors on Sixth Avenue, may be understandable. But when viewed in absolute terms, this is a rather flawed building. The granite-clad tower stands absolutely aloof, in a depressed "plaza" of its own making. The lack of an entrance from Sixth Avenue, where there are stairs down from the sidewalk placed as if only to tease, is especially galling. This is the building as pure object, not the building as a part of a complex, functioning city.

As an object, however, it is not without merit. The triangular columns covered in dark granite and rising without a break to the building's full 38-story height have a considerable dignity to them. Indeed, the whole building has a presence that makes it instantly clear that this is a serious piece of architectural business, and not a cheap make-a-buck game of real estate speculation, and for that, one should be grateful. But if only Saarinen hadn't felt he had to make this building stand so apart from its context, so assertive about the superiority to its neighbors that no one would deny it possesses. CBS standing in the middle of Sixth Avenue's mediocrity is like a duchess who goes to a sleazy party and, as if to minimize its impact on her reputation, refuses to talk to anyone.

II G 7 · ROCKEFELLER APARTMENTS
17 West 54th Street
Harrison & Fouilhoux, 1936

A very fine, very understated building. The rounded bay windows rise floor upon floor to create half-cylinders on the façade, bringing rhythm to the overall design; the detailing, especially of the front entrance, is spare but possessed of an appealing finesse. It is indeed a splendid backdrop to the garden of the Museum of Modern Art, which it faces. Together the Rockefeller Apartments and the museum garden create a remarkably serene urban presence.

II G 6 · *CBS Building*   **II G 7** · *Rockefeller Apartments*

II G 8 · UNIVERSITY CLUB
1 West 54th Street
McKim, Mead & White, 1899

This one was Charles McKim's, and it is more formal, more proper than what Stanford White would have wrought. But along with the Morgan Library (II C 10) it is McKim's best surviving work. This is an over-whelming Renaissance palazzo, with far more life to it than the Morgan Library has, and yet, as with all of McKim's work, no matter how much elegance there is, nothing is ever excessive, and there is never a hint of self-indulgence. Stanford White could occasionally go just over the line of restraint, though he did so with inventiveness and delicacy; McKim always stopped short.

The façade is worth a careful look. McKim has hidden a very high building of seven stories in what looks to be a three-story façade. And it *is* a three-story façade, by the Renaissance details which define it—three grand stories separated by string courses. The windows for the intermediate floors are slipped in as if they were ornaments atop the great arched windows of the main stories. The interiors, not open to the public, are especially notable: the dining room is among the great public rooms of New York.

II G 9 · RIZZOLI INTERNATIONAL BOOKSTORE
712 Fifth Avenue, between 55th and 56th streets
A. S. Gottlieb, 1908
renovation: Ferdinand Gottlieb, 1964

A good, typical Fifth Avenue building of its period, made into a most remarkable store—a bookstore that comes closer to being a club than a retail establishment. Rizzoli is warm and rich, with paneled walls and long corridors and tables full of books. There is a sort of central space, with arms extending east to Fifth Avenue and north to 56th Street, but what is remarkable is how well this store succeeds in establishing an aura of grandeur without any really major space at all. It feels as imposing in its way as the great rooms of the University Club feel in theirs, yet this is never cold, never intimidating, always able to strike the perfect balance between monumentality and warmth.

Rizzoli was at its best in its early days just over a decade ago, when one could stop there late at night, sip coffee and hear baroque music; now it is just the paneling, the chandeliers, and the books themselves that provide diversion.

II G 10 · SOLOW BUILDING
9 West 57th Street
Skidmore, Owings & Merrill, 1974

The richer, better-detailed uptown brother of the Grace Building (II E 2). The fact that more money was obviously spent here merely makes this

II G 10 · *Base of the Solow Building*

II G 8 · *University Club*

travesty of an urban building all the sadder—the developer, Sheldon Solow, wanted a very special office building and he was prepared to pay for it. Skidmore, Owings & Merrill partner Gordon Bunshaft wanted to play a game, and Solow bought it. The result is a swooping form that breaks the street line of 57th Street, inserting itself into that civilized block with extraordinary arrogance. There are many fine details here, but they can hardly make up for the fact that the scale and the shape of 57th Street can never be restored, and we have yet another part of Manhattan gone victim to the idea that a flamboyant form that may be interesting in itself is acceptable wherever it is put. From the north, incidentally, this forms a depressing black backdrop to the Plaza Hotel, so this building does double damage.

There was so much interest here in keeping the building sleek and cold that retail facilities were banished to a basement arcade. No store owner in his right mind wants to be underground (even Rockefeller Center's underground concourse, the best such place, has never been a complete success), and these stores were never rented. The arcade is empty and closed, a monument to the foolishness of trying to force retail uses off the street, where they belong.

II G 11 · SHEZAN RESTAURANT
4 West 58th Street
Gwathmey Siegel, 1976

This Pakistani restaurant is housed in what had been a dismal basement, and it presented a particular architectural challenge. Gwathmey Siegel met it with immense skill—the space is divided into a bar and dining room, with gray carpeted walls, travertine floors, aluminum acoustical tile reflecting candlelight so that the entire ceiling appears bronze in color, and imitation suede banquettes and Cesca chairs. The room manages the remarkable trick of being slick and cool and soft and gentle at the same time, and is among the very best of the few architect-designed restaurants in New York.

II G 12 · THE PLAZA HOTEL
Fifth Avenue at 59th Street
Henry J. Hardenbergh, 1907
addition: Warren & Wetmore, 1921

This has been pulled and pushed, twisted and turned, modernized and restored and expanded and altered more than any other building in New York, and it still comes out on top. The Plaza is a masterwork of Henry Hardenbergh, and it is surely the greatest hotel building in New York. By 1907, more than two decades after the Dakota (III B 9), Hardenbergh's style had softened somewhat. His sources had become more classical and more French than German and Flemish; hence the Plaza's great mansard, recalling a French Renaissance château, and its columned porticoes.

But what is most important here is that Hardenbergh's skill at pure composition, at the arrangement of masses and surfaces and details in original and visually pleasing ways, is as evident here as in any of his earlier work. The Plaza was built for a remarkable site—behind an open square and adjacent to a corner of Central Park, and it commands this double-fronted urban site as a great châateau commands a rural vista. There is a strong base of marble running along both the Fifth Avenue and Central Park South sides; central sections of white glazed brick, broken up by projecting end pavilions and splendid round corner towers; and a richly ornamented mansard, which evolves into large gables on Fifth Avenue to mark that avenue's more formal identity.

That sumptuous exterior is virtually intact, and after a recent cleaning, looks quite splendid. The interior, however, is in less happy shape—the Palm Court lost its Tiffany glass roof years ago during the Plaza's brief stint as a Hilton-chain hotel, and the other public spaces, such as the splendid parkside Edwardian Room, have had their ups and downs. Only Hardenbergh's great Oak Room, a somber and grand space which suggests that a treaty will be brought for your signature along with your meal, has remained wholly intact, and it is without question one of New York's incomparable public interiors.

The Plaza has been weakened in the overall urban scheme of things by the arrival of the General Motors Building (II F 26) and the Solow Building (II G 10). The Plaza's plaza, the great front yard containing the Pulitzer Fountain, is by no means the well-defined and impressive urban space it once was, though it is still pleasing. One is left with the sense that the Plaza has had to battle both enemies without in the form of hostile neighboring structures and enemies within in the form of well-meaning renovations, and that is a lot to ask of any building. This one, as well known to New Yorkers as Grand Central Terminal or the Empire State Building and more beloved, surely, than any other landmark in town, has kept its integrity.

II G 13 · CENTRAL PARK SOUTH

This is a part of town that was made for transients more than for residents. It seems always to be filled with tourists and visitors, in spite of its ample quantity of luxury apartment houses, which themselves seem to be occupied as pied-à-terre more than as full-time residences. There is, thus, a sense of movement and action here, very different from the repose of upper Park or upper Fifth avenues.

The street begins at the Plaza and ends at Columbus Circle, urban spaces of varying degrees of success, each demarking a corner of Central Park. The three blocks in between contain only one truly great building, the Plaza Hotel, but several very good ones, and the structures join together to create a street wall that is one of New York's best: a veritable cliff of masonry, solidly cutting a line between the hardness of the city and the softness of Central Park.

The first block of Central Park South contains, just after the Plaza Hotel, the Park Lane Hotel at No. 36 (Emery Roth & Sons, 1971), a 46-story tower of limestone that makes at least some of the right gestures—it is built out to the street, holding the all-important building line, and the arches of its base form a reasonably gracious echo of the base of the Plaza two doors away. The repeated arches at the top seem cheaply cute, however, and the overall design, including the Louis-the-Whatever lobby, is mediocre. Far better is the same firm's St. Moritz Hotel at No. 50 (1931), with its handsomely massed terrace setbacks and pleasant lobby, which still contains some fine original Art Deco lettering. Beside the St. Moritz is Rumpelmayer's, the celebrated ice-cream parlor that makes a design statement of its own—ice cream sodas combined with a stock of stuffed animals—that is imprinted on the memory of virtually every upper-middle-class child who grew up in Manhattan.

The next block, beyond Sixth Avenue, begins with a group of decent but unremarkable apartment houses and hotels. Two hotels farther west are significant, however: the Hampshire House (Caughey & Evans, 1931) and the Essex House (Frank Grad, 1930). Both are wonderful additions to the

II G 12 · *Plaza Hotel, with the Solow Building* (II G 10) *in the background*

II G 14 · *New York Cultural Center, with the monument to Christopher Columbus in the foreground*

skyline—the Hampshire House with its green peaked roof (recalling the shape of the mourned Savoy-Plaza, razed to make way for the General Motors Building) and the Essex House with its fine setbacks. The Essex House steps back grandly, like a mountain, a perfect realization of the romantic visionary drawings of skyscrapers as massed mountains done by Hugh Ferris in the 1920's. There is some fine Art Deco detailing on the façade (gone, alas, from the interior), whereas the Hampshire House has a black and mirrored lobby that seems incomplete without a lingering Carole Lombard. The block is completed by the New York Athletic Club (York & Sawyer, 1929) a 20-story version of an Italian Renaissance palace that may or may not work very well as a gym, but thanks to the fact that its design was done by New York's leading firm of bank architects in the 1920's, clearly makes its users feel at home.

Across Seventh Avenue, Central Park South becomes solely the province of apartment houses. Three of the six on the block are worth special note. No. 200, the extravagant curving façade at the corner of Seventh Avenue (Wechsler & Schimenti, 1964) has been laughed at for years as New York's best piece of Miami Beach architecture. It looks better and better upon close examination. The swooping curve is not a bad way at all for a large avenue to meet Central Park, and it does no harm to the line of buildings along Central Park South. The narrow tower on top is an amusing imitation (no doubt unintentional) of Frank Lloyd Wright's Johnson Wax Company tower. The details are a bit crude and the fountain in front is downright awful, but these aspects aside, 200 Central Park South is worth taking seriously.

The only building of distinction on Central Park South that belongs to the Plaza Hotel's generation is the Gainsborough Studios at No. 222 (Charles W. Buckham, 1908). This could be a bit of West 67th Street (III B 8) misplaced eight blocks downtown, but the façade is far more interesting than anything on 67th Street. There is a portal of Ionic columns, with bas-reliefs above and a bust above that. At that point the fun is only beginning—there are several floors of studio windows above that, and then for the upper few floors the façade bursts into mosaic and a flurry of ornament at the top.

The street's last building is one of its very finest, No. 240 Central Park South (Mayer, Whittlesey & Glass, 1940). Here, urbanistic concerns were paramount, and the solution chosen was altogether different, and far more subtle, than that for No. 200 at the other end of the block. There, the corner was turned in a single curve, whereas at No. 240 a complex form consisting of a pair of towers atop a zigzag, garden-topped base was used. The base brings variety to storefronts and rhythm to the building's Columbus Circle façade; the overall massing emphasizes park views and brings individuality to apartment layouts. It is a remarkably sophisticated design, substantially ahead of its time in its knowing response to a difficult urban site.

II G 14 · COLUMBUS CIRCLE: Intersection of Broadway and Eighth Avenue

This is a chaotic jumble of streets that can be crossed in about fifty different ways—all of them wrong. It is really just a big traffic intersection, not a civic square or a park corner or any of the other things it pretends to be. Edward Durell Stone once suggested putting the columns from the demolished Pennsylvania Station around the circle, and that would have made tremendous sense, for it would have given this place some sense of definition and order. As it is, there is none—there are just three wretched buildings, two of which arrogantly ignore the shape and meaning of the circle and the third of which is so silly that, like an innocent child, it can hardly be blamed for its misbehavior.

The child, of course, is the old Gallery of Modern Art, a Huntington Hartford gift to New York designed by Edward Durell Stone. It was completed in 1965, and it is a marble box full of round holes and slender arches and set on spindly legs. The jokes about it being a Persian whorehouse are all tired now, but they *do* make sense; this surely does not look like anything Western—except perhaps a Western architect's misguided idea of what the Near East thinks is architecture.

The building is now empty, awaiting conversion into a new headquarters for the City of New York's Department of Cultural Affairs. It is probably as good a use as any, since the structure never worked even remotely well as a museum. It does, however, look surprisingly decent when viewed at a distance from upper Central Park West or Broadway—it becomes a bizarre, funny kind of monument from there, closer than anything New York has to the wonderful jokes of Claes Oldenburg. If only Stone had *intended* it that way.

The New York Coliseum (Leon & Lionel Levy, 1956) is a mass of gray brick that is stunningly banal, but so large that its ordinariness becomes a monumental intrusion into the cityscape. Almost as dull, and perhaps more disturbing still, is 15 Columbus Circle, or One Gulf & Western Plaza (Thomas E. Stanley, 1970), a slender tower that makes not the slightest attempt to relate to the complex shape of the site on which it sits. Instead, the architect chose to try to simplify the site by creating a "plaza" and placing the building's official front door on it; it is rarely used, and the whole thing is both ugly and pointless.

Some visual relief is provided by the Maine Memorial, H. Van Buren Magonigle's monumental sculpture of 1913 at the entrance to Central Park— it is a pedestal that provides a firmer anchor than any of the larger buildings, and the boat containing sculptor Attilio Piccirilli's figures seems about to sail right into the center of the circle. It is a grand, if sentimental, presence, which is more than can be said for the statue of Columbus, by Gaetano Russo (1892), which sits atop a column in the very center of the square, with Columbus looking as if he had been waiting since 1892 for a break in the traffic so that he might go somewhere more comfortable.

II G 15 · CONSOLIDATED EDISON PLANT / originally IRT POWERHOUSE
58th to 59th streets, Eleventh to Twelfth avenues
exterior: McKim, Mead & White, 1904

This is monumental industrial architecture—New York's version of the Battersea Power Station, as Robert Stern calls it. Shorn of its smokestacks, it is not quite so imposing as it once was, and, of course, it lacks the sense

II G 15 · *Detail of IRT Powerhouse (now Consolidated Edison plant)*

of raw, industrial power of so many such buildings. Indeed, the objective of Stanford White was to achieve a lightness that would belie the building's true function: hence the ornate decoration that recalls a McKim, Mead & White club. White's efforts were heroic, though today we tend to appreciate the very industrial side of this building that he was trying to obscure as much as his act of obscuring. But this nonetheless set a pattern for the collaboration of engineers and serious architects on such public works that is all too rarely repeated in our time.

II G 16 · HEARST MAGAZINE BUILDING
959 Eighth Avenue, SW corner 57th Street
Joseph Urban, 1928

Gloriously Hearstian—it could have been part of the movie set for *Citizen Kane,* so much does it fit the fantasy image that surrounded the legendary publisher. Joseph Urban's six-story pile, vaguely reminiscent of the architecture of the Viennese Secessionist movement, is utterly pretentious, with its seven-story columns rising up the façade and over the roof line, but this is a wonderful folly. Legend has it that the building was intended as the base for a higher skyscraper. Urban's plans did call for another seven stories, which were never built, but apparently that was all—the building really *was* intended to look as wonderfully bizarre as it does.

II G 17 · 225 WEST 57th STREET
Shaw, Waid & Willauer, 1909

A nice surprise, this piece of knockoff Louis Sullivan on 57th Street. It is extremely heavy-handed, but a lot of Chicago School ideas are here—

horizontal groups of windows with abstracted ornament in between. It's a good reminder that influence trickles down in architecture in funny ways, yielding objects that embrace and reject the ideas of a particular style at the same time.

II G 18 · ART STUDENTS LEAGUE
215 West 57th Street
Henry J. Hardenbergh, Walter C. Hunting, John C. Jacobsen, 1892

Hardenbergh after the Dakota and before the Plaza, here trying out his French Renaissance wings. This is a handsome structure, exceedingly well proportioned. The triple arch of the second floor, echoed on top in the forms of three square windows, and the expanse of sparsely ornamented façade at each end all join to make a composition that, as with most Hardenbergh, is a poem of balance.

II G 16 · *Hearst Magazine Building*

II G 18 · *Art Students League*

II G 19 · OSBORNE
205 West 57th Street
James E. Ware, 1885
· ALWYN COURT
180 West 58th Street
Harde & Short, 1909

Two of the city's best apartment houses. The Osborne seems at one moment classical, the next Chicago School, and it is such a deft mixture that it leaves one puzzled as to why Chicago skyscraper architecture seems such a dramatic break from classical styles. What does it, of course, is the very rough, heavily rusticated exterior of reddish stone, which creates a texture that seems to cover all stylistic aspects of the building like a blanket. There is a splendid rich lobby in original condition; unfortunately, the entrance no longer has its original portico and the ground floor has been converted into storefronts.

The Alwyn Court, one of three fine Manhattan buildings by the early twentieth-century's most appealingly named architects, is like a stone tapestry, so rich and intricate is its French Renaissance terra-cotta detailing.

Again, the ground floor has been altered, and the cornice is gone, but the overall loss is offset by the good condition of the rest of the structure.

II G 20 · CARNEGIE HALL
SE corner, 57th Street at Seventh Avenue
William B. Tuthill; William Morris Hunt, Dankmar Adler, consultants,
1891

Better as a piece of the city's cultural history than as architecture. The Italian Renaissance design is awkwardly proportioned, to say the least, and the 15-story tower of offices and studios adds awkward massing to so-so detailing. But this is important as an early example of mixed-use construction in the city—stores, studios, offices, and apartments were all combined with a concert hall—and the significance of Carnegie Hall to the city's history is considerable. The simple white auditorium, with splendid acoustics, is the best feature of the building architecturally.

II G 21 · MARBORO BOOKSTORE / originally HORN & HARDART
57th Street west of Sixth Avenue
Ralph Bencker, 1938

There is just one functioning Automat left in Manhattan (see II D 12), and it is not in one of the original Horn & Hardart Automat buildings that once squatted so confidently all over town. This, however, *is* an original Automat building, although it has been converted to a bookstore. But it has been left intact, unlike virtually every one of its brethren around New York, and one can still see all of the glory that the quarters of this unusual restaurant chain once represented: rounded masses of pinkish stone with a distinct pretense toward monumentality. It is Art Deco, and more a showroom than a restaurant. There was no reason, Horn & Hardart appeared to believe, that you couldn't eat cheap food in a palace.

III/UPTOWN

Detail of 11 East 62nd Street

A/CENTRAL PARK

"The grand-daddy of all American landscaped parks," says the American Institute of Architects Guide to New York City, but this only begins to hint at the vital importance these 843 acres have had for the history of American urbanism. Central Park is at once an aesthetic, an engineering, and a social accomplishment; its physical form not only created a new model for what parks should look like, but it represented a new attitude toward their reason for being as well. To Frederick Law Olmsted, the co-designer of Central Park, the park's crowds gathered "with an evident glee at the prospect of coming together, all classes largely represented, with a common purpose . . . each individual adding by his mere presence to the pleasure of all others, all helping to the greater happiness of each . . . poor and rich, young and old, Jew and Gentile."

Olmsted's idea, thus, was to create a democratic place, a piece of geography on which social classes, joined by a common desire to free themselves from the tensions of the man-made city, might mingle comfortably. The physical design of the park is so brilliant as to be worthy, perhaps, of being called New York's greatest single work of architecture, but to Olmsted it was only a means toward a social end. The creator of Central Park saw the city as a healthy and civilizing influence under proper circumstances, but he foresaw the oppressive effect it could have on the poor, and he sought in the design of the park an antidote not merely to the harshness of the physical city but to its rigid way of life. "What we want to gain is tranquility and rest to the mind," he said. "A great object of all that is done in a park, of all the art of a park, is to influence the minds of men through their imaginations."

Today Fifth Avenue, Central Park South, Central Park West, and Central Park North are sheer walls of masonry, their buildings a tight ring of brick and stone around the park. It was not always so; in 1856, when work on Central Park began, the city had not yet grown far enough north to reach the park site, let alone surround it. The land that was set aside for the park was a messy sequence of rocky ledges, swamps, and fields, much of it empty but for a large portion containing squatters' shanties.

The decision to build a park came after prolonged public pressure—New York, it was said in the 1840's by people who considered themselves knowledgeable on such matters, had nothing in the way of public open space to compare with the great cities of Europe, and if the city was truly to become the international metropolis it took pleasure in seeing itself as, something had to be done. And it had to be done fast—the city in the mid-

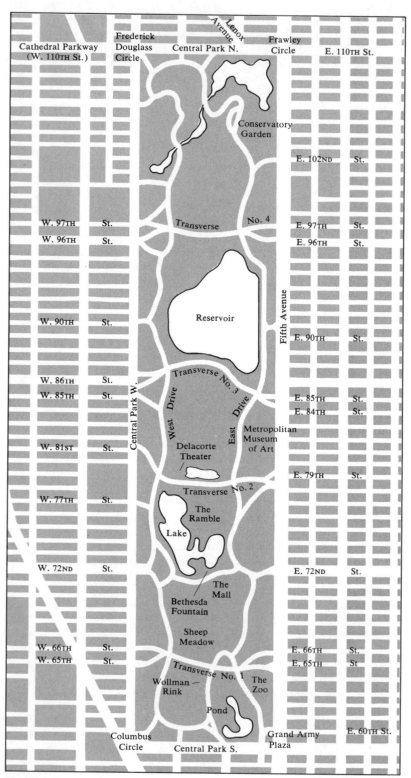

Cathedral Parkway
(W. 110TH St.)

Frederick
Douglass
Circle

Central Park N.

Lenox Avenue

Frawley
Circle

E. 110TH St.

Conservatory
Garden

E. 102ND St.

W. 97TH St.

W. 96TH St.

Transverse No. 4

E. 97TH St.

E. 96TH St.

W. 90TH St.

Reservoir

Fifth Avenue

E. 90TH St.

W. 86TH St.

W. 85TH St.

Transverse No. 3

E. 85TH St.

E. 84TH St.

Central Park W.

West Drive

East Drive

Metropolitan
Museum
of Art

W. 81ST St.

Delacorte
Theater

E. 79TH St.

W. 77TH St.

Transverse No. 2

The
Ramble

Lake

W. 72ND St.

E. 72ND St.

The
Mall

Bethesda
Fountain

Sheep
Meadow

W. 66TH St.

W. 65TH St.

E. 66TH St.

E. 65TH St

Transverse No. 1

Wollman
Rink

The
Zoo

Pond

Columbus
Circle

Central Park S.

Grand Army
Plaza

E. 60TH St.

nineteenth century was growing as Houston is in the mid-seventies; each year the need for a park was more urgent and the land available more scarce.

It was in 1853, after years of haggling, that the state legislature finally selected the present site, and it took another three years and $5.5 million to acquire all the land. Even before this process was finished, the gleam of increased real estate values shone in New York politicians' eyes: a movement started in the City Council to shave off a strip of land along the Fifth Avenue and Eighth Avenue (now Central Park West) borders for sale as villa sites.

Olmsted was on the staff as construction superintendent when the city decided to speed work along by holding a competition for a master plan for the park's completion. He at first hesitated to enter, fearful of conflict of interest, but he finally agreed and joined a young architect named Calvert Vaux in the preparation of a scheme they called "Greensward." They drew it on the dining-room table of Vaux's townhouse, and it took first prize.

"Greensward" went through some changes at the hands of Olmsted and Vaux, but it is essentially what was built. It is as dazzling a combination of landscapes as could be neatly compressed into a tight area; the genius of Central Park is that there is no single place, no particular kind of land, that could be called typical of it. We have the illusion that we are presented with an infinite variety of landscape experiences, each equally desirable. Olmsted and Vaux conceded in their initial report that "many types of natural scenery are not practicable to be introduced on the site of the Park—mountains, ocean, desert and prairie scenery, for example," but they balked at little else. Thus, there are dense, shrub-filled areas like the Ramble, where steep hills and twisted paths give way to surprise lawns; vast open areas like the Sheep Meadow, the Great Lawn, and the North Meadow; the formal Conservatory Garden at 104th Street; and the near wilderness of the ridges and woods at the northern end.

Somehow, this catalogue of landscapes is never too much. The meadows, gardens, and woods flow logically from one to the other. At the southern end, for example, one can enter at Scholars' Gate, at Fifth Avenue and 60th Street (all of the park entrances have such names; they are little used today, which, in the case of some of them, such as the Warriors' Gate in Harlem, seems just as well) and move up the East Drive, which rises gently as it curves into the park. The land drops off to the Pond at the left; the city gradually recedes to the right. It is becoming more and more pastoral, but just ahead, trees and statues aligned in a formal row appear. This is the park's one really ordered place, the one thing more French than English— a long promenade which opens out to a mall, then culminates in the elaborate terrace and sculptural group of Bethesda Fountain overlooking the lake.

Even this one touch of formality is set at a diagonal to the city's grid, as if to underscore Olmsted and Vaux's determination to keep every aspect of the park at a distance from the city's rigid order. And while the terrace's rich stonework (by Jacob Wrey Mould) and its luxurious steps and fountain could easily be part of a grandiose estate, they look not toward more order but across the lake toward the Ramble, one of the most pastoral of park views. In one sense, this is as romantic a place as there is in the park—an intricate terrace and fountain, set into a natural landscape as a springboard to a view. The view was given more drama by the erection in 1928 of the Beresford (III B 15), a massive apartment house at Central Park West and

III A · *View from the Pond including, from the left: 800 Fifth Avenue* (III D 3), *the Pierre and Sherry-Netherland hotels* (III D 2), *the General Motors Building* (II F 26) *and the Plaza Hotel* (II G 12)

81st Street whose three great towers loom over the trees like castles in the distance.

Views of the city from the park were something Olmsted and Vaux struggled to prevent, and when the city consisted of five- and six-story houses, they succeeded. Now, of course, the city imposes itself on park vistas constantly, but far from being a problem, this creates a sort of tension that brings drama to the landscape. The view of the midtown Manhattan skyline, spread out like an unfurled poster when seen from the north end of the Sheep Meadow, is as powerful as the great view of downtown from the harbor. Just as good is the same view from the bridge over the lake toward the Ramble. And from the southern end of the Sheep Meadow there is a rise topped by a rock or two; from there all of Central Park West, Manhattan's greatest linear skyline, becomes clear.

These views are spectacles of a sort. They have their more subtle counterparts: the Dakota looming over the foliage from the path that climbs the hill from the West Drive to the Central Park West and 72nd Street entrance; the San Remo apartment towers visible from the dense Ramble; the Guggenheim Museum seen from the west side of the Reservoir, looking as if it were floating on the water.

If Olmsted's fear that the intrusion of city buildings into park vistas would be harmful has turned out to be wrong, we have had no such luck with his companion, and more serious, fear—that of destruction to the landscape itself by buildings within the park. He struggled valiantly to keep them out, while every politician and philanthropist, it would seem, has struggled to put them in. The result is more or less of a draw: Olmsted lost on the Metropolitan Museum (he gave in to political pressure and officially approved its presence in the park, and would no doubt be horrified at its expansion in our time) and he, or his spirit, lost on the insertion of the Wollman Memorial Rink, the Delacorte Theater, several playgrounds and, most horribly of all, several parking lots. Vaux designed some structures, including the Belvedere Castle, a splendid folly that is now, alas, a near ruin, and the Dairy, a fine little Gothic Revival building that was originally built to provide milk for nursing mothers in the park. Vaux and Mould were responsible for the Ladies' Pavilion, an enchanting cast-iron Victorian gazebo now restored and placed on a promontory overlooking the Lake's west shore, and Mould himself designed the sheepfold, the building near West 67th Street that has been expanded into the Tavern on the Green restaurant.

The recent renovation (Warner LeRoy and Paul K. Y. Chen, 1976) has given Central Park its most spectacular structure and one of the city's most remarkable eating places from a visual standpoint: a glass-enclosed room of chandeliers and pink and white and blue plaster ornament that makes you feel as if you had somehow gotten inside of a birthday cake. It is something out of the mind of that eccentric genius Warner LeRoy, and

III A · *Bethesda Fountain and the Lake*

much as one regrets the flow of commerce into the park, there is no question that it is dazzling. And the garden terrace beside the restaurant, with its view across the park to the Fifth Avenue skyline, is splendid.

Far more destructive to the park landscape than the Tavern have been the Wollman Rink, a concrete skating rink opened in 1951 that would be more appropriate as a bunker than an object in a park, and the Central Park Zoo, erected in 1934 behind the Arsenal on Fifth Avenue (III D 5). The zoo's central pool of seals has by now become a part of the city's legacy, but the whole place is an awkward intrusion into the park's rural atmosphere—and especially cruel to the animals forced into its cramped quarters. The zoo and the rink are both needless leftovers from the days when it was believed that the open space of the park was fair game for any civic use, an idea whose time should be long gone.

That notion has brought not only too many structures into the park, but too much pavement of any kind. The Tavern on the Green is surrounded on two sides by asphalt, making it, as Henry Hope Reed has observed, more like Tavern on the Parking Lot when viewed from the west or the south. And the park drives, which Olmsted and Vaux intended for leisurely carriage promenades, have been doubled in mileage since 1920 to accommodate automobile traffic interested not in seeing the park but in getting to the other side of it.

The roads and pedestrian paths cross over and under one another on bridges that are almost all different. Most are made of stone, but the best is of cast iron—Vaux's Bow Bridge, completed in 1979 and restored in 1974. It connects the Ramble with the main park area near the Bethesda Fountain by spanning the Lake with a form that curves so gracefully that it does not leap, or soar, or span; it seems to pour over the water.

The park is richer still in underpasses, of which the best is Vaux's Trefoil Arch under the East Drive in the mid-Seventies. Its form joins three curves into a sort of cloverleaf opening, and the effect is rather like walking through a fleur-de-lis. The underpasses, obviously, serve a functional purpose as well as an aesthetic one, but it is more than the routine avoidance of an occasional intersection: one of the crucial aspects of the Olmsted and Vaux plan was its complete separation of several kinds of traffic. Most significant here are the four transverse roads, which cut across the park below ground level, like open tunnels; the rest of the park landscape moves over and around them, so that the crosstown traffic which must move through the park is virtually invisible. The transverses never intersect with the drives at ground level, intended for more leisurely carriage rides, and a bridle-path system and a set of pedestrian paths are granted almost complete separation from intersection as well. It sounds not all that unusual today; it was radical planning indeed for the 1850's.

The park, in its hundred-odd years of existence, has in some ways succeeded beyond anyone's dreams. The paths and roads overflow with crowds on summer weekends; the Sheep Meadow fills to capacity for musical events; the athletic fields are almost constantly in use. The park drives, which have come so often in recent years to resemble another encroachment Olmsted fought against—a speedway—are now closed to automobile traffic during weekends and summer days for the benefit of bicyclists. The park has managed to attract all social classes as much as Olmsted had hoped—if one now hears Spanish as much as English on a Sunday afternoon, that is

III A · *Bow Bridge and the Lake, with the Majestic* (III B 10) *in the background*

merely an affirmation of the park fulfilling its role of cutting across class boundaries.

But the park's success has come at a price. The physical condition is abominable and getting worse, and ironically, the more successful the park is at fulfilling Olmsted's ideal of it as a democratic mixing place, the more difficult the problem of maintaining it will become. The crowds today are heavier than ever before; the more use the park gets, the farther it drifts from Olmsted's vision of pastoral order. The city's budget is now strained to the point where even routine maintenance is difficult, let alone the extreme maintenance, and in some cases rehabilitation, that the aging park requires. So today much of the park is awash with litter after a day of good weather, and in some areas like Bethesda Fountain, crowds are so heavy that Olmsted's pastoral dreams become a laughable joke. The sense is more of a subway crowd without the subway—and all too often with the subway's dirt, noise, and crime.

But these problems, too, are not just of our age. Olmsted foresaw them all, and the early archives of the park are full of references to crowd control, physical damage, and the lack of adequate budget for physical upkeep. In 1875 Olmsted wrote to the president of the park board to complain of inadequate maintenance funds—the park, he said, "has been in the condition of a farm 'running down.' " And a letter from 1877 reports on an unruly crowd that had trampled plantings, smashed benches, and stolen flowers.

Olmsted was conscious most of all of the social problems that can ensue when large groups of people from different cultures share a piece of common ground, and it is not likely that he would be surprised to hear a dispute in the park today between Puerto Ricans wishing to play their transistor radios and whites demanding silence. In 1863 the Board of Commissioners wrote that the park's population was "reared in different climes, and bringing to the metropolis ideas of social enjoyment differing as wildly as the temperature of the various countries of their origin . . . the amusements and routine of the daily life of the Sicilian and the Scotsman are dissimilar. Each brings with him the traditions and habits of his own country."

III A · *Northern half of Central Park, with the Receiving Reservoir at the bottom left*

The answer, the commissioners concluded, was what Olmsted had been calling for all along—"There is, however, a universality in nature that affords a field of enjoyment to all observers of her works." Leaving the park free as a natural landscape, uncluttered by organized activities of any kind, was the only way to keep social peace—the only way, in Olmsted's words, "to produce a certain influence in the minds of the people, and through this to make life in the city healthier and happier."

B/CENTRAL PARK WEST TO COLUMBUS AVENUE

III B 1 · LINCOLN CENTER FOR THE PERFORMING ARTS
Broadway to Amsterdam Avenue, 62nd to 66th streets
· **AVERY FISHER HALL (originally Philharmonic Hall)**
Max Abramovitz, 1962
interior reconstruction: Johnson/Burgee, 1976
· **NEW YORK STATE THEATER**
Philip Johnson and Richard Foster, 1964
· **VIVIAN BEAUMOUNT THEATER**
Eero Saarinen & Associates, 1965
· **LIBRARY AND MUSEUM OF THE PERFORMING ARTS**
Skidmore, Owings & Merrill, 1965
· **METROPOLITAN OPERA HOUSE**
Wallace K. Harrison, 1966
· **JUILLIARD SCHOOL OF MUSIC**
Pietro Belluschi, with Eduardo Catalano and Westermann & Miller, 1968

Travertine here covers a multitude of skins. These are, for the most part, banal buildings, dreary attempts to be classical that took the form they did not out of any deep belief in the values of classicism, but out of a fear on the part of the architects that their clients, the conservative boards of directors of the center's constituent organizations, would not accept anything else. This is the progenitor of every little "cultural center" in every upwardly mobile city everywhere, from Maine to California, but unlike New York's other notable prototype, Rockefeller Center (II G 1), Lincoln Center is merely the first, not the best.

Of the three façades that join to form the central plaza—the Metropolitan Opera House in the center, the New York State Theater to the left, and Avery Fisher Hall to the right—surely the best is Johnson's New York State Theater. Its paired columns play off against the even grid of the windows behind to bring at least some subtlety to the composition, whereas Abramovitz's Avery Fisher Hall is prissy and overdelicate, its columns

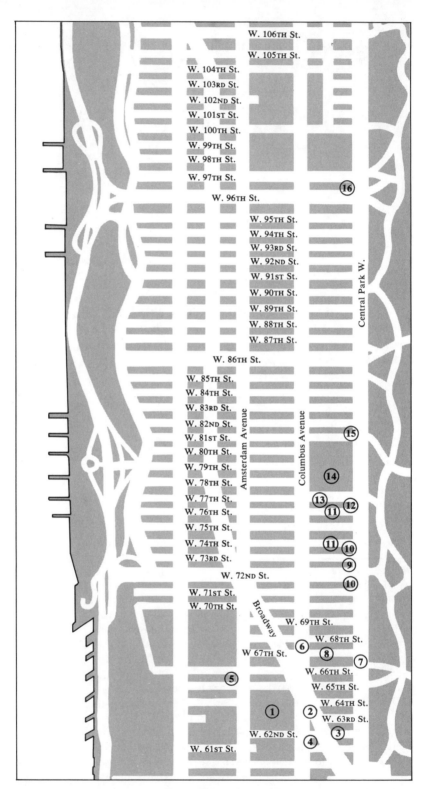

W. 106TH St.
W. 105TH St.
W. 104TH St.
W. 103RD St.
W. 102ND St.
W. 101ST St.
W. 100TH St.
W. 99TH St.
W. 98TH St.
W. 97TH St.
W. 96TH St.
W. 95TH St.
W. 94TH St.
W. 93RD St.
W. 92ND St.
W. 91ST St.
W. 90TH St.
W. 89TH St.
W. 88TH St.
W. 87TH St.
W. 86TH St.
W. 85TH St.
W. 84TH St.
W. 83RD St.
W. 82ND St.
W. 81ST St.
W. 80TH St.
W. 79TH St.
W. 78TH St.
W. 77TH St.
W. 76TH St.
W. 75TH St.
W. 74TH St.
W. 73RD St.
W. 72ND St.
W. 71ST St.
W. 70TH St.
W. 69TH St.
W 67TH St.
W. 68TH St.
W. 66TH St.
W. 65TH St.
W. 64TH St.
W. 63RD St.
W. 62ND St.
W. 61ST St.

Central Park W.
Amsterdam Avenue
Columbus Avenue
Broadway

III / UPTOWN   B / CENTRAL PARK WEST TO COLUMBUS AVE.

III B 1 · *Lincoln Center for the Performing Arts, from the left: New York State Theater, Metropolitan Opera House, Avery Fisher Hall*

narrowing toward the ground in a gesture that seems exhibitionistic and false. Harrison's Metropolitan Opera House is merely a pompous and simplistic form, made tolerable by a pair of unexceptional but colorful Chagall murals. The space between these three buildings, punctuated by a splendid fountain, is good, and can be especially pleasing on a warm summer night as café tables sprawl out from Avery Fisher Hall across the pavement.

Saarinen's Vivian Beaumont Theater would seem a bit heavy-handed in another context, but at Lincoln Center it is a veritable breath of fresh air. It is a building that sits handsomely at the west end of a reflecting pool, its austere lines aided significantly by a fine Henry Moore set within the pool; the siting creates the illusion that the building, which is in fact tightly crowded onto its site, has expansive space around it. The structure is shared by the Lincoln Center branch of the New York Public Library, which is tucked neatly in and around the Saarinen theater, surely the only time Skidmore, Owings & Merrill has been so willing to defer to the work of another architect.

The Juilliard School is probably the best building at Lincoln Center, but one says that reluctantly, because here, too, architecture is being graded on the curve. This would be a ho-hum Brutalist building if it were done in concrete and located somewhere else; here, the travertine brings a warmer texture, and the determination of Pietro Belluschi not to play the same two-bit classicizing game as the architects of the buildings on the main plaza did is appealing.

The strongly classical direction of these buildings was attacked quite sharply in the early 1960's, when, with modern architecture still an ideological force to be reckoned with, these structures appeared brazenly reactionary. Now it is not so easy to attack them on those grounds—the intellectual context today is more hospitable to buildings that allude to historical styles, and one is not so quick to condemn a building merely for not being "modern." But this change of intellectual climate hardly justifies Lincoln Center, for its fault never was in its classicism itself. What is wrong with these buildings is not that they are classicizing, it is that they are so bad at it—they are mediocre and slick classicism, with a heavy-handedness of form and a vulgarity of detail. (Indeed, lest it be thought that classicism is itself the villain, it is the State Theater, the most classical building here, that is the best.)

The interiors, like the buildings, range from a sort of ordinary corporate modern style of the 1960's (the auditoriums within the Juilliard School) to something far more embarrassing. The Metropolitan Opera House's red-and-gold auditorium has a shrillness to it that suggests Woolworth's more than the opera houses of old that it feebly imitates, and the New York State Theater—which has a magnificent sequence of spaces leading from low entrance to monumental entrance hall to auditorium—is, sadly, little better in its details. Philip Johnson's redesign of the auditorium of Avery Fisher Hall, done in association with the acoustician Cyril Harris, is lively and more tasteful, and, by default at least, is the best of the three large auditoriums.

III B 1 · *Plaza of the Vivian Beaumont Theater, sculpture by Henry Moore*

III B 1 · *North wall of the Metropolitan Opera House, sculpture by Alexander Calder*

III B 2 · AROUND LINCOLN CENTER

The economic impact of Lincoln Center has been enormous—this project may indeed break from sensible planning notions by its exile of theaters into a separate cultural enclave, away from the rest of the city, but it surely has worked in accord with urban renewal theory in terms of the effect it has had on its surroundings. Property values have soared, and what had been a slum has become, for better or for worse, a place for the rich.

Lincoln Center is one long block from Central Park West, and back in 1966 a plan was proposed to clear that site of buildings and create an immense mall connecting the complex with Central Park. It was a Beaux-Arts scheme of a grandeur rarely seen in present-day New York, and it had a charming naïveté to it—although the Metropolitan Opera House is not nearly big enough or good enough to have controlled the end of such a long and formal vista, there would have been something rather nice about trying to drop a bit of Paris into this one part of New York. Strong opposition from the YMCA and the New York Society for Ethical Culture, both of which would have been required to give up their buildings to the plan, put an end to it.

This bit of history is relevant because, had the mall actually happened, we would not have had to look at the gangling hulk of brown brick called One Lincoln Plaza (Philip Birnbaum, 1972). This is a 43-story wedge set directly across from Lincoln Center Plaza, on a site that had been empty and would have formed the western edge of the mall to Central Park. Now it is one of the city's very largest apartment buildings, and one of its most disturbing: it towers over Lincoln Center, making the buildings of the cultural complex look even weaker and more fragile than they are, and it wreaks havoc with the Central Park West skyline as seen from Central Park.

One Lincoln Plaza (when, oh when, will the affectation of calling everything One Something Plaza end?) is a mixed-use structure—it combines retail facilities, office space, and apartments in a single building. The developers were encouraged to produce this mix by the city's Lincoln Center Special Zoning District, yet another of the clever schemes of New York's planners to get a little bit of quality out of developers by giving away a lot of building bulk in the form of bonuses. Here the exchange involved not only the willingness of the builders to program mixed use into the building, but also their agreement to build a covered arcade in the front of the building. Presumably every building in the area will have such an arcade, and while it is true that, as planner Alexander Garvin has observed, you can't build the rue de Rivoli in increments, the arcade nonetheless brings to the building its one element of civilized urbanity.

Just up the street, No. 2 Lincoln Square (these builders can't even agree on their affectations, let alone their architecture), completed in 1973 to the designs of Schuman, Lichtenstein & Claman, pulls down the quality of the area yet another step. This is a plain slab set on a travertine base; for some inexplicable reason, the city planners approved a scheme by which the arcade would be under a cantilevered section of the building's base instead of supported by columns, thus making it not only ugly but inconsistent with the arcade at One Lincoln Plaza as well.

One Lincoln Plaza, which advertised unobstructed views when it was built, has just gotten a new neighbor—a near twin one block to the south, a building which at least has the virtue of continuing the covered sidewalk arcade, but about which nothing else positive can be said. On balance, the best building directly opposite Lincoln Center is the Bankers Trust branch bank at 66th Street and Columbus Avenue (Oppenheimer, Brady & Lehrecke, 1962), an urbane little Miesian exercise that brings a welcome note of understatement.

III B 3 · LINCOLN PLAZA TOWER
44 West 62nd Street
Horace Ginsbern & Associates, 1973

One of the few pieces of luxury housing built since World War II in New York that try. Here, the motif is striated concrete with rounded bay windows and rounded balconies. It is straight out of Paul Rudolph—one of New York's best examples, in fact, of the trickle-down aspect of contemporary architecture, in which a good architect invents a form and it is copied in increasingly simplified, picturesque, and less rigorous ways. Ironically, the Rudolphian models are housing in New Haven and the Bronx for subsidized tenants; it is the rich in New York who get the watered-down version.

III B 3 & 4 · *Lincoln Plaza Tower, at the left, and Sofia Brothers Warehouse*

III B 4 · *Detail of Sofia Brothers Warehouse*

III B 4 · SOFIA BROTHERS, INC. (originally Kent Columbus Circle garage)
47 Columbus Avenue between 61st and 62nd streets
Jardine, Hill & Murdock, 1930

Industrial architecture that is not only powerful, but full of humane, inviting life. This is always a surprise to come upon on a dreary stretch of Columbus Avenue, with the emptiness of Fordham University's downtown campus on one block and the heaviness of Roosevelt Hospital on the next. Here, Art Deco was used imaginatively for a new kind of program—a high-rise parking garage—and the style, and the architects, proved their versatility well. It is unfortunate that the otherwise respectable Lincoln Plaza Tower (III B 3) edges up against this handsome mass with rather more bravado than necessary.

III B 5 · MARTIN LUTHER KING, JR., HIGH SCHOOL
122 Amsterdam Avenue, between 65th and 66th streets
Frost Associates, 1975

Real dignity in a public-school building, a rarity indeed in New York. Rusty, naturally weathering steel, reddish quarry tile, and glass join to create a handsome façade, a building-front that achieves a notable balance between slickness and solidity: this is sleek and yet at the same time it feels like a substantial object. The classrooms are in the interior, for flexibility, while all of the corridors ring the periphery. That may be a way of teasing students with views of the world for just a moment or two at a time—rather sly, but the architecture is good.

III B 5 · *Martin Luther King, Jr., High School*

III B 6 · COLUMBUS AVENUE IN THE SIXTIES AND SEVENTIES

Columbus Avenue has sprouted up from Lincoln Center like an eager, aggressive weed. This was once one of New York's tenement streets, the dreary back alley of Central Park West. Workingmen's bars and *bodegas* and hardware stores were the main retail outlets, and it looked rather as though the old El had just been torn down.

No more. East Side-ier than Thou is now the theme; there are boutiques with designer objects and antique shops with cut glass and singles' bars with exposed brick walls. Each day, it seems, an old shop disappears without notice and in no time at all a health-food store or a cheese shop or an antique establishment is in its place. This is not by any stretch of the imagination Madison Avenue; but it has become just what Second and Third avenues were before they were completely taken over by white-brick boxes with names like the Versailles.

Most of the buildings are tenements, with not too much in the way of architectural interest—the contrast they strike with the proper middle-class houses of the side streets, such as those at 69th Street, is the most important aspect here. But there are a few buildings of note: the Romanesque block on the east side of the avenue from 68th to 69th streets (Edward Kilpatrick, 1894), with splendid brickwork but now, alas, only half a cornice; the decent former home of the Park & Tilford retail establishment at the southwest corner of 72nd Street, an 1893 McKim, Mead & White structure now nicely converted into housing; and the ponderously classicizing Rochelle Apartments (Lamb & Rich, 1896), a benign if heavy-handed gaggle of columns at the northeast corner of 75th Street.

III B 7 · CENTRAL PARK WEST

This is, plain and simple, New York's finest street at large scale. It is better by far than Fifth Avenue, for it is wider and has a much finer complement of buildings; it is better than Park Avenue, for it has Central Park. Below 96th Street it is also, with two exceptions, precisely as it was in 1931, when the Century at No. 25, the last of the twin-towered apartment buildings that give its skyline such drama, was finished. (The exceptions, the apartment tower at No. 80 and the additions to the New-York Historical Society, are blessedly small and restrained, and thus cause nowhere near the upheaval they might.) The buildings of Central Park West span several generations, in spite of the fact that most are, by our standards, old; the Dakota at 72nd Street was nearly fifty when the Century was built. But they manage, for all of their differences and for all of their individual strengths, to work together as a coherent whole. It is the difficult unity of different kinds of objects deferring to one another, not the easy unity of imitation, that gives this boulevard its true majesty.

It is best of all in the morning, when the sun shines from the east and brings a bright, optimistic light to the wall of masonry that the buildings of Central Park West make. And it should be seen from its southern end just above Columbus Circle, from which the two miles of the boulevard stretch out in a deceptively clear order. The Mayflower at No. 15, a decent but ordinary apartment hotel (Emery Roth, 1926), fills the block from 61st to 62nd streets and marks the street's beginning, but it is with the Century (Office of Irwin Chanin, 1931) that Central Park West moves into high gear. Here, twin towers culminate in handsome, machine-inspired Art Deco tops, lifted thirty stories into the sky. This building, along with its cousin, the Majestic at No. 115 (III B 10), and the Ardsley at No. 320 represent the best Art Deco apartment-house architecture in Manhattan—towers that romanticize modern imagery as skillfully, not to mention as earnestly, as any Renaissance palazzo romanticized the Medici. This is the New World, the Century tells us, it is the glory of height bringing you views and the glory of technology bringing you corner windows (the corner window, unbroken by a column, was a great sign of progress in the 1930's), and, of course, it is the glory of chic, too, for these buildings were fashionable indeed in their early years.

The Century's spirit is also captured in 55 Central Park West (Schwartz & Gross, 1929), a handsome Art Deco mass that utilizes the pleasing conceit of brick shaded in tone from red at the base to light tan at top—done, it was

III B 7 · *Eldorado and the Central Park West skyline*

said, to give the impression that the sun was always shining on the building. In considerable stylistic contrast at the lower end—but again, as with everything on this street, never in disagreeable clash—are Robert Kohn's New York Society for Ethical Culture at 2 West 64th Street (1910), a huge piece of limestone furniture that manages the contradiction of being at once Art Nouveau and utterly somber, and Charles W. Romeyn and Henry R. Wynne's Prasada apartments at No. 50 (1907), an overdecorated limestone pile.

Lower Central Park West might be said to end around here; just above 66th Street the street becomes a bit quieter in terms of both its traffic and its architecture. This stretch, running up to the Museum of Natural History at 77th Street, is Central Park West's most fashionable half-mile, the section of the street that has the most socially desirable apartment houses on it and the pleasantest sections of the revived Columbus Avenue (III B 6) behind it. The museum's great open square provides a respite at just the point at which the even line of buildings marching uptown from 60th Street might become a bit tedious; at 81st Street, above the museum site, the Beresford (III B 15) sits nobly, a final burst of glory before Central Park West allows itself to become a notch more plebeian in the Eighties and Nineties. The streets on the south and north of the museum square, 77th Street and 81st Street, are both themselves built to the large scale of Central Park West, but unlike most wide cross streets, they seem not like intersections of Central Park West but folded-back sections of it, as if the line of buildings along the park had simply been given a great turn at two crucial corners.

The Eighties are a relatively tranquil portion of the street, with fine buildings but nothing of unusual distinction. The terrain of Central Park raises a bit here, creating a rock cliff across the street that makes for a landscape markedly different from that of Central Park West in the Seventies. The beginning of the Nineties is marked by the double exclamation point of the Eldorado at No. 300 (Margon & Holder, 1931), the northernmost of the twin-towered apartment buildings and a fine Art Deco work, with towers that resemble those of the Empire State Building in profile. Just beyond at No. 320 is the Ardsley (Emery Roth, 1931), a Mayan-influenced pile that is, in terms of façade decoration, Central Park West's most elaborate Art Deco work. The massing, however, is conventional, as it is at No. 336 (Schwartz & Gross, 1929), where an undulating cornice suggests certain vague—very vague—Egyptian influences. The fine Christian Science Church (III B 16) marks the corner of 96th Street; above, from 97th Street to 100th Street, are the boring freestanding towers of the Park West Village urban-renewal complex, and while there are a few buildings of note farther to the north—most particularly, the voluptuous round castle of the Towers Nursing Home at 106th Street (Charles C. Haight, 1887)—by this point the special quality of Central Park West is lost.

A few of the places on Central Park West worth considering in more detail follow.

III B 8 · WEST 67TH STREET, OFF CENTRAL PARK WEST

A block that gets more special the more you look at it. It consists of several high, older buildings—in itself something unusual for a narrow street—

virtually all of which were created as artists' studios. Only the façades of No. 1 West 67th Street (the Hotel des Artistes) and No. 2 show them, but there are double-height spaces hidden behind the façades of most of these buildings, rooms intended for painters but now, thanks to the economics of New York real estate, occupied largely by writers, lawyers, architects, executives, and the like. They all look as if they were designed as sets for *La Bohème,* and they are a special category of New York housing unto themselves.

The façades of the buildings work together well, although only the gloriously blown-up Elizabethan manor-house front of the des Artistes (George Mort Pollard, 1918) is significant in itself. What is most remarkable about 67th Street as an urban environment is the sense of enclave it has, the dense, tight quality that makes it resemble a mews more than a street of large structures. The two new buildings inserted onto the street recently for ABC Television (Kohn Pederson Fox, 1978) are thoughtful and respectful of the street's significant qualities, although it would have been far better had they been built of limestone or gray brick instead of the yellow brick that was used.

Also worth a look: the chapel-like lobby of No. 15 (Simonson, Pollard & Steinam) where the Gothic allusions common to many buildings of the period become delightfully literal.

III B 9 · DAKOTA
1 West 72nd Street
Henry J. Hardenbergh, 1884

Nowhere has the idea of the apartment house as symbol of community been so well expressed as in the Dakota. It was among the first luxury apartment buildings in New York (though not, as is often claimed, the very first), and its organization suggests a group of townhouses turned on their sides, so that the rooms are stretched horizontally instead of piled vertically, and then arrayed around a central courtyard. The courtyard provides the building at large with a sense of both privacy and unity, not to mention bringing light and air to inside rooms; the layout on the entryway system, with four corner elevators, gives apartment entrances almost the degree of privacy of separate houses. Service elevators, among the first in any multiple dwelling, run up the middle of each side to connect directly with apartment kitchens.

These innovations alone would have made the Dakota significant in the history of American architecture. But the building is justly remembered for Hardenbergh's absolutely splendid façades, exteriors that at once have great power and utter graciousness. The building is an elaborate, eclectic composition, sort of a mix of Germanic, châteauesque, and English Victorian details. Like all of Hardenbergh's work, it is most impressive as composition—in this case as a brilliant balance of gables, dormers, arches, balconies, oriel windows, finials, and miscellaneous stone ornaments. Hardenbergh kept all of these disparate elements in control, yielding a product that is both lively and disciplined, utterly lacking in the fussiness and pretense of many of its imitators.

The apartments themselves are grandly scaled—most have 13- to 14-foot

III B 9 · *Entrance of the Dakota*

III B 9 · *Dakota*

ceilings—but the layouts fail to show the remarkable originality of the façades. Most are simply collections of rooms strung out along corridors—although the rooms themselves are grandly proportioned and discreetly ornamented, benign spaces able to comfortably accommodate far more than the Victorian furniture for which they were originally designed.

The Dakota was developed by Edward S. Clark, head of the Singer Sewing Machine Co., who had considerable faith in the potential of the West Side for residential development. He purchased the Dakota's site when the area was still a mass of shanties and Central Park was not yet finished; one of the city's most beloved bits of lore involves the choice of name for the building, an ironic reference to its distance from anything resembling the center of town in those days. Clark also developed a row of rental townhouses on West 73rd Street which Hardenbergh also designed; they are a lively, polychromed alternative to the brownstone that was so ubiquitous in the 1870's and 1880's. Unfortunately, the middle of the Hardenbergh row on the north side of 73rd Street between Central Park West and Columbus Avenue was removed to make way for the mediocre Park Royal Hotel, but enough remains to indicate clearly that Hardenbergh's compositional skill was hardly limited to large-scale works.

III B 10 · MAJESTIC
115 Central Park West, SW corner 72nd Street
Office of Irwin Chanin, 1930

· SAN REMO
145–146 Central Park West, between 74th and 75th streets
Emery Roth, 1930

Two contemporaries from Central Park West's golden age, separated by two blocks and by miles of stylistic difference. Underneath, they are essentially the same building: a solid base running a full block in width, with two towers rising at either corner up to a height of about thirty stories. And inside, the apartments have the same sort of generous size, central foyer–oriented layout and elaborately tiled bathrooms characteristic of all of the best New York apartments of the late 1920's and early 1930's.

There the similarity ends. Emery Roth chose to sheathe his form in classical details, with a rusticated limestone base, cartouches above the entrances, and a columned, finialed temple crowning each of the two towers. Chanin opted to be modern—or at least *moderne*. He covered his similarly massed structure with orange-colored brick and terra-cotta tile arranged in the streamlined patterns that, by 1930, were a common American interpretation of Art Deco. Like its companion building, the Century (III B 7), which followed it by just a year, the Majestic sought to romanticize futurism with sleek, sharp lines, dramatic corner windows, and tower tops molded as abstract sculpture. One building romanticized the future, the other the past—in each case they were stage sets, and both now have the charm of quaint revival.

III B 10 · *Majestic*

III B 10 · *San Remo*

III B 11 · WEST 74th STREET, OFF CENTRAL PARK WEST
· WEST 76th STREET, OFF CENTRAL PARK WEST

West 74th Street is one of the most remarkably unified groups of townhouses anywhere in New York—eighteen neo-Georgian manses, an ordered rhythm of limestone and red brick, completed in 1904 to the designs of Percy Griffith. The smoothness of the composition is uncharacteristic of New York and invites comparison with London—a comparison that seems obvious, yet serves as a reminder of how basically different the attitude toward the street is in the two cities. In London, Nash's ordered rows set a pattern followed by more modest architects and builders in less desirable areas; in New York, playing down the individual house was not quite so favored. The result is a block like West 76th Street, more typical of New York in spite of the fact that the limestone used here creates a white block instead of the common New York brown row—these houses are decorative, dissimilar, and largely classicizing, and they join together to create a coherent and handsome whole. West 76th Street has a liveliness to it that is also typical of New York side-street blocks—the order never becomes so all-pervasive as to feel confining, as it does on the Anglophilic West 74th Street.

III B 12 · NEW-YORK HISTORICAL SOCIETY
170 Central Park West, between 76th and 77th streets
Central portion: York & Sawyer, 1908
wings: Walker & Gillette, 1938

A dry building and a dry museum, but a source, often enough, of pleasant surprises anyway. The formality of the building is a bit disappointing, for there is so much more life to the rest of Central Park West, and one almost suspects that the society knew back in 1908 that Central Park West was not going to turn out to be quite another Fifth Avenue and felt it had to assert its social credentials with a bit of stuffy architecture. That may be why York & Sawyer, the city's leading architects of banks, were asked to do this museum—although, oddly enough, the banks that York & Sawyer did generally turned out to be a lot livelier.

The additions by Walker & Gillette are completely in character, but drier still. Not only are they among New York's last Beaux-Arts work, but they were virtually contemporary with the original International Style building of the Museum of Modern Art, which opened in 1939.

III B 13 · 44 WEST 77th STREET
Harde & Short, 1909

A gloriously silly Gothic fantasy of an apartment house, far more exuberant than 15 West 67th Street (III B 8). Much of the ornament was removed in 1944, but enough is left to make this one of the city's gingerbread centers. No. 44 West 77th Street, like most of the West 67th Street buildings, was designed for artists, and there are many high studio spaces within the large, rambling, and generally awkwardly laid-out apartments.

III B 11 · *West 74th Street, between Central Park West and Columbus Avenue*

III B 14 · *American Museum of Natural History, 77th Street façade*

III B 14 · AMERICAN MUSEUM OF NATURAL HISTORY
Central Park West, 77th to 81st streets
original wing: Calvert Vaux and Jacob Wrey Mould, 1877
West 77th Street wings: J. C. Cady and Cady, Berg & See, 1892–99
Columbus Avenue wing: Charles Volz, 1908
Central Park West wings: Trowbridge & Livingston, 1924–33
Theodore Roosevelt Memorial wing, Central Park West: John Russell Pope,
*   1935*

An immense, sprawling set of fortresses built on a vast plot of land that, in the 1870's, was a messy landscape of squatters, goats, and mud far from the center of town. When the initial wing by Calvert Vaux was opened, the location cut the museum's popularity considerably; the superintendent wrote that "the next day after our grandly successful opening we experienced the depressing effect of finding our spacious exhibition halls nearly deserted."

But things improved steadily for the museum, much as they did for the developing West Side, and by 1889 plans were under way for an expansion along West 77th Street. J. Cleveland Cady produced a Romanesque Revival structure of considerable grandeur that is still one of the city's finest examples of Romanesque architecture. It is of pink Vermont granite, with a massive central entrance intended originally for carriages. There are turrets and dormers and corner towers, a grand, sweeping staircase and a fine seven-bay arcaded porch. Cady also designed a master plan for the completion of the museum which can only be called imperial—it specified a repetition of the Romanesque design for the museum's entire site from Central Park West to Columbus Avenue and 77th Street to 81st Street, with a central pyramidal tower rising to twice the height of the present building.

If it had been built, that decision would surely have been one of Manhattan's more staggering landmarks, but the museum opted instead to continue building piecemeal. There are some undistinguished sections by Trowbridge & Livingston and a wing by Charles Volz; the construction has been so substantial that the Vaux wing is barely visible in the midst of the sprawl. All too visible, unfortunately, is John Russell Pope's Theodore Roosevelt Memorial, a massive Beaux-Arts entrance on Central Park West marked by a huge arch flanked by four Ionic columns. The Roosevelt Memorial has become the museum's symbolic front door, which is rather a shame, since it is pompous, overscaled, and generally inferior to the Beaux-Arts work of comparable scale elsewhere in town, such as the New York Public Library and Grand Central Station. The great hall inside has a spectacular, barrel-vaulted space that is so huge as to make even the most self-assured visitor certain that he has somehow trespassed in the vestibule of Olympus. There is no great interior space inside the Cady wings, but there is a far greater feeling of welcome to them.

III B 15 · BERESFORD
211 Central Park West, NW corner 81st Street
Emery Roth, 1929

It's a site you can't go wrong with—a corner, with Central Park to the west and the open square of the American Museum of Natural History to the south. In that sense, this is a plot not unlike that of the Plaza Hotel, and indeed, one thing tying the Beresford to the Plaza is that they are both among the very few major New York buildings to have two façades. And if the Beresford does not quite approach the remarkable level of the Plaza (II G 12), it is nonetheless designed with complete understanding of its crucial role in the cityscape.

The Beresford is a cousin to Emery Roth's San Remo (III B 10), and it

III B 15 · *Beresford*

III B 16 · *First Church of Christ, Scientist*

uses a similar classical vocabulary—rusticated limestone base, brick mid-section, some spare bits of classicizing ornament, and a subtle pattern of setbacks and terraces. But where the San Remo consists of two slender towers leaping from a relatively tight base, the Beresford is a single great, sumptuous pile, its top marked not by long, high towers but by three crowns, vaguely Baroque, which give it a remarkable and romantic silhouette. This is one of the few large urban buildings anywhere that sit with as much grandeur and ease as a country villa—not an easy trick at all when you realize how truly enormous this building is.

III B 16 · FIRST CHURCH OF CHRIST, SCIENTIST
1 West 96th Street
Carrère & Hastings, 1903

This is a daring, powerful surprise—classicism made stark and robust and startlingly fresh. The entrance is flanked by a pair of Ionic columns set all the way within a mass of clean stone; only a rich cornice zips across this mass, but not quite at the top. The tower plays Baroque games rather neatly, and the whole composition calls to mind the great London churches of Nicholas Hawksmoor. Hawksmoor was a genius whose work was beyond imitation, and Carrère & Hastings were merely very good Beaux-Arts architects, so this is a structure of nowhere near the depth and meaning of Hawksmoor's work. But it is more than just an interesting attempt—it is one of New York's best churches.

C/THE BROADWAY SPINE, WEST END AVENUE, RIVERSIDE DRIVE

III C 1 · BROADWAY

The main street of the Upper West Side, and the greatest example anywhere of the street as spinal cord. It is throbbing with that sort of sleazy vitality which is so characteristic of New York. This is a monumental street, or at least it tries to be—there are wide malls in the center, and the buildings are for the most part formal and large in scale. But Broadway could not be Park Avenue, even if every fruit stand and supermarket and hardware store and delicatessen were to disappear overnight, for there is an iconoclasm to this street that strikes deep at the heart of the order represented by the likes of Park Avenue. Broadway is a jumble, not merely of commercial establishments but of kinds of people and kinds of architecture. There are richly ornate apartment houses, somber hotels, flamboyant theaters, and loudly painted storefronts; walking through and past them are housewives and students and derelicts and lawyers and homosexuals and writers. It is all very dirty, it is often very loud, and it is somehow very relaxed, like a child's room that is permitted to remain in disorder by parents who feel that children should be permitted to have their own mess. Broadway is the West Side's indulgence, and if you doubt the economic wisdom of letting a street be that way, count the empty storefronts: there are virtually none from Lincoln Center to Morningside Heights.

The center-island malls tend to be rather dowdy, which is not disturbing at all, since Broadway—at least when it reaches high gear above 72nd Street—is pretty dowdy itself. The refurbished sections, at Lincoln Square, 72nd to 74th streets and 95th to 96th streets (Glasser & Ohlhausen, 1972), bring a self-conscious modernism to Broadway in the form of concrete kiosks and straight-backed benches and absurdly heavy chains as fences, and this feels about as right as a shopping-bag lady dressed in a Halston.

Like Central Park West (III B 7), Broadway has its distinct sections. The leg that moves uptown from Lincoln Center has not much of an identity at all; it is a mix of commercial and residential structures, all a bit neater and cleaner than the street gets further uptown. Here, the first major

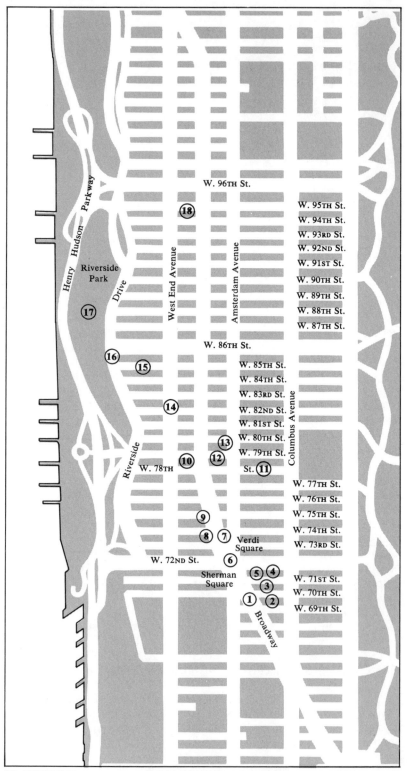

W. 96TH St.

W. 95TH St.
W. 94TH St.
W. 93RD St.
W. 92ND St.
W. 91ST St.
W. 90TH St.
W. 89TH St.
W. 88TH St.
W. 87TH St.

W. 86TH St.

W. 85TH St.
W. 84TH St.
W. 83RD St.
W. 82ND St.
W. 81ST St.
W. 80TH St.
W. 79TH St.

W. 78TH St.

W. 77TH St.
W. 76TH St.
W. 75TH St.
W. 74TH St.
W. 73RD St.

W. 72ND St.

W. 71ST St.
W. 70TH St.
W. 69TH St.

Henry Hudson Parkway

Riverside Park

Riverside Drive

West End Avenue

Amsterdam Avenue

Columbus Avenue

Riverside

Verdi Square

Sherman Square

Broadway

III C 1 · *IRT station at 72nd Street*

III C 2 · *Christ and St. Stephen's Church*

privately developed luxury apartment building to ride the wave of increased property values brought to the neighborhood by Lincoln Center was built: the Dorchester at 155 West 68th Street (S. J. Kessler & Sons, 1965), a pile of white brick that, thanks to zoning laws, has a rather interesting setback massing when viewed from a block or two to the east. The Dorchester is otherwise undistinguished, but it is worth comparing with one of its progeny, the altogether wretched Nevada Towers (never mind the plural, there is only one), built on a triangular site between Broadway and Amsterdam Avenue at 70th Street (Philip Birnbaum, 1977). Here, a dull shaft of brown brick rises straight up, with no setbacks and almost no acknowledgment in its form of the unusual shape of the site. More disturbing still is the virtual absence of windows on the north side, where there is a spectacular view to Sherman Square and the march of Broadway to the north.

Above West 72nd Street are a few masterpieces, such as the Ansonia (III C 8) and the Central Savings Bank (III C 7), and the stretch from here to 86th Street is probably Broadway's best architecturally. There are small hints of diminishing prosperity as one moves gradually northward and shopping-bag ladies begin to be more in evidence and well-dressed customers rushing toward Zabar's less so, but it is not until above 96th Street that Broadway registers a real drop in voltage. The street seems more fragile up there, quieter and more somber. But it goes into this phase with a splendid burst of energy at 96th Street, a corner second only to 72nd Street in vitality. Here, as at 72nd Street, there are drug dealers and news dealers, working all night and often struggling for the same customers; there are crowds constantly milling about, and there is always a sense—even though Broadway this far north is in line with the Manhattan grid and therefore creates no "squares" at its intersections—that this is a significant public space. It is no accident that it is around this intersection that New York got one of its first Szechuan restaurants and its very first McDonald's.

III C 2 · CHRIST AND ST. STEPHEN'S CHURCH
120 West 69th Street
William H. Day, 1880
renovation: J. D. Fouquet, 1897

A country church in the middle of Manhattan. It goes back to the days when the Upper West Side *was* country, or at least empty space, and it is a remarkable survival. The building is quaint without in any way being cute, as such remnants can be in the midst of large and tough cities; one thing that makes this building so appealing is that it does not seem very innocent or very surprised by what has grown up around it. St. Stephen's is a self-assured little building, holding on to its green front yard with a certain toughness. Like the old lady who refuses to move to make way for the demolition contractor, St. Stephen's manages to be both demure and iron-hard.

III C 3 · BOROUGH OF MANHATTAN COMMUNITY COLLEGE, BUILDING M (originally Pythian Temple)
135 West 70th Street
Thomas W. Lamb, 1927

Zap! Zap! Zowie! To call this immensely ornate mass flamboyant would be like calling the Empire State Building tall. This building defines flamboyance, not the other way around. It is not, really, a particularly skillful design, and all of those vaguely Near Eastern details have an odd flatness to them, in spite of the welcome polychromy. And the site, hidden away on a narrow side street, makes it hard to see. But the energy and exuberance created here by Lamb—whose practice consisted largely of designing theaters—are tremendous, and might have been too much for a prominent site anyway. As it is, there is a wonderful sense of surprise whenever you turn a corner and catch even a partial glimpse of this Cecil B. De Mille wonder.

III C 4 · BLESSED SACRAMENT CHURCH
152 West 71st Street
Gustave Steinback, 1921

The details are not nearly as good, but this nonetheless deserves to rank with Bertram Goodhue's St. Thomas (II G 4) as an exemplary model of an urban Gothic church. Blessed Sacrament's site is even more difficult than St. Thomas's—it is in the middle of a block, with neither a corner nor a wide avenue to provide space and a chance for the form to be viewed as a totality. Steinback understood the limitations of this site and did not try to fight them; instead, he piled his church behind a great, smooth façade that defines the street wall as well as any Park Avenue apartment house functions as part of its larger wall. There is some texture and rhythm to this light stone façade, but the overall effect is still one of a Gothic church that was somehow compressed into something very thin and taut—the church as plane instead of volume.

III C 3 · *Pythian Temple (now Borough of Manhattan Community College, Building M)*

III C 5 · *Dorilton*

III C 5 · LUCANIA
235 West 71st Street
Gaetan Ajello, 1910
· DORILTON
171 West 71st Street
Janes & Leo, 1902

Two ways of dealing with the medium-to-large Upper West Side apartment building, eight years apart. The difference was largely in styles: Ajello was one of the city's most skillful makers of controlled eclectic compositions, whereas Janes & Leo went all over the place. The Dorilton, in fact, inspired a column in the *Architectural Record* which spoke of "the gross excess of scale throughout, the wild yell with which the fronts exclaim, 'Look at me,' as if somebody were going to miss seeing a building of this area, twelve stories high! . . . How everything shrieks to drown out everything else!" Now the building seems more to be pitied than censored, a rather too eager-to-please piece of Second Empire foppery. Once, someone thought that a mansard roof and a lot of sculpture and cartouches made a building French; now we know better. Still, it is sad to see this building, for all its foolishness, in the sorry state of decay it has descended to, with unsympathetic storefronts along the Broadway side and a façade that clearly has not been cared for in years.

Ajello's building is, by contrast, so quiet it is easily overlooked. But this is the sort of richly textured composition that is worth a second glance—a strong base of two stories, with a third story given slightly more detail than the bulk of the façade to ease the transition upward; cartouches set neatly onto the façade, the balconies placed to give a sense of balance and rhythm to the midsection. A fine cornice, unfortunately, has been lost.

III C 6 · SHERMAN SQUARE / VERDI SQUARE
Broadway, 70th to 73rd streets

Here, Broadway crosses Amsterdam Avenue to create one of the symbolic hearts of the Upper West Side. This is the West Side of *Mr. Sammler's Planet,* of old men who are tired and of junkies who are tireder; it is also the West Side of secretaries and lawyers and upward mobility. But even where paths cross, this seems a long way from the gentrified Columbus Avenue—the image of this intersection is slow to change.

Sherman Square, the southern portion of the crossroads, has lent its address to one aggressively mediocre new apartment tower one block to the south, One Sherman Square (S. J. Kessler, 1971), a building which, like the Nevada Towers (III C 1), makes hardly a gesture at all toward its unusually formed site. Not too well crafted to its site either, but nonetheless far more appealing, is the subway kiosk in the middle of Sherman Square (Heins & La Farge, 1904). Here is a reminder of the days when the subways were a noble way to travel: a fine masonry box, bringing a confident monumentality to the intersection. A recent cleaning and painting have made this a pleasanter part of the cityscape, though the kiosk—the only one remaining in Manhattan—functions poorly indeed in today's heavy subway traffic.

Verdi Square, the northern triangle of the intersection, is an attempt at a park. It is surrounded by benches which seem as confining as fences, but the Pasquale Civiletti statue of Giuseppe Verdi is pleasing, and it is always worth wondering what Verdi would have made of this attempt to honor him in this particular part of New York—would he have considered the scene that swirls about him a tragic or a comic opera?

III C 7 · CENTRAL SAVINGS BANK
2100 Broadway, 73rd to 74th streets
York & Sawyer, 1928

New York's best bank architects, and one of New York's best banks. York & Sawyer knew that Florentine palaces were the places to keep your money, and what was good enough for the Federal Reserve (I A 35) was good enough for the Central Savings Bank.

But beyond the overall majesty of this building and its splendid interior space, there are good urbanistic lessons here. The site, thanks to Broadway's diagonal, is trapezoid, and the building fills out the trapezoidal shape to carry out what the architects understood were its responsibilities to its surroundings. But since great vaulted banking halls don't feel too comfortable as trapezoids, the hall itself is a perfect rectangle. How? A set of alcoves and mezzanines, covered by great arches, fills a triangular cut-off space from the banking hall.

III C 8 · ANSONIA HOTEL
2109 Broadway, 73rd to 74th streets
Graves & Duboy, 1904

What a shame that Janes & Leo couldn't have waited another two years before designing the Dorilton (III C 5), for here, just two blocks uptown, is the way splashy "French" façades are properly done. In the vast Ansonia, all of the heaviness of the Dorilton is turned to lightness; the façades are covered with ornament and balconies and marked by splendid corner towers and topped by mansards, and never for a moment does any of it become overbearing. This building, like a well-endowed soprano, sings with a grace that belies its size. That the ground floor has been altered and the lobby turned into a drab gathering place for a set of characters that resembles a George Price cartoon is a sadness, but one that does not destroy the Ansonia's lyrical glory.

This has the added virtue of superb siting. The round tower that marks the southeast corner also marks a slight turn in Broadway, so the building is able to command the vista both up Broadway from the south and down Broadway from the north. It anchors that vista with considerable strength, but at no cost to the building's overall lightness.

III C 8 · *Detail of the Ansonia Hotel*

III C 8 · *Ansonia Hotel*

III C 9 · BERKLEY GARAGE
201 West 75th Street
C. Abbott French & Co., 1890

Once a stable, and a fine piece of Richardsonian Romanesque. But it takes the influence of H. H. Richardson's great works, most notably the Marshall Field Wholesale Store of 1887 in Chicago, and heads in two directions—toward a much rougher style in the heavy stone base around the three half-round arches on 75th Street, and toward a more decorative style in the cornice. The dichotomy prevents this from being a first-rate building, but it serves as an important reminder of how influence in architecture is rarely translated neatly or, for that matter, ideologically. This is a very anti-Richardsonian use of Richardson.

The Amsterdam Avenue façade is dull and has been badly junked up with storefronts. But it is worth noting the red stripe painted onto the north end of the brick façade as a gesture to tie this building to its altogether different neighbor, a porcelain gas station and office building that has the same pleasing banality as the Water Street fire station (I A 23).

Across the street, the back of the Beacon Theater (Walter Ahlschlager, 1928) is a glorious explosion into monumental scale. It is all the more impressive because the front of this theater and hotel building, designed to express only the hotel, gives no sign of the splendors within. But the back tells all.

III C 10 · APTHORP
390 West End Avenue (2207 Broadway)
Clinton & Russell, 1908

· BELNORD
225 West 86th Street
H. Hobart Weekes, 1908

· ASTOR COURT
Broadway, 89th to 90th streets
Charles A. Platt, 1916

The West Side's three great courtyard buildings, all descendants of the Dakota (III B 9). The Apthorp is the best known, and in some ways the finest—surely Clinton & Russell's noble Renaissance façade of limestone has few equals in the history of multiple dwellings. And the arched entrance with its ornate iron gatework and coffered ceiling is among the best monumental entrances anywhere in New York. The landscaped courtyard of the Belnord, however, makes for a richer interior there, although the façade cannot equal the Apthorp's and the huge size makes for a rather unwieldy feeling overall. The Astor Court is more spare; Charles Platt saved everything for the splendid cornice, which has that sort of ice-cold luxury one associates with the best work of Charles McKim. All of the buildings share the liability of courtyard apartment houses, which is poor light in all too many of the units, but they also share the ability of all good courtyard buildings to create—far more than conventional buildings could—a sense of a private, secure world.

III C 11 · WEST 78th STREET, COLUMBUS TO AMSTERDAM AVENUES

A block that is at once civilized, tranquil, and lively. Its east end is closed by the pink-granite mass of the American Museum of Natural History, so there is a sense of quietness and isolation here that would make West 78th Street different from most other West Side blocks even if there were no

III C 11 · *121–131 West 78th Street*

III C 10 · *Courtyard of the Belnord*

architecture of note at all. The block looks typical at first glance: there are larger buildings marking the corners of Columbus Avenue, and brownstones filling most of the midblock. But the old apartment house at 101 West 78th (Emile Gruwé, 1886) is a powerful and unusual composition in red brick, and among the houses is a sextet that is one of the liveliest row-house groupings anywhere in the city.

The Gruwé building is an odd mix of clean, almost stark masses and elaborate details. The central section is simple and marked by very little ornament; most of the decoration is focused on two ornate side pavilions. The main floor at either end is a particularly inventive composition—arched windows are framed by Ionic columns set deeply into the façade; they are topped with overscaled keystones and cherubs and angels in terra-cotta panels set into the brick façade above the windows. The brick is itself set in unusually deep grooves, creating a sleekness that is startling in its contrast to the other elements of the façade.

The real triumph of West 78th Street, however, is the group of six houses at Nos. 121–131 (Rafael Guastavino, 1886). They are bright red, with white stone trim, and utterly cheerful details that are whimsical and delicate, making the group appear almost toylike. The details are not so impressive as craftsmanship in themselves as they are indicators of Guastavino's desire to tie all of the houses into a symmetrical composition. Thus the two end houses, the second and fifth, and the two center houses match. There was a desire that the houses appear unified as well, hence the knoblike details set into the façades where two houses join, snapping each set of neighbors together like a do-it-yourself toy. They are bizarre little constructions, these joints: zigzag brick patterns with terra-cotta lions' heads set into them and pitched roofs on top. Guastavino was celebrated for his great tiled vaults, but this grouping shows that his inventiveness could extend to other realms as well.

III C 12 · GLOUCESTER
200 West 79th Street
Schuman, Lichtenstein & Claman, 1976

Nowhere near Gloucester, and there is nothing seafaring about this new apartment building. But it is worth noting because it is the only building in a generation or more to use old-fashioned six-over-six multipaned windows. Here, they are set into a warm red-brick façade, and the difference the windows make is remarkable. There are also brick quoins, and together these devices bring texture and life to a building that, in every other aspect, is as banal as all of its high-rise brethren. This is testament to the ability of tiny details to act as savior.

III C 13 · HOTEL LUCERNE
201 West 79th Street
Harry B. Mulliken, 1904

The Upper West Side is full of apartment hotels, and it is full of buildings that lean vaguely toward the Baroque. But this one stands out, in part because of the wonderful richness of its brownstone. It could almost be wet mud, so alive and sharp is the color, or child's clay, molded carefully and then baked. The detailing is heavy and thick, making the building seem all the more like clay, but it is skillful enough so that it never feels overbearing. The entrance is one of the West Side's finest, thanks to the banded columns, but the entire mass stands nobly on its corner.

III C 14 · *West End Avenue, from 76th to 77th streets*

III C 13 · *Hotel Lucerne*

III C 14 · WEST END AVENUE

This is a dull, proper sort of street, the urban equivalent of the banal middle-class suburbs of Long Island. West End Avenue is long and absolutely straight, and its buildings line up neatly and properly, all behaving themselves quite well. What it needs is something to give it life—either the commercial activity of Broadway, the curves of Riverside Drive, or even the noble width and central mall of Park Avenue, West End Avenue's closest equivalent architecturally. Without any of these things, and even with a great many fine buildings, West End Avenue plods. Even the long, unbroken vista up or down its length—one of New York's true endless landscapes—seems lacking in the drama it should be capable of.

Developers of the Upper West Side expected that West End Avenue would be a commercial street and Broadway would be a great residential boulevard, and thus it was Broadway, not West End, that was given a central mall. That arrangement might have made more sense, for West End Avenue commercial development would have been equally accessible from both Broadway and Riverside Drive. But in the rush of development on the West Side following the opening of the Ninth Avenue elevated railroad in 1880, the expected order did not materialize.

Much of West End Avenue's "first growth," however, consisted of excellent row houses, most of which were Romanesque or Queen Anne, but which tended toward a lively eclecticism determined, above all, to prove its architects' distance from the formal and planar Anglo-Italianate of the brownstones of a decade before scattered throughout midtown and the Upper East Side. The Upper East Side was a divided quarter at this time: the very rich were on Fifth Avenue, and the working class settled east of them. The West Side turned out to serve those in the middle—middle- and upper-middle-class New Yorkers who could fit into neither of the East Side's extremes.

A few remnants of this phase of West End Avenue's development remain. The best is the complete blockfront of houses from 76th to 77 Street (Lamb & Rich, 1891), a remarkably varied grouping that mixes limestone, tan brick, and red brick in an array of gables and dormers and bay windows and arches that, for all its liveliness, preserves a sense of general order and symmetry.

Most of West End now consists of second-generation buildings, the apartment houses that began to replace the row houses as early as the years leading up to World War I and continued until 1930. Very few of them are bad, and most of them have generous, well-conceived apartments within. But they are built on a street scaled to the houses they replaced, and they end up looking far heavier than they deserve to.

But if West End Avenue in its present incarnation can be faulted for toeing the line just a bit *too* well, better that than a complete break, as came in 1975 with the Calhoun School (Costas Machlouzarides) at the southwest corner of West 81st Street. This is a box of travertine with four-story glass cutouts facing the street, looking for all the world like giant television screens. It is an arbitrary form, full of silly exhibitionism, and totally lacking in understanding of its urban context. There is not even the sort of wit here that might have found it amusing to make a school for small children into a real television set by adding a few details to symbolize knobs and such— no, the architect seems to have thought he was making a truly serious form, and no irony was intended at all.

III C 15 · THE RED HOUSE
350 West 85th Street
Harde & Short, 1904

This is an absolute gem, a total surprise on a block of typical West Side row houses—a six-story Elizabethan manor house, crossed with English red-brick row houses. The detail is Gothic, but the ambience is entirely that of those rows and rows of English houses, brought up to New York scale and purged of the bourgeois dullness that style so often symbolizes. This is full of life and color and joy, all the way up to the dragon cartouche near the top.

III C 16 · RIVERSIDE DRIVE

In a just world, this would have been New York's finest street. Charles Schwab, who built a vast mansion on the Drive at 73rd Street (demolished in 1948), bet that it would be, and so did others, but society could not be diverted from Fifth Avenue's manufactured status even by the genuine élan of river and Palisades views. Riverside Drive was developed first as a street of private houses, a few of which approached Schwab's ornate château in elegance, but most of which were similar to the upper-middle-class rows of West End Avenue. As with West End Avenue, the houses had largely given way to apartment buildings by the 1920's, but here the transformation was never so complete—Riverside Drive remains a bumpy combination of four- and five-story houses and 15-story apartment blocks.

III C 15 · *The Red House*   III C 16 · *173–175 Riverside Drive*

Still, this is a masterpiece of urban design. It curves gently, one of the few New York streets to break from the grid, and the best buildings curve along with the street, such as J. E. R. Carpenter's 173–175 Riverside Drive between 89th and 90th streets. Riverside Drive is a more consistent composition above 91st Street, where the drive dips down a grade and there is a narrow lane running in front of the apartment buildings and remaining row houses; a small strip of park separates the lane from the busier main section of Riverside Drive below, creating a wonderful sense of quietness and isolation in front of the buildings.

As on West End Avenue, virtually all of the buildings are good, and virtually none of them are exceptional. It is the *tout ensemble,* or at least the aspiration toward it, that matters. Styles range from the ornate, overdecorated brick and limestone of the Chatsworth at the drive's base at 344 West 72nd Street (John E. Schlarsmith, 1904) to the Renaissance/Art Deco mix of the Normandy, No. 140 Riverside Drive at 86th Street (Emery Roth, 1939). The last is a particularly interesting transitional building— Roth, whose Beresford (III B 15) and San Remo (III B 10) are among the city's very finest classically inspired apartment houses, seems to have known that the jig was up by 1938. He dipped his toe cautiously into the Art Deco water, then pulled it out to top the building with very conventional towers. Better in terms of its effect on the skyline is the Master Apartments at 103rd Street (Helmle, Corbett & Harrison and Sugerman & Berger, 1929), built as an early mixed-use building containing apartments, a school, and the Roerich Museum. This is a heavy, dark warehouse from close up, and a splendid Art Deco profile from afar, a nicely massed top that can hold its own with many a midtown skyscraper.

There are some houses of note remaining in the lower sections of the drive—most particularly, Yeshiva Chofetz Chaim, originally the Isaac L. Rice residence, Villa Julia, at the corner of West 89th Street (Herts & Tallant, 1901). This is a freestanding mansion as imposing as the Andrew Carnegie house, now the Cooper-Hewitt Museum (III D 44), but more pleasantly eccentric. The porte cochere, one-half of it scooped into the mass of the house, one-half of it projecting outward, is especially nice. But the best place to get a sense of the old Riverside Drive as a totality is between 105th and 106th streets—there, a full block of fine French Beaux-Arts townhouses, built between 1899 and 1902 to the designs of, variously,

Janes & Leo, Mowbray & Uffinger, Hoppin & Koen and Robert D. Kohn, remain as a complete, and completely florid, composition.

III C 17 · RIVERSIDE PARK
original design: Frederick Law Olmsted, 1873–1910
additions: Calvert Vaux and Samuel Parsons, Jr., 1888
reconstruction: Clinton F. Lloyd, 1937

This is nothing like Central Park in quality, but it is very good nonetheless, with its sharp grade providing visual drama in a confined space. This is a linear park, a place that never attempts, as Central Park does, to create the illusion of being a complete natural world unto itself. Here, you are always conscious of the rest of the world, either in the form of the undulating wall of Riverside Drive apartments to the east or in the smooth plane of the Hudson River to the west.

One is also, unfortunately, reminded of the presence of the world in the form of the automobile, for the Henry Hudson Parkway, a six-lane highway, has cut through the park since a reconstruction in 1937. That reconstruction had its good points, however: it covered the freight tracks of the New York Central line which had run through the park for years, and it led to the creation of the intricate and handsome round, triple-level interchange at West 79th Street that contains the automobile entrance and parking area for the 79th Street boat basin as well as a series of pedestrian paths and auto ramps.

The park's most notable architectural element, save for Grant's Tomb (IV A 13) is the Soldiers' and Sailors' Monument at West 89th Street (Stoughton & Stoughton and Paul Duboy, 1902). Based on the Choragic Monument of Lysicrates in Athens, the columned tower comes off in this context as a rather appealing folly, brought up to grand urban scale. And

III C 17 · *Soldiers' and Sailors' Monument*

III C 16 · *Master Apartments*

III C 18 · *Pomander Walk*

the terraces surrounding it are a nice counterpoint to both Riverside Drive and the park itself.

But the monument is best seen from the south, at about 88th Street. From there it provides a strong foreground focus for the curving form of 173–175 Riverside Drive which forms a benign curtain behind it. The Soldiers' and Sailors' Monument, the apartment house, and the trees of the park join to form the Beaux-Arts–inspired image of the City Beautiful so dreamed of in the early years of the century, here brought even to a middle-class residential quarter.

III C 18 · POMANDER WALK
94th to 95th streets, between Broadway and West End Avenue
King & Campbell, 1922

A sweet little row of tiny townhouses, an unashamed English stage set. They huddle rather sadly together, as if to protect themselves from the big bad buildings of the rest of the Upper West Side, and the place comes off as quaint and hollow, all at the same time. It is a lovely notion, but too fragile in both its idea and its physical makeup for the neighborhood of upper Broadway, and instead of growing strong over the years, it has grown shabby.

D/THE WEST EAST SIDE: FIFTH TO LEXINGTON

Once, a sociologist's map of the Upper East Side would have had it as an array of vertical stripes—the rich clustered to the left, on Fifth Avenue along the border of Central Park; the middle class beside them, east of Park Avenue; and the working class in tenements on the other side of Lexington Avenue. It is all a neighborhood of the well-to-do now, but the quarter's physical appearance belies its new economic consistency. It is not hard to tell that Fifth Avenue and the blocks just east of it were developed for the rich in a time when the architecture of New York was shamelessly ornate and self-indulgent, whereas the blocks farther to the east came later and were more modest. Lexington Avenue still remains the most reliable dividing line, although the border between the old-money West East Side and the new-money East East Side shifts occasionally. But nowhere in the two-mile length of the neighborhood, from 60th Street to north of 96th Street, does one ever stop feeling that this part of town still divides itself most logically with a vertical line, not a horizontal one. The West East Side is the land of brownstone and limestone, punctuated by discreet boutiques; the East East Side is white-brick apartment houses and made-over tenements, and the commerce is in singles' bars.

It is in these western blocks of the East Side, stretching nearly to Harlem, that the eclectic architecture that characterized New York residential design early in the twentieth century reaches its apex. Here, the sense that history was a great buffet table from which one could pick and choose anything—a sense that has always been crucial to the formation of New York's architectural identity—is the dominating idea. The architectural fantasies of freewheeling eclecticism are what everyone wanted and what the rich got, and, for the most part, they got it in this part of town.

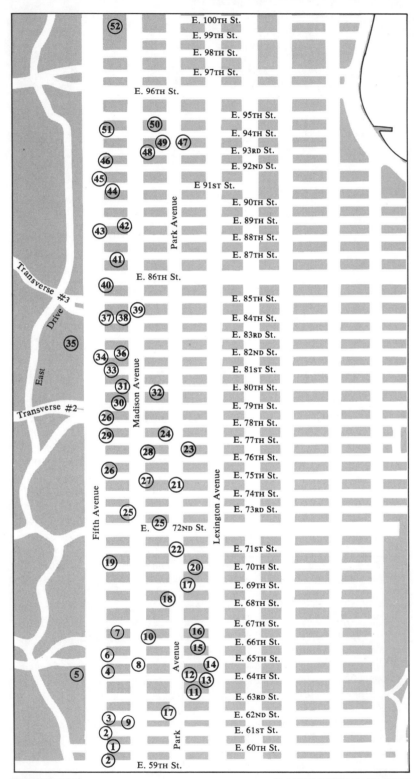

III D 1 · METROPOLITAN CLUB
1 East 60th Street
McKim, Mead & White, 1893
east wing: Ogden Codman, 1912
· HARMONIE CLUB
4 East 60th Street
McKim, Mead & White, 1906

These are both Stanford White's efforts, and they are worth contrasting not only with each other but with White's partner McKim's University Club down Fifth Avenue (II G 8). The Metropolitan Club has none of the University Club's sternness; it is exuberant as White himself was, and it is one of the few buildings of its decade which suggest that perhaps there really was such a period as the gay nineties. The exterior is not so skillfully proportioned as that of the University Club—the row of tiny windows near an overscaled cornice at the top throws the whole composition off a bit— but the colonnaded entrance on 60th Street is a splendid ceremonial gesture, a grand gateway worked cleverly and respectfully into the demands of a Manhattan side street. The idea of entrance is glorified, and the tiny court suggests that the building stands noble and apart from its neighbors on the street, whereas all the while it is standing close to them and adhering to the context that they create. The interior, like the exterior, is more inventive than that of the University Club—there is an opulent marble hall, two stories high, with a double staircase—but there is not the sense of a brilliant, cool intellect that one feels was at work at the University Club.

The Harmonie Club across the street was commissioned by the city's German-Jewish community, and one senses that White was asked to create something that equaled the Metropolitan Club in stature and style. He did not do so: the Harmonie, for all the grace of its cornice and fluted pilasters, comes off looking more like a bank than a club. The base is unusually heavy and institutional-looking. In fairness, part of the problem is the tight midblock site. But White was usually more imaginative; this time, he seems only to have wanted to play a game with his mix-and-match set of classical details, and the result is a two-dimensional arrangement, not a first-rate building.

III D 1 · *Metropolitan Club*

III D 2 · SHERRY-NETHERLAND HOTEL
Fifth Avenue at 59th Street, NE corner
Schultze & Weaver, 1927
· PIERRE HOTEL
Fifth Avenue at 61st Street, SE corner
Schultze & Weaver, 1929

Two of the city's finest old hotels, and the remaining two-thirds of the trio that, when it included the Savoy-Plaza (where the General Motors Building, II F 26, now stands), created a skyline profile for the southeast corner of Central Park that was as potent a symbol of romantic New York as existed anywhere. For the Sherry, Schultze & Weaver topped a slender tower with a steep peaked roof culminating in a lantern; the Pierre was given a stretched-out mansard, while the Savoy-Plaza, which had been completed in 1927 to the designs of McKim, Mead & White, had a high peaked roof topped by two chimneys. The Savoy was lower, and its loss would not have been too destructive to this remarkable pinnacle grouping had its replacement not been the garish General Motors Building, which assures that both the Pierre and the Sherry-Netherland are now seen from Central Park against the backdrop of a white marble box. The hard lines of the General Motors Building jeer at the delicacy of the two old hotels and its mass is belittling to them.

But the Sherry and the Pierre are good enough so that their integrity remains. Schultze & Weaver were to hotels in the 1920's what York & Sawyer were to banks: the magicians who translated clients' fantasies into the reality of historical architectural style, and they did it with imagination and skill. Both buildings rise with slender grace from solid bases which respect the urbanity of Fifth Avenue. The Pierre's, with its great arched windows set into rusticated limestone and freestanding urns as finials, is especially good. Neither hotel has anything approaching the monumental public space of the Plaza (II G 12) but the lobby of the Sherry-Netherland is an exquisite marble box, and the Sherry's café is one of the city's best pieces of mirrored 1930's elegance.

III D 3 · 800 FIFTH AVENUE
NE corner, 61st Street
Ulrich Franzen & Associates, 1978
· KNICKERBOCKER CLUB
SE corner, Fifth Avenue at 62nd Street
Delano & Aldrich, 1914

The Knickerbocker is the finest New York club to have come from the office of Delano & Aldrich, the firm that eventually took over the Manhattan club-building monopoly from McKim, Mead & White. It is a graceful Georgian manse of limestone and red brick, with an absolutely splendid tautness to it—there is something so tight and disciplined about this building that it makes virtually every other Manhattan club look overblown. It is not that the Knickerbocker is simple—it is, indeed, quite elegantly detailed— it is that the surface seems stretched and thin, like a perfectly made upholstery cover.

Ulrich Franzen was trying to respect the Knickerbocker in his design for 800 Fifth Avenue next door, and he paid careful attention to the Pierre (III D 2) as well. This is a building that rejects the modernist principle that the building must be a pure object, and seeks instead to accommodate itself to its surroundings, at the price of consistency or even at the price of any rigid ideology at all.

III D 3 · *Entrance of 800 Fifth Avenue*

All well and good, as a theoretical approach. The problem here is that the building is so big that ideas and principles don't matter. A 33-story mass, set parallel to the street (unlike the tower of the Pierre, which is set perpendicular to Fifth Avenue to reduce its apparent bulk), is too big for this part of Fifth Avenue, and it is bound to do harm, even if the architect has set the tower back a bit from Fifth Avenue and created a screen wall of limestone that attempts to carry the mass of the Knickerbocker Club and that of the base of the Pierre across the block, as Franzen has done. The limestone front is handsome, and a welcome attempt at craftsmanship in a day when putting a chandelier in the lobby is considered fancy apartment-house design, but it cannot do enough to offset the immense mass behind it. And it is so obviously a screen wall, or false front, that it becomes a bit disturbing when seen from the south—do we want to have such games played, even by self-proclaimed "post-modernists" like Franzen? It would have been better if the limestone wall had appeared to be something more solid, and it would have been better still if limestone had been used to sheathe the entire tower instead of the banal yellow brick (which was selected because of its similiarity to the brick used on the Pierre, where it looks a lot better). The east, or rear, façade of 800 Fifth Avenue is probably Franzen's most successful gesture—a stepped-back wall with an attractive pattern of half-round balconies, a pleasing break from conventional apartment design.

III D 4 · 834 FIFTH AVENUE
NE corner, East 64th Street
Rosario Candela, 1931

One of the masterpieces of New York's unsung hero of luxury apartment design. Candela did a number of buildings for the Anthony Campagna firm of builders, among others; they are invariably the best built and the best designed of the Upper East Side's luxury buildings. Most Candela buildings, like 834, are sheathed entirely in limestone; the façades contain discreet hints of ornament, always understated—a fluted base here, a cartouche or two there. There is never the heavy rustication of Emery Roth's buildings, such as the San Remo (III B 10) or the Beresford (III B 15); these are smoother masses, as if the entire building were designed to resemble a perfectly polished floor. The windows are vast, not so much out of a desire to bring light in as because the rooms themselves are immense and the windows are scaled to them. This is architecture that represents not aspiration but arrival, a self-assuredness that earlier, more ornate buildings could only strive toward. It is a bit reserved but, in the same way that McKim's buildings are, it brings admiration rather than irritation; you know that this is strong enough so that the whole image of elegance would not fall apart if the doorman forgot to wear white gloves one day.

III D 5 · THE ARSENAL
in Central Park, W side of Fifth Avenue at East 64th Street
Martin E. Thompson, 1848

This was the first home of the American Museum of Natural History, among its other early careers, and now serves as headquarters for the city's Department of Parks. It is one of the few buildings that seem to have a right to be in Central Park, not only because it predates the park, but because its stark brick form seems comfortable amidst the park landscape. It is entered from a plaza a bit below the grade of Fifth Avenue, obscuring it slightly, and permitting the trees to strike a balance with its hard lines. This is not the overdone, fanciful castellated architecture of most city armories, which came a few decades later; it is a businesslike fortress, and its straightforwardness is appealing, almost timeless.

III D 6 · TEMPLE EMANU-EL
1 East 65th Street, NE corner of Fifth Avenue
Robert D. Kohn, Charles Butler and Clarence Stein, with Mayers, Murray & Philip, 1929

A hushed mass of gray limestone, with the dignity and authority of an Episcopal church. The great arch of the Fifth Avenue façade is Romanesque in its origins but fairly original in its interpretation here, monumental and stark. The entire exterior seems like a great solid block, and one almost expects that the sanctuary within was hollowed out, not constructed. It turns out to be a generous space, though, with a certain Byzantine influence, very impressive and very cold.

III D 6 · *Temple Emanu-El*

III D 7 · *11 East 62nd Street*

III D 7 · THE EAST SIXTIES: THE BLOCKS OFF FIFTH AVENUE

Most of these blocks have remained remarkably free of large-scale intrusion or dramatic change of any sort since the 1920's, by which time most of the side-street mansions there today had been built. Fifth Avenue had the largest houses, but high property values and park frontage led to their demise in favor of apartment development during the 1920's, 1930's, and 1940's. The side streets had somewhat smaller buildings on somewhat less valuable land, and thus have been able to avoid falling prey to the perils of real estate speculation.

Each of these blocks from 62nd Street up is remarkable as an ensemble of individual, not matching, elements. These are not brownstones, one the same as the other, and they are not neatly tied-together rows of houses designed as a block-long composition. They are for the most part unique. But as with the best architecture everywhere in the city, they are responsible parts of a larger whole—there is no sense of clashing, no sense of jostling and fighting for position, on these blocks of the East Sixties. An Italian palazzo sits next to a Georgian manor house, which in turn is beside a Beaux-Arts mansion—it is all of history, spread out as in a catalogue so that each millionaire might be able to take his pick, and yet it is all New York, too, an eclectic jumble that maintains a clear and strong sense of continuity and sense of place. Materials play a certain role in this success—virtually everything here is limestone or brick—and scale helps, too, since nothing is substantially larger or smaller than anything else. Out of diversity comes a subtle unity that is the essence of New York.

Among the many houses between Fifth and Madison worth a special look:

——11 East 62nd Street (Haydel & Shepard, 1900), a large and elaborate French *hôtel* with especially nice iron balconies, forms over the second-floor arched windows that almost suggest Art Nouveau, and a strong rusticated base.

——3 East 64th Street (Warren & Wetmore, 1903), a grand, voluptuous palace, with huge dormers and oval windows—something of a cross between Warren & Wetmore's fantasy-like New York Yacht Club (II E 8) and that firm's later, more sober work.

——17 East 65th Street (George Nelson and William Hamby, 1941), one of Manhattan's few significant modernist townhouses. No. 17 East 65th, built originally for Sherman Fairchild, has two separate wings, one on the street and one in the rear, with a courtyard in between. The façade with its louvers is harsh and mechanical, although it fits a bit more discreetly into the streetscape than the International Style townhouses of William Lescaze.

——Lotos Club, 5 East 66th Street (Richard Howland Hunt, 1900), a grand Second Empire mansion, which piles an ornate two-story mansard on top of a red-brick midsection on top of a rusticated limestone base. The detailing is lavish, and comes tantalizingly close to excess. The ability of Hunt, who was the son of Richard Morris Hunt, to push this design right to the edge and yet never lose control is impressive.

——13 East 67th Street (Henry Allen Jacobs, 1921), a grand homage to Palladio (or, to be more precise, to the Palladian follower Serlio) in the form of a huge Palladian arch and triple window on the second floor which takes over the entire façade. There is a deep, cave-like entrance at street level to complete this handsome and unusual composition.

III D 7 · *13 and 15 East 67th Street*   **III D 7** · *9 East 68th Street*

————15 East 67th Street (Ernest Flagg, 1904), the Regency Whist Club. The name alone would justify it, but this is a gracious and handsome French house, mixing delicate ironwork with strong masonry in the same manner as Flagg's Singer Building (I F 7) and his Scribner's store (II D 4).

————16 East 67th Street (John H. Duncan, 1906), a heavy, heavy, heavy limestone mass that makes one think Duncan never stopped designing Grant's Tomb (IV A 13). But it makes for a nice and not disruptive contrast with its more subtle neighbors.

————9 East 68th Street (Heins & La Farge, 1906), one of the strangest houses in all Manhattan. Four engaged columns sit on bases almost a story high; they support nothing except a balustrade far too light in weight for them to make any sense. The columns loom over you as you approach the house, completely out of scale; one moment you wonder if they will not tumble over toward you, the next moment the whole thing looks like nothing but a trick to take your eyes off the rather pedestrian façade behind this colonnade. But the trick works—this building shouldn't be as appealing as it is.

III D 8 · *Storefront sign at 809–811 Madison Avenue*

III D 8 · MADISON AVENUE

There is almost no architecture worth anything here, and yet this is still one of the great visual experiences of this or any other city. Above 59th Street, Madison Avenue is a staggering array of elegant shops and galleries and boutiques, set in a jumble of old brownstones and apartment houses. It works because the pace is slow, the style refined, the scale small. The stores are varied and interesting, and always effective at pedestrian scale, and there is throughout the length of Madison Avenue a sense of balance. The objects one sees both in store windows and on the façades above are different enough to provide variety and continual visual interest, yet never so different as to be jarring. Obviously, a McDonald's outlet would no more fit among the stores of Madison Avenue than it would in the middle of Central Park, but the wonder of Madison Avenue is that it does not swing too far in the other direction—it is not too prissy and genteel, and the storefronts are never in search of a too easy similarity.

Occasionally something breaks the gentlemen's agreement here and forces itself too brazenly into one's line of vision, such as the slanted storefront at the northeast corner of 68th and Madison. But for each of these there is a piece of unusual dignity to offer balance, such as the exquisite matched metal storefront address signs over Nos. 809–811 Madison Avenue (F. B. and A. Ware, 1925), at the southeast corner of 68th Street, which bring a refinement and order to the streetscape at no loss to its spirit.

III D 9 · CARLETON HOUSE
674–680 Madison Avenue, 61st to 62nd streets
K. B. Norton, 1951

This must have been considered quite rear-guard when it was finished— after all, the United Nations Secretariat Building was up and the glass wall of Lever House was on the way. To erect an apartment hotel of red brick on a three-story limestone base complete with pilasters could only have seemed like a slap in the face of history. A quarter-century later, however, this looks not only appealing but impressive—it is a nicely massed pile of red brick that earnestly and conscientiously merges a conservative, Art Deco–influenced sort of modernism with a classical impulse. The ornament is a remnant, and it lacks the strength and energy of its precursors in houses and old apartment buildings of a generation before, but no matter: this is a fine transitional building, full of civilized intentions.

III D 10 · 45 EAST 66th STREET
NE corner, Madison Avenue
Harde & Short, 1906

From the folks who brought you the Alwyn Court (II G 19) and 44 West 77th Street (III B 13), more of the best gingerbread in town. This one is the best of the trio—a richly ornamented apartment house with a round tower that powerfully anchors the corner of Madison Avenue. The detail is an eclectic mix of Elizabethan and Flemish Gothic, and it is just elaborate enough to be showy, but restrained enough not to compete with the separate, secondary level of texture created by the dozens of 12-over-12 double-hung windows, a veritable curtain of tiny square panes. The round tower once contained the entrance, the relocation of which to the 66th Street side to allow more retail space is no help at all. But the building otherwise remains in splendid shape—an Elizabethan dance, ending with a gesture of joy as its rich cornice meets the sky.

III D 11 · HALSTON HOUSE
101 East 63rd Street
Paul Rudolph, 1970

Technically, this is a remodeling of a carriage house, but Rudolph's renovation was so total that it is, for all practical purposes, a new building. The interior is a set of complex spaces marked by a skillful balance of floating planes, stairways, balconies, platforms, and windows, and the façade hints as it should at the drama within. It is a subtle composition of steel and dark glass, with a gently projecting upper floor as a cornice-like horizontal element, a strong vertical center, and a solid base. The façade reflects interior functions perfectly, yet it works equally well as a composition in its own right. It is strong, yet always restrained, which permits it to blend gracefully into its older surroundings; rarely has any New York

III D 11 · *Halston House*

III D 10 · *45 East 66th Street*

building-front managed to make so powerful a statement of its own and yet achieve such quiet urbanity at the same time.

III D 12 · ASIA HOUSE
112 East 64th Street
Philip Johnson, 1959

A Mies-inspired glass skin, on the scale of a large townhouse rather than a skyscraper. The glass is dark and the steel frame is white, creating a sleek grid pattern that Mies himself would have found too decorative, but which helps make this a comfortably scaled object for this side street of brownstones and row houses. It is discreet and neat, very disciplined—but, ultimately, most interesting for the suggestion it offers that glass skins can work at this comfortably small scale.

III D 13 · former EDWARD DURELL STONE HOUSE
130 East 64th Street
Edward Durell Stone, 1956

Well, what *should* Edward Durell Stone's house look like, after all? Stone, dizzy with the success of the lacy concrete grillwork he used in his American embassy in New Delhi, started covering everything in sight with the same material—including his own brownstone. The building is small enough and the grille light enough so that this affectation does no real harm to the block, but it hardly upgrades it, either. It all comes off rather like a parody of Ed Stone done by a clever and malevolent student.

III D 12 · *Asia House*

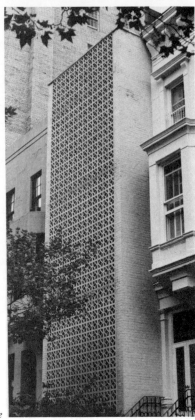

III D 13 · *Former Edward Durell Stone House*

III D 14 · FIRST OF AUGUST
860 Lexington Avenue, between 64th and 65th streets
George Ranalli, 1977

Of all the renovated—which is to say added to, twisted, and contorted—brownstone storefronts of the Upper East Side, this is the best. George Ranalli's façade for the First of August boutique consists of a two-story glass extension, made up of a grid of black steel. The extension is somewhat sculptured, in that it has a cut-in doorway and a couple of angled sections toward the top, but it is essentially a simple form. What makes it special is the pattern of the grid itself—square panes of glass, small enough so that the steel mullions coming every few inches create a rich and lively texture. The grid creates a scale that huge, unbroken panes of glass could not do, and hence it relates this very new design to the tradition of the brownstone of which it is a part. The addition seems at once daringly new and pleasantly old-fashioned; it is in the spirit of the tight grid to absorb contradictions, for one might also say that this glass storefront seems both solid and open, both opaque and transparent, both a wall and a window. Within, there is a handsome, if a bit chopped-up, store area, and a splendid space at the front of the shop within the two-story glass extension with a spiral stair that makes you feel suspended over the sidewalk.

III D 15 · 131–135 EAST 66th STREET
NE corner, Lexington Avenue
Charles A. Platt and Simonson, Pollard & Steinam, 1907

This is one notable exception to the mediocre level of apartment-house design in the eastern blocks of the Upper East Side. Platt's building is a grand house, a self-assured mass of limestone with fine Italian Renaissance detailing, skillfully wrought to reduce the structure's apparent height. There is a friendliness to this building that is missing in its equally grand contemporaries such as 998 Fifth Avenue (III D 33), which comes in part from the use of small-scaled 6-over-6 Georgian windows on the façade, and in part from the marvelous three-story pedimented doorways, which bring grandeur to the façade without ever altering the building's overall scale. Platt's entrances here, which are composed of Ionic columns supporting broken pediments, are themselves scaled larger than the building. But they are placed over the façade like vast pieces of classical jewelry, letting the body beneath show through. They are so welcoming that it is difficult to pass them by without going in.

III D 16 · SEVENTH REGIMENT ARMORY
Park Avenue, 66th to 67th streets
Charles W. Clinton, 1880

The ramparts of Park Avenue, here guarded by a fort whose architect seemed to know that the very idea of an armory in the middle of this part of town was not to be taken entirely seriously. So the Park Avenue façade is light and friendly, marked by a crenellated top that, though it is clearly based on medieval French fortress precedents, seems to make the building an enchanted prince's castle as much as a battle station. The rich red brick brings it back to nineteenth-century New York, but gently enough so as not to destroy the illusion of the prince's presence. On the Lexington Avenue side, there is more of a Victorian matter-of-factness—the great drill hall within is expressed by huge scale without.

III D 15 · *Entrance of 131–135 East 66th Street*

III D 16 · *Seventh Regiment Armory*

III D 17 · COLONY CLUB
564 Park Avenue at 62nd Street
Delano & Aldrich, 1924
· UNION CLUB
101 East 69th Street, at Park Avenue
Delano & Aldrich, 1932

The Knickerbocker Club's architecture (III D 3) suggests a membership that is svelte and athletic. The ladies of the Colony Club and the gentlemen of the Union Club, if their buildings are to be metaphors for their bodies, must be portly and slow-moving. For these are two of the most bloated buildings in Manhattan—mansions that seem to have been inflated with air and made bulbous and almost roly-poly. You just *know* the Colony Club is filled with Helen Hokinson ladies.

For all of that, the Georgian Colony Club and the eighteenth-century English Union Club are good buildings. Delano & Aldrich could capture a certain spirit in good details and good planning that makes not only for functional buildings, but for pleasant ones inside and out. But the dryness of both of these buildings is considerable—for all of the impressiveness of scale and the quality of detail here, these buildings still seem held up by hot air.

III D 18 · CENTER FOR INTER-AMERICAN RELATIONS
680 Park Avenue, NW corner 68th Street
McKim, Mead & White, 1911
· SPANISH INSTITUTE
684 Park Avenue
McKim, Mead & White, 1926
· ITALIAN CULTURAL INSTITUTE
686 Park Avenue
Delano & Aldrich, 1919
· CONSULATE GENERAL OF ITALY
690 Park Avenue
Walker & Gillette, 1917

When the Center for Inter-American Relations was owned by the Russian delegation to the United Nations some years ago, Nikita Khrushchev made a celebrated public appearance on the balcony over the front portico, bringing the house to the front page of newspapers from here to Zanzibar. Not long after—in 1965, to be exact—the house, originally built for Percy Pyne, and some of its distinguished neighbors were threatened with demolition by a developer wishing to erect an apartment house. Then, just in the nick of time, in rushed the Marquesa de Cuevas, a Rockefeller, who rescued the houses with a generous gift and presented them to the organizations which now occupy them.

The drama of the story is not, unfortunately, matched by the architecture. These are all very, very good houses, nicely wrought mixes of Federal and Georgian details, but none of them in any way leads the heart to skip a beat. They achieve an impressive unity, a vital lesson to architects today

III D 17 · *Colony Club*   **III D 17** · *Union Club*

in the virtues of working within the bounds prescribed by their neighbors, and, of course, they have great value for Park Avenue today as the only full block-front of townhouses left. But that is all—these are more important for their value as symbols than for their value as real architecture.

Worth comparing is Delano & Aldrich's Council on Foreign Relations, originally the Harold I. Pratt house, on the southeast corner of 68th Street and Park Avenue just beside this block. Completed in 1920, this is a fine English town mansion of limestone, tight and cool and possessing a strength that the Georgian and Federal mansions just up the way lack. As with all good urbanistic relationships, of course, the presence of the fine row to the north strengthens the Pratt House, just as the Pratt House strengthens the other buildings to the north. The loss of any of these structures would diminish all the others.

III D 19 · FRICK COLLECTION
1 East 70th Street
Carrère & Hastings, 1914
renovation and addition: John Russell Pope, 1935
east wing: Harry Van Dyke and John Barrington Bayley, 1977
garden: Russell Page, 1977

A member of Community Board 8, which is the local planning group passing on matters concerning the Upper East Side, was once told by a psychiatrist that he sent his troubled patients to relax at the Frick Collection. That should not have been surprising: this limestone palace, expanded into a museum by John Russell Pope in the 1930's, is a place of such serenity that it carries most visitors worlds away from New York. Pope's central court with fountain is one of New York's finest public spaces, far more inviting than almost anything else that architect ever produced, let alone than most other museums. The original house by Carrère & Hastings is less exceptional—it is large, yet, from the Fifth Avenue façade, seems the victim of a failed attempt to reduce its scale via small upstairs windows and modest details, and the whole thing looks as if it had once been another story high but had sunk into quicksand.

III D 19 · *Frick Collection*

Inside, Pope's spaces continue to come off better than Carrère & Hastings'. This is not the glimpse into life in a Fifth Avenue millionaire's mansion it is often thought to be; Pope did turn the place into a real museum, and it is better to think of the Frick as the smallest and pleasantest museum you can visit rather than the largest house you can see. The most recent addition, designed by classicist John Barrington Bayley, contains one 34-by-91-foot room, inspired by the Grand Trianon at Versailles, a seventeenth-century model somewhat bolder than the finely detailed eighteenth-century precedents on which the original Frick house and Pope additions were based. It was a daring idea, creating a true classical pavilion in the 1970's, and a lot of folks—mostly architects—laughed. It has turned out, with the exception of some rather heavy interior details that look as if they were made of Fiberglas instead of wood, to be quite a success. The addition not only integrates itself well with the rest of the Frick complex, it fits comfortably with the neighbors of the Collection along 70th Street. And it is handsome in itself, sitting rather proudly as it does beside Russell Page's overmanicured garden. Maybe there is a future to the Beaux-Arts, after all.

As a further reminder that limestone pavilions can be made decently in our time, the new addition is far superior to Pope's addition to the Frick complex on the north, the Frick Art Reference Library at 10 East 71st Street. Here, the magic of the interior court is gone, and Pope is cold, wildly overscaled, and utterly pompous.

III D 20 · EAST SEVENTIETH STREET, PARK TO LEXINGTON AVENUES

There are excellent houses on 70th Street all the way to Fifth Avenue, but this stretch, east of Park Avenue, is the best block of the Upper East Side, for here what happens commercially on Madison Avenue happens in residential architecture—a perfect balance between individuality and an overall order. Seventieth Street has lots of trees, a few large mansions, some plain brownstones, one International Style townhouse, and one gentle piece of fluff that is so good you have to take it seriously: the "French Provincial" fantasy of the Paul Mellon House at No. 125 (H. Page Cross,

1965) that brings lightness and—dare one use this word seriously?—charm to the block.

The 1941 International Style house is by William Lescaze, at No. 124, and it does not have charm. It is similar to his own stark house on East 48th Street in Turtle Bay (II D 6). Two such buildings would be an intolerable intrusion on this block; one brings a tolerable degree of variety, for it is checked by the array of Georgian houses around it. The grandest are the immense palaces at No. 115 (Patrick J. Murray, 1922) and No. 117 (Frederick Rhinelander King, 1932). The only somber, off-key note on the block is struck by the former Thomas W. Lamont House at No. 107, now occupied by the Visiting Nurse Service of New York (Walker & Gillette, 1921), a big and heavy Gothic pile that resembles nothing so much as a college dormitory. But even it cannot quash the spirit of this gentle, graceful block.

III D 21 · PARK AVENUE, ABOVE SEVENTIETH STREET

Here, Park Avenue works. The center island is too narrow, but otherwise the scale is right—the ambience is dignified and classy, in spite of the bigness of it all. It is fashionable to deride it, as Lewis Mumford has done rather eloquently in essays such as his "The Plight of the Prosperous," in which he pointed out the absence of light, views, and air in so many of these apartments. The criticisms have some truth; there is surely not much imagination to the design of the average building of upper Park Avenue. But Park Avenue was a product created for (and largely by) a social class that did not value imagination. It wanted solidity, security, and a reasonable amount of commodity, and that is what it got.

Almost everything is roughly fourteen stories tall, and most of the buildings are of dark brick in contrast to Fifth Avenue, which is predominantly light in tone. There are usually limestone bases to add a certain lightness to the street level as well as to avoid the sense that these façades

III D 20 · *Paul Mellon House; East 70th Street*

III D 22 · *Entrance of 740 Park Avenue*

are just sheer walls; there is usually enough ornament, however, so that the threat of starkness is not Park Avenue's most serious danger.

The newer buildings, such as No. 733 (III D 22), are encouraged by the current zoning law to rise as sheer towers rather than as masses built out to the street, and thus they break with the spirit of the avenue. No. 900 at the northwest corner of 79th Street (Philip Birnbaum, 1973) breaks most seriously, for it creates a sense of void at a crucial intersection. That building is where Birnbaum, architect of most of the boring Second Avenue high-rise towers, goes arty, and the results are dismal indeed.

But for the most part, upper Park Avenue consists of almost identical structures, each coated in an entirely different appliqué of historical detail. Often the eclecticism is so strong that styles are mixed within a single building. The mix is Georgian and Renaissance at the two formidable apartment houses that stand at the southwest and northwest corners of Park and 73rd Street, Nos. 770 and 778 Park Avenue (Rosario Candela, 1930). At No. 778 there is a fabulous four-story limestone base, and both buildings culminate in handsome towers, which, when viewed from the West Side, look like great gate-towers flanking East 73rd Street. An eqally interesting blend is the Georgian and Art Deco mix of No. 895 Park at the southeast corner of 79th Street (Sloan & Robertson, 1930); it is Park Avenue with just a hint of a 1930's flair. Across the street at No. 898 at the southwest corner of 79th and Park (John Sloan and Adolph E. Nast, 1924) the style becomes Lombardy Romanesque; elsewhere it is variously Renaissance, Georgian, and Gothic.

III D 22 · 740 PARK AVENUE
NW corner, 71st Street
Rosario Candela, Arthur Loomis Harmon, 1930
· 733 PARK AVENUE
SE corner, 71st Street
Kahn & Jacobs, Harry F. Green, 1971

Two generations of luxury apartment houses confront each other diagonally across an intersection, and a comparison is telling. No. 740 is another of the buildings by Rosario Candela, architect of 834 Fifth Avenue (III D 4), and it is in many ways his best—a solid, sumptuous mass that sits on a corner with absolute authority. The building is sheathed entirely in limestone, and the fluted base and entrance details suggest a hint of Art Deco, but made very, very tame, for nothing would be worse than to have the gentry of Park Avenue think they were being given the style of Central Park West and the Grand Concourse. The front doorway tells all: it is cut through a granite slab, topped by finials, which contains lettering that announces the address thus: 740 PARK AVENVE.

No such Roman affectations across the street. No. 733 Park was an attempt to construct an apartment house in the grand manner of buildings of a generation previous, such as No. 740, but it is nothing but a tower of red brick. The apartments within are generously laid out, but there is little except a few showy entrance details—travertine, chandeliers, and the like—to tell us that this place is something special. The tower itself is set back from both Park Avenue and 71st Street, breaking the street line that No.

740 holds so well—this building stands aloof, while No. 740, which has a much greater right to do so, acts as a willing and gracious neighbor.

III D 23 · URIS PAVILION, LENOX HILL HOSPITAL
Park Avenue, east side, 76th to 77th streets
Rogers, Butler, Burgun & Bradbury, 1975

A little harsh, but this red-brick box understands what it is doing in terms of its relationship to what goes on around it. It holds the line of Park Avenue and it has a discreet sort of dignity. Most important, finally, it is a reminder that some architectural firms are capable of learning from their mistakes, for it was the Rogers firm that designed the garish pink wing of Lenox Hill just next door, a coffee shop turned into a high-rise tower.

III D 24 · 870A PARK AVENUE
west side, between 77th and 78th streets
Robert A. M. Stern and John S. Hagmann, 1976

Within, this does as much as Philip Johnson's East 52nd Street house (II F 3) to kill the stigma of the New York townhouse as a place of dark and dull rooms. There is brightness and color and a complex interplay of spaces inside. The façade manages to achieve both a street-oriented formality and an expression of those activities within. Its base, midsection and cornice subtly allude to traditional townhouse façades; more important, they give this house a strength that allows it to hold its own on a street of far bigger neighbors. There is movement within an ordered frame here—and that, in theory at least, is as good a model for a contemporary townhouse façade as one could ask for.

The house is a drastic—which is to say total—remodeling of an 1899 house by A. M. Welch, part of a larger group of middle-class residences, of which two remain around the corner on the north side of East 77th Street just west of Park Avenue.

III D 25 · MANUFACTURERS HANOVER TRUST COMPANY
35 East 72nd Street, between Madison and Park avenues
Cross & Cross, 1931
· THE BANK OF NEW YORK
909 Madison Avenue, SE corner of 73rd Street
Schultze & Weaver, 1932

The great banks of York & Sawyer, like the Bowery Savings Bank on East 42nd Street (II D 15), make you feel secure. These two banks make you feel liked. The Cross & Cross building is a startlingly potent and creative interpretation of the eighteenth-century English style of the brothers Adam, marked by a high fanlight over the door, exaggerated quoins running up the edges, a second floor with a three-part window framed by engaged columns,

III D 25 · *Manufacturers Hanover Trust Company*

III D 24 · *870A Park Avenue*

and a third floor with just a single double-hung window in the middle of a solid wall. A pediment tops the composition, which, as a whole, is remarkably energetic and creative for a narrow building on a midblock site.

The Bank of New York is somewhat more modest in aspiration, but not in detail—it is a skillfully wrought Georgian business building, a branch bank that seeks to establish credibility not by awesome scale or massive solidity, but by an image of true domesticity. This is a bank made for the inhabitants of Park Avenue apartment buildings and East Seventies townhouses to cash a check or discuss a trust account—in every way an extension of their domestic worlds. The handsome fireplace right on axis with the front door sets the tone. No safes visible here.

III D 26 · COMMONWEALTH FUND
1 East 75th Street, NE corner Fifth Avenue
Hale & Rogers, 1905
· INSTITUTE OF FINE ARTS
1 East 78th Street, NE corner Fifth Avenue
Horace Trumbauer, 1912
interior alterations: Robert Venturi, Cope & Lippincott, 1958
interior alterations: Richard Foster, 1978

Taken together, these houses comprise one of the best lessons anywhere in the meaning of scale. They are both huge limestone palaces, located in equivalent positions vis-à-vis Fifth Avenue three blocks from each other. The Institute of Fine Arts is somewhat larger, but Trumbauer's immense scale makes it appear almost overwhelming. The Commonwealth Fund is only slightly smaller, but James Gamble Rogers' tight, small details make it appear far more modest. It is a reminder that scale is not so much size as appearance of size, and the relationship of size to the elements that make up its context.

The houses are equally good, although it is the Commonwealth Fund—built originally as the city residence of Edward S. Harkness, the great patron of Yale and Harvard—that is the more responsible building urbanistically. Rogers' ability to make a large building seem smaller and more discreet through the use of small (but never too small) windows, doors, porches, lintels, and cornices was unusual and impressive; there is a tightness and a discipline to this Renaissance composition that is appealing. This building wants to be on a tight city site, and for all its richness—and it is a very elaborate house indeed—it wants to defer to what is around it.

The Institute of Fine Arts, originally the James B. Duke house, shows less discretion. It is a great French neoclassical palace, and if it wants to be anywhere, it is back in France, viewed down a long and formal avenue of trees. It needs and deserves an axis for approach and some land around it for breathing, neither of which it gets on Fifth Avenue. On the other hand, Trumbauer's skill was such that the detailing here is superb, with a lyricism that goes a long way toward offsetting the image of utter immensity that this building projects. It is handsome and fairly welcoming—not nearly so cold as a limestone mass this huge might be.

The house was given to New York University for its Institute of Fine Arts by the Duke family in 1957, and renovated by Robert Venturi in one of his earliest and least-known jobs. Venturi endeavored to leave the original interior detail alone and insert matter-of-fact industrial materials, such as library stacks, into the rooms for contrast. Richard Foster's later renovation, made necessary by the Institute's growth and changing program, is handsome but more eager to be posh.

III D 27 · WHITNEY MUSEUM OF AMERICAN ART
Madison Avenue, SE corner 75th Street
Marcel Breuer, with Hamilton Smith, 1966

You aren't supposed to do such things, at least not in the post-modern 1970's—constructing a granite fortress in such a way that it steps out, floor by floor, so as to cantilever itself over its own front door. It is an arrogant, utterly abstract form, concerned more with its own shape than with any role it plays in the streetscape of Madison Avenue. The deliberately askew window on the top floor summarizes the overall attitude—abstraction before common sense. Oddly, it is right on center over the front door, preserving the building's symmetry and thus supporting the very classical impulse it seems intended to destroy.

Yet, for all this, the Whitney is almost all right. The gallery spaces are ample and flexible (although the side rooms tend to get in the way of many curators' ideas for exhibition layouts), and there is a general air of smooth functioning to this building. And even the overbearing, rather brutal form, when you have seen it once or twice, gets less threatening and seems to strike a cautious détente with the rest of Madison Avenue. This will never be the ideal building either for its site or for its program, and it will never

III D 27 · *Whitney Museum of American Art*

fully overcome that sense that all Marcel Breuer buildings give of being objects before they are buildings, but it deserves, after a decade, a grudging respect.

III D 28 · CARLYLE HOTEL
35 East 76th Street, NE corner Madison Avenue
Bien & Prince, 1929

If the Plaza is New York's best hotel building but not New York's best hotel, this may be the reverse—the best hotel housed in not the best building. But the Carlyle has its architectural merits nonetheless—the tower rising to thirty-eight stories is a handsome East Side landmark, one of the few skyscrapers of real visual interest in this part of town, its conical-topped crown bringing a sense of life to a skyline too much defined by white-brick boxes. The Carlyle's top is floodlit at night, enhancing its significance as a neighborhood—and citywide—symbol. At ground level, the Ludwig Bemelmans murals in the Bemelmans bar are a whimsical treasure, but the absence of any sort of truly elegant public space befitting a hotel aspiring to such grandeur is unfortunate.

The great brownstone tenement next door at No. 55 East 76th Street (F. T. Camp, 1883) is one of the city's earliest apartment buildings. It is a handsome relic built for a less privileged economic class than now occupies this quarter, and it is pleasing to see that it has been able to join the upwardly mobile rather than fall prey to the wrecker's ball.

III D 29 · 960 FIFTH AVENUE
NE corner, 77th Street
Rosario Candela, Warren & Wetmore, 1929

Rosario Candela (III D 4, III D 22) again, this time in partnership with the architects of Grand Central Terminal. Two things distinguish this building from Candela's other efforts. First, this was created as a cooperative building, and prospective buyers were permitted to purchase large blocks of space and have them designed according to their wishes; hence the somewhat erratic façade, on which it is easy to pick out the pattern of certain double-height living rooms, etc. What is interesting is how Candela and Warren & Wetmore managed to create a sense of overall order in spite of the freedom permitted to individual tenants; the triple-arched window and balustrade near the top has a significant role to play in anchoring the entire façade. Also worth noting is how the residents of 960 Fifth Avenue managed to avoid the problem of deciding whether one of the great, formal iron marquees of old or a newfangled canvas canopy is the better thing to have—they have always had both, one fitting neatly under the other.

III D 30 · HANAE MORI
27 East 79th Street, between Fifth and Madison avenues
alteration: Hans Hollein and Baker & Blake, 1969

This reconstruction of an old brownstone, done for the Richard Feigen Gallery and since turned into a fashion emporium, is the only New York work of Hans Hollein, the distinguished Austrian architect. The white stucco composition of the façade is dominated by a double column of chrome, which comes down just off center in a two-story entrance cut in the sleek white façade. The chrome column suggests the right degree of commercialness, just enough to let us know that this is not a house without suggesting too much more than that, either. It is a significant recent addition to a block that once could claim one of the city's proudest collections of townhouses, and still today, in spite of the replacement of the Brokaw Mansion on the northeast corner of 79th Street and Fifth Avenue in 1966 by a mediocre apartment tower (980 Fifth Avenue, Paul Resnick and Harry F. Green), has an impressive row of mansions on the south side of the block.

III D 31 · EAST 80th STREET, PARK TO LEXINGTON AVENUES

The best and biggest Upper East Side houses tend to cluster toward Fifth Avenue, but here are four exceptions, and together they make a splendid block, exactly the sort of sprightly Georgian row that the houses at Nos.

680–690 Park Avenue (III D 18) aspire to but fail to make. These houses are thinner, tighter than the Park Avenue group, which may be why they work better; they are also each more distinct in their design, and thus strike a far better balance between unity and diversity.

These are all urban versions of the search for the colonial good life as it was being sought in places like Greenwich and Locust Valley—Georgian-inspired mansions, very proper and straitlaced, just right for a generation of bankers who were appalled at what they then considered the vulgarity of the Beaux-Arts. No. 116 East 80th Street (Cross & Cross, 1922) is the most modest of the group, a restrained and welcoming neo-Federal house of red brick topped by a wide pediment. There is a lovely interplay between the main entrance on the left and the service entrance on the right—the service door has been squeezed down and the main door given an elaborate frame to enhance its symbolic importance, yet the two doors occupy precisely symmetrical places in the composition of the façade, almost exactly what Le Corbusier was to do just a few years later in the celebrated International Style façade of his Villa Stein at Garches, France.

No. 120 East 80th Street, one door to the east (Cross & Cross, 1930), is a Georgian and Federal mix, somewhat grander than No. 116, its entrance marked by a fine semicircular Doric porch. No. 124 (Mott B. Schmidt, 1930) is pure Georgian, with brick quoins and a heavy rounded pediment over the doorway. The easternmost house, No. 130 (Mott B. Schmidt, 1928), is sheathed in a tweedy, rough sort of limestone instead of the red brick of the other houses, and has overtones of the English Regency. The façade here is an especially fine composition—a strong base with an Ionic-columned porch; a two-story midsection, in which four Ionic pilasters support a cornice (its line carried across all four houses, by the way), and a fourth floor and pediment on top.

III D 32 · MANHATTAN CHURCH OF CHRIST
48 East 80th Street, between Madison and Park avenues
Eggers & Higgins, 1968

This is a surprisingly successful midblock church—not profound but sensitive. The massing of the façade is a mix of horizontal and vertical elements that strikes the sort of balance achieved in Paul Rudolph's Halston House (III D 11), although Eggers & Higgins hardly achieved Rudolph's subtlety. And the proportions are not as good here—the building should have been taller and thinner. But it is the sort of attempt to rise above the ordinary that is all too rare in New York, and it is worth viewing.

III D 33 · 998 FIFTH AVENUE
NW corner, East 81st Street
McKim, Mead & White, 1910

Fifth Avenue consisted mostly of mansions when No. 998 was built, and it must have been thought something of an intruder: apartment houses were still not considered welcome in the districts occupied by the very rich. But the design of W. S. Richardson of the McKim, Mead & White firm not only brought the occupants of this building the sort of luxury and space that townhouses provided, but brought to the streetscape every bit of the design skill shown by the best Fifth Avenue mansions. No. 998 is an Italian Renaissance palazzo, blown up to the size of an apartment house but scaled carefully to relate to what is around it. Much as Charles McKim did in the design for the University Club (II G 8), the façade of No. 998 is divided into three horizontal sections to reduce the scale—a heavy base of rusticated stone, and then two midsections separated by ornamental plaques and balustrades. An elaborate cornice tops the building off.

This is not, however, by any definition a delicate or a modest building. The great iron-and-glass canopy, which makes for as imposing an entrance as in any apartment building in Manhattan, alone would assure that. No. 998 is formal, grand, and imposing. What it is not—and here is the real sign of design skill—is intimidating.

III D 34 · 1001 FIFTH AVENUE
between 81st and 82nd streets
Johnson/Burgee, 1978
apartment layouts: Philip Birnbaum

Philip Johnson and John Burgee were called in to fix up what was to have been a cheap, standard Philip Birnbaum apartment house, sort of like Abe Burrows fixing up a play on the road. They chose to redesign the façade as a "post-modern" statement—as a polemic against the austere International Style and as a testament to the renewed acceptance of ornament among current-day architects. So they used limestone, along with rounded ornamental moldings running across the façade to carry across the lines of ornament from No. 998 Fifth Avenue next door (III D 33), and the whole façade was topped with a mock-mansard roof—a wall in the shape of a mansard that looks like a mansard from across Central Park but looks like a limestone billboard from Fifth Avenue.

The intent was admirable, but, as in Ulrich Franzen's similar attempt to break out of the standard apartment-house mold at 800 Fifth Avenue

III D 35 · *Metropolitan Museum of Art, at the foot of East 82nd Street* (III D 36)

(III D 3), the execution falls short. The biggest problem here is that Johnson and Burgee's façade suffers from a conflict between the strong verticality of the strips of windows and the horizontality of their stone ornamentation. Thus the building becomes almost vertical, and ends up fighting the distinguished neighbor at No. 998 that it is trying so hard to accommodate itself to.

III D 35 · METROPOLITAN MUSEUM OF ART
Fifth Avenue, west side, 80th to 84th streets
original building (rear façade visible within Lehman wing): Calvert Vaux
and Jacob Wrey Mould, 1880
south wing: Theodore Weston, 1888
north wing: Arthur L. T. Tuckerman, 1894
central wing, Fifth Avenue façade: Richard Morris Hunt, 1902
side wings, Fifth Avenue façade: McKim, Mead & White, 1906
Thomas J. Watson Library: Brown, Lawford & Forbes, 1965
Fifth Avenue façade and Great Hall renovation: Kevin Roche John
Dinkeloo and Associates, 1970
Robert Lehman Collection: Kevin Roche John Dinkeloo and Associates,
1975
Sackler Wing: Kevin Roche John Dinkeloo and Associates, 1978

It keeps on growing, and there is more to come, for a master plan prepared by Kevin Roche calls for the construction of more Roche wings (some now under way) to create an entirely new western façade for the museum in Central Park. One would not be surprised if the next announcement were of a new delivery entrance on Central Park West, so huge and so deeply entrenched in Central Park is the museum already. It was put into the park only after the grudging approval of Frederick Law Olmsted, Central Park's designer (III A), who felt he could not resist the pressure from civic leaders eager to join the national trend toward placing art museums in bucolic surroundings, far from the crass quarters of commerce. Olmsted called the decision in 1890 "an act generally regretted," and one suspects he would be shocked to realize that his partner Calvert Vaux's original wing has now grown into one of the largest museum complexes in the world.

Vaux's pleasant Ruskinian Gothic beginning for the Met is now largely invisible, although its red and white rear façade can be seen in overly cleaned-up, sterilized form through Roche's Lehman wing. The Weston and Tuckerman sections are also obscured, and to most of the public the image of the Metropolitan Museum is that created by Hunt and expanded by McKim, Mead & White on the Fifth Avenue façade. This is a grand Beaux-Arts façade, textured and jumpy in the case of Hunt's midsection, rather too austere in the case of McKim, Mead & White's end wings. The composition of the Hunt façade recalls the diminutive Public Baths on Asser Levy Place (II A 16) more than it does the city's other Beaux-Arts façades of comparable size, like that of the New York Public Library (II E 1). Roche's redesign of the façade is generally pleasing—his immense stair sprawls generously where Hunt's went up and down too tightly, and it has become a real urban place of its own, a Fifth Avenue version of the Spanish Steps, where people congregate on almost any pleasant day. Unfortunately, where Roche giveth urbanism, he also taketh away, for the front on either

III D 35 · *Great Hall of the Metropolitan Museum*

side of the great stairs is stark and unwelcoming. Fountains cannot make up for trees.

Inside, Hunt's Great Hall, the museum's main lobby, one of the city's great interior spaces, has been cleaned up and prettified by Roche, and the results are disquieting. The hall once had a certain air of mystery to it, an air of Piranesian shadow, and now it is filled with planters and brass kiosks and wooden benches and soft lighting. The effect is something like that of a virile workman made to wear makeup.

Roche, whose Ford Foundation (II D 10) and United Nations Plaza Hotel (II D 7) are among the city's very finest recent buildings, somehow has just been unable to give the Metropolitan his best work, for his Lehman wing, completed in 1975, is a further disappointment. There is just too much architecture here: the centerpiece is a diamond-shaped court, with its ceiling a skylight pyramiding up to a central point; there is a double limestone wall around the court, a promenade around that, a set of rooms from the Robert Lehman residence on West 54th Street around that, and a set of galleries on the lower level. It is all elegant, but the pictures are somewhat overwhelmed. It is hard not to feel that the overall concept of this building emerged as much from a desire to create a pyramid of glass as from a desire to create functional gallery space. The gallery spaces were simply strung out along the edge—although that, of course, may be the only thing to do with galleries that are "decorated" period rooms taken from a townhouse. It is all like displaying art in Bloomingdale's.

Roche's other major completed section, the Sackler wing on the north side of the museum housing the Temple of Dendur, is less frantic, but equally disappointing. Dendur is a good work of Egyptian architecture, but it is not the most extraordinary artifact to have come out of that culture, and by placing it alone in a vast room, a room that feels far bigger than the Great Hall at the museum's entrance, the temple is at once made to feel overly important and utterly unimportant. It does not deserve such immense surroundings, and they do not flatter it—the temple in Roche's huge space looks as awkward as a person dining alone in an enormous banquet hall.

It is austere and chilling, and it makes you want to rush to the comfort of the other, cluttered galleries.

The other interior gallery spaces are, for the most part, large and conventional, although some galleries in the older wings, most notably the Islamic and Egyptian collections, have been reinstalled with considerable finesse and skill. As of this writing, the other Roche wings were not complete; it can be said in their favor that they attempt to create a unified west façade facing Central Park, something the museum has never had in the past. But they are all, like the Lehman wing, abstract structures of glass, contrasting sharply with the Beaux-Arts wings which they abut.

III D 35 · *Sackler Wing of the Metropolitan Museum, with the Temple of Dendur*

III D 36 · EAST 82nd STREET, FIFTH TO MADISON AVENUES

Another superb block of townhouses, this time with a special function: to form a visual approach to the Metropolitan Museum. New York has only a handful of vistas that mean anything, and this is one of them. Richard Morris Hunt's arched entrance, framed by pairs of Corinthian columns and set on Kevin Roche's fine flowing staircase, is tightly enclosed from half a block down East 82nd Street, and the view has considerable drama. The street is far too narrow to succeed at offering the sort of grand axial vista the Beaux-Arts architects dreamed of, but it is far more interesting as it is than it would have been had the street been wider, for you can feel the space, compressed by the tightness of the street, burst out at the end when it comes to Fifth Avenue and the museum. The fact that the narrow street allows you to see only the center of the museum enhances the experience still further—you know there is more to it, and you are pulled toward the building to find out what it is.

It is worth contrasting the 82nd Street view with the vista toward the museum from 81st Street or 83rd Street. From there, there is no columned entrance pavilion to frame the view and focus it; the huge masses of the side wings merely float at the far end of the vista, as if they were ships capable of gliding down the avenue.

One building on the 82nd Street block is of special note in and of itself: the fine French *hôtel* at No. 1009 Fifth Avenue (Welch, Smith & Provot, 1901), an exceptionally graceful Beaux-Arts house, whose curved bays and iron-and-glass marquee give it a real lyricism.

III D 37 · 3 EAST 84th STREET
between Fifth and Madison avenues
Raymond Hood, 1928

A tiny, little-known gem, this ranks with 350 West 85th Street (III C 15) as one of the best small apartment houses in the city. It is a little slice of Rockefeller Center moved to the Upper East Side—there is a gray-stone front, generous and simple double-hung windows, and recessed metal spandrels in an elaborate Art Deco pattern. What this is, in fact, is not Rockefeller Center copied but Rockefeller Center foreshadowed—for this was finished years before Rockefeller Center was ready, and one can see Raymond Hood in practice here.

III D 38 · 17 EAST 84th STREET
between Fifth and Madison avenues
George F. Pelham, 1923
· 24 EAST 84th STREET
between Fifth and Madison avenues
renovation: R. Marshall Christensen, 1969

Two real curiosities. No. 17 East 84th Street is a nine-story apartment house with a strange Tudor base and upper floors that are more or less Georgian—but set into them is a five-story mock façade of mock half timber! This is the building to keep art historians awake all night, and as good a reminder as any that New York eclecticism doesn't much like playing by the rules.

No. 24 East 84th Street is a brownstone renovation of equal oddity. The stoop has been removed, as in many such alterations, and the door put into the former ground level. But instead of a window on the parlor floor above, the frame of the door continues to create the illusion of a vast two-story door, as if the owners intended only to enter and leave on stilts. It is a nice visual surprise.

III D 39 · 21 EAST 84th STREET
NW corner, Madison Avenue
· 1130–1140 MADISON AVENUE
John H. Duncan, 1892

This is a powerful row of houses in which sandstone and brick and terra cotta join in a more or less Renaissance composition, but with a starkness and a strength that are striking. There is a hint of Sullivan in the frieze, although he would never have tolerated such a simplistically decorative pattern, not to mention the sawtooth molding above. There are Ionic pilasters in brick and Doric columns in the window bays; the whole grouping is a complete hybrid in the New York tradition of complete hybrids. But also in the New York tradition is the fact that it is the architect's compositional sense that excuses the historical confusion and makes the whole thing work. Bad alterations for retail use on the Madison Avenue side have hurt the row a fair amount.

III D 40 · YIVO INSTITUTE
SE corner, Fifth Avenue and 86th Street
Carrère & Hastings, 1914

This is Louis XIII, an earlier French style for a later New York house—that is, a house postdating many of the New York mansions which take their inspiration from later French styles. This is fine, however, for reasons far beyond the reminders it offers of the Place des Vosges in Paris, of which it could almost be a sliced-out section; the red-brick and limestone façade works excellently on Fifth Avenue, anchoring a corner with a relaxed self-assurance. That cheerful peacefulness of the Place des Vosges is echoed here, with Carrère & Hastings' usual compositional skill.

III D 41 · 12 EAST 87th STREET
between Fifth and Madison avenues
George and Edward Blum, 1910

A sumptuous eight-story apartment house, an early gem that is one of the more unusual examples of terra-cotta ornament around. The patterns are geometric, and they foreshadow the fashions of Art Deco that were not to come to New York for almost another two decades. Like 3 East 84th Street (III D 37) or 235 West 71st Street (III C 5), this has a size that is especially appealing—it is a shared residence for a number of families, not a vast and impersonal block. In some ways it is little buildings like this, rather than the still more elegant structures like the Dakota (III B 9) or 998 Fifth Avenue (III D 33), that continue the ambience of townhouses best. And this building feels as if it *belongs* on a side street—it is not like an unwelcome intruder from an avenue.

III D 42 · 22 EAST 89th STREET
SW corner, Madison Avenue
Thomas Graham, 1893

What an entrance! A two-story arch flanked by two sweeping curves, supported by two tightly compressed engaged columns. It is Sullivan and Richardson and Furness and Guimard, all contorted into one architectural statement. It comes at the expense of the ideas of all of these architects, of course, just as the triangular lintels up above are at the expense of real Georgian lintels and the Romanesque details here and there are at the expense of real Romanesque details. Graham seemed to want to do everything, all at once, and he had none of the gift for gracious and subtle synthesis possessed by architects like Henry Hardenbergh or Gaetan Ajello. What Graham did have was a certain vulgar energy, and it shows everywhere in this apartment building, enough so that, in the end, it begins to win you over. There is nothing right about this building except its earnestness, and after a while you think of it in terms of sincerity instead of audacity.

III D 43 · *Solomon R. Guggenheim Museum*

III D 43 · *Interior of the Guggenheim Museum*

III D 43 · SOLOMON R. GUGGENHEIM MUSEUM
1071 Fifth Avenue, between 88th and 89th streets
Frank Lloyd Wright, 1959
addition: East 89th Street, Taliesin Associated Architects, 1968
Aye Simon Reading Room: Richard Meier & Associates, 1978

Absolutely the wrong building in the wrong place and no matter: the interior space is one of the great architectural experiences. Late Frank Lloyd Wright buildings tended to be a bit on the fantasy side, and this has the wild spirit of the master's last works, along with much more discipline—the entrance sequence is brilliantly controlled, from a low vestibule area into the great high rotunda. The drama of movement into that space, as the great stripes of the spiral galleries suddenly swirl over you and the skylit dome appears over your head, is incomparable.

Does it work as a museum? Not particularly well, although it is splendid when the exhibit contains large, color-field abstraction, Calder mobiles, or Pop Art. The architecture does, alas, fight the art much of the rest of the time, not only in the larger sense of the building's insistence upon being the foreground element in one's consciousness instead of the paintings, but also in minor ways such as problems with lighting, limitations on picture sizes, and the fact that the continuous spiral gallery forces visitors to follow a particular sequence. But it is worth the distractions, the limitations, the confusions it causes to have that rush of joy that the great space brings.

The addition, by the successors to Wright's practice, is dreadful—as good a reminder as one could ask for that genius cannot be copyrighted and mass-produced. It is sloppy, cheap imitation Wright, unworthy of the building of which it is a part. On the other hand, Richard Meier's tiny reading room off the main gallery ramp, added just recently, is less literally Wrightian, yet far more respectful of Wright's, and the building's, spirit. It is a modest and well-crafted study in the use of natural light and the interplay of curving spaces against one another—just what the Guggenheim itself is about.

III D 44 · COOPER-HEWITT MUSEUM
2 East 91st Street, at Fifth Avenue
Babb, Cook & Willard, 1903
renovation into museum: Hardy Holzman Pfeiffer Associates, 1977

This was originally the Andrew Carnegie mansion, and Carnegie's arrival pushed the borders of upper-class Manhattan into the then not too fashionable Nineties. It is notable more for its quality as a freestanding house than for its architectural distinction—the detail of this Renaissance-Georgian mix is heavy and overbearing, and the design overall has little grace, save for the pleasant glass conservatory at the east end of the main floor. Perhaps it is what Carnegie wanted—he told Babb, Cook & Willard that he envisioned "the most modest, plainest and most roomy house in New York." It is surely not the first of these, it is not the second, either, but it may well be the third.

The house was renovated with care by Hardy Holzman Pfeiffer Associates after it was taken over by the Cooper-Hewitt Museum, the Smithsonian Institution's new National Museum of Design, appropriately located in New York. The rooms inside do not make ideal gallery spaces, but they suffice, and the experience of viewing objects in the house is more relaxed than living there could have been.

III D 45 · CONVENT OF THE SACRED HEART
1 East 91st Street, at Fifth Avenue
J. Armstrong Stenhouse, with C. P. H. Gilbert, 1918
· DUCHESNE RESIDENCE SCHOOL
7 East 91st Street
Warren & Wetmore, 1902
· CONSULATE OF THE U.S.S.R.
9 East 91st Street
Carrère & Hastings, 1909
alteration: William B. Gleckman, 1976

Three of the city's greatest Renaissance mansions, each fine enough to command a Manhattan block on its own and together able to make one of New York's noblest rows. The Convent of the Sacred Heart is the most unusual—built originally for Otto Kahn, the banker, philanthropist, and patron of the arts, it is a somber exercise in Italian Renaissance palazzo design, rigid and cool but beautifully disciplined. It is one of the largest private houses ever built in Manhattan, with elaborate reception rooms and courtyards and vestibules and stair halls all arranged rather asymmetrically behind the neat and ordered façade. Most unusual is the carriageway cut into the mass of the house, a full driveway that enters in one arch and exits through another; it tells us not only that there is space to spare, but that this is a true fiefdom, a private world cut off from the city around it not by the easy device of a fence, but by the far more self-assured gesture of a private gateway.

Stenhouse was English, and one can feel it in the crisp detachment of the Kahn house. Carrère & Hastings and Warren & Wetmore were American eclectics, and their Renaissance mansions tended more toward the picturesque. The Warren & Wetmore house at No. 7 is the better of these two, less showy than No. 9 but in no way less luxurious. Its second floor is a true *piano nobile,* a great formal level sitting atop a street-level base. The house at No. 7 was built originally for James A. Burden; it complemented its neighbor, No. 9, built for John Henry Hammond. The gate in the driveway between the two houses, added when No. 9 became a Russian consulate, hurts the composition substantially.

III D 46 · 1107 FIFTH AVENUE
SE corner 92nd Street
Rouse & Goldstone, 1925

This would be an ordinary, though decent, Fifth Avenue apartment house were it not for a quirk—the fact that it once included a 54-room triplex built for Marjorie Merriwether Post, the evidence of which can be seen at a couple of crucial points on the exterior. The great Palladian window near the top of the center of the façade opened into the apartment's main foyer (there were separate men's and women's coatrooms off to either side); the apartment filled all of that floor and all of the two floors above that, too. And so that its owner—who back then was married to E. F. Hutton, the stockbroker—would not have to mix with the common folk of Fifth Avenue, she ordered a private porte cochere cut into the 92nd Street side of the building, which gave entrance to a private elevator direct to her suite. The apartment has long ago been divided into several smaller units, but the porte cochere and huge window remain as evidences of a very curious approach to the idea of apartment life.

III D 47 · 1185 PARK AVENUE
east side, 93rd to 94th streets
Schwartz & Gross, 1929

This is the only East Side attempt at a West Side form, the full-block courtyard apartment house (III C 10). Here, Schwartz & Gross, one of the most active firms of apartment-house architects of the 1920's, chose to sheathe the structure in a vaguely Gothic sort of ornament—although, as if fearing that too much medievalism would frighten the gentry of Park Avenue, they specified the multipaned double-hung windows common in

III D 47 · *Entrance of 1185 Park Avenue*

Georgian buildings. But the Gothic entry is splendid and the apartments are good—this is what happens when you design a medieval castle for a Park Avenue market.

III D 48 · SMITHERS ALCOHOLISM CENTER, ROOSEVELT HOSPITAL
56 East 93rd Street, between Madison and Park avenues
Walker & Gillette, 1932

What an exquisite thing this is—an Adamesque mansion of limestone that swoops and curves in the most wonderful, unusual way. The house is a wide mass of three full stories and one dormer floor, and its lower two floors project out at either end in a curving shape, leaving a front entrance area shaped, in plan, like a concave curve. The end wings feel like great arms reaching out to embrace you as you walk toward the front door; indeed, they pull you toward the door as you approach the house from either direction. There is an oculus over the front door, a Palladian window

III D 48 · *Smithers Alcoholism Center, Roosevelt Hospital*

on the front of each of the end wings and a great double-hung window set into each of the curving walls, all of which make the composition seem all the more unusual. But everything here, as well as the fine Adamesque detailing, so light it could be ornamental plasterwork, is a classical element. The brilliance here is not in the invention of daring, showy new forms—it is in the ability of Walker & Gillette to take an existing vocabulary and start moving it around until it becomes magic.

III D 49 · SYNOD OF BISHOPS OF THE RUSSIAN ORTHODOX CHURCH OUTSIDE OF RUSSIA
69–75 East 93rd Street, NW corner Park Avenue
Delano & Aldrich, 1918
addition: Delano & Aldrich, 1928

This is how you make a city—carefully. This is a vast mansion, an eclectic mix of the Federal and relatively similar Georgian styles, and the respect it shows for the cityscape is unusual. The house was originally built for Francis F. Palmer as a severe, squarish structure on the Park Avenue corner; when George F. Baker, Jr., purchased it in 1928, he wisely went to the original architects and let them handle his request for an immense addition to contain a ballroom. Delano & Aldrich's solution was an L-shaped wing, beginning on Park Avenue north of the original house and extending west, then turning to meet 93rd Street. A garden court was created in the space on 93rd Street between the wings, and it is a magnificent open space, grand and relaxed at the same time, the new ballroom wing forming a strong and sensitive backdrop. The court became the ceremonial entrance, and the Park Avenue side now functions as a quiet mass, holding the avenue's building line. So there is an overall order to this grouping that relates well to the overall order of the city, and within that strong order is liveliness and diversity.

III D 50 · HUNTER HIGH SCHOOL
Park to Madison avenues, 94th to 95th streets
Morris Ketchum, Jr., 1971
· FAÇADE OF SQUADRON A ARMORY
Madison Avenue, 94th to 95th streets
John Rochester Thomas, 1895

Once, the immense castle of Squadron A Armory filled the entire block, a massive presence that, unlike the Seventh Regiment Armory (III D 16) had a no-nonsense air about it, a sense that defending the populace was serious business and, hence, serious architecture. Bravado like that cannot last forever, and Squadron A was on the verge of being torn down for a new school when, in 1966, community pressure kept the western wall as a remnant. Architect Ketchum responded valiantly, and designed a school that echoes the old armory's castle-like air. The juxtaposition of old and new saves the new section from possible oppressiveness, as does the inherent playfulness in Ketchum's round towers, not to mention the general appropriateness of a heavy masonry solution for this Park Avenue site. If only brickwork these days could be a quarter as good as it was in the 1890's.

The finest aspect of the design, however, is not the school building itself but the play area at the Madison Avenue end. It skillfully uses the old armory façade as a backdrop, something which the old wall is not only admirably suited for visually but which makes it a benign and useful presence in the minds of the children of the neighborhood.

III D 51 · INTERNATIONAL CENTER FOR PHOTOGRAPHY
1130 Fifth Avenue, NE corner 94th Street
Delano & Aldrich, 1914
renovation: Robert Simpson, 1974

Neat, clean and immensely likable. It was Delano & Aldrich's ability to be both disciplined and welcoming when they wished to be, as in the Knickerbocker Club (III D 3), and overblown and pompous when they wanted to be that, as in the Union Club (III D 17). Happily, they were in their better period when Willard Straight, the original client of No. 1130, commissioned this house, and the result is a grand Federal-style house, bigger than anything the Federal building ever produced but at no sacrifice of that style's usual grace. The proportions are especially fine, and the row

III D 51 · *International Center for Photography*

of bull's-eye windows on the fourth floor brings a real movement to the façade; it lilts upward in a wonderful way. The conversion of the house into a museum in 1974 has been successful and sympathetic.

III D 52 · ANNENBERG BUILDING, MT. SINAI HOSPITAL
Fifth Avenue, between 98th and 101st streets
Skidmore, Owings & Merrill, 1976

This is a mass so huge, so brutal, as to make everything around it seem pitiful and weak. One wonders if this building was in fact commissioned not by the hospital at all, but by the builders of some of the overblown high-rise apartment towers nearby, so as to make their own offenses pale by comparison. The Annenberg Building is 436 feet tall and sheathed in Corten steel, a naturally weathering material with a rusty texture that can look handsome at small scale but becomes dark and threatening only at this immense size. In true Skidmore, Owings & Merrill fashion, this is a box, making no concessions whatsoever to anything around it, but bursting into the neighborhood and thrusting itself onto the skyline like the town bully. Why Skidmore partner Roy Allen felt that he had to make this not only so bulky but so dark as well, thereby compounding everything that is wrong with the building, is a mystery.

E/THE EAST
EAST SIDE: LEXINGTON
TO THE RIVER

There are a few isolated patches of attractiveness here, but for the most part the eastern section of the Upper East Side is an uncomfortable mix of tenements gone fancy and new high-rise apartments. Most of the new buildings were quickly and cheaply constructed, with something of the air of Quonset huts thrown up to house military personnel—only, this time there is no war, just a complete surrender of territory to the upper-middle class. The newer apartments fall into two categories—those built before 1964, which for the most part are bulky boxes built out to the street with lots of little setbacks, often catty-cornered, at the top; and those built after that year, which tend to be sheer towers, set back from the street at ground level. Zoning laws, not architects, made the decisions here, and in each case, unfortunately, builders eager to capitalize on the postwar switch of this neighborhood from a working-class quarter to an upper-middle-class one built rapidly and poorly, on the assumption that a chandelier in the lobby and a name like the Regency on the door would be sufficient indication of luxury.

The Sixties around Second and Third avenues were developed first, and they contain more of the earlier generation of postwar buildings, plus the most generous array of singles' bars anywhere in town. The Seventies are similar, only a bit quieter and less frenetic, but the Eighties, where development at large scale came later, are surely the most visually chaotic, for here the apartment houses are almost all isolated towers, clashing violently with the older tenements and townhouses which remain. It is all a jumble, and a loud, tense one—cleaner and richer than the jumble of Broadway on the Upper West Side (III C 1), but also more frenetic, more desperate, less relaxing. It all came very quickly, and you feel it may all disappear tomorrow.

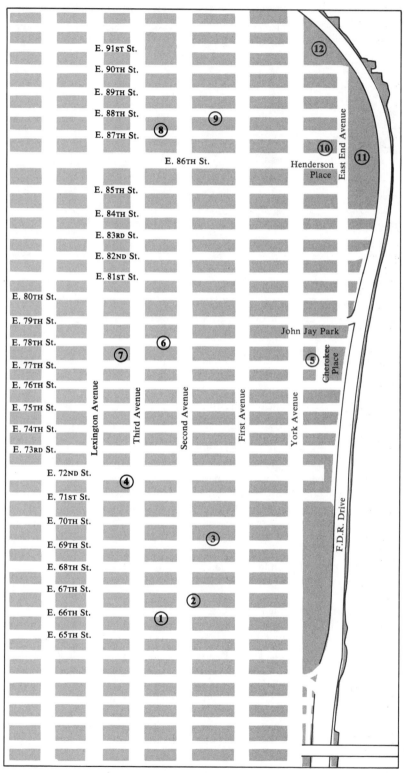

E. 91ST St.

E. 90TH St.

E. 89TH St.

E. 88TH St.

E. 87TH St.

E. 86TH St.

E. 85TH St.

E. 84TH St.

E. 83RD St.

E. 82ND St.

E. 81ST St.

E. 80TH St.

E. 79TH St.

E. 78TH St.

E. 77TH St.

E. 76TH St.

E. 75TH St.

E. 74TH St.

E. 73RD St.

E. 72ND St.

E. 71ST St.

E. 70TH St.

E. 69TH St.

E. 68TH St.

E. 67TH St.

E. 66TH St.

E. 65TH St.

Lexington Avenue

Third Avenue

Second Avenue

First Avenue

York Avenue

East End Avenue

Henderson Place

John Jay Park

Cherokee Place

F.D.R. Drive

III E 1 · *Manhattan House*

III E 1 · MANHATTAN HOUSE
200 East 66th Street, between Second and Third avenues
Skidmore, Owings & Merrill and Mayer & Whittlesey, 1950

This is a very fine building and a very bad model. An early urban renewal effort sponsored by the New York Life Insurance Co., it led the way for the postwar development of Second and Third avenues as a sea of white-brick high-rise apartment towers. But just as the wretched progeny of the Seagram Building should not be permitted to obscure that building's merit, so the ubiquitous white-brick boxes of the Upper East Side should not get in the way of the respect due Manhattan House.

For the first thing worth noting is that this is not a white-brick building in the first place. Its façade is a handsome shade of gray brick, and the metal window frames are white, creating a much more subtle pattern of colors than the white brick and aluminum window-frame combination of Manhattan House's imitators. And other details are carefully considered as well—the balconies are deeper than usual, and do not begin until a high enough floor for them to make sense. The lobby is generous in size with windows in both front and rear, and the apartments themselves are well laid out.

This is, of course, an entire block's worth of apartment building, and it can reasonably be argued that any apartment building that takes up an entire block is too big to start with. True, but the designers of Manhattan House made real efforts to accommodate this building's bulk to the functioning of the city at large. East 66th Street was widened, permitting a private automobile entranceway, and commercial development was kept to wings on Second and Third avenues, where the building is built out to the street line. A garden area stretches behind the slab on the south, and the lobby opens onto it.

Of course, much of the value of Manhattan House came at first from the expansive views that virtually every apartment had when the building was new and the vistas on all sides were clear. Now, intensive development in the neighborhood has cut off views from many apartments. But even the most cursory look at Manhattan House's neighbors—especially the directly imitative Imperial House at 150 East 69th Street (Emery Roth & Sons, 1960)—will reveal how much better this is than all the copies. The slab in open space is not the best way to make a city, but at least this time it was a good way to make a building.

III E 2 · 265 EAST 66th STREET
Second Avenue, 66th to 67th streets
Gruzen & Partners, 1978

A cry in the wilderness for better apartment design. Unfortunately, it is too little and too late—the idea of a rounded-corner glass-curtain-wall apartment house seems, in these energy-conscious late 1970's, passé, and it is a sign of how backward things are in Manhattan apartment design that this building looks avant-garde. (It was in fact designed in 1969, but not built until 1978.)

On the other hand, the 47-story shaft is a nice counterpoint to Manhattan House across the street, and the tower is by any standard a vast improvement over the white-brick rabbit warrens that dot these parts of town. The curved wall yields especially attractive corner apartments with rounded glass-walled rooms; there are round columns descending through these spaces, and they are a surprisingly positive element, not an intrusion at all. The skin is not good enough to allow this building to rank with the best glass buildings in town, but it unquestionably deserves an A for effort.

III E 3 · PREMIER
333 East 69th Street, between First and Second avenues
Mayer, Whittlesey & Glass, 1963

Here, at last, a real architect gave some real thought to what a midblock apartment façade should be. The designer was William Conklin of the Mayer, Whittlesey firm, who also did Butterfield House (I H 8), one of the

III E 3 · *Premier*

III E 2 · *265 East 66th Street*

other buildings on that very short list of decent postwar luxury housing in Manhattan. The Premier's façade is a grid of exposed concrete with brick infill; it is a strong, rhythmic presence on East 69th Street. The windows are large and well detailed, and instead of the silly balconies that project from most newer apartment houses, there are protected open pavilions set into the façade of this building. Unfortunately, the apartment layouts themselves are ordinary—but what the public sees is excellent.

III E 4 · TOWER EAST
190 East 72nd Street, SW corner Third Avenue
Emery Roth & Sons, 1962

The first apartment building to go up under the "new zoning"—the revised 1961 zoning ordinance, which encouraged sheer towers instead of setback buildings. Like Manhattan House (III E 1) and so many other New York prototypes, the first was the best; the quality of apartment towers went sharply downhill after Tower East. And Tower East is not in itself anything all that special—it is only by comparison with what has followed that this building's exposed concrete-and-glass façade looks good. The one-story commercial podium on which the building sits is a good design element, however—it brings storefronts right out to the street line, where they belong, and it avoids another useless "plaza."

III E 5 · CHEROKEE APARTMENTS
507–523 East 77th Street, at Cherokee Place east of York Avenue
Henry Atterbury Smith, 1912

This six-story apartment complex is one of the city's most significant examples of model housing built to improve the lot of the working class. The quality starts on the outside: triple-hung windows, ironwork railings on narrow French balconies. It gets better within—the apartments are arranged around open courts, with open stairwells in each corner that have vaulted tile ceilings and lovely little balconies looking back from each landing onto the courts, each possessing a tiny bench and glass canopy. The courts themselves are entered through Guastavino tiled vaults, austere but full of drama, for the coutyards become the light at the end of the tunnel.
　　The Cherokee would be a good building anywhere, but it is especially appealing here, where it is abutted by John Jay Park, a tiny neighborhood park, with which it joins to create the sense of a very special enclave. If it looks too institutional at first glance, despite the grace of the iron balconies, compare it with the Pavilion apartment house across the street at 500 East 77th Street (Philip Birnbaum, 1960), one of the largest white-brick blockbusters anywhere in town. At the Cherokee one senses an order and a place for each resident that makes him, as he stands at his balcony or crosses through the courtyard, feel unique. At the Pavilion one is only a number disappearing into a slot in a vast, undifferentiated façade.

III E 5 · *Entrance of the Cherokee Apartments*

III E 6 · *208–218 East 78th Street*

III E 6 · EAST 78th STREET, SECOND TO LEXINGTON AVENUES

A pair of blocks that both charm and instruct. If one begins at Second Avenue, the mix of tenements and very modest—though now very expensive—townhouses indicates the social composition that once prevailed in this part of town. The street becomes gradually more elegant as it moves west, rising in even stages. Across Third Avenue, townhouses are interrupted not by tenements but by a pair of fine old studio-apartment buildings. And then across Lexington Avenue 78th Street becomes truly grand, a street of large and formal townhouses to rival the Park-Lexington block on East 70th Street (III D 20).

The eastern block, between Second and Third avenues, has a relaxed air that suggests the better blocks of Greenwich Village. It is wider, and thus a bit more stately than most West Village blocks, but the same mix of fine, small old houses and larger, six-story buildings prevails. This is among the very few side streets to have stores, and to make this block more special still, they are almost all old stores with little glass display windows, not shiny prefabricated storefronts. Surely this is as close as you can come to a sense of what this part of town was like thirty or forty years ago.

The houses on the north side, Nos. 233 to 241 and 255 to 261, are delightful, Italianate in feeling, and utterly gracious. Their row is broken by the two six-story tenements at Nos. 243 and 253, which surely were considered a gross intrusion when they were built, probably quite near the end of the nineteenth century; today they seem to get on quite comfortably with the old houses, and their nicely detailed front and lovely bow-fronted storefronts merely serve to make the charm of this block more catholic.

What is really exquisite, however, is the row of six Italianate houses across the street at Nos. 208 to 218. They are all three stories high, continuing the generally modest size of most of the old houses on the street, and they are all in perfect shape, complete with intact stoops. Their windows form a lovely rhythm of arches down the street, and although this row is clearly the star of the block, it is typical of the civilized attitude buildings on East 78th Street have toward each other in that these houses in no way take attention away from their neighbors.

The houses at Nos. 157 to 165 on the block between Third and Lexington avenues are not quite so neat and perfect a group, but they are equally charming—a lovely row of red-brick townhouses, mostly with Italianate details, that have a grace and understatement far more common to Federal-period houses downtown in the Village.

III E 7 · 180 EAST 78th STREET
Third Avenue, 77th to 78th streets
E. H. Faile, Robert B. Thomas, 1938
· 177 EAST 77th STREET
between Lexington and Third avenues
Boak & Paris, 1941

The good spirit of East 78th Street extends even to storefronts on Third Avenue and apartment houses on 77th Street, it would seem. This is a splendid, civilized urban complex—a row of storefronts on Third Avenue with apartments above, accessible not from the avenue but from a common garden behind the stores. It is not quite as secluded as Turtle Bay Gardens, the Manhattan enclave it most suggests (II D 6), but with its elaborate plantings and central fountain, it creates that same feeling of enchanted, undeserved peace in the middle of Manhattan. The apartments are really more like cottages; each has its own entrance from the garden and a private terrace overlooking it, making the approach to their front door like heading toward a bungalow in the back of the Beverly Hills Hotel.

The 77th Street connection comes through the apartment house at No. 177, whose residents both overlook the garden and have access to it. No. 177 is out of scale with the cottage row, but it is a decent late 1930's building that clearly makes an attempt to fit in. The garden is not open to the public, although a portion of it can be glimpsed from the 78th Street gate; what the public can view is the Third Avenue façade of the cottage row, which is lined with glass blocks—a wise device to keep out noise when Third Avenue had the El, but now a bit dreary.

III E 8 · JEWISH BOARD OF GUARDIANS GROUP RESIDENCE FOR YOUNG ADULTS
217 East 87th Street, between Second and Third avenues
Horace Ginsbern & Associates, 1968

This wants to be La Tourette, Le Corbusier's great monastery in France that set architects all over the place playing games with raw concrete and led ultimately to the Boston City Hall. Here, the Brutalist style, as it has been called, is used to considerable success, and the mode is not too slavishly Corbusian. It is an odd image for a residence, for it is openly and proudly harsh as a style, but this building does manage to do what Brutalism often fails at, which is to work comfortably with its neighbors. A strong projecting upper floor and a continuous wall around the first floor give this building a powerful horizontality, which helps it hold on to the street line and work into its context. Unfortunately, a wretched apartment tower just to the west has been given a plaza which scoops out an open space just beside this building, leaving it more exposed and making it appear to be the end of a row instead of a building set within a row, as it was designed to be.

III E 9 · CHURCH OF THE HOLY TRINITY
316 East 88th Street, between First and Second avenues
Barney & Chapman, 1897

This is a château with hints of French Gothic, built of exquisite golden-brown Roman brick, and it works brilliantly. The tower is stunning—it rises tall and straight, with four-story-high vertical openings, then bursts into an exuberant crown. It is one of the few buildings anywhere that manage to be at once sleek and intricate.

But the siting of this church is every bit as impressive. The nave is parallel to the street, set back behind a carefully landscaped yard, like a country church, while the parish house to the west and the parsonage to the east come out like arms to meet the street. They and the nave enclose the garden on three sides, giving the space a tight, urban quality. The tower rises above the church entrance, and it is placed near, but not at, the west end of the church, thus giving the entire composition a subtle asymmetrical rhythm. The design is creative aesthetically and civilized urbanistically—there are few churches anywhere that succeed so well both as art objects and as gracious additions to the streetscape.

III E 8 · *Jewish Board of Guardians Group Residence for Young Adults*

III E 9 · *Church of the Holy Trinity*

III E 10 · HENDERSON PLACE
off East 86th Street, north side, between York and East End avenues
Lamb & Rich, 1882

What is the value of half a mews? This was once a charming, isolated enclave of thirty-two Queen Anne houses, all designed as a group by Lamb & Rich under the sponsorship of John C. Henderson, a fur merchant who decided to speculate in row houses for the middle class. Now twenty-four of the houses remain, but the eight which disappeared were replaced by a large apartment house, on East 86th Street, the side of which fills the entire west side of Henderson Place. The character of what is left is thus so compromised that the original design intent of the grouping is lost.

Still, even if there is no longer a sense that this is a private little cluster of houses, cut off from the tensions of the city, the architectural quality of the remaining houses is clearly apparent. They are a carefully wrought composition, each house not an isolated element but a part of a larger whole. Thus entranceways are often shared, and bay windows and stoops and turrets are located not as part of a single façade, but as pieces of a block-long composition.

III E 11 · CARL SCHURZ PARK and JOHN FINLEY WALK
East End Avenue to the East River, 81st to 90th streets
reconstructed for the F.D.R. Drive: Harvey Stevenson and Cameron Clark,
1938

Now, this is urbanism—a stroll from an avenue, East End, of fine apartment houses through a pleasant park and up a gentle rise to the edge of the East River, where there is a long promenade and not a car to be seen. The city falls away, the trees and the river views take over, and the automobiles are where they belong—speeding through a shelf underneath the park. Why, oh why, could this civilized solution not have been done everywhere?

The park itself is unexceptional, but unusually pleasing in size—just big enough so that it feels as if it contains a number of distinct sections, small enough so that it retains the feeling of a neighborhood open space, not a place meant for the city at large. Carl Schurz Park is big enough to encompass and shelter Gracie Mansion, the Federal-style country house of 1801–1810 that has served as the residence for New York's mayors since 1942. It is an appropriate part of the East End Avenue neighborhood, a quarter which always has the sort of hushed grandeur about it that one associates with the presence of embassies and consulates—there are none of those here—and for that reason the presence of police guards and limousines never seems startling.

East End Avenue and its companion street just south of Carl Schurz Park, Gracie Square, are a cross between the mood of Park Avenue and that of Sutton Place. Blocks of quietly dignified apartment houses make them feel large and formal, yet the sense of isolation here—this is two full blocks east of First Avenue, and far from any through-traffic route—creates the illusion that the scale is smaller and the feeling more intimate than it really is. The real treasure of the neighborhood, on balance, is the long riverfront promenade, John Finley Walk, which not only brings river views to users of Carl Schurz Park but continues south for several blocks beyond the park, its very existence even more impressive when, slipped over the highway between the buildings and the river, it becomes just an entity unto itself.

III E 12 · *Former Municipal Asphalt Plant*

III E 12 · former MUNICIPAL ASPHALT PLANT
Between York Avenue and Franklin D. Roosevelt Drive, 90th to 91st streets
Kahn & Jacobs, 1944

A soaring parabolic arch of reinforced concrete, and New York's great piece of mid-twentieth-century industrial architecture. It really was a case of the old modernist doctrine of form following function, for the arch form was a way of covering asphalt-making equipment with minimal-waste space; it was easy to see how Kahn & Jacobs could justify the form further as an appropriate expression of the flowing yet monolithic quality of reinforced concrete. The only real comparison one can make is with the huge grain elevators that assert themselves across the Middle Western landscape: they are inadvert but great pieces of monumental architecture, and so is this. It is empty pending the raising of funds to convert it into a gymnasium and community center, and one cannot imagine a more nearly perfect sort of re-use than an athletic facility, for the soaring concrete arches have as their very essence a feeling of movement and power.

IV/UPPER MANHATTAN

George Washington Bridge (IV E 7)

A/MORNINGSIDE HEIGHTS

Morningside Heights is where cultural institutions do not pretend to pastoral illusions—urban reality surrounds them at every turn. The mix here is a curious one: no New York neighborhood is as rich in centers of learning and places which the rest of the nation likes to think of as Great Institutions—such as Riverside Church and Grant's Tomb—but Morningside Heights also has its share of welfare families, dirt, and crime. Most of the neighborhood looks like the Upper West Side in the blocks below 110th Street; it is heavily

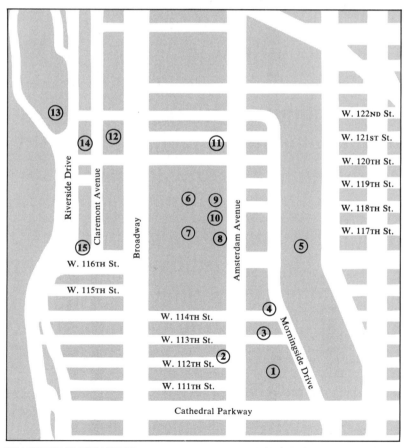

built up with apartment houses dating from the first two decades of this century, and Broadway is both its physical and its spiritual center.

But there is something that makes Broadway in Morningside Heights noticeably different from Broadway in the Eighties or the Nineties. It is poorer here, but it is more alive. The only physical differences are a few more bookstores here and a younger clientele in the bars, but there is a sense above 110th Street of a neighborhood that is a little bit more self-assured, a little bit less interested in remaking itself to look like someplace else. There will be no white-brick high-rise apartment houses here, even if economics did make them feasible, for what residents of this neighborhood fear most of all is the tendency of so much of Manhattan to look like the Upper East Side. To Morningside Heights, the Village sold out long ago and the rest of the West Side is in the process of doing so now; here, residents believe, is where city life remains real.

Morningside Heights is, in a sense, New York's equivalent of Hyde Park in Chicago, where the University of Chicago sits amidst urban decay. But the neighborhoods are not the same at all, in spite of the fact that Columbia University is surely Morningside Heights' controlling presence, for in New York the spirit of the city is as strong as the spirit of the university. The city does not stand at bay, allowing the cultural institution within it to maintain an effete, aloof presence; it rushes in with all its force, and it stamps its personality upon all of the institutions in the area. The result is that Morningside Heights is like neither any other university neighborhood nor any other city neighborhood anywhere. It is a classic New York standoff, in which no force actually dominates.

IV A 1 · CATHEDRAL CHURCH OF ST. JOHN THE DIVINE
Amsterdam Avenue at 112th Street
Heins & LaFarge, 1892–1911
Cram & Ferguson, 1911–1942

If it were ever finished, it would be the world's biggest cathedral. Now it is the world's biggest hybrid—a Byzantine-Romanesque apse, choir, and crossing, and a French Gothic nave and front. The original design was for a Byzantine-Romanesque cathedral by Heins & LaFarge, who won the commission in a competition. By 1911 both architects and the cathedral's original sponsor, Bishop Henry Codman Potter, had died, and Ralph Adams Cram, the nation's most ardent Gothic Revivalist, had persuaded his successor to discharge the original architect and let him take over the job. Cram offered a new design for a Gothic cathedral, and until World War II put an end to construction altogether; all subsequent sections of St. John the Divine were constructed in Cram's style.

The cathedral is so large—it is 601 feet long and, at the transept, 320 feet wide—that the clash of styles is rarely visible. It is awkward indeed at the crossing, where the rough, almost primitive feeling of the Heins & LaFarge section makes an awkward joining with Cram's delicate Gothic, but for the most part you have a sense of being in one section or the other, and you do not notice the shift.

Cram deeply believed that Gothic was the only acceptable style for a church; he may have been American architecture's most rigid ideologue.

Much of his work was stuffy and dry, giving credence to the theory that religious ritual meant more to him than architectural creation, but St. John's is different. The great nave is an immense, narrow space, with side aisles rising all the way to the full height of the room; it is dark, brooding, and vast, with the ethereal quality of all great Gothic cathedrals. Cram somehow managed to enhance rather than kill the sense of religious awe with his huge scale, and more impressive still is the sense of intimacy that this enormous space manages to convey. Here, Cram's passion finally broke through, and he allowed himself to make a church that has both lyricism and majesty.

Neither Cram's great crossing tower nor his façade towers were ever built, and as a result, the cathedral is more obviously unfinished on the outside than it is within. Plans were recently announced for the completion of the towers, but that is years, if not decades, off. The façade is awkward and ill-proportioned in its present state, and the joining of the Heins & LaFarge section to the Cram nave on the north side, visible from 113th Street, seems especially jarring, as if it had been done last month rather than more than sixty years ago. But the towerless façade still forms a remarkable terminus to the vista eastward along 112th Street, a narrow canyon of tenements that suddenly breaks wide open for the cathedral front; it is as dramatic a juxtaposition of the commonplace and the realm of God as exists anywhere in France.

IV A 1 · *Cathedral Church of St. John the Divine*

IV A 2 · AMSTERDAM HOUSE
1060 Amsterdam Avenue, NW corner 112th Street
Kennerley, Slomanson & Smith, 1976

Housing for the elderly, and far, far above the usual norm. The façade is of gray brick, and one can hardly call this building uninstitutional, but one detail does wonders—plate-glass windows framed in natural wood. The rich wood plays off nicely against the gray brick, and more important, it creates a domestic air that must help considerably in making the building's occupants feel at home.

Indeed, this building is well detailed all the way through. The windows are set in pairs, flush to the brick wall, with ventilating grilles set neatly into the façade beneath them. On the Amsterdam Avenue side, groups of three horizontal windows join together into large bays; the brick slopes gently down on the windowsills and gently up over doors and ground-floor windows, symbolizing their different roles. A pleasing garden and terrace is at street level, permitting residents privacy but giving them the chance to become part of the life and activity of the street at the same time. This is humane and sensitive—one of those rare reminders that architecture and social concerns need not always be in conflict.

IV A 3 · ST. LUKE'S HOSPITAL
north side, West 113th Street between Amsterdam Avenue and Morningside Drive
Ernest Flagg, 1896

The central wings of St. Luke's, like the Singer Building in SoHo (I F 7), stand as a monument to Ernest Flagg's creative imagination. What is this,

IV A 2 · *Amsterdam House*

IV A 3 · *Central entrance pavilion of St. Luke's Hospital*

Baroque? Second Empire? Classical? There is something here for everyone, but it was Flagg's gift to be able to meld stylistic influences together into a composition original enough so that you feel it is something new, and something meant to be what it is, not a warmed-over echo of some historic style.

What is most appealing here is the central entrance pavilion, a projecting tower topped by a Baroque drum and dome and ornamented in its midsection by a two-story colonnade topped by a broken pediment and at its base by an elaborate entrance porch. A bit fussy, yes, but the entrance porch's wide arms reach out as if to let you know this building wants to take care of you. By contrast, see how much sympathy the newer wing to the west (for which the western side of Flagg's building was demolished, destroying its symmetry) will give you.

IV A 4 · CHURCH OF NOTRE DAME
Morningside Drive, NW corner 114th Street
apse: Dans & Otto, 1910
church: Cross & Cross, 1915, 1928

This is one of New York's finest classical churches, a handsome and utterly dignified structure that brings real monumentality to a tight and domestically scaled site. The plan of the church is based on a Greek cross, with a Corinthian portico on the front; the whole thing is nestled in a neighborhood that hardly leads one to expect the grandeur of Napoleonic France, which is what this church suggests. Inside is a stone grotto. Cross & Cross's original plans called for a drum and dome to bring light into the sanctuary; these were never built, necessitating artificial light outside—but permitting the building to blend more gracefully into the streetscape than it probably would have done otherwise.

IV A 5 · MORNINGSIDE DRIVE / MORNINGSIDE PARK

Morningside Drive winds its way uptown from 100th Street to 122nd Street, forming the eastern border of Morningside Heights and the western border of Morningside Park, a cliff that serves as the no man's land between the Heights up top and Harlem down below. The street aspires to be Riverside Drive, and almost makes it visually, although it is now dreary and drab. The President's House (Morningside Drive, NW corner 116th Street, 1912) of Columbia University, a Renaissance mansion designed by McKim, Mead & White to be the equivalent of any of their midtown palazzos for merchant princes is the best remnant of Morningside Drive's once proud hopes.

Now, the most potent image of the Drive is not a building but the view east across the park and down into Harlem. There is no mystery to the meaning of this view today; the symbolism is clear—the rich high on a cliff, the poor down below. Perhaps it is poetic justice that the street up high is, today, almost as troubled as the streets below.

The park that divides Morningside Heights and Harlem is unsafe and always has been; Frederick Law Olmsted, who designed it, argued against the conversion of this land into a park, for even in the nineteenth century that great prophet realized the difficulties that policing a park on a cliff would entail. The park became a famous battleground in 1968, when Columbia University's proposal to build a gymnasium on park land touched off the student riots; the park land was saved, but today it is rarely used.

IV A 6 · *Columbia University campus, looking north toward Low Library, center*

IV A 6 · COLUMBIA UNIVERSITY
Main Campus: Broadway to Amsterdam Avenue, West 114th Street to West 120th Street
master plan: McKim, Mead & White, 1893

Columbia has never been able to figure out whether it wants to be a city college or look like campuses everywhere else, and the result has been an unresolved struggle between the urban and rural impulses. Charles F. McKim, who did the master plan and most of the early buildings, had no doubts: he envisioned an urban campus of dense, tight courtyards between identical classroom buildings, and of City Beautiful vistas to major monuments, such as the library. But nothing quite turned out that way, for only a few of McKim's buildings and only one of his compressed courts, that between Avery and Fayerweather halls, were built. Sprawl came instead, with buildings popping up all over the place, and open space forced in where it didn't seem to want to be. In spite of the true grandeur of the great central open space in front of McKim's centerpiece, the Low Library, this campus never escapes the city around it. There is nothing wrong with that— it is only that the post-McKim architects seemed always to be trying to fight this place's basic urban nature.

McKim's classroom buildings are imposing but dull Italian Renaissance structures of red brick and limestone trim. They have a stuffiness to them that must have provided the inspiration for many of the later architects who worked on the campus—James Gamble Rogers' Butler Library, which closes the vista at the south end of the campus, is heavy and graceless, and the slightly reduced scale that makes such Rogers buildings as the Commonwealth Fund (III D 26) appealing is of little help here. Far more disturbing are the postwar efforts on this campus. Moore & Hutchins' Uris Hall is a limestone-and-metal box that provides a harsh and scaleless backdrop for Low Library; the inside is a place of terrazzo floors and fluorescent lights that feels like an airport. In its utter banality it may well be trying to tell us something about the building's occupant—the business school—but if so, the price of such irony is high indeed.

Not much better are a pair of white boxes on a campus extension east of Amsterdam Avenue, the Law School at the northeast corner of 116th Street (Harrison & Abramovitz, 1963) and the School of International Affairs at the southeast corner of 118th Street (Harrison & Abramovitz, 1971). They are tied to the original campus area via a block-long bridge over Amsterdam Avenue, an immense and ugly "mall," which probably marks the high point of Columbia's attempts to deny its surroundings. The buildings themselves look like small-scale rehearsals for the same architects' Albany Mall.

IV A 7 · LOW LIBRARY
main campus, Columbia University
McKim, Mead & White, 1897

This is McKim's centerpiece, and far and away the high point of his Columbia designs. In fact, Low Library is one of New York's great pieces of monumental architecture, period. It never worked too well as a library, and served as one only until 1934. It has all of the severity and cool restraint one expects of McKim, but all of the opulence, too—it is not a building that inspires love, but it is one that brings a certain sense of awe no matter how many times you see it.

The inventiveness that McKim brought to the classical vocabulary here is considerable. The library has an Ionic colonnade at its entrance, a low dome, and a Greek-cross plan, but the base of the dome is set on an octagonal base, bringing a sense of roundness and fullness to the overall mass. Most impressive of all is the setting of the building atop three tiers of steps—a device that could have been imposing and distant, yet works superbly as a welcoming gesture. The stairs function like a piazza, more like the Spanish Steps in Rome than like any stairway in New York; they lead grandly to the building, yet they also exist as a destination in themselves. It all works because the campus is terraced upwards around and behind the Low Library, and the stairs serve not only as an approach to the building but as a means of moving to the north end of the campus beside and behind Low. One thus has the wonderful experience of ascending a monumental staircase and then, instead of entering the building at its head, slipping off to the side into an entire group of buildings that only then comes into view. Here, absolutely, McKim's plan succeeds.

IV A 8 · ST. PAUL'S CHAPEL
on main campus, Columbia University
Howells & Stokes, 1907

It is Greek-cross time again, but despite the similarity of the floor plan, this building could not be more different from Low Library. Howells & Stokes' chapel is largely Byzantine, with an overlay of Renaissance detail, and a cylindrical drum supports the dome. The details, the proportions, and the general air of this building, a neat combination of modesty and self-confidence, make it one of the best—perhaps the best—early building on the Columbia campus. There is none of the Low Library's arrogance here, yet there is every bit as much dignity. This building knows what it wants to be, which is its own mixture of styles, and it has great integrity. The interior has fine Guastavino tile vaults.

IV A 9 · FAIRCHILD CENTER FOR THE LIFE SCIENCES
on main campus, northeast of Low Library
Mitchell/Giurgola Associates, 1977

An unusual and subtle façade that makes for Columbia's finest postwar building by far. Fairchild occupies a crucial site on the Columbia campus, terminating a major visual axis north of McKim's Low Library; it is a site that calls for something significant, but the closeness of this building's neighbors—it is squeezed in between McKim's Schermerhorn Hall and Uris Hall, the business school—makes monumentality difficult.

Giurgola responded with a façade of quarry tile, a material that almost precisely matches the brick walks of Columbia's campus in its color. But instead of being set directly on the façade, the tile is set into large panels that are placed in front of a glass-and-metal building to act as screens. The effect is of a building that is at once massive and light: the color and the material make the building strong enough to hold its own against the large structures beside it, yet the delicacy of the façade functioning as a screen brings lightness to the building at the same time. The façade has depth and texture, like the older McKim buildings nearby, and the patterns of the screen wall act in a way as latter-day equivalents of ornament. Romaldo Giurgola has written frequently and well about his belief that buildings must function as fragments of greater wholes, not as objects in themselves, and here his theories are brought to eloquent reality.

IV A 8 · *St. Paul's Chapel, Columbia University campus*

IV A 9 · *Fairchild Center for the Life Sciences, Columbia University campus*

IV A 10 · AVERY HALL
on main campus, northeast of Low Library
McKim, Mead & White, 1912
Avery Library extension: Alexander Kouzmanoff & Associates, 1977

The original building is another McKim, Mead & White Italian Renaissance classroom box, with one exception—the great Avery Library, the finest architectural library in the nation, is on the main floor. The expansion is another of Columbia's recent efforts, like the Fairchild Center, to bring quality architecture to a campus that has seen little of it for generations. This one does not come off quite so well, in spite of the fact that Kouzmanoff's planning—which works classroom, lecture, exhibit, and library space into unused below-ground space—is a masterly three-dimensional jigsaw puzzle. The problems are a certain blandness in the interiors of the new section, and the placement of the large stairway that descends into the expansion space right along the central axis of the old Avery Library reading room, turning that once grand space into a sort of leftover corridor. And the rear courtyard over the addition, the only courtyard to have been built under the original McKim plan, has been fussed up with different kinds of brickwork and planters, giving it a bit of the air of a suburban shopping mall.

IV A 11 · BANCROFT HALL
509 West 121st Street
Emery Roth, 1911

This is mad, powerful eclecticism, a myriad of styles thrown together and then held in check—Roth, here, taunted chaos the way a good bullfighter taunts a bull, and he managed to emerge unscathed. The building consists of a central wing behind a forecourt and two projecting side wings, and while the ornament is basically Beaux-Arts in derivation, there are hints of Art Nouveau, Spanish Mission, and even, if you will, something that might be called Japanese-California Bungalow. It all works, in part because Roth abstracted everything—the cartouches are not real Italian Renaissance cartouches but abstract versions of them, for example. The side wings are the best thing of all—there are six-story bays running up the center of each, with spandrels and mullions all in elaborately molded copper, now a rich green; above the bay is an abstracted balustrade, topped by an arch; above the arch is brickwork with terra-cotta diamonds and squares set into it, and above that is a low, sprawling pitched roof out of a California bungalow or early Frank Lloyd Wright. The roof is echoed in miniature below and to the right and left of the six-story bay. The building is dark, and deserves to be cleaned, but even on its tight, compressed midblock site, it gleams.

Bancroft Hall faces the rear of Teachers College of Columbia University, and just west of it and across the street is the back of one of Teachers College's best buildings, Macy Hall (William A. Potter, 1904), a splendidly rich essay in red brick.

IV A 12 · UNION THEOLOGICAL SEMINARY
Broadway to Claremont Avenue, West 120th to West 122nd streets
Allen & Collens, 1910

This is an entire complex of collegiate Gothic, and it provides the same sort of startling shift from the world of the city to the privacy of a quadrangle that the General Theological Seminary does in Chelsea (II B 1). The buildings here are not as exquisitely detailed as the Gothic works of Yale, nor so lively and rough as the Gothic fifteen blocks uptown at City College (IV D 2). But they are handsome, and they provide the one exception to the general rule at Morningside Heights that the city never gives way to the institutions—here there is isolation and privacy.

Claremont Avenue, which also contains the banal limestone home of the Manhattan School of Music (originally the Juilliard School of Music, 120 Claremont Avenue, NW corner of West 122nd Street, designed by Donn Barber, 1910), breaks away from the messy vitality of the rest of Morningside Heights for much of its length. But it is so heavily built up, so dense with institutions and apartment buildings, that the street itself never manages to provide the pastoral illusion its institutions seem to be seeking. It is just well-behaved urban instead of rambunctious urban.

IV A 13 · *General Grant National Memorial (Grant's Tomb)*

IV A 14 · *Riverside Church*

IV A 13 · GRANT'S TOMB
Riverside Drive at West 122nd Street
John H. Duncan, 1897
surrounding benches: Pedro Silva, Cityarts Workshop, 1973

A site high above the river is the ideal place for a monument, but oh, this one is pompous indeed, and the neighborhood has responded by covering much of this immense mausoleum with graffiti. The architecture is best inside, where four coffered-ceilinged vaults support a circle with an Ionic colonnade on which rests a dome. The interior is noble and not without some good theatrics: the bodies of Ulysses S. Grant and his wife lie on polished black sarcophagi at ground level, but you view them from the monument's main interior floor one level above. That is reached via a great flight of outside steps, so that you proceed majestically up, go through a pair of bronze doors, then look down through a circular cutout to the level you have just left.

At least as good as anything Duncan wrought, however, are the recent benches in bright mosaic tile surrounding the monument. They are a continuous, flowing form, truly Gaudi-esque, undulating in and out and up and down around three sides of the building. The mosaics depict views of the city, people, automobiles, and animals, and their color and movement are just the right counterpoint to the humorless monument. The benches are full of laughter, but they are set far enough back, so that rather than poking fun directly at the building, they offer a more welcoming alternative. The benches were done by community residents; they are perhaps Manhattan's finest piece of folk art of our time, and it is no surprise that graffiti-prone vandals have chosen to leave them alone.

IV A 14 · RIVERSIDE CHURCH
Riverside Drive, West 120th to 122nd streets
Allen & Collens and Henry C. Pelton, Burnham Hoyt, 1930
south wing: Collens, Willis & Beckonert, 1960

This Rockefeller gift to New York is solid and clean, with nothing mysterious or fussy to it—a church built by money that had seen the best of European Gothic architecture and made a cool, intelligent business decision to reproduce a bit of it here. The building is strongly institutional, for by 1930 there was not too much passion left for Gothic Revivalists, and these architects, unfortunately, had only minimal inventiveness to offer in exchange for passion. The exterior is especially dull, save for the 392-foot tower; it is really a steel-framed office building with a carillon inside, and it is so big in proportion to the nave that it makes the nave look like the rear end of two men playing a horse. (The 1960 addition brings the overall composition into slightly better proportion, however.)

In the nave at least a little excitement finally breaks through. The room is immense, and cool as it is, it has a serene, confident quality that cannot but inspire a certain respect. St. John the Divine suggests a great faith in a mysterious God; Riverside suggests that its designers had a clearer idea of what God was up to, and even if you do not quite see it that way, you admire their confidence.

IV A 15 · COLOSSEUM
435 Riverside Drive, SE corner West 116th Street
Schwartz & Gross, 1910
· 29–35 CLAREMONT AVENUE
north of 116th Street
Gaetan Ajello, 1910

Colosseum would be just another pretentious, overdecorated apartment house if it were shaped like most of its contemporaries. But its entire façade is a great, sweeping curve, a lovely gesture to turn the corner from Riverside

IV A 15 · *29–35 Claremont Avenue*

IV A 15 · *Colosseum*

Drive into 116th Street. The curve both enhances 116th Street's role as an approach to Columbia University's main gate and brings more much needed light and view to 116th Street itself. A similar building across the street at 440 Riverside Drive—3 Claremont Avenue (also by Schwartz & Gross) echoes the curve in another direction; the two buildings play off against each other in plan like the curving lines of a Miró. They are both significant antecedents of 200 Central Park South (II G 13), the only attempt to celebrate a corner with a curve in postwar apartment design. In each case, the decision to break away from the traditional 90-degree corner makes sense because both streets at the intersection are significant, and the intersection deserves the enlargement of this grand gesture. It wouldn't work at a conventional corner, but it is splendid here.

The Ajello buildings around the corner on Claremont Avenue are less creative urbanistically, but have absolutely first-rate façades—lush white brick and white terra-cotta ornament, wonderfully rich and textured, yet able to feel like a strong, solid plane at the same time. They are among the most joyous buildings in the Morningside Heights area, and if Ajello's ornament could have been joined to Schwartz & Gross's curves, we would have ended up with one of the great buildings of New York.

B/CENTRAL HARLEM

The Harlem that exists today is neither the nightclub fantasy of the 1920's nor the seething ghetto of the 1960's. But it remains poor, troubled, and tense. Harlem was developed in the late nineteenth century as a middle-class suburb, and it contains some of the city's finest row housing. The neighborhood became black shortly after the turn of the century when, after overbuilding had led to high vacancies, an enterprising black realtor named Philip A. Payton persuaded landlords to let him rent to blacks, who were then being squeezed out of the slums in the West Thirties and West Fifties by commercial development. Payton's plan worked, perhaps better than he had ever expected: in just a few years Harlem was almost entirely black.

The bourgeois origins of the neighborhood make for a minimum of conventional tenements—one could not mistake Harlem for the Lower East Side. The streets are wider, and there is a sense of the overriding order of the Manhattan street grid with its long side-street blocks and wide avenues. But Harlem's aura is not one of grandeur or even of faded grandeur: there are so many vacant buildings, vacant lots, and red-brick public-housing towers that the blocks of old, intact row houses, though still considerable in quantity, nonetheless come as a surprise. The neighborhood has been decimated by social policies and by economic forces, and it has now come to resemble less the center that it is than the tired outskirts of a city, where gas stations and bars and boarded-up storefronts make up the streetscape.

Had more prosperity come to Harlem in recent years, much of its remarkable stock of row houses, churches, and commercial buildings would have disappeared. Enough have gone anyway, not to progress but to despair—hence the streets of vacant lots and abandoned houses. It is a sad view, for much of the city's best architecture is here, waiting for help. It is hard to feel hopeful: this is a place where, while the building scale is small enough and the streets are wide enough so that you can always see the sky, there is an almost overpowering sense of enclosure.

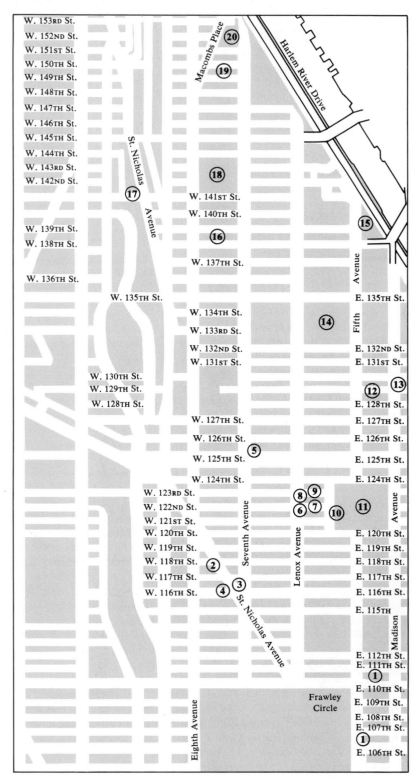

W. 153RD St.
W. 152ND St.
W. 151ST St.
W. 150TH St.
W. 149TH St.
W. 148TH St.
W. 147TH St.
W. 146TH St.
W. 145TH St.
W. 144TH St.
W. 143RD St.
W. 142ND St.
W. 141ST St.
W. 140TH St.
W. 139TH St.
W. 138TH St.
W. 137TH St.
W. 136TH St.
W. 135TH St.
W. 134TH St.
W. 133RD St.
W. 132ND St.
W. 131ST St.
W. 130TH St.
W. 129TH St.
W. 128TH St.
W. 127TH St.
W. 126TH St.
W. 125TH St.
W. 124TH St.
W. 123RD St.
W. 122ND St.
W. 121ST St.
W. 120TH St.
W. 119TH St.
W. 118TH St.
W. 117TH St.
W. 116TH St.

Macombs Place
Harlem River Drive
St. Nicholas Avenue
Seventh Avenue
Lenox Avenue
St. Nicholas Avenue
Eighth Avenue
Fifth Avenue
Madison Avenue

E. 135TH St.
E. 132ND St.
E. 131ST St.
E. 128TH St.
E. 127TH St.
E. 126TH St.
E. 125TH St.
E. 124TH St.
E. 120TH St.
E. 119TH St.
E. 118TH St.
E. 117TH St.
E. 116TH St.
E. 115TH
E. 112TH St.
E. 111TH St.
E. 110TH St.
E. 109TH St.
E. 108TH St.
E. 107TH St.
E. 106TH St.

Frawley Circle

IV / UPPER MANHATTAN   **B / CENTRAL HARLEM**

IV B 1 · FIFTH AVENUE LAKEVIEW APARTMENTS
Fifth Avenue, 106th to 107th streets
Gruzen & Partners; Castro-Blanco, Piscioneri & Feder, 1976
· ARTHUR A. SCHOMBURG PLAZA
Fifth to Madison avenues, 110th to 111th streets
Gruzen & Partners; Castro-Blanco, Piscioneri & Feder, 1975

One of these housing projects, Schomburg Plaza, is a showy pair of octagonal towers; the other is a restrained set of boxes discreetly worked into the streetscape. Both are excellent, and it is easy to overlook the thoughtful and intelligent Lakeview Apartments in the shadow of its more flamboyant neighbor by the same architects.

Schomburg's 35-story towers were intended as markers for the northeast corner of Central Park, and they function well in that role, like great posts announcing the meeting of the park and Harlem. One might wish that the design were a bit more conscious of the need to bring definition to the area at ground level as well as in the skyline, for Frawley Circle, the intersection of Fifth Avenue and 110th Street, is a diffuse jumble, and this project might have helped give it order. But the multilevel open space within Schomburg Plaza is excellent, a good mix of intimate, sheltered spaces and large, open ones, with stairs, ramps, trees, wooden gazebos, and a hexagonal paving block that alludes nicely to the octagonal tower forms as well as to the traditional sidewalk paving around Central Park. The towers themselves are reduced in scale by the handsome balconies inset into their mass in pairs every few stories; the balconies create a pleasing rhythm and texture as well.

IV B 1 · *Arthur A. Schomburg Plaza*

IV B 2 · *St. Thomas the Apostle Church*

IV B 2 · ST. THOMAS THE APOSTLE CHURCH
260 West 118th Street, SW corner St. Nicholas Avenue
T. H. Poole, 1907

This is a wild masterpiece, the power of Frank Furness merged with the delicacy of King's College Chapel. It is, alas, in terrible shape, with graffiti in as much profusion as Gothic ornament, but that does not obscure this remarkable building's quality. There is something sumptuous, almost bulbous, about the massing here that is not Gothic at all. A great stairway begins the façade composition at ground level, with one flight up in the center giving way to flights going up another story off to the right and left, up to a magnificent porch of paired columns and trefoil arches. The forms here have the sense of the absolutely raw energy of Frank Furness's great Victorian buildings in Philadelphia, but the detail itself is much lighter than Furness's, more reminiscent of French or English Perpendicular Gothic than Ruskinian. This is one of those buildings that represent eclecticism at its best—the different styles are not hitched together like boxcars but are merged into something altogether new and makes you wonder why you never saw such a thing before.

IV B 3 · GRAHAM COURT
Seventh Avenue, NW corner 116th Street
Clinton & Russell, 1901

A lovely rehearsal for the same architects' later Apthorp (III C 10), Graham Court is Harlem's finest old apartment house. The scale is curious—the building is eight stories high, significantly smaller than the Apthorp, and in fact it feels little enough so that one is constantly reminded of the façades of tenements, for all the obvious excellence and care of this building's design. The entrance into the central courtyard is via a barrel-vaulted passageway with a tile roof, each end of which is a handsome Palladian arched composition. The grandeur of the entrance reminds you that this is someplace special, just as the vast scale does in the later Apthorp.

IV B 4 · EL NIDO APARTMENTS
121 St. Nicholas Avenue, NW corner 116th Street
Neville & Bagge, c. 1900

This ornate apartment house is typical of a certain turn-of-the-century-building type common in many middle-class precincts in Manhattan—seven stories, a rusticated base, elaborate lintels over doors and windows and a heavy cornice. Somehow all of the ornament never quite convinces you that this building was meant for the rich, but it does remind you that, whatever its present state, it was most assuredly not built to be a slum.

No. 121 St. Nicholas is of special interest, however, for its skillful handling of a difficult corner. The intersection of St. Nicholas Avenue and 116th Street yields an acute angle, and this building controls that tight site well. The undulating façades, delightfully rhythmic in themselves, come to

IV B 3 · *Graham Court*

IV B 5 · *New York State Office Building*

a rounded point of focus at the corner. The form of the building thus ennobles the corner by focusing on it, and yet defers to the corner at the same time by letting the pattern of the streets be the major design factor. This era never tried to pretend that fitting into context stifled creativity— here, you can have deference and flamboyance, too.

IV B 5 · NEW YORK STATE OFFICE BUILDING
163 West 125th Street, NE corner Seventh Avenue
Ifill-Johnson-Hanchard, 1973

Well, if nothing else, this proves that the State of New York is evenhanded— it is willing to give Harlem the same mediocre architecture it dishes out everywhere else. This is a huge glass-and-concrete tower, sitting on a vast, empty site of its own making. A portion of the site is paved, and we are expected, therefore, to consider it a "plaza," even though there is virtually no seating space or landscaping. The rest of the site is a vacant lot, awaiting further development that seems less and less likely as time goes on.

The tower consists of a huge concrete frame with sections of glass curtain wall set into it. The building thus has two scales—the enormous scale of the concrete frame itself and the smaller scale of the curtain wall which denotes individual floors. Top sections project outward on the sides, and the concrete columns are splayed out at the bottom, both of which seem to be reminding us that this is Architecture, not just a building. It doesn't work—it tries much too hard, and in the end, all this looks like is not big architecture but big government.

IV B 6 · ST. MARTIN'S EPISCOPAL CHURCH
West 122nd Street, SE corner Lenox Avenue
William A. Potter, 1888

Arguably the city's finest Richardsonian Romanesque church—rich, mysterious, and powerful. St. Martin's is more of this world than Richardson's transcendent creations, but it is still masterful, a strong, somber group of masses skillfully arranged around a tower. The whole composition feels compressed, as if it were making a special effort to pull itself in and hold tight to the lines of the street and its neighboring buildings; the tower thus comes as a sort of punctuation mark, a surprise in the midst of these restrained masses. The Brown Decades, as Lewis Mumford named this building's era, produced little that struck as fine a balance between urbanistic concerns and the molding of sculptural form.

IV B 7 · WEST 122nd STREET, MOUNT MORRIS PARK WEST TO LENOX AVENUE

One of the several fine blocks in the Mount Morris Park Historic District, where there are townhouses to equal the best in Manhattan. The row made up of Nos. 4–16 West 122nd Street is especially fascinating—it is a complete composition of six houses, with the two end houses and one in the center set forward and the others set back but for flattened two-story, oriel windows projecting forward. Nos. 6 and 8, as if to anchor the center of the composition, have a massive double stone stoop. The detail is typical of the late nineteenth century, with panels set into the façade of an ornament that one can only call watered-down Sullivan. There is a lovely and far more original cornice of brick set in a geometric pattern.

IV B 8 · BETHEL GOSPEL PENTECOSTAL ASSEMBLY
36 West 123rd Street, SE corner Lenox Avenue
Lamb & Rich, 1889

One of the finest remnants of Lenox Avenue's days as a stately Harlem boulevard. This was originally the home of the Harlem Club, and if it is a bit too decorative to be a really first-rate piece of Romanesque architecture on the level of nearby St. Martin's Church (IV B 6), it nonetheless stands as an articulate relic of the period when Harlem was a neighborhood of the gentry. The neighborhood's great speculative boom came in the years following 1878—hence the abundance of late Victorian Gothic, Romanesque, and Queen Anne structures hereabouts. Also worth noting is the nearby Ephesus Seventh Day Adventist Church at 267 Lenox Avenue (NW corner 123rd Street; J. R. Thomas, 1887), with its splendid Victorian spire; this was originally the Reformed Low Dutch Church of Harlem, and like the Pentecostal Assembly, its new tenancy stands as a further reminder of Harlem's evolution.

IV B 9 · WEST 123rd STREET, MOUNT MORRIS PARK WEST TO LENOX AVENUE

Another first-rate townhouse block, beginning with the former Dwight Mansion at No. 1, now occupied by a congregation of Ethiopian Jews (Frank H. Smith, 1890). It is a grand Renaissance mansion, with a curious

IV B 6 · *St. Martin's Episcopal Church*   **IV B 9** · *6-26 West 123rd Street*

façade of one rounded bay and one flat one, and it makes a good beginning to the splendid brownstone row at Nos. 6-26 West 123rd Street. The brownstones are intact but for the replacement of many of their stone entrance balustrades with newer iron rails, a sad and unnecessary attempt to modernize what had no need for modernization.

But worth the trip is the view to the west down this block—there, right on axis with 123rd Street and way off in the distance atop the cliffs of Morningside Heights, is Grant's Tomb. The vista is completely upplanned, it comes as a total surprise, and it is a splendid piece of accidental order.

IV B 10 · MOUNT MORRIS PARK WEST

A strong Romanesque row anchors the west side of Marcus Garvey Park (formerly Mount Morris Park), and even the intrusion of a community services center at No. 10 does not alter the general aura of bourgeois contentment which emanates from this architecture. The service center, a rehabilitation by Russo & Sonder, has flush windows and a solid brick wall, but manages to feel welcoming in spite of this break from the block's style. It joins with the houses at Nos. 11 to 14 across 121st Street to form a good gateway to 121st Street, a block not quite up to the level of 122nd and 123rd, but excellent nonetheless—especially because its even brownstone rows neatly frame the tower of Riverside Church in the far distance, much as Grant's Tomb is framed by 123rd Street.

IV B 11 · MARCUS GARVEY MEMORIAL PARK
Madison Avenue to Mount Morris Park West, 120th to 124th streets

Purchased by the city as an open square in 1839, this is a rock outcropping with true drama, a hill that seems to have been squeezed out of the tight, flat blocks around it. Harlem's drastic open-space needs would have been better served by a flat park, but this land—called Mount Morris Park until it was renamed in honor of black leader Marcus Garvey in 1973—creates a visual experience that exists nowhere else in Manhattan, that of a square that, because of the high land in its center, can never be seen as a totality.

It is as if the sides of Washington Square were cut off from one another, something that would totally change the identity of that square as a unified place.

The fire tower atop the mount, a cast-iron frame structure engineered by Julius Kroehl and erected in 1856, is remarkably elegant—an octagonal form, having an open-columned frame with a spiral stair that creates a lyrical movement within. The sweep of the stair plays off gently against the rigid geometry of the structure; it is all absolutely first-rate urban sculpture, a man-made object that actually improves the rock upon which it sits.

Not as much can be said for the Mount Morris Recreation Center and Amphitheater along Mount Morris Park West in the park (Lundquist & Stonehill, 1969), a sharply geometric structure with slanted roofs that is better than most city-parks-department design by far, but still seems out of place in this quarter of old buildings. But it is far better than the harsh swimming pool and bathhouse (Ifill & Johnson, 1969) within the park just to the north.

IV B 12 · *15–29 East 129th Street*

IV B 11 · *Fire tower in Marcus Garvey Memorial Park*

IV B 12 · EAST 129th STREET, FIFTH TO MADISON AVENUES

This block has tenements, brownstones, a crumbling asphalt-shingled house, abandoned row houses, a tiny church in an old house, and a couple of vacant lots—a mix that might delight the sociologist in the perfect summary it offers of the condition of Harlem, but can only sadden anyone else. The best portion of the block is the fine row of brownstones at Nos. 15 to 29, an excellent reminder not only of the dignity this quarter once had, but of the extraordinarily rhythmic, textured streetscape the New York brownstone could produce. As in most of Harlem, the stoops have remained on the houses, making the street lively in spite of the the unintended harshness created by the absence of trees. There is a nice trio of Italianate houses at Nos. 12–16; they, along with the brownstone row, are the only sections of the block in decent shape.

IV B 13 · ALL SAINTS CHURCH
Madison Avenue, NE corner East 129th Street
Renwick, Aspinwall & Russell, 1894
· RECTORY
47 East 129th Street
Renwick, Aspinwall & Russell, 1889
· SCHOOL
52 East 130th Street
W. W. Renwick, 1904

An excellent Gothic grouping in the tradition of the very best work of James Renwick, Jr., founder of the firms that did All Saints—better, in some ways, than Renwick's own St. Patrick's Cathedral (II F 19). For the main church here manages to be at once grandiose and delicate, and the composition is inventive. The 129th Street façade is symmetrical, with a single portal, a large rose window, and a central gable above flanked by a pair of delicate towers. The top part of this composition is reproduced in miniature on each side—a smaller rose window is topped by a smaller gable with a single tower. The side aisles do not go to the height of the nave, and thus clerestories are visible, and they are not conventional windows but a series of rose windows. The rose windows are the only first-rate aspect to the Madison Avenue façade—it is otherwise all too clearly a side rather than a front; the building's design pays little attention to its role as a corner element, focusing everything on the 129th Street façade, in spite of the fact that the Madison Avenue side is far more conspicuous. (An interesting contrast is St. Thomas Church at Fifth Avenue and 53rd Street (II G 4), where the act of turning the corner becomes the controlling force of the entire composition.)

The subsidiary buildings of the All Saints grouping vary in quality. The rectory is a very handsome Gothicized row house, with an exceptionally lovely balustrade of pinwheeling stone carving. By the time the school was built, however, something had been lost—in spite of the fact that it is considerably smaller than the main church, it feels far bulkier. It is a stocky mass given an overlay of delicate details, like a stout woman wearing finely detailed jewelry, while the church is a delicate mass in itself, and its details do not seem to be trying to cover up for anything. The comparison between the two is instructive.

IV B 14 · LENOX TERRACE
Fifth to Lenox avenues, 132nd to 135th streets
S. J. Kessler & Sons, 1957

This is "hi-rise lux drmn" housing for the upper class of Harlem, a reminder that aspirations here are no different from those anywhere else. It is most definitely not public housing, in spite of the fact that these are towers of red brick set apart from one another on an open site, just like the projects that surround Lenox Terrace's neighborhood—it would not be surprising if the physical similarity between New York luxury housing and New York public housing causes more pain here, to these residents, than it does anywhere else.

IV B 15 · *Riverbend*

IV B 13 · *All Saints Church*

IV B 15 · RIVERBEND
Fifth Avenue, 138th to 142nd streets
Davis, Brody & Associates, 1967

This might look ordinary at first glance, but it is in fact one of the most distinguished housing complexes of our time. Davis, Brody and the HRH Construction Company under Richard Ravitch joined forces to try to improve the design quality of publicly assisted housing in the mid-1960's, and the result is thoroughly intelligent and civilized. Two towers contain small apartments, thrust high in the sky for generous views; eight lower buildings contain duplex apartments, reached by outdoor corridors which perform double-duty as private terraces with river views. The arrangement of the ten structures on a tight and difficult site is superb—there is shared open space, yet never that sense of empty and wasted space that exists between the towers of most public housing projects. The buildings here bind tightly together to hold the street line on Fifth Avenue, to assure the best river views for the maximum number of apartments, and to make a handsome sculptural composition as well.

The buildings are built of a giant reddish brick, 5½ inches by 8 inches, which was developed by Davis, Brody for this job as a means of reducing labor costs. It has become a standard part of the housing vernacular in New York in the decade since Riverbend, and has a bit of a clichéd air to it in some of its applications. Here, however, it was new, and in conjunction with the crisp concrete frame of Riverbend, it still appears fresh and vigorous. These buildings are *housing,* not institutions, and they feel that way through and through.

IV B 16 · KING MODEL HOUSES (STRIVER'S ROW)
138th to 139th streets, Seventh to Eighth avenues
202–250 West 138th Street, 2350–2354 Seventh Avenue
James Brown Lord, 1891
203–271 West 138th Street, 2360–2378 Seventh Avenue, 202–272 West 139th Street
Bruce Price and Clarence S. Luce, 1891
203–267 West 139th Street, 1380–2390 Seventh Avenue
McKim, Mead & White, 1891

The blocks of West 138th Street and West 139th Street stand in stunning contrast to the decay around them. Most of Seventh Avenue here is a mix of tenements, neon-sign-fronted bars, cheap stores, and vacant lots; you turn the corner onto these blocks and suddenly you are on a street that might be on the Upper East Side—but for the fact that there are no rows of townhouses as good as this on the Upper East Side. The King Model Houses, built by developer David King to show that architectural quality and urbanistic harmony could be achieved in speculative housing for New York's gentry, are unequaled.

King commissioned three different sets of architects to do segments of the development, and the results strike just the right balance between variety and unity. The scale of all of the blocks is similar, and the colors and materials, which are not the same in each section, harmonize well.

The northernmost row is by McKim, Mead & White, a street of solid Renaissance palaces of brick. The composition here is austere but elegant, with ground-floor entrances instead of stoops cutting into rusticated lime-stone bases and elaborate parlor floors with balconies below and medallions above a three-windowed composition. The block's houses frame the vista to the west of George B. Post's tower at City College (IV D 2) high off in the distance.

The south side of 139th Street, as well as the north side of 138th Street, was designed by Bruce Price and Clarence S. Luce. Here, the buildings are Georgian, with lusher ornament than McKim, Mead & White allowed themselves. The brick is buff-colored and the trim is of white stone, creating a subtle interplay of colors. There is a splendid rhythm to this block, with one especially pleasing aspect—every so often a house projects slightly out from its neighbors, and that projection is usually echoed with an indentation in the McKim, Mead & White houses across the street.

James Brown Lord's section is the simplest—red brick on a brownstone base. The ornament, again, is Georgian in derivation, but these buildings feel closer to a Victorian apartment house, brought down to row-house scale. They are very handsome, though, and the rich, deep coloration is a nice counterpoint to Price and Luce's softer tones.

Both of the blocks have service alleys running behind them, an eminently sensible gesture that has been common in cities like Baltimore and Boston but almost never used in New York. The alleys have occasional entrances

IV B 16 · *King Model Houses (Striver's Row), 203–267 West 139th Street*

IV B 16 · *One of the King Model Houses*

from the streets themselves, in between houses; it was indicative of Price and Luce's concern for quality that the houses bordering on the alley entrances were given wraparound cornices and a full complement of windows and ornament on the sides facing the alleyways, lest it appear that the alleys were merely leftover townhouse sites rather than an integral part of the composition. The houses came to be occupied by blacks not long after the rest of Harlem turned into a black neighborhood; the name "Striver's Row" came into fashion as the houses became a desirable residence for successful, ambitious blacks. They remain among Harlem's most prized housing, and deservedly so.

IV B 17 · HARLEM SCHOOL OF THE ARTS
645 St. Nicholas Avenue, at West 141st Street
Ulrich Franzen & Associates, 1977

Rather too harsh on the outside—one wonders why this was not called the Harlem Fortress of the Arts—it becomes suddenly welcoming and gracious within. Franzen fashioned out of limited space and still more limited budget not only a grand and pleasant central hall, but a myriad of lively class and practice rooms. The whole building is oriented around an attractive exterior courtyard that backs up against the cliffs of St. Nicholas Park, skillfully turning the existing topography to architectural advantage.

IV B 18 · DREW HAMILTON HOUSES
141st to 143rd streets, Seventh to Eighth avenues
Katz Waisman Weber Strauss, 1965

Worth looking at as an indication that it is possible to do bad things a little bit better. This is a public-housing complex of towers on a superblock, which is a way of building we have by now outgrown, and one we should have outgrown by 1965. But these architects did understand something about the urban fabric, and thus the towers have been kept to the major avenues, and not thrust into the middle of the site where they would have left gaping holes in the streetscape; further, the midblock area has been made into a mix of different uses instead of being left as one unwieldy space. A couple of old buildings on the midblock portion were allowed to remain, and they combine well with community facilities to create a good central space.

The towers are set at a diagonal—an attempt to enliven the streetscape that is a bit arty. But this, too, works, because the diagonal towers rise from an oblong base full of stores that tightly holds on to the street line. The major shortcoming is in the design of the towers themselves—the attempt to express the vertical circulation spine in metal instead of brick is a tired modernist cliché that, unfortunately, adds to rather than detracts from the complex's institutional qualities. And the switch from red to tan brick in the different slabs of each T-shaped tower isn't much help, either— it should have been done in really contrasting bright color or left in a single tone.

IV B 19 · PAUL LAWRENCE DUNBAR HOUSES
149th to 150th streets, Seventh to Eighth avenues
Andrew J. Thomas, 1928

Developed by John D. Rockefeller, Jr., as a cooperative for low-income black families, Dunbar is New York's first garden-apartment complex. The six-story brick structures, with a few rather stingy hints of Spanish Renaissance ornament on the façades, are arranged around central landscaped courts, and the dullness of the buildings themselves is made up for by the sense of the place as a relaxed and private enclave. The buildings have wings that project into the central space symmetrically, thus making one's movement through that space a splendid rhythmic procession of openings and closures. Like so much subsidized housing of a later era, it proved popular but not economically viable; when tenants could not meet payments during the depression, Rockefeller foreclosed and turned the building into a rental property.

IV B 20 · HARLEM RIVER HOUSES
151st to 153rd streets, Macombs Place to Harlem River Drive (site
bisected by Seventh Avenue)
*Archibald Manning Brown with Charles F. Fuller, Horace Ginsbern,
Frank J. Forster, Will Rice Amon, Richard W. Buckley, John L.
Wilson; Michael Rapuano, landscape architect, 1937*

Why, oh why, doesn't all public housing look like this? Harlem River Houses ranks with Williamsburg Houses in Brooklyn, its contemporary, as the finest public housing in New York City, where so often a prototype's quality is never reflected in its successors—as in Rockefeller Center being our best and first skyscraper grouping, as in Lever House and Seagram being our best and first glass-curtain-wall buildings.

Harlem River Houses consists of four-story red-brick walkups skillfully

IV B 20 · *Entrance of the Harlem River Houses, sculpture by Paul Manship*

strung around a large central open space in the section west of Seventh Avenue, and stretched out along the Harlem River in the section east of Seventh Avenue. The buildings have a vaguely International Style quality to them, but they are at best a neutral presence bearing decent, light apartments within. It is the arrangement of the complex itself that is so impressive.

The open space is at once massive and intimate, thanks to the projecting wings of the buildings themselves, which create a series of sheltered little court areas beside the large central area. There is thus a feeling of community to the project at large, and a sense of privacy in each little area near each entryway. The project is oriented entirely to this central space—its lack of connection with the street is a shortcoming—and there are entrances into the central space from all four sides. The space thus becomes a crossroads, a public square knitted into the fabric of the neighborhood, and yet it still feels special and private. The section east of Seventh Avenue has a less clear sense of organization, and there is less of a proprietary feeling to it— it is not surprising that, here, residents seem less concerned about outsiders wandering in and out and less quick to perform routine acts of maintenance themselves. There is no big space on this side, and there is far less of a sense of community.

Open space alone does not make a project work, of course—indeed, much public housing is compromised by too much open space, not too little. Here, a comfortable domestic scale and a relatively low density help considerably to avoid the aura of institutional tension that pervades much public housing elsewhere. So does art: there is a fine Paul Manship statue inside the 151st Street entrance to the court. There is virtually no graffiti here, by the way, and the general level of maintenance is so high that it is only the size of the trees and the hints of International Style detail that give away this place's age. Otherwise, there is something almost timeless in its solidity, general attractiveness, and sense of an architecture concerned with decency and community.

C/EAST HARLEM

In central Harlem one senses the tragedy of a rich architectural past being lost, in East Harlem the sadness of a neighborhood that never had the chance to achieve distinction in the first place. This was once an Italian slum, and is now the center of New York's Puerto Rican community; at its best it was a quarter of the working class, not the middle class, and the quality of the housing is therefore markedly different from that of central Harlem. There are tenements with fire escapes and graffiti obscuring the façades, and a handful of industrial buildings and garages, and a lot of vacant lots. Nowhere in East Harlem is there row housing of the quality of the good Harlem brownstones, and there are few parks, with what open area there is coming from the spaces in between the red-brick towers of public housing. One project of publicly assisted housing, 1199 Plaza (IV C 7) is among the city's most distinguished, and some of the other projects fall above the norm, but they are not enough to offset the general dreariness of this place, a neighborhood that has never managed to reflect in its physical form the liveliness and spirit of the Hispanic culture within it.

IV C 1 · PARK AVENUE: NORTH FROM 96th STREET

There is perhaps no other place in the United States where the necessity of tolerance is made so visible as the intersection of Park Avenue and 96th Street, for there is no other place in which the very rich live in such proximity to the very poor without a hint of the middle-class buffer upon which they both depend. Park Avenue below 96th Street is a boulevard of the rich, who live in great apartment houses made desirable by the fact that the train tracks running to and from Grand Central Terminal are buried way out of sight beneath the street; above 96th Street these very tracks burst out of their tunnel and ride atop an immense stone structure that is an ugly presence in the middle of the avenue, and the street thus instantly becomes a slum. The view from expensive cooperative apartments is one of tenements, and the view from tenements is one of luxury, and the two exist in a cautious state of détente.

The stone viaduct supporting the tracks is more like a wall than a base for an elevated train; it is heavy and dark, and streets cross it by tunneling through its mass. It would be handsome in a somber, mysterious sort of way were it not so threatening a barrier, a wall cutting East Harlem off from

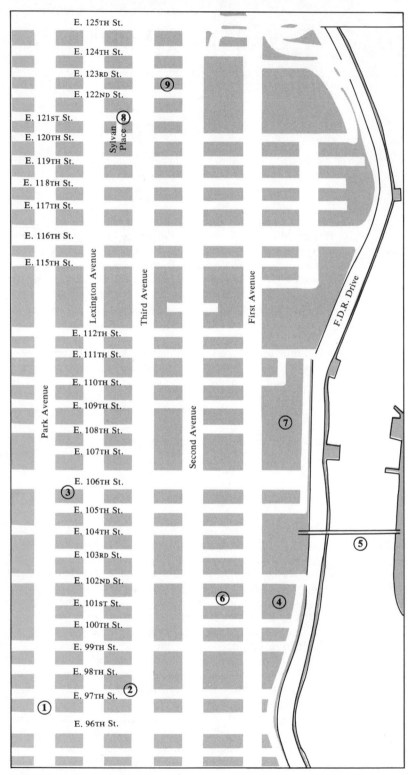

IV C 1 · *Railroad viaduct on Park Avenue*

Harlem to the west; further, it tells the people of this quarter that the railroad did not care to undertake the expense of shielding them from the ugliness of the tracks. Save for a segment between 111th and 115th streets, where a market under the tracks turns this intrusion into a joyous asset, the stone wall stands as a reminder that sometimes mass transit can be as destructive to a city as a highway.

IV C 2 · FLORENCE NIGHTINGALE NURSING HOME
1760 Third Avenue, NW corner 97th Street
William N. Breger Associates, 1974

A strong and solid composition of red brick, with a bravado that never becomes overstated. It brings a considerable degree of style to this neighborhood, standing as a reminder that red brick, that material associated here with the banal towers of public housing, can be used to create sculptural masses of real richness. The only problem is that this building, for all its obvious design quality, does not transcend its institutional identity—it looks like a hospital, albeit a very sensitively designed one, more than it looks like a place for people to live.

IV C 3 · ST. CECILIA'S CHURCH
120 East 106th Street, between Park and Lexington avenues
Napoleon Le Brun & Sons, 1887

This elaborate, vaguely Romanesque church is a curiosity more than it is a building of real distinction, in spite of the general quality of the work of the LeBrun firm, architects of the Metropolitan Life Tower (II A 9) and of so many of the city's fine early firehouses. But St. Cecilia's is surely the

IV C 4 · *Metro North Plaza*

IV C 2 · *Florence Nightingale Nursing Home*

best church of its era in East Harlem, and its ornate red terra-cotta ornament is delightful. The composition of the façade, anchored by a triple portal and by low side wings, is active yet oddly tame—somehow, here, the idea of balance doesn't work. There is not enough intellect and brilliance to the control of it, and not enough passion to the emotion of it, and it all comes off not as heavy-handed, as a poorer building of the time might, but as rather bulbous. The whole thing is saved by the amusing conceit of a bas-relief one and a half stories high, a billboard-sized version of St. Cecilia.

IV C 4 · METRO NORTH PLAZA
· VITO MARCANTONIO SCHOOL
First Avenue to Franklin D. Roosevelt Drive, 100th to 102nd streets
Conklin & Rossant, 1976

This is not truly innovative, but it is very good—a reminder of how vastly the standard of publicly assisted housing has improved in recent years. Metro North and its accompanying school are a set of low- to medium-rise buildings, constructed of concrete frames with ribbed concrete-block infill and arranged around a central corridor, a private pedestrian street. The street runs through the project at an angle perpendicular to First Avenue, with the school at its far end and a hint of a gate at its entrance—nice symbolism indeed for a housing project that wishes to impress upon its occupants the sense that they are part of a village within the greater city. The complex is roughly symmetrical around this central street, with low wings set next to the corridor and higher wings back across landscaped courts, thus enhancing the sense of the place as village-like. The buildings may not be unusual in themselves, but the careful attention here to scale, open space, and general urbanity mark this as a significant project.

IV C 5 · WARDS ISLAND PEDESTRIAN BRIDGE
East River at 103rd Street
repainting: Conklin & Rossant, 1976

Well, it was a wonderful idea, at least, when architects William Conklin and James Rossant suggested to the city's Department of Highways that the slender Wards Island Bridge be repainted in bright, contrasting colors. And it showed a certain degree of gumption when the bureaucracy went along and agreed to let the bridge have purple towers, a yellow span, and vermilion trim. After all, it was thought, this would liven up the dreary views along the Franklin D. Roosevelt Drive and give the East Harlem neighborhood a needed boost.

It may do that, but it doesn't work architecturally. The bright colors force this bridge, once a handsome background element in the urban environment, into the foreground, and they make it shriek and scream. The use of different colors for each part of the bridge makes the whole structure appear disjointed, as if the parts had started fighting with each other. The bridge becomes not a real element of the cityscape but a child's toy, a colorful plaything. All of the intentions were right—the East Harlem community does need something bright and happy, and the entire city does need more color—but this effort just doesn't come off. It is too much color, too zealously applied, and the result is that whatever integrity the bridge once had is lost.

IV C 6 · CHURCH OF THE RESURRECTION
325 East 101st Street, between First and Second avenues
Victor Lundy, 1965

This wedge-like sculpture in red brick might be considered poor man's Eero Saarinen—it strives toward drama at the expense of any obvious relationship to its context. But Lundy avoids letting the form be too theatrical, which saves it, and one passes this church convinced that the sculptural form is a correct choice for this situation. It is a deliberate contrast to the oppressive red-brick public-housing towers nearby, and it speaks strongly of the notion that a religious house should stand for a certain irrationality of form—how else to know it from its banal neighbors?

The interior, like the exterior, has a restraint that brings dignity and prevents this from being as showy as one senses it might almost have been. A ramp leads up to the sanctuary, a tentlike space that climbs with a wood-ribbed roof to a corner skylight. You enter the space under a low ceiling, and only as you move into it do you see the soaring roof line, with the spot of natural light at its climax.

IV C 7 · 1199 PLAZA
First Avenue to Franklin D. Roosevelt Drive, 107th to 111th streets
The Hodne/Stageberg Partners, 1975

This is truly noble housing—perhaps the closest Manhattan has come to the monumental housing projects for the poor constructed in Vienna in the

1920's. The architects are a Minneapolis firm, which got the commission in 1963 as the result of a competition to develop the site; it took twelve years of red tape and so much redesign that the present scheme bears little resemblance to the original, but it was all worth it.

1199 Plaza (the name comes from health-care workers' District 1199, the sponsor) consists of four 32-story towers of red brick, each shaped like a U in plan, with the open side of the U facing the East River. The towers are stepped down toward the river, so that the arms of each U reduce progressively to ten, eight, and six stories as they move toward the end. The towers themselves have a lively, angular form that adds considerable visual interest without in any way detracting from the buildings' functional rationale, and there are balconies with solid brick railings to enhance both the sense of mass and the general texture of the façade.

There is attractively designed open space within the center of the U of each tower, given privacy by the fact that the building wraps around it, yet is open to the view of the river. On First Avenue the façades are more formal—here the towers reach their full height, and they are grand and imposing, yet, as is characteristic of every aspect of this fine project, never oppressive.

The apartments themselves are well designed, with attractive duplexes for families grouped in the lower wings and smaller apartments properly in the high-rise sections. The brightly colored doors opening onto outside corridors are one of the project's few shortcomings—there is nothing wrong with the color per se, but it seems like a crutch, as if the architects did not have enough sense in the inherent value of their forms and felt they had to toss in some color just to maintain our interest.

They need not have worried. These buildings, especially from their best vantage point (alas, visible only from a moving car) on the Franklin D. Roosevelt Drive, sit with a self-assurance and a graciousness that are rare in contemporary housing. They manage to be both monumental and welcoming, both grand and comfortable—pleasing places to live and landmarks for the entire city, all at once.

IV C 8 · HARLEM COURTHOUSE
170 East 121st Street, SE corner Sylvan Place
Thom & Wilson, 1893

An odd Romanesque structure, this seems almost fearful of asserting its stylistic tendencies—it is not so much a great solid mass, like Richardsonian Romanesque buildings, as a conventional nineteenth-century brick building with Romanesque details sprinkled lightly, like salt and pepper, across it. It is too delicate and fussy to be Richardsonian, too shy to suggest the work of Frank Furness, yet at the same time it is too powerful to be anything like Victorian Gothic.

There is a tautness, a cleanness, to this entire form that is immensely appealing, though—the skin has been stretched thin around the form, and it fits just right. The round tower is not distinguished by any means, but it is handsome, and just right as a symbol of 1890's civic dignity. Indeed, what this is, is not a New York building at all, but a courthouse in the great

IV C 7 · *1199 Plaza*

IV C 8 · *Harlem Courthouse*

tradition of county courthouses of the Middle West, those splendid buildings that mixed styles so well and served as the centerpieces of town squares with all of the self-assurance of the town eccentric—he knew his position in town was unassailable, and so did the courthouse. That Harlem could have had such a place is a reminder of how far removed it once was from the press of the rest of the city downtown.

IV C 9 · TAINO TOWERS
Second to Third avenues, 122nd to 123rd streets
Silverman & Cika, 1977

Glass and very white concrete, in 35-story towers, Taino Towers was a daring scheme to put a lot of community-housing funds into a true luxury

IV C 9 · *Taino Towers*

development for low-income residents. There are floor-to-ceiling windows, balconies detailed so well they look as if they could have been done by Skidmore, Owings & Merrill, and concrete corners detailed to look almost like heavy timber. What it all looks like is rich people's housing in Caracas, a vision of sophisticated Latin richness. Here it is in the middle of Latin squalor, however, and the project's utter lack of relation to its context is disturbing—not the least of the reasons for this being that it gives the sense that the project's sponsors (and its architects) were taking as the basis for their design a total rejection of all that now exists in East Harlem.

The project has not been finished as of this writing, and financial problems make its opening date still uncertain. It will cost huge sums to operate under any sort of financial arrangement, even under the original plan by which community-services organizations would rent the lower commercial floors and hence subsidize the project. What is clear is that Taino Towers is far superior to the wretched boxes being passed off as "luxury" housing to people downtown, but how much good that will do for East Harlem remains doubtful.

D/HAMILTON HEIGHTS

Several worlds, joined neither in topography nor in sociology, make up Hamilton Heights. City College, the central campus of the City University of New York, is the neighborhood's institutional anchor, and it struggles to stand aloof from the slums that surround it. Like Morningside Heights to the south, Hamilton Heights is set on a bluff overlooking Harlem, but here the juxtaposition is not so dramatic, for much of Hamilton Heights is as deprived as the Harlem it overlooks. But there are sections of this neighborhood that are economically healthy and visually handsome—the Hamilton Heights Historic Dictrict around Convent Avenue just north of City College is one of Manhattan's finest townhouse groupings, with Alexander Hamilton's country house, Hamilton Grange, sitting forlornly in the midst of late nineteenth-century speculative splendor. And just north of the historic district is "Sugar Hill," praised in Harlem lore as the black man's Grand Concourse, the land where the blacks who made it could look down off the bluff at the ones who didn't.

Landscape makes for more drama here than in almost any other part of Manhattan, for the lower end of the district, the old village of Manhattanville, is set in a deep valley, which separates the rest of Hamilton Heights from Morningside Heights to its south. The terrain above Morningside Heights takes a drop so sharp that the West Side IRT subway, quite firmly underground as it passes Columbia University, suddenly becomes elevated. A steel viaduct carries the subway across the valley to 133rd Street, where it plunges again into its dank tunnel; the viaduct itself is a splendid latticework arch, which leaps across 125th Street with a raw, mechanistic power equaled in Manhattan only by the Queensboro Bridge (II F 6).

Manhattanville itself was an industrial quarter, and it grew up early enough to have more the air of a New England mill town than that of a great ciy. Solid brick factory buildings nestle close to one another and to the riverfront that made them possible; unfortunately, they lack the quality of the great brick industrial structures of the nineteenth century, such as the mills of Fall River, Mass., or Lowell, Mass. These are dingy hulks, with little of the grace of their New England counterparts, which require a certain degree of rural tranquillity to achieve their aesthetic value. That, in fact, may be the crucial problem—Manhattanville is a harsh cityscape, with nothing around to bring these buildings to a sense of repose. It comes off looking more like a warehouse district than anything else, and one moves with a certain relief up the hill toward the lively mix of slum, school, and brownstone that is the rest of Hamilton Heights.

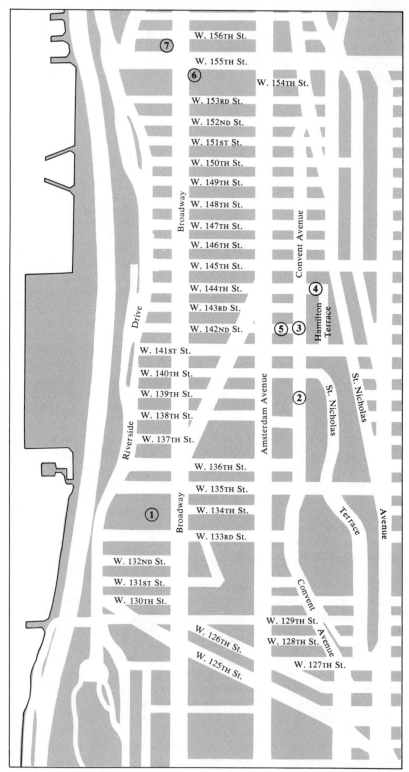

W. 156TH St.

⑦

W. 155TH St.

⑥

W. 154TH St.

W. 153RD St.

W. 152ND St.

W. 151ST St.

W. 150TH St.

W. 149TH St.

Broadway

W. 148TH St.

W. 147TH St.

Convent Avenue

W. 146TH St.

W. 145TH St.

W. 144TH St.

④

W. 143RD St.

Hamilton Terrace

W. 142ND St.

⑤ ③

W. 141ST St.

W. 140TH St.

Amsterdam Avenue

Drive

W. 139TH St.

W. 138TH St.

②

St. Nicholas

St. Nicholas

W. 137TH St.

Riverside

W. 136TH St.

W. 135TH St.

Broadway

W. 134TH St.

Terrace

Avenue

①

W. 133RD St.

W. 132ND St.

W. 131ST St.

W. 130TH St.

Convent Avenue

W. 129TH St.

W. 126TH St.

W. 128TH St.

W. 125TH St.

W. 127TH St.

IV D 1 · RIVERSIDE PARK COMMUNITY APARTMENTS
3333 Broadway, between 133rd and 135th streets
· INTERMEDIATE SCHOOL 195
625 West 133rd Street
Richard Dattner & Associates, Henri A. LeGendre & Associates, and Max Wechsler Associates, 1976

A set of far too big red-brick slabs, joined to form five-eighths of an octagon, with the neighborhood's school in the center. The slabs are of different heights, with the tallest facing southwest to catch river views and light; the whole thing looks like a pair of arms outstretched to protect the prize in its center. The project looks dreadful from Riverside Drive, where the contrast between its huge size and that of everything around it is, curiously, more disturbing than from close up on local streets. From the Broadway front these are merely banal towers, newer and cleaner than the tenements that face them on 135th Street, but otherwise not as conspicuous as one might expect. The reason is that one cannot see all five slabs from the surrounding streets (or from most areas within the complex); only to transients speeding by is the entire shape—and thus the threatening size—clear. The unorthodox solution here is probably better than putting the same number of apartments into four equal towers would have been—but not by much.

IV D 2 · CITY COLLEGE: NORTH CAMPUS
West 138th to West 140th streets, Amsterdam Avenue to St. Nicholas Terrace

The original City College campus—expanded in 1952 by the purchase of the brownstone Romanesque campus of Manhattanville College just below 135th Street—is startlingly bucolic. The curve of St. Nicholas Terrace, the presence of trees, and the detached buildings all make the tensions of the city recede far more than they do at, say, Columbia or New York University. Those campuses could only be in the midst of a throbbing metropolis; this one is hardly in a New England village, but it could pass for a campus on the outskirts of a small Midwestern city.

Part of the reason the illusion of non–New Yorkness is sustained so well is the choice of Gothic architecture for the North Campus's original structures. The main campus was completed in 1905 to the designs of George B. Post, and it is genuine, bona-fide, 100 percent American Gothic, just like the college in your hometown. Actually, it isn't quite like the college in your hometown: Post used Manhattan schist excavated from the construction of the IRT subway which passes up Broadway near the campus, and the stone yields a heavy, rough gray texture, startlingly robust. The details are all white terra cotta, and they are sufficiently ornate to establish a strong contrast to the harsh gray body of the façades, so the overall effect is rather like that of a bear wearing jewelry.

Post's main building—Shepard Hall—is the most distinguished. Its façade follows the curve of St. Nicholas Terrace with a generous curve of its own, proving once again how good the American eclectics could be at breaking with stylistic precedent in the name of good urbanism. The center of the curve, and the anchor of the entire structure, is a high Gothic tower, behind which is an immense barn of a hall—truly a nave for the City College cathedral.

This place saw itself as the people's Harvard, and for a time before World War II, it was. Now it remains the place where the children of the city's working classes seek an inexpensive (no longer free) education, but the social makeup of the student body, unlike the physical ambience of the campus, stands as a reminder of urban change.

There has been a great deal of construction on the campus since the original Post grouping, and virtually all of it is ponderous and dull. The worst building by far is Mahoney Hall (Skidmore, Owings & Merrill, 1971) a science building of reinforced concrete that sits on a squat base of its own making. The building bears no relation whatsoever to the terrain or to any of the structures anywhere near it; it seems to be trying, like so much of Skidmore's work, to evoke an image of corporate suavity. It ends up, instead, being not corporate at all, but pretentiously and arrogantly institutional.

There is much more promise in the huge and unfinished academic complex between 135th and 138th streets and Convent and Amsterdam avenues by John Carl Warnecke & Associates, which at least attempts to honor the existing geometries of the campus, and in the Aaron Davis Hall on the southeast corner of Convent Avenue and 135th Street by Abraham W. Geller & Associates and Ezra Ehrenkrantz & Associates, a sensitively designed performing-arts complex.

These are buildings that at least equal, if they do not surpass, the current standards of campus architecture around the nation, and they show a true respect for what has come before at City College. It will be difficult, however, for them to echo the original spirit of the campus, a place that today seems born in a spirit of innocence as much as anything else: the noble academy high atop the hill far away from the bustling city. Now the view down off the hill is of Harlem, and yet the plaque inside the lobby of Shepard Hall still bears the words of this oath of devotion: "We will never bring disgrace to our city by any act of dishonesty or cowardice . . . we will strive to transmit this city not only not less but greater, better and more beautiful than it was transmitted to us."

IV D 1 · *Riverside Park Community Apartments*

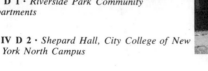

IV D 2 · *Shepard Hall, City College of New York North Campus*

Convent Avenue runs through the City College campus, but it comes into its own as it passes through the fanciful Shepard Archway, which spans it at the campus's north end. For the next five blocks Convent Avenue turns into a dignified, utterly pleasing street, with fine limestone-fronted houses, good churches, and clean, proper-looking apartment houses. One senses here not so much a place that has prospered as a place that has not changed—an urban neighborhood with all of the scrub-down-the-sidewalks earnestness so much of the city had in the 1920's and 1930's. This is one of Manhattan's finest enclaves, a place apart from the traffic, noise, and tension of so much of the rest of the city.

The best-known building here is perhaps the least interesting: Hamilton Grange, the country house of Alexander Hamilton at 287 Convent Avenue between 141st and 142nd streets (John McComb, Jr., 1801). The Grange was one of the city's earliest Federal houses, and old photographs show it to have been handsome, but since 1889 it has been subjected to the indignity of its present site, squeezed tightly between a Romanesque church and a brick apartment house and shorn of its porches. Were it not for a sign to remind you that this is a historic site under the jurisdiction of the National Park Service, you would think this to be occupied by the proverbial little old lady who refused to move away when the real estate developers came knocking at her door. The house cries out for both loving care, which it may someday get, and land, which it will probably never get.

The Grange's neighbor, St. Luke's, completed in 1892 to the designs of R. H. Robertson, is one of the city's better Richardsonian Romanesque churches, with a splendid curved entrance porch of half-round arches. It faces a good row of limestone-fronted Beaux-Arts houses at Nos. 280–298 Convent Avenue (Henri Fouchaux, 1902). Above 143rd Street, Convent Avenue seems to take a cue from St. Luke's and the houses turn Romanesque, and some of them are absolutely superb. The row at Nos. 311 to 339, for example, between 143rd and 144th streets (Adolph Hoak, 1890), is a dazzling mix of colors, materials, and geometric forms, all controlled by a general Romanesque leaning but full of Flemish and Tudor elements as well. A picturesque aesthetic was the true guiding spirit here—a mix of hipped roofs and gables and dormers, a mix of smooth stone and rough, a mix of straight stoops and L-shaped ones. Hoak's restraint kept the whole thing from becoming cacophonous, and the composition, like many good townhouse groupings, was further controlled by an overall symmetrical arrangement—a unique house forms the centerpiece, and matching designs flank it in twin sets receding away from the center house to the right and left.

The houses across the street at Nos. 320 to 328 (Horace B. Hartwell, 1890) are more restrained than the Hoak row, but equally skillful. Hartwell's houses were Romanesque as well, but he seemed to be making cautious movements into a newer world—the ornament on No. 324 is almost Sullivanesque. The next group, Nos. 330–336 (Robert Dry, 1892), carry the notion of picturesqueness further by using brick and brownstone to simulate half-timbering. It is typical of the order and serenity of Convent Avenue that the switch to the Tudor style creates hardly a moment of visual unease—the street enforces a general order that overrides stylistic differences and turns them into harmonies. The keys here, besides the consid-

IV D 3 · *280–298 Convent Avenue*

erable compositional skill and each of the architects involved, are the wide street and generous setbacks of the houses, the consistent scale, and the trees—contributors to civilization all.

Worth noting is the block of houses just off Convent Avenue on West 144th Street between Convent and Amsterdam avenues (Nos. 453–467 West 144th Street, William E. Mowbray, 1886–1890; Nos. 468–474, Harvey L. Page, 1889; Nos. 452–466, William E. Mowbray, 1890). These houses equal the picturesque compositional skill shown in the Convent Avenue houses, and they are all placed behind raised terraces to set them off from the sidewalk—a device that brings to row houses a hint of the grandeur of the freestanding mansion.

IV D 4 · WEST 144th STREET, HAMILTON TERRACE TO CONVENT AVENUE

Eclecticism gone wild. But in the spirit of the fine Convent Avenue blocks which it adjoins (and the Hamilton Heights Historic District, of which both this block and its neighbors are a part), it is all held in control, and the product ends up being exhilarating rather than excessive.

The row on the north side, Nos. 413–423 West 144th Street (T. H. Dunn, 1898), is a mix of Venetian Gothic, Italian Renaissance, and French Renaissance elements—yet another reminder of how pointless it is to try, at least in New York, to classify styles precisely. All of history is here for the taking; there was no belief that the Venetian Gothic style *meant* anything except delicate arches, so there was no reason—at least in this architect's mind—not to combine it with the ornamental pilasters and decorative shields of Renaissance architecture. The controlling idea here was visual, not ideological, and because Dunn had a good as well as an imaginative visual sense, it all works.

The houses on the south side, Nos. 418–426 (Neville & Bagge, 1897), make up a strongly ordered row, with strong, large end pavilions. Most unusual here, though, are the Second Empire overtones mixed with Renaissance composition—these houses are Renaissance townhouses with Second Empire mansard roofs to jazz them up. More rules are broken, and once again the score here is architects 100, rules zero.

IV D 5 · OUR LADY OF LOURDES CHURCH
467 West 142nd Street, between Convent and Amsterdam avenues
O'Reilly Brothers, 1904

Here, eclecticism is given new meaning altogether. One wonders if the O'Reilly Brothers misunderstood what was said about eclectic architecture in class one day, and when they were told that eclecticism meant the combination of different styles, they thought it meant the combination of different buildings. In any case, these architects took the idea of eclecticism so literally that they made Our Lady of Lourdes out of portions from three demolished buildings: the National Academy of Design, which once stood at 23rd Street and Park Avenue South; the Madison Avenue side of St. Patrick's Cathedral which was removed to make way for the Lady Chapel; and the A. T. Stewart residence, which stood at 34th Street and Fifth Avenue.

The National Academy of Design, a gray-and-white façade of marble and bluestone (Peter B. Wight, 1865), was New York's most significant piece of Ruskinian Gothic architecture, and it is the controlling influence in this born-again hybrid. The St. Patrick's elements have gone into the apse and part of the east wall of the church, while the Stewart remnants (John Kellum, 1867) are part of the church entrance.

It all could be silly, and yet it all works just fine—it does not come off as a piece of whimsy at all, but as a serious architectural gesture. The Wight façade works well with the limestone houses surrounding it, and would be a decent street façade almost anywhere. Here it is a magnificent piece of urban rescue—why is there not another Our Lady of Lourdes for a later generation of lost buildings?

IV D 6 · CHURCH OF THE INTERCESSION
SE corner, Broadway and 155th Street
Bertram Grosvenor Goodhue, 1914
· TRINITY CEMETERY
Riverside Drive to Amsterdam Avenue, 153rd to 155th streets
Gatehouse and Keeper's Lodge: Vaux & Radford, 1883
Grounds: Vaux & Co., 1881

Goodhue's wonderful massing made his churches seem to push up from the ground like organic objects. Here, even more than in St. Thomas Church on Fifth Avenue (II G 4), you sense the play of masses, molded as skillfully as a sculptor molds clay. And one can feel, as in Goodhue's much later St. Vincent Ferrer (1923) at 66th Street and Lexington Avenue, the abstract forms of his Nebraska State Capitol, the posthumously completed building

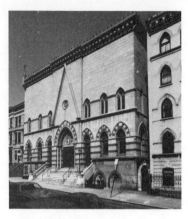

IV D 6 · *Church of the Intercession*

IV D 5 · *Our Lady of Lourdes Church*

that would establish him at the front rank of American eclectics searching for an acceptable backdoor entrance into modernism.

The Church of the Intercession sits on a country hillside, in the midst of the large and rural Trinity Cemetery. It is thus in a sense closer than anything else in New York to the idealized country church of the Gothic Revival. But Goodhue's forms and detailing were crisper and more urban (in spite of the fine cloister here) than a rural Gothic church could have been; he had a ruralist's sense of siting but an urbanist's sense of materials. That the massing is a bit suggestive of Hugh Ferris' great renderings of 1920's skyscrapers in its ability to be both soaring and sumptuous ties this building further to city rather than country Gothic traditions.

IV D 7 · AUDUBON TERRACE
Broadway, west side, 155th to 156th streets
master plan: Charles Pratt Huntington, 1908
· MUSEUM OF THE AMERICAN INDIAN
Charles Pratt Huntington, 1916
· former AMERICAN GEOGRAPHICAL SOCIETY
Charles Pratt Huntington, 1916
· HISPANIC SOCIETY OF AMERICA
West Building: Charles Pratt Huntington, 1908
East Building and West Building additions: Charles Pratt Huntington, Erik Strindberg and H. Brooks Price, 1910–26
· AMERICAN NUMISMATIC SOCIETY
Charles Pratt Huntington, 1908
· NATIONAL INSTITUTE OF ARTS AND LETTERS AND AMERICAN ACADEMY OF ARTS AND LETTERS
Administration Building: William M. Kendall, 1923
auditorium and gallery: Cass Gilbert, 1930

A sad and rather silly dream, this Beaux-Arts grouping that was intended to create an American Acropolis at 155th Street. West 155th Street never quite wanted such glory, and the neighborhood, rather tawdry by now, seems to do its best to reject this infusion of culture altogether.

But even without the ironic juxtaposition of classical temples in the midst of Puerto Rican *bodegas,* this would provide one of New York's very strangest architectural experiences. The museums comprise two rows of limestone-fronted temples, all opening onto a brick-paved court. None of the buildings are especially distinguished, and the proportions of the court are not a little awkward. But something works here anyway, and I think it is the scale. This place doesn't come upon you with any great drama—it is not like turning a corner on dingy 41st Street and seeing the Public Library loom up at you. Audubon Terrace never looms—its scale is no bigger than that of the neighborhood bank (and its architecture, in truth, is no better). But this tiny scale adds an element of surprise, for we are not accustomed to seeing Beaux-Arts buildings that are so little. As at the Appellate Division on East 25th Street (II A 12), there is a delicacy that confers unexpected charm.

The court, uneasily proportioned though it is, nonetheless has a pleasing quality of street about it. The classical buildings line up side by side to make a little town all their own, rather as they must have done in Charles McKim's happier dreams. The west end of the court is blocked, unfortunately, by the back side of an apartment house which obscures the river view that the court itself was undoubtedly intended to have, but the east end is open to Broadway, and the constant traffic gliding by provides just the right sense of connection with the street, a window open to the city.

E/WASHINGTON HEIGHTS TO INWOOD

This is the sliver at the top of Manhattan, the narrow north end that remained largely rural through the nineteenth century. Now it is only the very tip—Fort Tryon Park and Inwood Hill Park—that stay green and wooded. But the topography is still dramatic, with river views and steep ridges giving most of this quarter a very different aura from its downtown counterparts.

Washington Heights below 181st Street, a main east–west axis, has become a troubled neighborhood in recent years; although it lacks the utter poverty and desolation of parts of East Harlem, it is clearly a place in which the welfare class has taken over a neighborhood originally settled by the working class. Once, all of Washington Heights was a quarter of the upwardly mobile immigrant class, and it is still ethnically diverse, but a clear division has arisen in recent years at 181st Street: the blocks above remain isolated, tranquil, and even—in a few cases—elegant, while the blocks below seem under greater and greater strain. The presense of the massive Columbia-Presbyterian Medical Center complex from 165th to 168th streets along Broadway to Riverside Drive serves to anchor the southern end of the neighborhood somewhat.

In its best times, this was never a distinguished neighborhood architecturally—development came too late for first-class row houses, and most of the buildings are apartment houses from the years after World War I which are superior to tenements in terms of amenity but hardly in terms of architecture. They create a dense, tight cityscape, and the result is that virtually all of Washington Heights, except for the blocks near a park or facing the river, seems drab and monotonous, with little of the eccentricity that makes the streets of, say, Harlem so stimulating.

The average is higher in Inwood, the blocks above Dyckman Street which comprise the northernmost end of Manhattan Island. The forest of Inwood Hill Park, Manhattan's only true wilderness, fills Inwood's western half; the rest of the neighborhood is dense, but full of good, medium-sized Art Deco apartment houses from the late 1920's and early 1930's. Payson and Seaman avenues here are miniature versions of the Grand Concourse, and if they never quite reached the splendor of the Concourse in its heyday, they have been far better maintained in the years since.

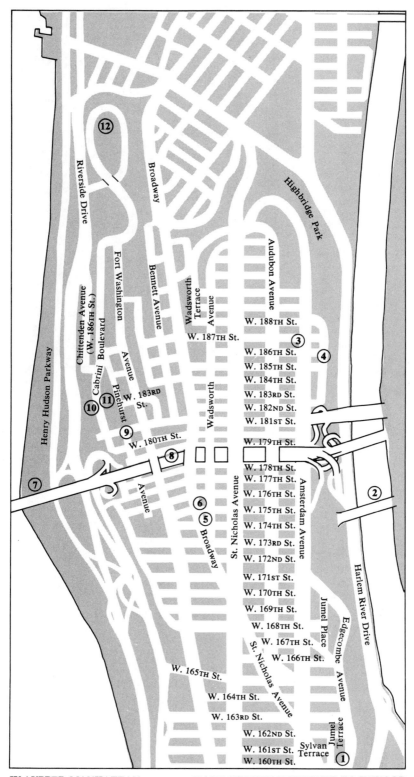

IV E 1 · *Morris-Jumel Mansion*

IV E 1 · MORRIS-JUMEL MANSION
Edgecombe Avenue, NW corner 160th Street
c. 1765
portico added, c. 1810

Every city needs the sort of place in which proper ladies tell you how George Washington slept here, and, well, this is New York's. It is really a fine Georgian mansion with a Federal portico added to bring it up to nineteenth-century fashion; its grand, open site is as uncharacteristic of New York as is the very idea of a house-museum such as this.

But the Morris-Jumel mansion serves as a crucial reminder of how rural Upper Manhattan once was. It was built as a summer residence by Colonel Roger Morris, and it did indeed serve as George Washington's headquarters for a period during the Revolution. Later it served as a British headquarters, then as a tavern, before being purchased in 1810 by Stephen Jumel, whose wife later lived there with her second husband, Aaron Burr. Before apartment buildings were constructed to the south of the house it had a splendid view; the blocks surrounding the house, however, remain full of small-scaled houses that form a pleasing backdrop for the mansion. Worth noting is the imitation stonework on the façade: the quoins in the front corners are of wood, not stone, and to further deflate the myth of nineteenth-century architectural integrity, the rear façade was finished in economical shingles.

IV E 2 · HIGH BRIDGE
West 174th Street at Highbridge Park
John B. Jervis, 1839–48
new central span: 1923
· HIGHBRIDGE TOWER
West 173rd Street in Highbridge Park
attributed to John B. Jervis, 1872

High Bridge was New York's great Roman aqueduct, and although the removal of some of its central arches to facilitate ship traffic in the Harlem River in 1923 has altered its proportions substantially, it remains one of the city's finest pieces of surviving nineteenth-century engineering. Not quite the Pont du Gard, but very handsome nonetheless, with a fine, active rhythm to the masonry arches. The Romanesque water tower, which was used originally to create water pressure to assist the water that had just come through the aqueduct in moving the rest of the way downtown, deserves to rank with the great eclectic water towers of the nineteenth century around the nation—its stretched, energetic form is both contemporary and equal to the famous Chicago water tower, for example. Today other structures and other bridges make both the tower and High Bridge less conspicuous elements on the cityscape than they deserve to be.

IV E 2 · *High Bridge*

IV E 2 · *Highbridge Tower*

IV E 3 · YESHIVA UNIVERSITY, Main Building
Amsterdam Avenue, SW corner 187th Street
Charles B. Meyers, 1928

What is it about Upper Manhattan that brings eclecticism to such a frenzy? Is the air thinner so far uptown? Yeshiva's Main Building is a mad mass of orange stone, with towers and minarets and arches and balconies and buttresses and details of brass and ceramic tile. The outside is a mix of Near Eastern eclecticism and New York institutional architecture, as if a public school had been given a Byzantine overlay. The interior, on the other hand, is a curious and enchanting mix of Near Eastern details and expressionism, something that ends up looking like Near Eastern Art Deco. There are shiny brass doors, walls of marble and granite stripings, and an auditorium with wild mirrored chandeliers and orange and yellow glass windows which is brilliant, powerful fantasy architecture.

The outside is only slightly less dazzling, and is remarkable purely as a formal composition. The central entrance on Amsterdam Avenue is through a flattened and intricately decorated arch topped by a balustrade which is itself the base of a two-story arch containing one high window. Five narrow perpendicular windows are above that, with the central one highest and the others stepped down to reflect the shape of the arch below them. This entire composition is pulled slightly out from the façade; a miniature tower is pinned on to the right, and further to the right there is a four-story wing, its central two floors projecting slightly forward and its end marked by the high, domed tower that is the controlling element of the entire building. There is a similar mass to the left, but with fewer windows, so that there is an impression of more mass to balance the huge tower to the right; for further balance, a delicate minaret prances atop the far left corner.

There is more, but that's the idea—one thing balances another, and the game is, you add one element, I add the next, and the loser is the one who throws the composition off balance. Here, nobody did, and the architect, praise be he, wins.

The rest of Yeshiva up and down Amsterdam Avenue is sadly lacking in the architectural skill shown by the Main Building. Some of the structures look almost identical with the banal suburban hospitals that their donors doubtless also endowed; others, such as the Belfer Science Center (2495 Amsterdam Avenue at 184th Street; Armand Bartos & Associates, 1968)

IV E 3 · *Main building of Yeshiva University*

and the Gottesman Library (Amsterdam Avenue between 185th and 186th streets; Armand Bartos & Associates, 1967), are dark brick fortresses that appear to be a response to the declining neighborhood. Belfer is a high tower with strong vertical articulation at a few points, but so few that it looks more like a windowless brick box with stripes. The library plays off projecting and receding masses in an attempt to get arty, but the boxy forms set in and out at intervals come off looking rather as if they were Moshe Safdie's Habitat put through a compressor.

IV E 4 · LAUREL HILL TERRACE

Laurel Hill Terrace curves off Amsterdam Avenue at 182nd Street and comes back to meet it at 188th Street, and what it does in the meantime is jut out into Highbridge Park. It is a remarkable enclave, not so much for its architecture—it is mostly seven-story buildings, some of them Art Deco but none of them better than average—as for the fact that the street is like a private balcony perched over the park and the Harlem River. There is a sense of isolation here, for there is no traffic and very little noise; the buildings occupy only the west side of the street, while across the east side is the steep drop into overgrown, ill-kempt Highbridge Park.

The view is open to the park, to the Harlem River, and to the world beyond and around that—Davis, Brody & Associates' immense River Park Towers on the Bronx side of the river, the train tracks, the multilayered traffic interchange of the Alexander Hamilton and Washington bridges. One sees cars, trains, buildings, bridges, a constant rush of movement, all from a quiet bench on this quiet street. It is like a view through a keyhole, but instead of looking into a room, here you are looking out.

IV E 5 · FORT WASHINGTON PRESBYTERIAN CHURCH
21 Wadsworth Avenue, NW corner 174th Street
Carrère & Hastings, 1914

Sir Christopher Wren on one of his rare visits to New York. English Baroque was not normally Carrère & Hastings' *métier,* but as in the Christian Science Church (III B 16) at 96th Street and Central Park West, the firm here proves itself skillful and reasonably inventive. Like most good American adaptations, this makes up for its lack of academic finesse with a certain pleasing picturesqueness and an eagerness to adapt to urbanistic demands. Here, the portico has been compressed to bring the mass of the building almost to the street line; the tower, normally prominent, becomes even more important. The tower itself is a bit too large and fussy for Wren himself to have ever let it come to be, but its overeagerness can be excused as a gesture intended to compensate for the relative dreariness of this section of Washington Heights.

IV E 6 · *Loew's 175th Street Theater (now the United Church)*

IV E 5 · *Fort Washington Presbyterian Church*

IV E 6 · UNITED CHURCH (originally Loew's 175th Street Theater)
Broadway, NE corner 175 Street
Thomas W. Lamb, 1930

Almost every neighborhood has something big, special, and deliciously excessive. For the Upper West Side it's the Ansonia, for the East Forties it's the Chrysler Building. Here, it is this theater, a grand movie palace that, unlike most of its contemporaries, looks like a grand movie palace from the outside as well as the inside. The 175th Street and Wadsworth Avenue façades are both decorated in lavish terra-cotta ornament that has hints of Egyptian, Aztec, Mayan, and Spanish architecture; what it really is, of course, is a great terra-cotta curtain, making not only moviegoers but all passersby wonder what delights are about to be revealed behind it.

Lamb did not stop with the façades. There is a tower at the 176th Street and Wadsworth Avenue corner, carrying the building's eclectic motifs further. It has no purpose other than to accent the theater's role as a place of dreams in what its designers surely knew was a fairly dreamless neighborhood; it must have been a teasing element indeed to those who lacked the resources to go inside.

On Broadway a row of stores skillfully continues the motifs of the building once more, this time to fill out the awkwardly shaped site, a reminder that urbanistic responsibility need not get in the way of fantasy fulfillment.

IV E 7 · GEORGE WASHINGTON BRIDGE
Hudson River at 178th Street
Othmar H. Ammann, engineer, 1931

The George Washington Bridge is to the twentieth century what the Brooklyn Bridge was to the nineteenth—a brilliant synthesis of art and engineering that at once sums up a period and spurs it onward. Both bridges leap over space in a way that still causes the heart to skip a beat; there is a balance between power and lyricism in both designs that is extraordinary.

The George Washington, unlike the Brooklyn, is all of steel, and that, combined with its great size, tempts us to consider it the archetypal modern statement. It is not; there is a solid conservatism to the arched form of those great, high towers, which were almost to have been covered in concrete (Cass Gilbert even designed a Beaux-Arts encasement, rejected for reasons of economy). Even in their raw-steel condition the towers speak of the formality of established ways, not the adventurousness of technological experimentation.

But the bridge is no less a piece of poetry for this. Le Corbusier was right: "Here, finally, steel architecture seems to laugh." This is not the delicate poetry of, say, the Golden Gate Bridge—it is something broader, solider. It is what New York is to San Francisco, a thing slightly less graceful but vastly less precious, a thing not quite as beautiful but much more strong.

The bridge's relationship to the city is as important as the structure itself. The bridge is not seen easily from most of the surrounding area, and this is a real drawback. It is one of the true symbols of the city, and its relationship to Washington Heights should be like the Eiffel Tower's relationship to the 15ᵉᵐᵉ arrondissement in Paris, visible from so many blocks both near and far that it is impossible not to think of it as the protective presence, the patron saint, of the neighborhood.

For the most part, only those in speeding cars along the Henry Hudson Parkway or residents lucky enough to live on Riverside Drive or on high floors of other Washington Heights buildings can see the bridge. To pedestrians, unfortunately, it is almost always hidden by bulky, unsympathetic buildings, and the pattern of the streets is such as to bring the bridge into almost no walker's line of sight.

There is one remarkable exception to this on 181st Street, just west of Fort Washington Avenue. West 181st Street begins to curve downhill at this point, and just as the curve begins the west tower of the bridge comes into the far end of the view. As you walk farther down the hill, it disappears; a moment later the east tower, much larger and much closer, looms up

IV E 7 · *George Washington Bridge*

suddenly. By Cabrini Boulevard the east tower has become a massive presence over the old brick apartment houses; it is a strong focus, yet never an oppressive or threatening object. The entire sequence is the perfect way for a city to relate to a monument—the great structure appears powerful yet benign, and the curve and hill of the street conspire to play a game of cat and mouse with you, hiding the bridge one moment and exposing it the next.

To really understand the bridge, one must see it from afar, from the 181st Street vantage point, and from within as well: a walk across is as necessary here as at the Brooklyn Bridge. The wide pedestrian walkway is reached by crossing Fort Washington Avenue; it brings great views that help you understand the city as much as the bridge itself. Once, the New Jersey side was all rural, and the great arches of the towers really were a gatway from city to country. Now, high-rise sprawl on the Fort Lee side has removed the dramatic contrast and made the bridge a roadway between what are really just two different generations of cityscape.

But oh! to stand underneath the gray steel towers, looking straight up at the web of metalwork as the sound of automobiles becomes a distant whir, is to celebrate structure as you can nowhere else in New York. You feel the soaring cables, their curving lines sharp against the sky; they move and push, and the structure holds, frames, enforces. The towers are the rational conscience, the cables the romantic impulse, and together they make harmony.

IV E 8 · *George Washington Bridge Bus Station*

IV E 8 · GEORGE WASHINGTON BRIDGE BUS STATION
Fort Washington to Wadsworth avenues at 178th Street
Pier Luigi Nervi and Port of New York Authority, 1963
· BRIDGE APARTMENTS
between Wadsworth and Audubon avenues, West 178th and 179th streets
Brown & Guenther, 1964

Two attempts at bringing innovation to the development just east of the George Washington Bridge, and both are failures. The butterfly form of concrete which Nervi used as the roof of the bus station is a decent counterpoint to the form of the bridge and a good closing element to the vista of the bridge's eastbound roadway, but it is still showy and exhibitionistic. And the interiors are wretched, merely a newer version of the dreary, institutional Port Authority Bus Terminal downtown (II E 12).

The Bridge Apartments are constructed over the bridge-approach highway, and while one may praise this early attempt to utilize air rights, the buildings themselves are utterly banal. The four towers are identical, poorly detailed slabs, with no concern for light and views. And worst of all, the bridge approach was not fully decked over, so there are immense holes between each tower, bringing the residents a gift of fumes, soot, and noise.

IV E 9 · PINEHURST AVENUE, 181st TO 183rd STREETS
stair constructed: 1924

This is so tiny it is easy to overlook, but it is as civilized an amenity as exists anywhere in Upper Manhattan. Pinehurst Avenue stops dead 75 feet north and 25 feet above 181st Street, and a tiny park with a long stair fills the gap. It is a lovely urban gesture, oriented entirely to the needs of the pedestrian instead of the automobilist, and one of the few street-stairway combinations in New York. It functions as a secluded gathering place and as a passageway, all at once; one can only think in comparison of the tiny stair-passages in Montmartre.

IV E 10 · CASTLE VILLAGE
120–200 Cabrini Boulevard, between 181st and 186th streets
George F. Pelham, Jr., 1938

This is a landmark in New York City housing—because of its location, perhaps the least known of New York's first-rate housing complexes. Castle Village is a set of 14-story red-brick cruciform towers set on open lawns high above the Hudson River. Its site plan suggests the disastrous model of Le Corbusier's Ville Radieuse, but wait—here the towers are all set close to the street, with street entrances, and the huge, beautifully kept green lawn is behind, with a bench-lined promenade overlooking the water. So this is good urbanism, a part of Cabrini Boulevard rather than a rejecter of the street, yet it is open to air and views and light. It is as if Pelham had reconciled the irreconcilable—towers in the park and the old-fashioned street.

The towers themselves are attractive, with chamfered corners and 6-over-6 windows, and a mix of Georgian and castle-like detailing, so they look nothing like institutional red-brick housing towers at all. The land, incidentally, is the former estate of Charles Paterno, one of the city's more enlightened real estate developers; a plaque in his memory on the side of the Castle Village building at No. 180 Cabrini Boulevard says that "He . . . lifted the spirit," and for once this sort of public-relations language approaches truth.

IV E 9 · *Pinehurst Avenue, between 181st and 183rd streets*

IV E 12 · *The Cloisters*

IV E 11 · HUDSON VIEW GARDENS
116 Pinehurst Avenue, between 183rd and 185th streets
George Fred Pelham, 1924

Here are more civilized multiple dwellings, these by the senior Pelham and in half-timbered dress. The seven-story structures, tightly massed together like the cottages of a medieval English town, are arranged along a U-shaped lane which leaves and then returns to Pinehurst Avenue. The buildings on the inner side of the U are set higher, and the land is terraced down so that the buildings on the outside are lower, thus keeping river views open to the inner structures. There are private entrances for each section down tiny flights of steps, and the entire place is covered with vines—the closest thing Manhattan has to a tranquil country lane, and as good as the celebrated Forest Hills Gardens project in Queens, its larger but equally picturesque precedent.

IV E 12 · THE CLOISTERS
Fort Tryon Park, enter from 193rd Street and Fort Washington Avenue or from Riverside Drive
Charles Collens, 1938
alterations for Fuentadueña Chapel: Brown, Lawford & Forbes, 1961

The tower is modern, but altogether appropriate as a centerpiece for this grouping of French and Spanish cloisters brought to Inwood as a setting for the Metropolitan Museum of Art's medieval collection. Collens, of the firm of Allen, Collens & Willis, integrated several cloisters into a complex that seems neither disjointed nor cute, which, considering that he was pulling together real building pieces from twelfth- and thirteenth-century France and Spain and putting them in twentieth-century New York, is impressive. The tower resembles the towers of St. Michel de Cuxa, the twelfth-century French monastery from which one of the real cloisters came, and it is a respectful copy.

The siting is the most important thing here—the buildings sit high atop Fort Tryon Park, once the C. K. G. Billings estate and a gift to the city, along with the Cloisters collections, from John D. Rockefeller, Jr. There are splendid views to the Hudson, and since Rockefeller had the rare foresight to purchase considerable amounts of land on the Palisades across the river in New Jersey and to restrict development there, the pastoral illusion is almost complete. This is a place of illusion, in both its siting and its architecture: it has none of the quality of being a Great Institution that its parent, the Metropolitan, has. Its true colleague is the warmly eccentric Gardner Museum in Boston, and it ranks with the finest non-museum museums anywhere in the world.

V/ROOSEVELT ISLAND

Main Street, looking south toward Westview

It was Welfare Island until the 1970's, when the New York State Urban Development Corporation, the quasi-public urban-renewal agency that was eventually to suffer almost total financial collapse, renamed it in honor of Franklin Delano Roosevelt and started work on what was going to be the ultimate "new-town-in-town," but which ended up as merely being one of the better housing projects around. The island's site is extraordinary—right in the East River opposite the Upper East Side—and no place could be more logical for a residential community. What had prevented such development before then was the stigma of the island, which had been used since the 1830's exclusively for hospitals and jails, two institutions which the nineteenth century tended to think of as belonging together. The jails were

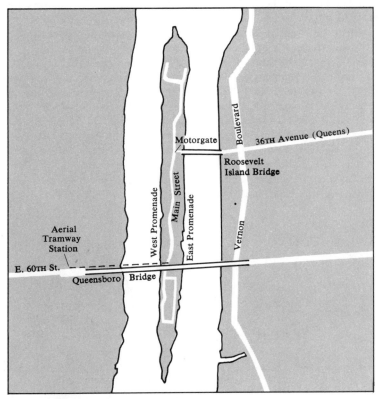

V / ROOSEVELT ISLAND

cleared out when the Riker's Island penitentiary was completed in 1935, but the hospitals still remain, now overshadowed by the new function of the central section of the island as a residential quarter.

The Urban Development Corporation's initial plan for the island was ambitious and not a little naïve: eighteen thousand people in two sections separated by a lively urban core, the whole place free of automobile traffic. What got built was something much smaller—a reduced version of just one of the sections, "Southtown," containing 2,138 apartment units in four separate buildings. The master plan was compromised but essentially followed, and wonder of wonders, there really is no automobile traffic—all cars entering the island on the 36th Avenue bridge from Queens (there has never been automobile access from Manhattan) are dispatched into a vast garage and kept there. Their owners switch to little red minibuses. The Motorgate garage, a reinforced concrete structure by Kallman & McKinnell completed in 1974, is one of the finest buildings on the island—the same Brutalist concrete vocabulary that was overbearing in works by these architects such as the Boston City Hall is just right for a combination garage and symbolic entrance to a community.

The master plan was by Philip Johnson and John Burgee, and it called for U-shaped housing to be arranged along a central, slightly winding street. What was built is far higher than what Johnson and Burgee called for— economics, the UDC said, dictated greater density—but otherwise it roughly matched their specifications. The U's are set along both sides of the street, rather coyly named Main Street, with the open side of the U facing the river. The backs of the U's thus join to form a tightly defined, very urban street; to further tie the street to Manhattan's canyons, the buildings are highest in the backs of the U's along the street, and step down gradually toward the river.

Ideally, the architecture would have resembled the distinguished 1199 Plaza project in Manhattan (IV C 7), but the results here are less praiseworthy. Two firms divided the task: Sert, Jackson & Associates designed Eastwood, the immense complex that occupies the entire east side of Main Street's developed section (Nos. 510–580 Main Street, 1976) and Westview on the west side of Main Street (Nos. 595–625 Main Street, 1976); both of these projects are for middle- and lower-middle-income tenants. The wealthier—the island's other naïve dream, that of truly mixing incomes, seems also to be working out—are housed in two structures designed by Johansen & Bhavnani, both completed in 1975 and both on the west side

V · *Eastwood*

V · *Main Street, looking north toward the Chapel of the Good Shepherd, left, and Eastwood, right*

of Main Street facing Manhattan: Island House, at Nos. 551–575 Main Street, and Rivercross, at Nos. 505–541 Main Street.

The rich get the best Manhattan views and the poor are left to look at Con Edison's "Big Allis" generator in Queens, but the poor may still get the better deal. The Sert, Jackson buildings are sharp and lively constructivist masses of ribbed concrete with sharp accents in red; there are well-defined court spaces within the various U's of the project, and many of the apartments themselves are duplexes, reached off glass-enclosed corridors.

The Johansen & Bhavnani buildings are sheathed in a dreary asbestos material, which proved efficient for construction but gives them a pallid look that is the very opposite of the elegance to which they strive. Yellow accents make the project look even sicklier, and the gangplank entrances come off as rather gimmicky. On the other hand, the courtyard spaces are decent, and in some cases excellent, and the same can be said for the apartments themselves.

But architecture itself is not the idea here. If this place works visually at all, it is because its designers held fast to two principles—first, that the street be a lively canyon that would reproduce the tightness of the existing city instead of the amorphous quality of most spaces between new housing projects, and second, that the riverfront be respected at all times.

And the street does work. Its curve is gentle, just enough to create a sense of curiosity as to what might be beyond the bend, not so much as to deny the island's fundamental longitudinal layout. It is paved in brick, which looks splendid, and it is beginning, slowly, to attract enough stores to make a promenade down its center feel like something other than a visit to a ghost town. (Early on, there was something of a Catch-22 problem—stores wouldn't rent space until enough people filled the housing, and people wouldn't rent apartments until enough stores were in place.) Both of the architects of the housing have dealt respectfully with the street, each firm in its own way. Sert, Jackson have built covered arcades, one of which, in the huge Eastwood building, yields a long and dramatic vista, a harsh concrete rue de Rivoli. Johansen & Bhavnani have built storefronts right out to the street, setting them at slight angles to create a constantly changing zigzag pattern, not unlike the successful storefronts across the river at 240 Central Park South (II G 13).

But it is the riverfront promenades that are best of all. The views to Manhattan, obviously, are superb, and nowhere else, except from the Brooklyn Heights promenade, can the city skyline be seen from such a tranquil vantage point. The river views play a kind of hide-and-seek with the passerby on Main Street that is excellent—there are sections of the Johansen & Bhavnani buildings extending across the riverfront side that have arcaded openings which frame the view, intensifying its drama.

It all serves to remind you, however, that this place is not the city at all but a kind of suburb poised delicately at the city's edge. The island, after a slow start, has turned out to be extremely popular—new housing by the architects Charles Gwathmey and Robert Siegel is now in design—but it seems clear that, for all the efforts made to make the place feel urban, it has succeeded not because it is relatively urban but because it is relatively rural. Main Street is very, very quiet; there are neither crowds nor dirt nor noise nor, it is said, much crime. That seems to be what a lot of people want, and they seem not to notice the fact that on Roosevelt Island there is none of the life, none of the mix of exhilaration and depression, that characterizes Manhattan. It is all even, precise, and ordered, like a place not within viewing distance of Manhattan but a place far, far away.

Most of the older buildings on the island are undistinguished, but there are a few exceptions. The pleasing Chapel of the Good Shepherd, a gracious Gothic Revival church by Frederick Clarke Withers (543 Main Street, 1889), has been turned into a community center by Giorgio Cavaglieri, and set in the midst of a fine plaza designed by Johansen & Bhavnani and Lawrence Halprin & Associates. The plaza is handsome and urbane, without a hint of the cuteness that affects so many such places, and it provides just the right degree of balance between the enclosure of Main Street and the openness of the riverfront walks.

Less successful is Cavaglieri's restoration of the Blackwell House, the little clapboard farmhouse of 1804 that sits in the midst of a pleasant riverfront yard, "Blackwell Park," on the east side of Main Street just south of Eastwood. The house was the original home of the Blackwell family, the family that gave its name to the island before the city called it Welfare Island; it is a modest, unpretentious farmhouse, and it has been sanitized here and made to look something like a model house for a new suburban tract development. Dan Kiley's landscaping is good, but cannot manage the impossible chore of bridging the visual gap between this poor, lonely little building and the huge housing blocks looming near it.

Most of the other buildings are now, unfortunately, off limits to the public. Far to the south is the original Smallpox Hospital; it is a haunting Gothic ruin, dating from 1856, by the gifted James Renwick, Jr. (south wing, York

& Sawyer, 1904; north wing, Renwick, Aspinwall & Owen, 1905). It deserves a better fate than its current abandonment, as does one other hospital remnant of quality, this one at the northern end of the island, the Octagon Tower by Alexander Jackson Davis of 1839. (Here, the mansard roof and entry stair were later additions by Joseph M. Dunn, c.1880.) Also significant, back behind fences at the southern end, are the harsh stone City Hospital of 1859, as much like a jail as an institution of charity, and the Renaissance-inspired Strecker Memorial Laboratory (Withers & Dickson, 1892).

Until a planned subway connection is finished in the 1980's, visitors and residents without cars will enter and leave Roosevelt Island on an aerial tramway that connects the island with Second Avenue and 60th Street in Manhattan. The tram's stations at either end were designed by Prentice & Chan, Olhausen and finished in 1976; they are industrial structures of aluminum and concrete with all of the tramway's great rotary machinery visible and painted all sorts of bright colors, a really lovely kindergarten version of *Modern Times* and absolutely the right beginning or end for a visit to the island, which is itself so much a combination of modern, industrial imagery and gentle game-playing.

The tram journey itself is extraordinary—gentle, soft, soaring, there could be no better way to traverse a river or a part of a city. It is a symptom of our times, no doubt, that you think first that you are in Disneyland and that someone has deviously pasted a photograph of the Manhattan skyline across the window of your tram car, but if the illusion lasts no more than a split second, there is greater pleasure still in perceiving the reality: this is not Disneyland at all—it is New York.

V · *Motorgate*

INDEX

References in boldface type indicate pages where the specified subjects are discussed in full.

ABOUT THE AUTHOR

PAUL GOLDBERGER received his B.A. from Yale and has been the architecture critic for *The New York Times* for several years. He has taught architectural history at Yale, lectured widely, and has written for many periodicals, among them *Esquire, Art News, New York* magazine and *Art in America*. He lives on the Upper West Side of Manhattan.

PHOTOGRAPHER'S NOTE

In the course of taking the photographs for this book, I have come to love this city more than I had ever imagined I could. This has something to do with the discovery of buildings, vistas and entire neighborhoods I'd never known before. It also has something to do with the rediscovery of old favorites—seen for the first time with a critical and appreciative eye. But beyond anything else, it has to do with the people in this town who opened rooftops, balconies, terraces and windows to me as I sought the perfect angle on New York's architecture. Not only unfailingly courteous and cooperative, these New Yorkers were utterly enthusiastic about sharing the special views that exist in such a vertical city. They cherish the panorama they behold every day and they were delighted that it was being chronicled. Their affection and appreciation were contagious. I could not begin to name the several hundred individuals and organizations who have helped me, but to all of them I extend my thanks—not only for their generosity but for the evidence they offered that this city's greatness rests as much in its soul as in its skyscrapers.

—DAVID W. DUNLAP